THE GOSPEL OF JOHN

This commentary presents full analyses on passages, key terms, and major motifs in the Gospel of John. One might say that the "big picture" is more important here than exacting detail. Readers will be invited into the Gospel by noting its typical literary patterns (chiasms, topic statements and development, patterns of double-meaning words), rhetorical commonplaces, and discourse (e.g., "the 'noble' shepherd"; forensic trials: accusations, defense, verdict, and sentence). In particular, this commentary brings readers into the cultural world of the Gospel by presenting materials such as honor and shame, challenge and riposte, gossip, secrecy, and sectarian character of the group. This is a very accessible reading of John.

Jerome H. Neyrey, S.J., is currently Professor of New Testament at the University of Notre Dame. Among his most recent books are *Paul: In Other Words, a Cultural Reading of His Letters* (1990); *2 Peter, Jude* in the Anchor Bible Commentary series (1993); *Portraits of Paul: An Archeology of Ancient Personality* (1996, with Bruce Malina); *Honor and Shame in the Gospel of Matthew* (1998); and *Render to God: New Testament Understandings of the Divine* (2004).

NEW CAMBRIDGE BIBLE COMMENTARY

GENERAL EDITOR: Ben Witherington III

HEBREW BIBLE/OLD TESTAMENT EDITOR: Bill T. Arnold

EDITORIAL BOARD:
Bill T. Arnold, *Asbury Theological Seminary*
James D. G. Dunn, *University of Durham*
Michael V. Fox, *University of Wisconsin-Madison*
Robert P. Gordon, *University of Cambridge*
Judith Gundry-Volf, *Yale University*
Ben Witherington III, *Asbury Theological Seminary*

The New Cambridge Bible Commentary (NCBC) aims to elucidate the Hebrew and Christian Scriptures for a wide range of intellectually curious individuals. While building on the work and reputation of the Cambridge Bible Commentary popular in the 1960s and 1970s, the NCBC takes advantage of many of the rewards provided by scholarly research over the last four decades. Volumes utilize recent gains in rhetorical criticism, social scientific study of the Scriptures, narrative criticism, and other developing disciplines to exploit the growing edges in biblical studies. Accessible, jargon-free commentary, an annotated "Suggested Reading" list, and the entire New Revised Standard Version (NRSV) text under discussion are the hallmarks of all volumes in the series.

ALSO IN THE SERIES
Exodus, Carol Meyers
Judges and Ruth, Victor H. Matthews
Paul's Letters to the Corinthians, Craig S. Keener
The Letters of James and Jude, William F. Brosend II
Revelation, Ben Witherington III

FORTHCOMING VOLUMES
Genesis, Bill T. Arnold
Deuteronomy, Brent Strawn
Joshua, Douglas A. Knight
1–2 Chronicles, William M. Schniedewind
Psalms 1–72, Walter Brueggemann and William H. Bellinger, Jr.
Psalms 73–150, Walter Brueggemann and William H. Bellinger, Jr.
Isaiah 1–39, David Baer
Jeremiah, Baruch Halpern
Hosea, Joel, and Amos, J. J. M. Roberts
The Gospel of Matthew, Craig A. Evans
The Gospel of Luke, Amy-Jill Levine and Ben Witherington III
The Letters of John, Duane F. Watson

The Gospel of John

Jerome H. Neyrey, S.J.
University of Notre Dame

CAMBRIDGE
UNIVERSITY PRESS

CAMBRIDGE UNIVERSITY PRESS
Cambridge, New York, Melbourne, Madrid, Cape Town, Singapore, São Paulo

Cambridge University Press
32 Avenue of the Americas, New York, NY 10013-2473, USA

www.cambridge.org
Information on this title: www.cambridge.org/9780521828017

First published 2007

Printed in the United States of America

A catalog record for this publication is available from the British Library.

Library of Congress Cataloging in Publication Data

Neyrey, Jerome H., 1940–
The Gospel of John / Jerome H. Neyrey.
    p.   cm. – (New Cambridge Bible commentary)
Includes bibliographical references and index.
ISBN 0-521-82801-5 (hardback) – ISBN 0-521-53521-2 (pbk.)
1. Bible. N. T. John – Commentaries.   I. Title.   II. Series.
BS2615.53.N49   2006
226.5′077–dc22   2006003319

ISBN-13   978-0-521-82801-7 hardback
ISBN-10   0-521-82801-5 hardback

ISBN-13   978-0-521-53521-2 paperback
ISBN-10   ₁0-521-53521=2 paperback

To The Context Group,
with respect, gratitude, and affection

Contents

Texts Cited, Translations, and Abbreviations

*T*he translation of the Bible used in this book is the New Revised Standard Version. All texts and translations of Greek and Roman authors come from the Loeb Classical Library, with one exception. George A. Kennedy's rendering of Aristotle's *Rhetoric* is used because of its clear understanding of epideictic rhetoric and its sensitivity to technical rhetorical terms. Abbreviations of journals and serials are taken from the style sheet of the *Journal of Biblical Literature*. For the convenience of readers, a list of abbreviations follows. Moreover, abbreviations of Greek and Roman writings are drawn from the list by the same journal.

Four texts of the rules for an encomium are used here: Aelius Theon (James Butts, *The "Progymnasmata" of Theon: A New Text with Translation and Commentary* [unpublished dissertation from Clarement Graduate School, 1987]), Apthonius of Ephesus (trans. Ray Nadeau, *Speech Monographs* 19 [1952], 264–85); Hermogenes of Tarsus (trans. C. S. Baldwin, *Medieval Rhetoric and Poetic* [New York: Macmillan, 1928], 23–38), and Menander Rhetor (trans. D. A. Russell and N. G. Wilson, *Menander Rhetor* [Oxford: Clarendon Press, 1981]).

ABBREVIATIONS FOR JOURNALS AND REFERENCE WORKS

ABD	*Anchor Bible Dictionary,* 6 vols., D. N. Freedman, ed. (New York: Doubleday, 1992)
AJP	*American Journal of Philology*
ANRW	*Aufstieg und Niedergang der Römischen Welt*
ARN	*The Fathers According to Rabbi Nathan* (trans. Judah Goldin [New Haven, CT: Yale University Press, 1955])
ATR	*Anglican Theological Review*
AusBR	*Australian Biblical Review*
BAR	*Biblical Archaeology Review*

BDAG	Walter Bauer, F. Danker, W. F. Arndt, and F. W. Gingrich, *Greek–English Lexicon of the New Testament*, 2nd ed. (Chicago: University of Chicago Press, 1979)
BI	*Biblical Interpretation*
BJRL	*Bulletin of the Johns Rylands University Library of Manchester*
BSac	*Bibliotheca Sacra*
BTB	*Biblical Theology Bulletin*
BTrans	*Bible Translator*
BZ	*Biblische Zeitschrift*
CBQ	*Catholic Biblical Quarterly*
CP	*Classical Philology*
CurTM	*Currents in Theology and Ministry*
CW	*Classical World*
DR	*Downside Review*
EBib	*Études biblique*
ETL	*Ephemerides Theologicae Lovanienses*
EvQ	*Evangelical Quarterly*
EvT	*Evangelische Theologie*
ExpT	*Expository Times*
G & R	*Greece and Rome*
HeyJ	*Heythrop Journal*
HR	*History of Religion*
HSCPh	*Harvard Studies in Classical Philology*
HTR	*Harvard Theological Review*
HUCA	*Hebrew Union College Annual*
IBS	*Irish Biblical Studies*
IDB	*Interpreters Dictionary of the Bible*
IEJ	*Israel Exploration Journal*
IESS	*International Encyclopedia of the Social Sciences*
JAAR	*Journal of the American Academy of Religion*
JBL	*Journal of Biblical Literature*
JECS	*Journal of Early Christian Studies*
JHS	*Journal of Hellenic Studies*
JRS	*Journal of Roman Studies*
JSJ	*Journal for the Study of Judaism*
JSNT	*Journal for the Study of the New Testament*
JSOT	*Journal for the Study of the Old Testament*
JTS	*Journal of Theological Studies*
LSJ	Henry Liddell, Robert Scott, and Henry Jones, *A Greek–English Lexicon* (Oxford: Clarendon, 1968)
LTP	*Laval théologique et philosophique*

M-M	James Moulton and George Milligan, *The Vocabulary of the Greek Testament* Illustrated from the Papyri and Other Non-Literary Sources (London: Hodder and Stoughton, 1952)
NTS	*New Testament Studies*
NovT	*Novum Testamentum*
PEQ	*Palestine Exploration Quarterly*
PRS	*Perspectives in Religious Studies*
PTR	*Princeton Theological Review*
RAC	*Reallexikon für Antike und Christentum*
RB	*Revue Biblique*
ResQ	*Restoration Quarterly*
RevExp	*Review and Expositor*
RSRev	*Religious Studies Review*
SBLSP	*Society of Biblical Literature Seminar Papers*
SJTh	*Scottish Journal of Theology*
ST	*Studia Theologica*
Str-B	H. Strack and P. Billerbeck, *Kommentar zum Neuen Testament* Aus Talmud und Midrash (Munich: Beck, 1922)
SVTQ	*St. Vladimir's Theological Quarterly*
TAPA	*Transactions and Proceedings of the American Philological Association*
TBT	*The Bible Today*
TDNT	*Theological Dictionary of the New Testament*, Gerhard Kittle, ed. (Grand Rapids, MI: Eerdmans, 1964)
TJT	*Toronto Journal of Theology*
TS	*Theological Studies*
TynB	*Tyndale Bulletin*
TZ	*Theologische Zeitschrift*
VT	*Vetus Testamentum*
WTS	*Westminster Theological Journal*
ZAW	*Zeitschrift für die Alttestamentliche Wissenschaft*
ZNW	*Zeitschrift für die Neutestamentliche Wissenschaft*
ZRG	*Zeitschrift für Religions-und Geistesgeschichte*

ABBREVIATIONS FOR CLASSICAL AUTHORS

Aristotle, *N.E.*	*Nicomachean Ethics*
Aristotle, *Poet.*	*Poetics*
Aristotle, *Rhet.*	*Rhetoric*
Cicero, *De Orat.*	*De Oratore*
Cicero, *Tusc. Disp.*	*Tusculan Disputations*
Exod. Rab.	*Exodus Rabbah*
Gen. Rab.	*Genesis Rabbah*
Gregory of Nyssa, *De Beat.*	*De Beatitudinis*

Gregory of Nyssa, *Or. Cat.*	*Oratorio Catechetica Magna*
Josephus, *Ant.*	*Antiquities*
Justin Martyr, *Dial.*	*Dialogue with Trypho*
m. Ket.	*Mishnah Kettuboth*
m. Shab.	*Mishnah Shabbath*
Philo, *Abr.*	*On Abraham*
Philo, *Cher.*	*On the Cherubim*
Philo, *Ebr.*	*On Drunkenness*
Philo, *Flacc.*	*Flaccus*
Philo, *Heres*	*Who Is the Heir*
Philo, *Leg. All.*	*Allegorical Interpretation*
Philo, *Migr.*	*On the Migration of Abraham*
Philo, *Mos.*	*Life of Moses*
Philo, *Mut.*	*On the Change of Names*
Philo, *Plant.*	*On Noah's Work as a Planter*
Philo, *Post.*	*On the Posterity and Exile of Cain*
Philo, *Q. Ex.*	*Questions of Exodus*
Philo, *Sac.*	*On the Sacrifices of Abel and Cain*
Philo, *Somn.*	*On Dreams*
Pliny, *H.N.*	*Natural History*
Quintilian, *Inst. Orat.*	*Institutio Oratoria*
Stobaeus, *Ecl.*	*Eclogae*
Tg. Ps.-J.	*Targum Pseudo-Jonathan*
Tg. Neo.	*Targum Neofiti*
Xenophon, *Mem.*	*Memorabilia*

A Word about Citations

*A*ll volumes in the New Cambridge Bible Commentary include footnotes, with full bibliographical citations included in the note when a source text is first mentioned in each chapter. Subsequent citations include the author's initial or initials, full last name, abbreviated title for the work, and date of publication. Most readers prefer this citation system to endnotes, which require searching through pages at the back of the book.

The Suggested Reading lists, also included in all NCBC volumes after the introductions, are not a part of this citation apparatus. Annotated and organized by publication type, the self-contained Suggested Reading lists are intended to introduce and briefly review some of the most well-known and helpful literature on the biblical text under discussion.

I. Introduction

L ike Goldilocks's three bears, introductions to the Fourth Gospel come in different sizes: small, medium,[1] and large.[2] Typically, they contain standard areas of investigation, such as: author, place of composition, and date; relationship of the Fourth Gospel to the synoptic Gospels; background, whether Israelite and/or Greco-Roman; sociological character of the readers of the Gospel (e.g., a sect in tension with the synagogue); unity of the document; and theories of its development over time and its changing perspectives. Many introductions, moreover, regularly give attention to theology by attending to special vocabulary (light, see, know), distinctive themes ("sacraments" and eschatology), topics (revelation, signs/miracles, knowledge), and Christology ("prophet," "king," "Messiah," "I AM," and "Son of Man"). The commentaries cited in the notes provide an excellent discussion of these topics, and readers are urged to consult them. But here I present a different kind of introduction, one more suited to the specific perspective of this commentary and the series in which it is published. The New Cambridge Bible Commentary series brings to readers a "socio-rhetorical" perspective for interpreting biblical documents,[3] drawing especially on literary/rhetorical and cultural perspectives. Therefore the topics discussed in this introduction are commensurate with the perspective of this commentary and the series to which it belongs: the social location of the author

---

[1] Robert Kysar, "The Fourth Gospel in Recent Research," *ANRW* 2.25.3 (1984), 2391–2480; and George Beasley-Murray, *John* 2nd ed. (Nashville, TN: Thomas Nelson, 1999), xxxii–xciii.

[2] Raymond E. Brown, *An Introduction to the Gospel of John*, ed. Francis J. Moloney (New York: Doubleday, 2003); and Craig S. Keener, *The Gospel of John: A Commentary* (Peabody, MA: Hendrickson, 2003), 1.3–330.

[3] As editor, Ben Witherington III (*Revelation* [Cambridge: Cambridge University Press, 2003]) described the focus of this series thus: "The NCBC takes advantage of many of the rewards provided by scholarly research over the past four decades. Volumes utilize recent gains in rhetorical criticism, social scientific study of the Scriptures, narrative criticism, and other developing disciplines to exploit the growing edges in biblical studies."

(what he knows); rhetoric, literary patterns, and language; Johannine characters in cultural perspective; and social-scientific models needed to interpret this ancient document.

THE SOCIAL LOCATION OF THE AUTHOR

Current scholarship distinguishes between a "writer" of this Gospel and an "author."[4] A writer may only take dictation, whereas the author imagines the project, organizes the materials, and establishes the editorial point of view. Despite the best labors of Johannine scholarship, we are still uncertain who the author is or where and when the document was written and revised. Nevertheless, we can learn much about the author by asking a new question: What does he know?[5]

Geography. The author knows about *Judea*[6] (Bethany, Jerusalem), *Samaria* (Sychar, Jacob's well, and the custom that Israelites and Samaritans "do not share things in common," 4:9), and *Galilee* (Bethsaida, Cana, Capernaum, Nazareth, Sea of Galilee/Sea of Tiberias). He is even aware of the negative cachet of Nazareth and Galilee (1:46; 7:31, 41–43). Within Jerusalem, he tells us of two pools, Bethzatha (5:1) and Siloam (9:7), the residence of the high priest Annas (18:13–18), and Pilate's praetorium (18:28). He knows much about the geography of Jerusalem's temple: He can identify the "treasury" (8:20), the "portico of Solomon" (10:23), and the place where the incident in 2:13–16 was described. In many of these things, he displays a unique and sharper knowledge than the authors of the synoptic Gospels (see 2:20).

Temple Feasts and Sabbath. Whereas the synoptic Gospels know of only one Passover in the career of Jesus, this author knows of three, two celebrated in Jerusalem and one in Galilee. He knows a range of pilgrimage feasts that span the year and the ritual objects characteristic of them: Passover and its specially treated lamb (2:13; 6:4; 12:1; 19:36); Booths (7:1–8:58) and its petitions for sunlight and rains; Dedication (10:22); and an unnamed festival (5:1). He knows of a conflict between "this mountain" in Samaria and its rival in Jerusalem as the legitimate place of worship. Finally, he treats Sabbath observance differently

---

[4] R. E. Brown, *An Introduction to the Gospel of John* (2003), 189–96.

[5] See Vernon K. Robbins, "The Social Location of the Implied Author of Luke-Acts," in Jerome H. Neyrey, ed., *The Social World of Luke-Acts: Models for Interpretation* (Peabody, MA: Hendrickson, 1991), 333–60; and Jerome H. Neyrey, "The Social Location of Paul: How Paul Was Educated and What He Could Compose as Indices of His Social Location," in David B. Gowler, L. Gregory Bloomquist, and Duane F. Watson, eds., *Fabrics of Discourse: Essays in Honor of Vernon K. Robbins* (Harrisburg, PA: Trinity Press International, 2003), 126–64.

[6] Ingo Broer, "Knowledge of Palestine in the Fourth Gospel?" in Robert T. Fortna and Tom Thatcher, eds., *Jesus in Johannine Tradition* (Louisville, KY: Westminster John Knox, 2001), 83–90.

from the other Gospels, for he argues that just as God works on the Sabbath, so does he (5:16–17), and that if Moses' authorization to circumcise on the Sabbath does not break the Law, then surely an act that made a man's body whole does not break it (7:22–23).

Scripture and Midrashic Interpretation. The author compares Jesus with two of Israel's great patriarchs ("greater than our father Jacob... greater than Abraham"), drawing not only on the Scriptures but also midrashic interpretations of them. As regards the Scriptures, he claims that Moses will change his traditional role of advocate to that of prosecutor of Israel (5:45), and he claims that Isaiah explains why so many did not become Jesus' followers (12:38–40). The author's knowledge of and use of the midrashic interpretations about psalms and patriarchs suggest that he has a school education, such as was found in the *bet ha-midrash*.[7] For example, it has been argued that John 6 is an elaborate midrash on Passover and manna.[8] A text, "He gave them bread from heaven to eat" (6:31), is cited and developed word by word, denying the text to Israel and claiming it for Jesus and his group. In the story of Abraham, the author distinguishes those who descend from Ishmael (the slave and illegitimate son, who did not remain in the house) from those descended from Isaac (the freeborn son and legitimate heir, who remains in the paternal house, 8:33–44), a school interpretation similar to that in Galatians 4:21–30. He utilizes the midrash that Cain is the firstborn of Satan and ancestor of the audience. They are all liars and murderers from the beginning (8:44).[9] And he knows the traditional midrash about Psalm 82:6 apropos of the charge that Jesus is equal to God.[10]

Literary Acumen. As far as his rhetorical skills are concerned, the author can write prologues (1:1–18; 13:1–3) and conclusions (12:1–50). From rhetorical handbooks, he knows the Greco-Roman principle of uniqueness[11] used for amplifying praise ("no one has ever but...," "he is the unique son...," "he is the first and only one to do..."); honor ascribed by comparison (Jesus vs. Moses, 1:17); and the use of questions as weapons. He is familiar with certain literary forms found both in Israelite and Greco-Roman literature: the miracle (5:2–9; 9:1–9; 11:1–44) and the farewell address (14:1–17:26). Most interestingly, the author

---

[7] Although the author insists that Jesus had no formal education (7:15), this does not exclude the author. For materials on midrash and schools of midrash, see Gary G. Porton, "Midrash: Palestinian Jews and the Hebrew Bible in the Greco-Roman Period," *ANRW* 2.19.2 (1979), 103–38; and also R. Alan Culpepper, *The Johannine School* (Missoula, MT: Scholars Press, 1975), 261–90.

[8] Peder Borgen, *Bread from Heaven: An Exegetical Study of the Concept of Manna in the Gospel of John and the Writings of Philo* (Leiden: Brill, 1965).

[9] See Nils A. Dahl, "Der Erstegebone Satans und der Vater des Teufels," in W. Eltester, ed., *Apophoreta* (Berlin: Töpelmann, 1964), 70–84.

[10] Jerome H. Neyrey, " 'I Said: You are Gods': Psalm 82 and John 10," *JBL* 108 (1989), 647–63.

[11] Jerome H. Neyrey, "Uniqueness: 'First,' 'Only,' 'One of a Few,' and 'No One Else': Rhetoric, and the Doxologies in 1 Timothy," *Biblica* 86 (2005), 59–87.

interprets Jesus' death according to the commonplace of a "noble death," celebrated in Greek funeral oratory (10:11–18), and he employs most of the elements
of the encomium taught in the second level of Hellenistic education: origins
(place and parents), nurture and training, virtues, and death and posthumous
honors.

Israelite and Greco-Roman Theology.[12] The author has a solid grasp of Israelite
God-talk. He utilizes the midrashic tradition that God has two basic powers
(creative and eschatological), both of which he bestows on Jesus. The author
interprets the name Jesus manifests, "I AM," in two senses (8:24, 28; 8:58). First,
"I AM" is the name of the appearing deity of the Scriptures, but since no one
has ever seen God (1:18), those receiving appearances must have seen the person
who properly bears the divine name, "I AM." Second, in several places, "I AM"
is juxtaposed with mortals who came into being and pass out of it (8:56–58).
Thus the author appreciates the Hellenistic topos that a true deity is eternal in
the past and imperishable in the future.[13] Whereas Jesus himself repeats the key
element of Israel's theology, namely monotheism (17:3), the crowds abandon
God who is King for King Caesar (19:15).

Political Scene. Although the author knows the form of Judean and Roman
trials, he especially appreciates the judge's examination of the accused in his
portrayal of two such scrutinies of Jesus by Pilate (18:33–38; 19:8–11). Not only
does he know that judges should judge justly and not according to appearances
(7:24; 8:15) but also that according to the law, a person accused has a right to
speak before the court (7:51). Of all the evangelists, the author most appreciates
patron–client relationships. He knows that Pilate is Caesar's "friend" (that is, his
client), and he records Jesus making his disciple-servants his "friends" (15:13–15).

Traditions in John and the Synoptics. Although modern scholarship has been
unable to prove Johannine dependency on any one of the synoptics, most admit
that the author frequently draws on traditions shared with those Gospels.[14]
Although this is not an exhaustive list, the author of the Fourth Gospel knows:
(1) John the Baptizer witnessing to Jesus; (2) healings (cure of the paralytic
and the blind man; raising of the dead); (3) the multiplication of loaves and the
walking on the water; (4) the entrance into Jerusalem; (5) anointing of Jesus' feet
at a banquet; (6) the challenge to the Temple; (7) the arrest, trial, and execution
of Jesus; (8) the burial and the empty tomb; and (9) resurrection appearances.[15]

---

[12] Jerome H. Neyrey, "'My Lord and My God': The Divinity of Jesus in John's Gospel,"
   SBLSP (1986), 152–71.
[13] Jerome H. Neyrey, "'Without Beginning of Days or End of Life' (Hebrews 7:3): Topos for
   a True Deity," *CBQ* 53 (1991), 439–55.
[14] For a convenient survey of this, see R. E. Brown, *Introduction to the Gospel of John* (2003),
   90–105.
[15] Other items include "the Twelve" (6:67–71); the name of the high priest, Caiaphas (11:49;
   18:28); and a miraculous catch of fish (21:5–11). See also Raymond E. Brown, "Incidents
   that Are Units in the Synoptic Gospels but Dispersed in St. John," *CBQ* 23 (1961), 143–60.

However one evaluates dependence or independence, the author knows a great deal about the Jesus tradition.

What, then, is the social location of the author? Because of all of the things he knows and composes, he would seem to have been educated at least to the second level of education in antiquity, the period during which students learned to compose according to certain genres. And because education was status-specific,[16] this argues that the author was not an illiterate peasant (Acts 4:13). Yet he gives little evidence of an elite formal training such as Luke and Paul had. He is likely the client or retainer of someone with resources sufficient to provide for the writing of such a document. Although his Greek may lack sophistication, the knowledge and craft of the author suggest a person of considerable education and social standing.

CHARACTERS

Scholarship on the dramatis personae of the Fourth Gospel has been both intense and productive. Readers have always sensed that its characters are symbolic in some sense, but Raymond Collins[17] shaped the discussion by considering them as "representative figures": They represent in a homiletic context traits either praiseworthy or blameworthy within the Johannine group. Alan Culpepper advanced this: "The characters represent a continuum of response to Jesus. . . . The characters are, therefore, particular sorts of choosers."[18] His continuum contains these responses: (1) rejection and tepid acceptance of Jesus; (2) scrutiny of reactions to Jesus' signs and wonders, noting that some people argue that God must be the source of these, whereas others see merely the eating of a surfeit of bread; (3) receptivity to Jesus' words, which distinguishes insiders or outsiders; (4) misunderstandings that end either in enlightenment of insiders or proof that the interlocutors simply lack the ability to learn; (5) select disciples, who might receive unique information, demonstration of Jesus' greatest gift (the raising of Lazarus), or simply be known as "beloved" disciples; and (6) defection (6:66) and treason, indicating hate, not love, of Jesus.[19]

Craig Koester added to this discussion insights about how characters were drawn in ancient speeches and drama.[20] He notes that although ancient characters were individuals (Nicodemus is *not* the Samaritan woman), they nevertheless manifest representative, formal ways of speaking and acting. Moreover, Koester cites Aristotle on "character": "Character is that which reveals choice,

---

[16] J. H. Neyrey, "The Social Location of Paul," in *Fabrics of Discourse* (2003), 156–61, and the literature cited therein.

[17] Raymond Collins, "Representative Figures in the Fourth Gospel," *Downside Review* 94 (1976), 26–46, 118–32.

[18] R. Alan Culpepper, *Anatomy of the Fourth Gospel* (Philadelphia: Fortress Press, 1983), 104.

[19] R. A. Culpepper, *Anatomy of the Fourth Gospel* (1983), 146–48.

[20] Craig R. Koester, *Symbolism in the Fourth Gospel: Meaning, Mystery, Community* (Minneapolis, MN: Fortress Press, 1995), 36–38.

shows what sort of thing a man chooses or avoids . . . so those speeches convey no character in which there is nothing whatever which the speaker chooses or avoids" (*Poet.* 6.24). Finally, he notes how characters provide positive and negative examples in the pursuit of a suitable manner of life. These studies have shaped the way readers of the Fourth Gospel interpret its dramatis personae. It is now accepted wisdom to examine the Johannine characters as representative of some trait important to the group or along some continuum of response to Jesus or according to the choices made concerning Jesus.

We gain, moreover, considerable benefit from the use of social-science studies of types of personalities, which radically contrasts modern individualists with ancient group-oriented persons.[21] Persons in ancient *bioi*, history, and encomia were praised according to fixed conventional canons, which are ideal places to discover the culturally accepted criteria of status and honor. An author would ask: Where was he born? Who were his parents and ancestors? Who were his teachers? What was his trade? What was his name? To what group did he belong? A noble and honorable person is born in a noble place (Tarsus, Acts 21:39; Jerusalem, Ps 87:5–6). Conversely, nothing noble can come from Nazareth (1:46), nor anyone important from Galilee (7:41–43, 52). People tended to be known in terms of their fathers (e.g., Simon, son of Jonah; James and John, sons of Zebedee).[22] They are presumed to be "chips off the old block" (John 8:38–44), for better or worse. Males are known by their trade (fishermen, carpenters, tax collectors) or role (high priests, priests, scribes, procurator, and Caesar). Except for Nicodemus (3:1), we do not know the names of any other Pharisees or scribes because to know their affiliation or group is to know all about them. Note, for example, what the Pharisees say to the man born blind: "You are his disciples. We are the disciples of Moses" (9:28). Thus, people are known in terms of the teacher[23] they profess to follow.[24] Persons, moreover, were always embedded in someone else; wives in husbands, children in parents, and the like. Plutarch provides an excellent example of this, which minimizes individualism in favor of embeddedness:

The nurse rules the infant, the teacher the boy, the gymnasiarch the youth, his admirer the young man who, when he comes of age, is ruled by law and his commanding general. No one is his own master, no one is unrestricted. (*Dialogue on Love* 754D).

---

[21] See Bruce J. Malina and Jerome H. Neyrey, "First-Century Personality: Dyadic, Not Individualistic," in Jerome H. Neyrey, ed., *The Social World of Luke-Acts: Models for Interpretation* (Peabody, MA: Hendrickson, 1991), 67–96; and their *Portraits of Paul: An Archeology of Ancient Personality* (Louisville, KY: Westminster John Knox, 1996), 153–201.

[22] See Bruce J. Malina, *The New Testament World: Insights from Cultural Anthropology* 3rd ed. (Louisville, KY: Westminster John Knox, 2001), 63–67.

[23] We call attention to scholars now using "social-identity theory" for studying Paul and John. See Philip F. Esler, *Galatians* (London: Routledge, 1998); and Philip F. Esler and Ronald A. Piper, "Lazarus, Mary and Martha as Group Prototypes: Social Identity, Collective Memory and John 11–12," forthcoming.

[24] On just this point, see R. A. Culpepper, *The Johannine School* (1975), especially 171–96.

John presents Jesus as a group-oriented person. He is and remains totally embedded in his heavenly Father, even resting on his heart (1:18). He speaks and does all, but only what his Father instructs him: His Father gives him his own powers (5:19–28), reveals only to him unique words and mysteries, and guides and directs his career from his descent from heaven to his "lifting up" and his "glorification" by God. Jesus, faithful and loyal to the one who sent him, never acts on his own. He is, moreover, God's broker; he is the one who is "sent" – that is, agent and intermediary.[25] It should be part of our reading of this gospel to note the group-oriented characteristics of friend and foe. Disciples, for example, hear Jesus' voice (10:3–5), accept his teachings (12:23–26), are instructed in his secrets (15:15), and imitate his behavior (13:12–17).

ROLE AND STATUS

Formal use of the social-science concepts of role and status is extremely helpful in assessing the dramatis personae of the Fourth Gospel. Because the Johannine group is a social organization, we need to know who plays what role and who enjoys what status.[26] "Status" differs from "role" in that status is "a recognized position that a person occupies within society . . . [which] determines where he or she fits in relationship to everyone else."[27] "Status" suggests verticality, a ranking of people according to some criteria of worth or excellence. "Role" has to do with behavior and is "the socially recognized position of a person which entails rights and duties."[28] Put simply, status defines who one is socially – male or female, slave or free, Judean or Gentile – whereas role defines what one is expected to do socially on the basis of status. Whereas one *has* status, one *plays* a role.

Roles in the Fourth Gospel are easier to identify than status. We learn of family members, those of Jesus and then of other characters.[29] Jesus' family consists of Joseph, his father (6:42); God, his Father; his mother (2:1–12; 19:26–27); his aunt (19:25); and his brothers (7:3–5). Apart from Jesus' blood relatives, other brothers and sisters appear: Andrew and Peter (1:40); Martha, Mary, and Lazarus (11:1); and the sons of Zebedee (21:2). All persons in familial roles have rights and duties, and their roles last as long as the relationship endures. Furthermore, the various roles of Jesus are either acknowledged or denied, such as "prophet" (6:14; 7:52; 9:17), "king" (6:15; 12:13; 18:33–37), "Messiah" (1:41; 4:25–26; 7:31, 41–42),

[25] Peder Borgen, "God's Agent in the Fourth Gospel," in Jacob Neusner, ed., *Religions in Antiquity* (Leiden: Brill, 1968), 137–48.

[26] A full exposition of this material is deferred until the commentary on John 20 because only then will readers have observed the characters well enough to make this analysis.

[27] Raymond Scupin and Christopher DeCorse, *Anthropology and Global Perspective* (Englewood, NJ: Prentice Hall, 1995), 280.

[28] A. Paul Hare, "Groups: Role Structure," *IESS* 6.283.

[29] On the family of Jesus, see Sjef van Tilborg, *Imaginative Love* (Leiden: Brill, 1993); and Jan G. Van der Watt, *Family of the King: Dynamics of Metaphor in the Gospel According to John* (Leiden: Brill, 2000), 304–40.

and "teacher" (1:38; 3:2; 20:16). Similarly, we know of other roles: that of a Judean leader (3:2), high priests (11:49–51; 18:13–26), a "royal official" (4:46), a Roman procurator (chs. 18–19), and Caesar, who is owed the loyalty of his "friend" Pilate (19:12). Moreover, we know that some people play the role of ill persons: a man crippled for thirty-eight years (5:5), a man born blind (9:1), and a dying/dead man (11:1–42). Finally, members of the Jesus group are sometimes ascribed a role, such as "the ones sent"; that is, people with duties either to acclaim Jesus or to purify in his name (17:17; 20:21). Finally, Jesus will designate one person the chief shepherd of the group (21:15–19). It is hotly contested whether the Samaritan woman and Mary Magdalene have formal roles.

But "status" seems to be more important in this Gospel than roles because a character can enjoy very high status without playing a role. In the gender-divided world of antiquity, status begins with knowledge that a person is either male or female.[30] Furthermore, gender, such as female, is never an abstraction because "Every woman is a sister, daughter, wife, mother or aunt, and it is the role and relationship that usually determines how she will be perceived and treated."[31] The same can be said of males, who are brothers, sons, husbands, uncles, and so on. Oddly, gender does not immediately suggest status in the Fourth Gospel, for on occasion males do female tasks (e.g., Jesus giving water to the Samaritan woman, 4:10, 15) and females do male tasks (e.g., Mary roaming about seeking to find and carry away a corpse, 20:13, 15). But the critical issue for assessing the status of the characters in John lies in discerning the criteria whereby status is awarded or denied. Although readers can only discover these criteria by working their way through the entire gospel narrative, we anticipate the discussion of this in the commentary on John 20 by listing six criteria for high status in the Johannine group: (1) physical closeness to Jesus (anointing his feet, reclining on his breast, clasping his feet, touching his hand and side); (2) bold public acknowledgment of Jesus; (3) reception of revelations, secrets, and special knowledge; (4) imitation of Jesus (grain of wheat; greater love . . . than to lay down one's life); (5) enjoying the label "beloved," and (6) being called by name.[32] The six criteria for high status uniquely apply only to distinctive Johannine characters (Lazarus, Martha, Mary, the man born blind, the Beloved Disciple, and Mary Magdalene). It would appear that although they

---

[30] In the ancient gender-divided world, males and females were separated according to space, time, task, and tools; see Jerome H. Neyrey, "Jesus, Gender and the Gospel of Matthew," *Semeia Studies* 45 (2003), 43–52.

[31] The quotation is from Lila Abu-Lughod's *Veiled Sentiments: Honor and Poetry in a Bedouin Society* (Berkeley: University of California Press, 1986), cited in John J. Pilch, *Introducing the Cultural Context of the Old Testament* (New York: Paulist Press, 1991), 117.

[32] Although not marks of the highest status just listed, certain characters enjoyed status as insiders because they moved from darkness to light and from "*not* in the know" to "in the know." The only blessing in the Fourth Gospel is pronounced over those who "have not seen but believed" (20:29). Finally, certain characters, such as Nathanael, struggle through difficulties in accepting Jesus (1:45–49).

enjoy very high status, they do not have formal roles. In contrast, traditional figures, such as Andrew and Peter and the sons of Zebedee, part of "the Twelve," have much lower status, even though they appear to be the only people with ascribed roles.[33]

REVEALING AND CONCEALING: LANGUAGE AND THE STRATEGIES OF SECRECY

Bultmann quipped that in the Fourth Gospel Jesus reveals[34] that he is the Revealer, but not much else. This "information control" emerges as a central phenomenon in John and provides significant clues to the social dynamics of the community for which it was written. Writing on secrecy, Stanton K. Tefft notes that all peoples engage in some form of secrecy or information control,[35] a point also made by Kees Bolle: "Not only is there no religion without secrecy, but there is no human existence without it."[36] "Information control" is the label for the process whereby secrets, information, and revelations are shared with some but not with others. "Information control," moreover, not only describes Jesus' activity but clues the audience in to distinguishing insiders from outsiders in terms of "who knows what and when."

The Revealer. God remains "unknown" by all except Jesus, for "no one has ever seen God" (1:18; 5:37; 6:46). Jesus speaks the words of God, even if many do not grasp their meaning (3:34). Some who receive Jesus' revelation then disclose it to others (1:35–50). Nevertheless, at all levels, we observe a process of selected disclosure.

Selective Disclosure. Given the strategy of information control and conceal-ment, a careful reader will ask who in the narrative knows what and when? The answer to these questions provides data for ranking and classifying insiders. In Samaria, the Samaritan woman is progressively told secrets by Jesus. She begins the story as a character to whom Jesus said, "If only you knew . . . who it is who said to you 'Give me to drink,' you would have asked him . . ." (4:10). Entrusted with more secrets, she asks Jesus to "Give me this water" (4:15). Later she receives remarkable information (4:20–24), even a revelation of Jesus as the Messiah (4:26). The man born blind is gradually enlightened, from merely knowing Jesus' name, to acclaiming him a prophet, and then arguing that he

---

33 This phenomenon has long puzzled commentators; see Raymond E. Brown, *The Com-munity of the Beloved Disciple: The Life, Loves, and Hates of an Individual Church in New Testament Times* (New York: Paulist Press, 1979), 69–91.

34 See Saeed Hamid-Khani, *Revelation and Concealment of Christ: A Theological Inquiry into the Elusive Language of the Fourth Gospel* (Tübingen: Mohr Siebeck, 2000).

35 Stanton K. Tefft, *Secrecy: A Cross-Cultural Perspective* (New York: Human Sciences Press, 1980), 39.

36 Kees W. Bolle, *Secrecy in Religions* (Leiden: Brill, 1987), 1.

must enjoy God's favor (9:30–33). Jesus himself catechizes the man to believe in
the "Son of man" (9:35–38). Martha receives special information from Jesus, "I
am the Resurrection and the Life" (11:25), which prompts her to acknowledge
Jesus as "Messiah, the Son of God." At the last meal, Jesus reveals the identity of
his betrayer, but only to the Beloved Disciple (13:23–26). After that meal, select
disciples enjoy Jesus' private disclosure of secrets during the Farewell Address:
the meaning of the footwashing (13:12–17); information about where he is going
(14:1–7); identification of his replacement, who will disclose still more controlled
information (14:26); prophecies of future hard times (15:18–19; 16:1–4, 31–33);
explanation of some of his statements that seem ambiguous (16:16–22); and a
time when "figures," or information control, will no longer be used (16:25–30).
The disclosure of secrets continues after Jesus' resurrection. Mary Magdalene
receives both a Christophany at the empty tomb and a revelation of a remarkable secret that she is commanded to disclose to Jesus' "brethren": "Go to my
brethren and say to them,'I am ascending to my Father and your Father, to my
God and your God'" (20:17). Finally, Peter is given special information about
the death he would die in order to glorify God (21:18–19). Information, then, is
selectively disclosed, but only to certain persons.

Asides and Footnotes. The author selectively discloses to his audience information not even known to the narrative characters. Besides the translation of
certain Semitic terms into Greek (1:38, 41, 42; 4:25; 5:2; 9:7; 19:13, 17; 20:16), we
are given "footnotes" and "asides."[37] As M. C. Tenny has shown (see n.37), some
of these inform the reader of times and places (6:4; 7:2; 9:14; 10:22–23; 11:17),
customs (4:9; 19:40), recollections of the disciples (2:22; 12:16), explanations of
actions or situations (2:9; 4:2; 7:5, 39; 11:51; 12:6; 19:36–37; 21:19), identification
of persons (6:71; 7:50; 11:2; 18:10, 14, 40; 19:38–39), and indications of what Jesus
knows (2:24–25; 6:6; 13:1, 3). The narrator, moreover, gives special information
about himself to this select audience (1:14b; 19:35; 21:24–25), and on one occasion
he corrects a popular rumor (21:22–23). Thus secrets are shared, but only with
special people. Information is always controlled.

Jesus Knows All Secrets. Even if people try to keep their thoughts secret, Jesus
can read hearts, pierce ambiguity and deception, and know all secrets. There
is no information that Jesus does not know. Early in the narrative, we are told
that he did not trust himself with people: "Because he knew all people ... he
himself knew what was in man" (2:24–25). The author demonstrates repeatedly
that Jesus knows the secret thoughts and motivations of those with whom he
speaks:

---

[37] J. J. O'Rourke, "Asides in the Gospel of John," *NovT* 21 (1979), 210–29; M. C. Tenny, "The
Footnotes of John's Gospel," *BSac* 117 (1960), 350–64.

5:42	"I know that you do not have the love of God in you."
6:26	"You seek me, not because you saw signs, but because you ate your fill of the loaves."
6:64	"Jesus knew from the first who those were that did not believe."
8:19	"You know neither me nor my Father."
8:37	"My words find no place in you."
8:43–7	"Why do you not understand? It is because you cannot bear to hear my word. You are of your father the devil."

By reading their hearts, Jesus knows who are insiders or outsiders, and who believe or who feign interest in him. No one can keep secrets from him.

The Concealer. If Jesus selectively discloses secrets to some, he also keeps secrets according to various language patterns characteristic of this gospel: (1) questions asked, but not answered; (2) double-meaning words; (3) the pattern of statement–misunderstanding–clarification; (4) anti-language (language designed to conceal rather than communicate); (5) irony; and (6) consideration of Johannine epistemology.

Question Asked and Maybe Answered. Although Jesus said "Ask and you shall receive" (Matt 7:7), he maintains extraordinary control of information in the way he does or does not answer questions. Four types of questions are asked of Jesus: (1) "Who are you?"; (2) "What is this? What are you doing?"; (3) "Why are you doing this?"; and (4) "How can you say . . . ?" All of these questions touch upon Jesus' authorization, his tasks, and his relationship to God – significant pieces of information but not necessarily available for all.

Who Are You? Officials conduct formal inquiries about Jesus. They first investigate the Baptizer concerning his own identity but then his relationship to Jesus (1:19–22). The man cured at the pool is queried about Jesus (5:12–13), as are the parents of the man born blind (9:21). Jesus himself is asked specific questions about his identity: "Who are you?" (8:25) and "Whom do you make yourself out to be?" (8:53). Either an empty answer is given or one that reveals very little. Information here is strongly controlled when questions are not answered.

What Is This? What Does This Mean? If Jesus responds to a question, it is a selective disclosure. Both foe (7:36) and friend (16:17–18) examine his words: "What does he mean?" But meaning is concealed from them and disclosed only to insiders.

Why? What Motive? Investigations search for the reasons that something is done. For example, people directly ask Jesus "why?" questions: "Why cannot I follow you now?" (13:37) and "Why is it that you will manifest yourself to us and not to the world?" (14:22; see also 1:25). Balancing this, we can observe Jesus himself retorting "why?" to his opponents' question. Such questions generally result in attempted concealment from Jesus: "Why do you seek to kill me?" (7:19); "Why don't you understand?" (8:43); "Why don't you believe?" (8:46); "Why do you strike me?" (18:23); "Why are you weeping?" (20:15).

How Can This Be? How Can You Say? Others ask questions introduced by the adverb "how," which indicate how little of Jesus' secret is understood. People who have listened to Jesus react in incomprehension to his words:

3:4	"How can a man be born when he is old?"
6:42	"How does he say, 'I have come down from heaven'?"
6:52	"How can this man give us his flesh to eat?"
12:34	"How can you say that the Son of man must be lifted up?"

The fact that people ask these questions indicates either that information is withheld from them or they are not privy to the secret meanings of Jesus' words.

Jesus' Own Questions. Clearly, Jesus controls information when questions are asked of him.[38] But when Jesus asks his own "how" questions, he reveals how little his audience knows; that is, how well controlled his information is:

3:12	"How can you believe if I tell you heavenly things?"
5:44	"How can you believe, who receive glory from one another and do not seek the glory that comes from the only God?"
5:47	"If you do not believe his [Moses'] writings, how will you believe my words?"

Questions such as these reveal why information is withheld. The epistemology of outsiders is such that they belong to earth and so can know only earthly things.[39] Theirs is a literal understanding, devoid of spirit. Thus, although Jesus says many important things to the crowds, his words find no home in their earthly hearts; because they are not his sheep, they do not recognize his voice. Jesus, then, maintains a strategy of selective disclosure and concealment.

Double-Meaning Words. With this we enter the realm of concealment, which is expressed in specific linguistic patterns of secrecy. Although the use of double-meaning words has been extensively studied and lists of them compiled,[40] a few examples may help us understand how information is controlled by them. Jesus tells Nicodemus that people must be born "*anothen*," a word that could

---

[38] Jesus himself asks his opponents "why?" questions, which generally result in concealment by them: "Why do you seek to kill me?" (7:19); "Why don't you understand?" (8:43); "Why don't you believe?" (8:46); "Why do you strike me?" (18:23); "Why are you weeping?" (20:15).

[39] Jerome H. Neyrey, "John III – A Debate over Johannine Epistemology and Christology," *NovT* 23 (1981), 118–127.

[40] D. W. Wead, *The Literary Devices in John's Gospel* (Basel: Reinhardt, 1970); D. A. Carson, "Understanding Misunderstanding in the Fourth Gospel," *TynB* 33 (1982), 61–91; E. Richard, "Expressions of Double Meaning and Their Function in the Gospel of John," *NTS* 31 (1985), 96–112; and S. Hamid-Khani, *Revelation and Concealment of Christ* (2000), 5–17, 46–60.

mean "again" or "from above." The correct meaning is a factor of Nicodemus' choice, which reveals his character, and of Jesus' strategy of concealment. The audience knows that Nicodemus is both incapable of understanding spiritual things and the object of concealment. Similarly, "lifting up" may mean crucifixion (12:32–34) or exaltation (3:14), depending on whether one is an insider or outsider. The blindness from which the man in John 9 is healed becomes not only physical sight but insight by virtue of Jesus' revelation to him (9:35–38), but the "sight" of the Pharisees is labeled "blindness" (9:39–41). When Jesus uses words with several meanings, his strategy is to reveal to some but conceal from others.

Statement–Misunderstanding–Clarification. Many times, Jesus *states* something, that is *misunderstood* and prompts him to *speak* again.[41] Jesus' discourse with the Samaritan woman provides an excellent sample of this:

Statement:	"If you knew the gift of God, and who it is that is saying to you, 'Give me a drink,' you would have asked him, and he would have given you living water."
Misunderstanding:	"Sir, you have no bucket, and the well is deep. Where do you get that living water?"
Clarification:	"Everyone who drinks of this water will be thirsty again, but those who drink of the water that I will give them will never be thirsty. The water that I will give will become in them a spring of water gushing up to eternal life."

Sometimes this pattern describes the progressive revelation of secrets to a person once "*not* in the know" but who receives a Christophany (4:26) or special information (11:13–15, 25–26). But the converse also occurs: Some who misunderstand Jesus never come "into the know" or have their questions answered, and so are confirmed as obtuse outsiders (3:3–10; 6:41–48; 8:21–30). Thus Jesus' clarifications may be revelations leading either to further disclosure or concealment, but in all cases they serve as "information control."

Anti-language. Normally language should communicate, but not anti-language. Certain groups find themselves estranged from or in conflict with the larger society in which they are embedded. They develop not only an anti-society but an anti-language. They use "ordinary terms from the ordinary language of the larger society but give them special in-group meanings that are understood only by insiders."[42] Anti-language, then, is a distinctive form of concealment

---

41 Jerome H. Neyrey, The Sociology of Secrecy and the Fourth Gospel," in Fernando Segovia, ed., *What Is John? Volume II: Literary and Social Readings of the Fourth Gospel* (Atlanta: Scholars Press, 1998), 107–8.

42 Bruce J. Malina and Richard L. Rohrbaugh, *Social-Science Commentary on the Gospel of John* (Minneapolis, MN: Fortress Press, 1998), 46–47. See also Norman R. Petersen, *The Gospel of John and the Sociology of Light: Language and Characterization in the Fourth Gospel* (Valley Forge, PA: Trinity Press International, 1993), 89–109.

from outsiders but disclosure to insiders. Anti-language has several character-istics: (1) overlexicalization, the piling up of words that mean virtually the same thing;[43] (2) new oppositional terminology distinguishing in-group from out-group (light vs. darkness, 1:5; above vs. below, 8:23; life vs. death, 3:36; truth vs. lie, 8:44–45);[44] and (3) emphasis on interpersonal relations ("beloved disciples," "remain!" "love!"). Although readers may be familiar with Johannine dualisms and boundary making, anti-language brings into play the element of conceal-ment, whereby Jesus has no intention of disclosure to some people and speaks in a way calculated to maintain secrecy to outsiders. Its choice of words is "con-centrated in precisely those areas that are central to the protest of the subculture and distinguish it most sharply from the surrounding society."[45] Hence, I argue, Johannine anti-language intends *not* to communicate but to hide and disguise its contents. It is *not* intended to be decoded or to reveal but rather to conceal and create distance.[46]

Irony. In plays or narratives, irony consists of some people sharing knowledge of which a character is ignorant. Thus the character acts in a way grossly inap-propriate to the actual circumstances, expects the opposite of what fate holds in store, or says something that anticipates the actual outcome – but not at all in the way he means it.[47] Hence, irony is another mode of secrecy and information control.[48] From the perspective of the author, Capernaum and Jerusalem are filled with people who seem to act intelligently and with power but are totally ignorant of the events taking place. For example, the council that meets after the raising of Lazarus ironically tries to forestall two things: Jesus' gain in respect and honor, and the destruction of their "place" by the Romans. Their leader ironically got it right when he said "You know nothing at all!" (11:49), but then neither did he.

Ambiguity and Deception. Outsiders in the narrative are convinced that Jesus is hiding something or disguising himself – what we are calling "information control." Friends and foes "think" they know something, but the audience knows better. People think they understand Jesus when he speaks about Lazarus being "asleep" (11:13); those who slaughter the disciples "think" they are offering worship to God (16:2); the disciples "think" that Judas leaves the table to give

[43] Richard L. Rohrbaugh, "What's the Matter with Nicodemus? A Social-Science Perspective on John 3:1–21," in Holly E. Hearon, ed., *Distant Voices Drawing Near* (Collegeville, MN: Liturgical Press, 2004), 344–45.

[44] G. E. R. Lloyd, *Polarity and Analogy: Two Types of Argumentation in Early Greek Thought* (Cambridge: Cambridge University Press, 1966).

[45] R. L. Rohrbaugh, "What's the Matter with Nicodemus?" in *Distant Voices* (2004), 344.

[46] R. L. Rohrbaugh, "What's the Matter with Nicodemus?" in *Distant Voices* (2004), 350.

[47] Paul Duke, *Irony in the Fourth Gospel* (Atlanta: John Knox Press, 1985), 12.

[48] Instances of irony in the Fourth Gospel include 2:9–10; 4:12; 7:22, 33–34, 52; 8:21–22; 11:16, 36; 13:37; 18:31; 19:5, 14, 19ff.; see D. W. Wead, *The Literary Devices in John's Gospel* (1970), 47–68.

alms (13:29), and Mary "thinks" she sees a gardener (20:15). Some falsely "think" that Moses will intercede for them (5:45), whereas Jesus knows that he will be their judge. Jesus himself is a major source of ambiguity to the crowds. He performs remarkable healings, but because they occur on the Sabbath (5:9–11; 9:14), they *apparently* violate the Sabbath law, despite Jesus' rationalization for his behavior (7:21–23; see also 9:30–33). Jesus tries to dispel this ambiguity by instructing his critics not to "judge according to appearances" (7:24; see also 8:15). Crowds regularly express their uncertainty about Jesus, and so become divided over him, some acclaiming and others denouncing him (7:12–13, 27, 31, 40–41; 9:16–17, 28–34). Jesus, moreover, is skilled in unmasking their deception (7:32, 47–48). Because he reads hearts, he can remove the deception or ambiguity of those who claim to believe in him (8:31) by systematically penetrating the layers of lies, finally exposing them as the sons of Cain and Satan, who were both liars and murderers (8:44). Both Jesus and the crowds appear to each other as ambiguous and deceiving, but whereas Jesus can completely read the truth in his opponents, they are limited in what they see and misunderstand even that.

Hiding. Occasionally the Revealer "hides himself." After revealing great revelations in 8:56 and 8:58, Jesus "hid himself" from the enemies seeking to stone him (8:59) – a strategic move, no doubt, but one fraught with ambiguity when compared with Jesus' revelation to the crowd in 12:27–35. He warned his audience: "The light is with you a little longer. Walk while you have the light" (12:35). The Revealer soon ceases telling the crowds the word of God, for the light fades: "When Jesus had said this, he departed and hid himself from them" (12:36b). Later Judas asked, "Why is it that you will manifest yourself to us and not to the world?" (14:22), to which Jesus replied that he continues to disclose things to them but hides them from others. Whereas concealment is acceptable for Jesus, it is not acceptable for characters who "hide" themselves to avoid censure from their peers. Nicodemus comes secretly to Jesus at night to avoid detection (3:2; 19:39); others who are attracted to Jesus disguised their affiliations (12:42; 19:38).

CULTURAL SCENARIOS: INSIGHTS FROM THE SOCIAL SCIENCES

Modern readers unknowingly take a great risk if they presume that they can simply take up the Fourth Gospel and read it with understanding. This two-thousand-year-old document was written in a time and place utterly foreign to us, embodying complex social dynamics unfamiliar to modern readers. If Euro-Americans cannot understand the modern inhabitants of the Middle East, all the more should the peoples from these same regions in the Fourth Gospel present severe problems for understanding. Trying to avoid the Scylla of ethnocentrism and the Charybdis of anachronism, we suggest the use of the following cultural scenarios for a more sensitive, accurate interpretation of this foreign document. We will treat in some detail two overarching models that should shape our perception of the cultural world of the Fourth Gospel: *pivotal values* (honor and shame) and *patronage* (roles of patron, broker, and clients; the types of reciprocity). Many other important concepts from anthropology will be itemized at the end with reference to their location in the commentary.

Honor and Shame. The dynamic of honor and shame is deeply rooted in both Israelite and Greco-Roman cultures. Put simply, "honor" refers to the worth or value of persons both in their own eyes and in the eyes of their neighbors. It refers to the public role and status that individuals enjoy.[49] Honor basically focuses on social perception and evaluation: What do people think of this person? How is he evaluated, and by what criteria? Thus, honor means reputation, renown, and fame; that is, a person's "glory" or "good name." Explaining honor as "worth," Aristotle described it as follows:

'Worthy' Now the greatest external good we should assume to be the thing which we offer as a tribute to the gods, and which is most coveted by men of high station, and is the prize awarded for the noblest deeds; and such a thing is honour, for honour is clearly the greatest of external goods." (*N. E.* 4.3.9–12)[50]

"Love of honor" (*philotimia*), was commonly acknowledged as the prize both Greeks and Romans sought. Xenophon described the Athenians as passionate for praise: "Athenians excel all others not so much in singing or in stature or in strength, as in love of honour (*philotimia*), which is the strongest incentive to deeds of honour and renown" (*Mem.* 3.3.13). Later, in his review of the history of Rome, Augustine commented on the Roman obsession with the love of praise and renown: "For the glory that the Romans burned to possess is the favourable judgment of men who think well of other men" (*City of God* 5.12).[51]

In the Fourth Gospel, praise and glory provide a native's perspective on the way honor is claimed and acknowledged. Jesus enjoys the highest respect and honor because God gave them to him. God highly favors Jesus and so gives him the two divine powers (5:19–28), God's names, and God's words and deeds. Thus all that God is and does Jesus is and does. In addition, in amplifying praise, rhetoricians from Aristotle to Quintilian instruct us to dwell on the uniqueness of someone's traits or exploits:

[W]hat most pleases an audience is the celebration of deeds which our hero was the first or only man or at any rate one of the very few to perform: and to these we must add any other achievements which surpassed hope or expectation. (*Inst. Orat.* 3.7.16)[52]

---

49 Johannes Schneider, "Tiun", *TDNT* 8.169–80.

50 Aristotle says more about honor: "The thing which we offer as a tribute to the gods, and which is most coveted by men of high station, and is the prize awarded for the noblest deeds . . . is honour. . . . It is honour above all else which great men claim and deserve" (*N.E.* 4.3.9–12).

51 Jerome H. Neyrey, *Honor and Shame in the Gospel of Matthew* (Louisville, KY: Westminster John Knox, 1998), 16–19.

52 J. H. Neyrey, "Uniqueness," *Biblica* 86 (2005), 59–87.

In the Fourth Gospel, when the author states that Jesus *alone* sees God (1:18; 6:46) and that *no one* else has ever gone up to heaven but he who came down from there (3:13), he presents strong warrants for highest honor because of Jesus' uniqueness. Jesus, moreover, is the only or unique son of God (1:14, 18; 3:16, 18).[53] Often we are told that God has glorified Jesus and will glorify him again (8:54; 12:23; 13:31–32; 17:1, 4). God, moreover, mandates that "All . . . honor the Son just as they honor the Father. Anyone who does not honor the Son does not honor the Father" (5:23). Furthermore, God allows Jesus to embody his special name, "I AM," thus giving him extraordinary status. Therefore, we know two things: Jesus enjoys the full respect of God, and true honoring of God means that all should honor Jesus "just as they honor the Father." Respect means appreciating Jesus' signs as his credentials from God, the grounds for calling him a "prophet" or "king."

But not all honor Jesus or accept his credentials. Like most prophets, Jesus receives no respect in his homeland (4:44). Some in his audience accuse him of being demon possessed (8:49), thus insulting God by rejecting his agent. The evangelist gives us a reason for this denial of honor: Many are more interested in what the synagogue or their neighbors think than what God thinks. Hence they prefer the "glory that comes from one another" (5:44) to praise from God. Denial of Jesus' honor is expressed by hostile labels against him (7:12; 9:24), incessant challenges to him,[54] frequent forensic processes against him, and ultimately by his torture, death, and mutilation. Yet Jesus has the last laugh, for in John's logic his shame is ironically honor. In his shame, Jesus is glorified (13:31–32; 17:1–5); the mock enthronement of Jesus by the Romans is ironically true: He is glorified and lifted up in his death (19:1–3, 19).[55] The killing of Jesus is the occasion for demonstration of his "noble" death and of the power God gave him to lay down his life and take it back (10:11–18).

Honor regularly attaches itself to a name (for it identifies family and clan), an attribute (favorable or unfavorable), or some behavior. Plutarch's summary of the honor attached to names is invaluable to us:

Caius was the proper name; the second name, in this case Marcius, was the common name of family or clan; and the third name was bestowed subsequently because of some exploit, or fortune, or bodily feature, or special excellence in a man. So the Greeks used to

---

[53] This term "only begotten" (*monogenēs*) should be detached from the context of procreation and located in the realm of role/status, honor, and uniqueness. See Paul Winter, "ΜΟΝΟΓΕΝΗΣ ΠΑΡΑ ΠΑΤΡΟΣ," *ZRG* 5 (1953), 335–65; and R. L. Roberts, "The Rendering of 'Only Begotten' in John 3:16," *ResQ* 16 (1973), 2–22.

[54] Honor may be acquired by military, athletic, or aesthetic prowess, but especially in the push and shove of daily social life; see Jerome H. Neyrey, "The Trials (Forensic) and Tribulations (Honor Challenges) of Jesus: John 7 in Social Science Perspective." *BTB* 26 (1996), 107–24, and his "Questions, Chreiai, and Challenges to Honor: The Interface of Rhetoric and Culture in Mark's Gospel," *CBQ* 60 (1998), 657–81.

[55] Jerome H. Neyrey, "Despising the Shame of the Cross: Honor and Shame in the Johannine Passion Narrative," *Semeia* 69 (1996), 113–37.

give surnames from an exploit, as for instance, Soter (Savior), and Callinicus ("Winner");
or from a bodily feature, as Physcon (Fat-paunch) and Grypus (Hook-nose); or from a
special excellence, as Euergetes (Benefactor) and Philadelphus (Generous); or from some
good fortune, as Eudaemon (Prosperous). And some of their kings have actually had
surnames given them in mockery, as Antigonus Doson ("Always Promising"). (Plutarch,
Lives: Coriolanus 11.2–3)[56]

In the Fourth Gospel, Jesus is pejoratively identified as "son of Joseph" (1:45)
and honorably as "son of David" (7:42) and especially "Son of God" (1:34, 49;
3:18; 11:4; 19:7; 20:31). We do not name Jesus son of Joseph or David because of
any actions he performed. But because he is a "chip off the old block," who is
his heavenly Father, God, he manifests the powers of his heavenly Father in all
he says and does. Thus he is the unique and only Son of God. Others, moreover,
call him many honorable names, ranging from the neutral ("teacher": 1:38; 4:28;
13:13) to names of greater honor ("King": 1:49; 12:13; 18:33–37; 19:3, 14, 19; "Lord":
13:13; 20:28; "Messiah": 1:40; 7:26; 10:24; 11:27; 20:31; "Prophet": 4:19; 6:14; 7:40;
9:17; and "Savior of the world": 4:42).

If others honor him with these names, Jesus on his own describes himself
by means of two other names. Coming from Jesus, we interpret them as claims
to very high honor and respect. First, although Jesus tells both insiders and
outsiders about the "Son of Man,"[57] only insiders can possibly understand that
this name refers to his descent from and ascent to God's throne (3:3–14). For
example, he promises the disciples that they will see this Son of Man enthroned in
heaven with angel courtiers streaming to him from all directions (1:51). Although
people on earth may see this "Son of Man" on earth, his destiny is to return to
his heavenly glory. Second, the Gospel says that God gave Jesus his own name,
"I AM." In his farewell address, Jesus twice declares that he has manifested this
name to his disciples (17:6, 26), and twice he prays that God will keep them
in this name (17:10–11). This name, moreover, expresses a unique quality of a
true God, namely eternal existence: uncreated in the past and imperishable in
the future. When talking about Abraham, who died, Jesus states that "Before
Abraham came into being, I AM" (8:58). Abraham was born and died; not so
Jesus, who was before creation and who ascends to God's realm.

In the middle level of Greco-Roman education, young men of some social
prominence learned to "write"; that is, to compose a variety of genres necessary
to produce a speech at court, assembly, and graveside. Of the collected exercises
called the *progymnasmata*, we focus on the encomium, in which students were
taught how to find grounds for praise of someone. The standard contents of
the rules for an encomium provide us with a unique view of what the ancients

---

[56] Plutarch's analysis of names is in total agreement with the anthropological study of names;
       see Dale Eickelman, *The Middle East: An Anthropological Approach* (Englewood Cliffs, NJ:
       Prentice-Hall, 1989), 181–87.

[57] See Francis J. Moloney, S.D.B., *The Johannine Son of Man* (Rome: LAS, 1978).

considered honorable. Students were instructed to find praise in four areas of a person's life: (1) origins (place and parents); (2) nurture and training; (3) display of a person's fortune, physical acumen, and virtue; and (4) death and posthumous honors.[58] In assessing a person's origins, attention is first paid to place of birth and then to parents, ancestors, and clan. The place of birth was highly significant in antiquity because places carried a certain cachet of nobility or baseness. We find this encoded in the stereotypes of various places and peoples,[59] which generally escape the notice of modern readers. Whereas Paul boasts that he is a citizen of Tarsus, "no low-status city" (Acts 21:39),[60] many disqualify Jesus because he comes from Nazareth, from which "nothing good can come" (John 1:46). If Jerusalem communicates the sense of a large, sophisticated city, Galilee, on the other hand, is too mean to produce a prophet or messiah (7:41–43, 52).[61] Based on earthly criteria for noble places of origin, Jesus fails to earn respect. However, those who are "in the know" appreciate that Jesus' true origin is heaven, God's kingdom, whence he descends to this world and to which he will ascend (1:1–18; 13:1–3). How outsiders assess his origins, then, is shallow and erroneous. True disciples, in contrast, know whence he comes and whither he goes, and thus greatly honor Jesus.

Honor may also be drawn from a person's descent from noble parents, family, and ancestors. It was thought that offspring would be "chips off the old block" and so embody and display the nobility of their fathers. Outsiders claim that Jesus is the "son of Joseph" (6:42), hardly a source of nobility and honor. But, as always, these people do not know the truth about Jesus, much less that he speaks of his true Father, who resides in a heavenly kingdom. It is no minor matter that Jesus is considered "equal to God" (5:18; 10:33) or that God demands that Jesus have equal honor with himself (5:23). His origins, both place and family, are extraordinarily honorable, but only to those who think correctly.

Honor may also be drawn from nurture and training. In the case of Greco-Roman elites, this referred to education under a famous teacher, training in philosophy, or prowess in military, athletic, and aesthetic skills. Unlike in Luke 2:41–51, the evangelist here has nothing to say about the way Jesus was raised or educated. The topic appears only in 7:15, where outsiders are surprised that Jesus presumes to have public voice: "How does this man have such learning, when he

---

[58] Jerome H. Neyrey, "Josephus' *Vita* and the Encomium: A Native Model of Personality," *JSNT* 25 (1994), 177–206; B. J. Malina and J. H. Neyrey, *Portraits of Paul* (1996), 23–63; and J. H. Neyrey, *Honor and Shame in Matthew* (1998).

[59] B. J. Malina and J. H. Neyrey, *Portraits of Paul* (1996), 117–24, 169–74.

[60] On the stereotyped evaluation of cities, see Jerome H. Neyrey, "Luke's Social Location of Paul: Cultural Anthropology and the Status of Paul in Acts," in Ben Witherington III, ed., *History, Literature, and Society in the Book of Acts* (Cambridge: Cambridge University Press, 1996), 251–79.

[61] See Richard L. Rohrbaugh, "The Pre-Industrial City in Luke-Acts: Urban Social Relations," in Jerome H. Neyrey, ed., *The Social World of Luke-Acts: Models for Interpretation* (Peabody, MA: Hendrickson, 1991), 125–37.

has never been taught?" But Jesus maintains that he was indeed taught by God. For example, "The son does only what he sees the Father doing. . . . The Father loves the son and shows him all that he himself is doing" (5:19–20); the words Jesus speaks are not his own (12:29), for he speaks the words of God (3:34); the Father has placed all things in Jesus' hand (3:35) such that the works Jesus does are those authorized by God (5:36; 8:47; 10:25; 17:4); "My teaching is not mine, but his who sent me" (7:16); and Jesus revealed God's name to his disciples (17:6, 11, 26). Because Jesus was nurtured, trained, and educated by the wisest of all teachers, he deserves great respect.

Third, praise may be drawn from consideration of a person's virtues. In the Greco-Roman world and in certain streams of Hellenistic Judaism, we find a commonplace of four cardinal virtues (wisdom, justice, courage, and temperance). In regard to Jesus' virtues, I focus on "justice" as piety to God:

> The parts of justice are piety, fair dealing and reverence: piety toward the gods, fair dealing towards men, reverence toward the departed. Piety to the gods consists of two elements: being god-loved and god-loving. The former means being loved by the gods and receiving many blessings from them, the latter consists of loving the gods and having a relationship of friendship with them." (*Menander Rhetor* I.361.17–25)

Unlike other writers who talk explicitly of Jesus' obedience (Phil 2:8; Heb 5:8), this author emphatically tells us throughout that Jesus was "sent" by the Father; all that he says and does, then, are mandated by God. Jesus is the unique and faithful agent of God. Jesus himself tells the crowds, but especially his disciples, that he has commands from God (10:17–18) and that he has faithfully fulfilled them (14:31; 15:10). The evangelist concentrates this material in the last part of the Farewell Address, in which Jesus prays to God, acknowledging his obedience. He speaks first a generalized statement of his obedience: "I glorified you on earth by finishing the work that you gave me to do" (17:4). He then tells God aspects of this "work." Jesus has given the disciples the words God gave him (17:8, 14) and he has manifested the name that God gave him (17:6, 26). And it can be said that Jesus is God-loving and God-loved: The Father loves the Son (3:35; 10:17) and glorifies him (8:54). Thus Jesus demonstrates the superior virtue of justice because of his faithfulness and obedience to God.

Fourth, many funeral orations and encomia dealt with the phenomenon of a warrior's or hero's death. Honor, the orators argue, can be drawn from death if it is "noble." A commonplace about what constituted a "noble" death then developed. Honorable deaths benefited the polis, displayed the virtues of courage and justice, were voluntarily chosen, and manifested victory even in death or received posthumous honors and even immortality. In 10:11–18, the author describes Jesus' role as shepherd in terms of the canons of a "noble" death. The Shepherd dies for the sheep, courageously faces the wolf, and shows loyalty to his flock. No one takes his life from him; he lays it down voluntarily. His death affirms this gospel.

Therefore, it seems one could hardly evaluate the character of Jesus appropriately without knowing the code of honor and shame. Only by knowing this native value system will the honorable roles and status of Jesus be made salient and understood in terms of the native value system of honor and shame. As Jesus himself said, "All may honor the Son just as they honor the Father. Anyone who does not honor the Son does not honor the Father who sent him" (5:23). There is no Johannine Christology apart from honor and shame.

Patron–Broker–Client. The ancient world both understood and engaged in some form of patron–client relationship, whether it was between centurions and villagers (Luke 7:1–10) or Caesar and procurator (John 19:12). "Patronage" is a broad concept that aids in understanding a series of relationships, such as God–man, saint–devotee, godfather–godchild, lord–vassal, landlord–tenant, politician–voter, professor–student, and so forth. But we need to know more about the characteristics of these relationships:[62]

1. *Asymmetrical relationships* occur between parties of different status, representing a vertical dimension of superior and inferior relationships.[63]
2. *Simultaneous exchange* of different types of resources occurs, above all instrumental, economic, and political ones by the benefactor, and from the client promises of reciprocity, solidarity, and loyalty.
3. *Interpersonal obligation* is prevalent, couched in terms of personal loyalty or attachment between patrons and clients.[64]
4. *Favoritism* is frequently present.
5. *Reciprocity.* As basic goods and services are exchanged, notions of *reciprocity* arise and clients generally incur a *debt*.
6. *"Fictive kinship glaze"* reduces the crassness of the exchange; the client becomes the "son" of his patron/father, and those who serve Jesus are no longer his slaves but "friends."
7. *Honor*, both given and received, is a significant feature of these relationships.

---

[62] A. Blok, "Variations in Patronage," *Sociologische Gids* 16 (1969), 366. See also Ernst Gellner and John Waterbury, eds., *Patrons and Clients in Mediterranean Societies* (London: Duckworth, 1977), 1–7.

[63] See E. Gellner and J. Waterbury, *Patrons and Clients* (1977), 4; and Richard P. Saller, *Personal Patronage under the Early Empire* (Cambridge: Cambridge University Press, 1982), 1–2.

[64] John Rich's "Patronage and International Relations in the Roman Republic," in *Patronage in Ancient Society,* ed. Andrew Wallace-Hadrill (London: Routledge, 1990), 128, describes the importance of loyalty/faithfulness in the patron–client relationship: "In one of the most important of its many uses *fides* means 'protection.' The weaker party is said 'to be in the *fides*' of the stronger. At the formation of such a relationship, the weaker party is said to give himself into or entrust himself to the *fides* of the stronger and the stronger to receive the weaker into his *fides*."

We also need to know what types of reciprocity characterize the exchange between patrons and clients; what "goods" are exchanged? Three types of reciprocity were practiced in the ancient Mediterranean: generalized, balanced, and negative.[65]

Types of Reciprocity	Comparative Aspects
Generalized	1. *characteristic:* give without expectation of return 2. *forms:* child rearing, hospitality 3. *recipients:* parents, children, kin 4. *biblical examples:* Matt 7:11; John 3:16; 11:3–6; 13:34
Balanced	1. *characteristic:* tit-for-tat, quid pro quo 2. *forms:* barter, assistance agreements 3. *recipients:* neighbors 4. *biblical examples:* 1 Cor 9:3–12; Matt 10:10; John 6:1–15
Negative	1. *characteristic:* exploitation; reap where one does not sow 2. *forms:* robbery, buy cheap, sell dear 3. *recipients:* strangers, enemies 4. *biblical examples:* John 19:8, 10; 12:6; 13:27–30

If parents express the solidarity extreme of altruistic generosity to their family and kin, then thieves and robbers exemplify the unsocial extreme to strangers, enemies, and others. But in villages where all know that "charity begins at home," all exchanges are made with the clear expectation of balanced reciprocity.

What is exchanged? Were we to catalog all that patrons and clients exchange, our list would stretch to the moon. Comprehensive, yes, but hardly comprehensible. Social scientists, however, provide models for classifying the materials in these exchanges by creating four abstract categories that serve as baskets into which all benefactions may be put:[66] power, commitment, material goods, and influence. When patrons such as kings protect and deliver their subjects, they provide power. Gifts of seed, food, dowries for daughters, and hospitality illustrate inducement. As regards influence, teachers give instruction to students as sibyls, oracles, and prophets provide secret knowledge to their petitioners. Commitment refers to faithfulness, loyalty, and obedience, as well as to fictive-kin bonds, grants of honor and respect (i.e., doxologies and hymns to the gods), and the language of "friends" and friendship.

---

[65] Marshall Sahlins, *Stone-Age Economics* (Chicago: Aldine-Atherton Press, 1972), 185–230; and Bruce J. Malina, *Cultural Anthropology and Christian Origins* (Atlanta: John Knox Press, 1986), 98–106.

[66] Talcott Parsons, *Politics and Social Structure* (New York: The Free Press, 1969). See also Terence S. Turner, "Parsons' Concept of 'Generalized Media of Social Interaction' and Its Relevance for Social Anthropology," *Sociological Inquiry* 39 (1968), 121–34; and B.J. Malina, *Cultural Anthropology and Christian Origins* (1986), 77–87.

Before we utilize these notions to interpret the patron–client phenomenon in the Fourth Gospel, we must distinguish two sets of relationships. On the one hand, God acts as patron to his client, Jesus; but Jesus himself acts as broker to God's clients on earth. It is now a commonplace to understand "Father" less as a gender label and more as a patron.[67] When Israelites, Greeks, and Romans call god "Father," they understand this title as referring to god as benefactor or patron, as Dio Chrysostom illustrates: "At that time, the Creator and Father of the World, beholding the work of his hands . . . " (*Oration* 36.60).[68] Its meaning, however, must derive from examination of the earthly paternal role; that is, the rights and duties of earthly fathers. Their duties include protection, nurture, and socialization of their children,[69] and their rights include obedience and respect, as in "Honor your father and your mother." Jesus' patron, moreover, bestows many benefactions on his son/client, including "works" (5:36), "words" (17:8, 14), a "name" (17:12), "glory" (17:3, 22), "honor" (5:23), and "all things" (13:3). In a series of verbs expressing God's commissioning and honoring of Jesus, God "sends" Jesus (3:34; 4:46; 7:28–29, 33), loves him (3:35; 15:9), gives him great powers (5:21–28) and peoples (6:39), and shows him all that he does (5:19–20).

In terms of the four classifications of things that might be exchanged, God gives Jesus *power* (5:19–28), especially power to lay down his life and take it back again (10:17–18); *commitment* in terms of kinship with God and honor from him (5:23); *inducement*, such as his access to abundant wine (2:6–7) and bread (6:11–13); and *influence* by virtue of his unique access to God, for he alone makes God known.

Jesus in turn "honors his father." Repeatedly he insists that he came to do his Father's will (4:34; 5:30; 6:38–40, 12:43) and seek only the Father's glory (7:18; 8:49–50). In this respect, Jesus models the ideal response of a client to a patron quite differently from many in his audience, who seek their own glory (5:41, 44; 7:18). Jesus fulfills the commands that he received from God (10:18; 12:49–50; 15:10). Thus the "Father" is revealed as a most generous patron to Jesus, who in turn totally honors and obeys his Patron-Father.

Jesus, however, functions also as broker to God's clients, the house of Israel. Whether we call Jesus "broker," agent, mediator, priest, or prophet, all of these variants function in the same way: They bridge, speak on behalf of, or serve as ambassador to or messenger between those who send and authorize them and

---

67 See Mary Rose D'Angelo, "Abba and 'Father': Imperial Theology and the Jesus Traditions," *JBL* 111 (1992), 611–30; and her "Theology in Mark and Q: Abba and 'Father' in Context," *HTR* 85 (1992), 149–74.

68 See Jerome H. Neyrey, "God, Benefactor and Patron: The Major Cultural Model for Interpreting the Deity in Greco-Roman Antiquity," *JSNT* 27 (2005) 465–92.

69 See Jerome Neyrey, "Father," in Carroll Stuhlmuller, ed., *The Collegeville Pastoral Dictionary of Biblical Theology* (Collegeville, MN: Liturgical Press, 1996), 315–19. See also John J. Pilch, " 'Beat His Ribs While He Is Young' (Sir 30:12): A Window on the Mediterranean World," *BTB* 23 (1993), 101–13.

the sender's clients.[70] Greco-Roman deities often employed intermediaries to communicate with mortals, such as Hermes/Mercury[71] or oracles, prophets, or sibyls. Mortals in turn employed persons whom we call "priests" to sacrifice, petition, and consult the deity for them. Mortals, moreover, used mediators and go-betweens for purposes of trade, politics, legal matters, and the like. A good broker was a person trusted by both patron and client. He had a foot in both worlds, so that he adequately represented the interests of both parties and strove to bridge them effectively. Brokers were necessary because both heavenly and earthly monarchs dwelt "in unapproachable light." Some go-between was necessary to safely and honorably approach the inaccessible One.

Brokers are known in terms of their function (i.e., priest), but in the Fourth Gospel Jesus the broker is called "prophet" (6:14; 9:14) and "king" (12:13; 18:33–37; 19:19). "Agent," although not an actual title, is the most frequent role that describes Jesus' relationship with the Father and with his followers, a role constantly in view. Concentrating only on John 14–17, we find a wealth of material describing Jesus' brokerage. In addition to announcing that "I go to prepare a place for you" (14:2–3), he claims that he is the unique broker: "No one can come to the Father except through me" (14:5–6). He tells us, moreover, why he makes an excellent broker: He has been in the presence of the Patron (1:1–18) and will return there (17:5; 20:17). He belongs as fully as possible in the world of the Patron, and to see him is to see the Patron (14:8–9). In fact, he should be considered "equal to God" (5:18; 10:33). Balancing this, we learn that he is also dedicated to the interests of his clients: "I kept them" (17:12); "I desire also, that those you have given me, may be with me where I am" (17:24). He also petitions the Patron on their behalf: "Protect them" (17:11, 15).

Patron–broker–client relations are most evident when we examine the language about "dwelling" and "being in." The brokerage of Jesus is expressed in the way God the Patron dwells in Jesus and the disciples remain in him. "Dwelling" occurs frequently in the Farewell Address, especially as the durability of all relationships seems questionable. Thus, in light of Jesus' approaching death, his relationship with his Patron-Father is reaffirmed: "Believe me that I am in the Father and the Father is in me" (14:10, 11). This mutual indwelling expresses profound confidence, for it claims that the relationship of patron and broker will most assuredly endure. Similarly, Jesus promises to "dwell" with his disciples (14:25), but he also demands that they "dwell" in the vine (15:4, 5, 7) – all of which express enduring brokerage relationships, for the branches who dwell in the vine will "bear much fruit." Moreover, the author speaks about

---

[70] On brokerage in patron–client relations, see S. N. Eisenstadt and L. Roniger, *Patrons, Clients and Friends: Interpersonal Relations and the Structure of Trust in Society* (Cambridge: University of Cambridge Press, 1984), 81–84, 226.

[71] John N. Collins, *Diakonia: Re-interpreting the Ancient Sources* (Oxford: Oxford University Press, 1990), 90–92.

persons "being in" others, which resembles the relationships noted earlier. For example, eventually the disciple will "know" the ultimate knowledge: "I am in my Father and you are in me and I in you" (14:20). Thus the patron continues his relationship with the broker, and if the clients remain in the broker, their access to the patron is assured.

If we ask what Jesus does when he brokers, he links both patron to clients and clients to patron. We noted that Jesus, the agent, brings to the clients God's works, words, the name, and power to heal and become children of God, as well as a surfeit of wine and bread. No one has ever seen God but the Son-Broker who has made him known. He is the unique Son-Broker whom the Patron sent into the world to save it. He brokers power, commitment, material goods, and influence; in short, all that God has and can do now resides in the Son-Broker. Alternatively, Jesus' brokerage facilitates the clients' access to the Patron. We observe this in the extensive remarks Jesus gives the disciples on petitionary prayer. These instructions on petitionary prayer are Jesus' brokerage because all such prayers will be made to the Patron "in my name": "If in my name you ask for anything, I will do it" (14:14), and "the Father will give you whatever you ask for in my name" (15:16). Moreover, Jesus is intimately involved in the Father-Patron's sending to them "another Advocate." Jesus states that "I will ask the Father, and he will give you another Advocate" (14:16), and in another place that the Patron will send this Advocate "in my name," presumably in response to Jesus' petition. Finally, "I will send to you [the Advocate] from the Father" (15:26). Jesus clearly functions as broker for the clients needing the Patron's assistance.

Although the terminology of patron–broker–client may be new to readers, most of us are familiar with the way prayer, praise, and glory in the New Testament are given to God *through Jesus Christ*, either through petitionary prayers (Rom 1:8, 7:25; 1 Cor 15:57) or doxologies (Heb 13:20–21; Jude 25). Jesus, then, mediates the heavenly patronage of God to us, even as he functions to mediate earthly petitions and praise to the heavenly Patron.

Therefore, examination of the Fourth Gospel by means of patron–broker–client relationships is another native model of social relationship that was common in the ancient world. By means of it we are able to appreciate roles and relationships in the Gospel, appreciating in particular the broker role of Jesus, which describes his relationship with God and with the Israel in whose midst he pitched his tent.

OTHER SIGNIFICANT CULTURAL CONCEPTS

Glory. Although technically this belongs in the "honor and shame" section, it deserves separate treatment because it is the author's favorite term to express the relationship between Jesus and God. Moreover, Jesus levels a steady criticism against the crowds for seeking their own glory rather than that of God. The social interpretation of "glory" may be found in the *Closer Look* "Give God the Glory" in the commentary at 12:27–36.

Gossip Network. To assess what roles various characters may play or not play, we need to study how information traveled in the age before the printing press and electronic media. Many people tell others various bits of information, but the issue raised is whether we should consider all who bring "gossip," which is news, not slander, as having a formal role. A general discussion of this topic may be found in the *Closer Look* "How Information and News Travels in a Pre-Media Culture" at 20:16–18. Two specific discussions of "gossip network" are presented in regard to the Samaritan woman at 4:27–30 and Mary Magdalene at 20:14–18.

Limited Good and Envy. One of the most pernicious sources of conflict in antiquity was envy, which arose because of the perception that as someone gained honor and respect, surely another was losing the same – probably me! John's disciples envy Jesus (3:22–30), just as the Jerusalem elites are provoked to envy over Jesus' raising of Lazarus (11:45–52). The *Closer Look* at 3:21–30 provides a cameo of this social phenomenon.

Names. Names, too, belong in the model of honor and shame, for they communicate role and status; they may acknowledge honor or label another as lacking respect and worth. A cultural discussion of names may be found in the *Closer Look* "The Meaning of Names" in the commentary at 17:6–12.

Role and Status. Some of this material appeared earlier in the discussion of characters. Because it can serve as a way to decide which character has a role to speak to outsiders or to speak to insiders, a cursory discussion of role and status occurs in the commentary at 4:27–30, in the *Closer Look* "Role and Status, What's the Difference?" at 11:20–28, in the extensive chart at 12:14–19, which classifies most Johannine characters, and in 20:15–18.

Secrecy. Despite the common claim that Jesus is the Great Revealer, in fact he is the man of many secrets, who lives in a world of lying and ambiguity. The model of secrecy is presented in two places, first in the *Closer Look* "The Revealer Keeps Secrets" at 11:45–53 and later in the commentary on 18:19–23.

Status Transformation Rituals and Ceremonies. The Fourth Gospel proposes several transformation rituals, at entrance into the kingdom (3:3–5), passage from ignorance to knowledge, illness to health, and death into life. Ceremonies are few in the Gospel, mainly accounts of meals such as that at the home of Mary, Martha, and Lazarus (12:1–6) and the final meal (13:1–17, 26). The commentary on the footwashing (13:4–11, 12–20) depends on knowing the difference between transformation and ceremony.

Territoriality. The author identifies many places and has a distinct interpretation of them. Galilee and Jerusalem stand for places and times where Jesus receives acceptance or not; "not on this mountain nor in Jerusalem" requires one to know more about fixed and fluid space. Territoriality is the social-scientific model for studying the cultural and social meaning given to places: classification (sacred/profane; mine/yours); communication of the classification (walls, doors, signs); and control of the space. The Johannine Gospel stands in opposition to the Temple and its fixed sacred space and so consciously opts for an understanding of fluid sacred space. This model is particularly helpful in the interpretation of 2:23–25 and 4:21–24.

Time. Just as with space, there are many references to time in the Fourth Gospel that require readers to interpret beyond chronological and calendar time. Although considering them in symbolic terms aids their interpretation, what is needed is a social-science mode of "telling time" in this Gospel, which is provided in the commentary on 2:4 and the *Closer Look* there.

Just as savvy travelers read up about a country and its customs before they travel there, so should readers have basic knowledge about the socio-rhetorical character of the Fourth Gospel. As respectful tourists, readers have a start on understanding the author of the Fourth Gospel and his characters on their own terms and in their own value system. The topics chosen for this introduction are by no means scholarly chit-chat but essential lenses for seeing what is really going on in the Gospel. They are chosen because they give readers the biggest bang for the buck. And because the size and scope of this commentary cannot answer every question, it can point readers into areas and authors of interest, both in the notes and in the Suggested Readings Section. But what is here should provide a fresh reading of John that although it contains material familiar to readers brings into the conversation exciting, interesting, and provocative interpretations – particularly from a socio-rhetorical perspective.

II. Suggested Reading on the Gospel of John

COMMENTARIES

Commentaries on the Fourth Gospel come in many sizes: extra large (Rudolf Schnackenburg, *The Gospel According to St. John*, 3 vols. [New York: Herder and Herder, 1968–1982]), large (Raymond E. Brown, *The Gospel According to John* [Garden City, NY: Doubleday, 1966–1970]), and manageable (Charles H. Talbert, *A Literary and Theological Commentary on the Fourth Gospel and the Johannine Epistles* [New York: Crossroads, 1992]). Brown's commentary still reigns as a most balanced work, even after thirty years. Still full of insight and good judgment is C. K. Barrett's *The Gospel According to St. John*, 2nd ed. (Philadelphia: Westminster, 1978). Francis J. Moloney's three-volume commentary, *Belief in the Word: Reading John 1–4* (1993), *Signs and Shadows: Reading John 5 –12* (1996), and *Glory not Dishonor: Reading John 13 –21* (1998), all published by Fortress Press, offers an informed, accessible, and theological reading. In evaluating commentaries, consult Margaret Davies, "Which Is the Best Commentary? XI: The Fourth Gospel," *ExpT* 99 (1987), 73–78. Other worthwhile commentaries are:

George Beasley-Murray, *John* (Nashville, TN: Thomas Nelson, 1999).
D. A. Carson, *The Gospel According to John* (Grand Rapids, MI: Eerdmans, 1991).
C. H. Dodd, *The Interpretation of the Fourth Gospel* (Cambridge: Cambridge University Press, 1968).
Craig S. Keener, *The Gospel of John: A Commentary* (Peabody, MA: Hendrickson, 2003).
John Painter, *The Quest for the Messiah: The History, Literature and Theology of the Johannine Community*, 2nd ed.(Nashville, TN: Abingdon Press, 1993).
Ben Witherington, *John's Wisdom: A Commentary on the Fourth Gospel* (Louisville, KY: Westminster John Knox, 1995).

LITERARY, RHETORICAL, SYMBOLIC, AND IRONIC STUDIES

The Fourth Gospel, written in simple Greek, emphasizes Jesus as Logos and Revealer. And many scholars keep reminding us of its irony, double-meaning words, symbolism, and riddles. Similarly, R. Alan Culpepper's *Anatomy of the Fourth Gospel* (Philadelphia: Fortress Press, 1983) invites us to read the Fourth Gospel in terms of contemporary narrative and literary theory. See also:

D. A. Carson, "Understanding Misunderstanding in the Fourth Gospel," *TynB* 33 (1982), 61–91.

Margaret Davies, *Rhetoric and Reference in the Fourth Gospel* (Sheffield: JSOT Press, 1992).

Paul Duke, *Irony in the Fourth Gospel* (Atlanta: John Knox Press, 1985).

Saeed Hamid-Khani, *Revelation and Concealment of Christ: A Theological Inquiry into the Elusive Language of the Fourth Gospel* (Tübingen: Mohr Siebeck, 2000).

Dorothy A. Lee, *The Symbolic Narratives of the Fourth Gospel: The Interplay of Form and Meaning* (Sheffield: JSOT Press, 1994).

Earl Richard, "Expressions of Double Meaning and Their Function in the Gospel of John," *NTS* 31 (1985), 96–112.

Tom Thatcher, *The Riddles of Jesus: A Study in Tradition and Folklore* (Atlanta: Society of Biblical Literature, 2000).

SOCIOLOGICAL AND ANTHROPOLOGICAL APPROACHES

Scholars have begun to interpret the Fourth Gospel from the perspective of the social sciences, focusing on one or another concept or model. Wayne Meeks authored a very influential article, "Son of Man from Heaven in Johannine Sectarianism," *JBL* 91 (1972), 44–72, although his social theory is minimal. The pioneering commentary for reading John in this manner is that of Bruce J. Malina and Richard L. Rohrbaugh, *Social-Science Commentary on the Gospel of John* (Minneapolis, MN: Fortress Press, 1998); its clarity and succinctness make it a convenient way into this type of reading. Recent attention has been given to the study of Johannine language, especially by Bruce Malina in his *The Gospel of John in Sociolinguistic Perspective*, Protocol of the 48th Colloquy (Berkeley, CA: The Center for Hermeneutical Studies, 1985), and by Richard Rohrbaugh in his "What's the Matter with Nicodemus? A Social Science Perspective on John 3:1–21," in Holly E. Hearon, ed., *Distant Voices Drawing Near: Essays in Honor of Antoinette Clark Wire* (Collegeville, MN: The Liturgical Press, 2004), 145–58. Other significant applications of social-science methods for reading John include:

Tricia G. Brown, *Spirit in the Writings of John* (New York: T & T Clark, 2003).

Bruce J. Malina, "John's Maverick Christian Group – The Evidence of Sociolinguistics," *BTB* 24 (1994), 167–82.

Jerome H. Neyrey, *An Ideology of Revolt: John's Christology in Social-Science Perspective* (Philadelphia: Fortress Press, 1988).

"The Sociology of Secrecy and the Fourth Gospel," in Fernando Segovia, ed., *What is John? Volume II: Literary and Social Readings of the Fourth Gospel* (Atlanta: Scholars Press, 1988), 79–109.

"What's Wrong with this Picture? John 4, Cultural Stereotypes of Women, and Public and Private Space," *BTB* 24 (1994), 77–91.

"Despising the Shame of the Cross: Honor and Shame in the Johannine Passion Narrative," *Semeia* 69 (1996), 113–37.

"Spaces and Places, Whence and Whither, Homes and Rooms: Territoriality in the Fourth Gospel," *BTB* 32 (2002), 60–74.

Jerome H. Neyrey and Richard L. Rohrbaugh, "'He Must Increase, I Must Decrease'(John 3:30): Cultural and Social Interpretation," *CBQ* 63 (2001), 476–81.

Norman R. Petersen, *The Gospel of John and the Sociology of Light: Language and Characterization in the Fourth Gospel* (Valley Forge, PA: Trinity Press International, 1993).

BACKGROUND: ISRAELITE AND GRECO-ROMAN

Rarely do scholars give much attention to the Greco-Roman environment as an influence on the Fourth Gospel. Peder Borgen's survey, "The Gospel of God and Hellenism: Some Observations," in R. Alan Culpepper and C. Clifton Black, eds., *Exploring the Gospel of John* (Louisville, KY: Westminster John Knox, 1996), 98–123, is all the more important. Some individual studies examine John's use of Hellenistic commonplaces, such as Jerome H. Neyrey's "The 'Noble' Shepherd in John 10: Cultural and Rhetorical Background," *JBL* 120 (2001), 267–80. But most attention is given to John's engagement with feasts and customs, especially knowledge of Judean midrash and arguments. The premier scholar in this regard is Peder Borgen; see especially his *Bread from Heaven: An Exegetical Study of the Concept of Manna in the Gospel of John and the Writings of Philo* (Leiden: Brill, 1965). See also:

C. K. Barrett, *The Gospel of John and Judaism* (Philadelphia, PA: Fortress Press, 1975).

Peder Borgen, "God's Agent in the Fourth Gospel," in Jacob Neusner, ed., *Religions in Antiquity* (Leiden: Brill, 1968).

Raymond E. Brown, "Proposed Influences on the Religious Thought of the Fourth Gospel," in his *An Introduction to the Gospel of John* (New York,: Doubleday, 2003), 115–50.

W. D. Davies, "Reflections on Aspects of the Jewish Background of the Gospel of John," in R. Alan Culpepper and C. Clifton Black, eds., *Exploring the Gospel of John* (Louisville, KY: Westminster John Knox, 1996), 43–64.

Hugo Odeberg, *The Fourth Gospel: Interpreted in Its Relation to Contemporaneous Religious Currents in Palestine and the Hellenistic-Oriental World* (Amsterdam: B. R. Grüner, 1974).

HISTORY OF INTERPRETATION

It is a regular feature of scholarship to produce surveys of recent interpretations of biblical literature, and the Fourth Gospel has by no means been neglected. Admitting that modern studies are limited by contemporary scholarship, Robert Kysar's survey "The Fourth Gospel in Recent Research," *ANRW* 2.25.3 (1984), 2391–2480, is the exception to the rule. Each of the following articles contributes something different to readers who wish to be brought up to speed on the Gospel of John:

David Ball, "Some Recent Literature on John: A Review Article," *Themelios* 19 (1993), 13–18.

D. A. Carson, "Selected Recent Studies of the Fourth Gospel," *Themelios* 14 (1989), 57–64.

Colleen M. Conway, "The Production of the Johannine Community: A New Historicist Perspective," *JBL* 121 (2002), 479–95.

R. B. Edwards, "John and the Johannines: A Survey of Some Recent Commentaries," *BTrans* 43 (1991), 140–51.

C. R. Koester, "R. E. Brown, and J. L. Martyn: Johannine Studies in Retrospect," *BTB* 21 (1991), 51–55.

R. Kysar, "The Gospel of John in Current Research," *RSRev* 9 (1973), 314–23.

The Fourth Evangelist and His Gospel: An Examination of Contemporary Scholarship (Minneapolis, MN: Augsburg Publishing House, 1975).

Klaus Scholtissek, "Johannine Studies: A Survey of Recent Research with Special Regard for German Contributions," *Currents in Research: Biblical Studies* 6 (1998), 227–59.

THEOLOGY

Writings about the Fourth Gospel that have "theology" or "theological" in their titles use these terms in regard to three quite different aspects of the Gospel of John: (1) the God of Jesus Christ; (2) Christology; and (3) practices in the Johannine group, such as sacraments. Thus, on "God" who is Father, see Marianne Maye Thompson's *The God of the Gospel of John* (Grand Rapids, MI: Eerdmans, 2001). On Johannine Christology, see on the Israelite background of the declaration that Jesus is "equal to God" Jerome H. Neyrey's "'My Lord and My God': The Divinity of Jesus in John's Gospel," *SBLSP* (1986), 152–71. Finally, on sacraments in this gospel, see Raymond E. Brown's "The Johannine Sacramentary Reconsidered," *TS* 23 (1962), 183–206, and follow this up with Francis J. Moloney's "When Is John Talking about Sacraments?" *AusBR* 30 (1982), 10–33. Of particular note are the following books and articles:

Paul N. Anderson, *The Christology of the Fourth Gospel: Its Unity and Disunity in the Light of John 6* (Valley Forge, PA: Trinity Press International, 1996).

Mark L. Appold, *The Oneness Motif in the Fourth Gospel: Motif Analysis and Exegetical Probe into the Gospel of John* (Tübingen: Mohr, 1976).

David M. Ball, "I Am" in John's Gospel: Literary Function, Background and Theological Implications (Sheffield: Academic Press, 1996).

Marinus de Jonge, "Variety and Development in Johannine Christology," in his *Jesus: Stranger from Heaven and Son of God* (Missoula, MT: Scholars Press), 193–222.

James F. McGrath, *John's Apologetic Christology: Legitimation and Development in Johannine Christology* (Cambridge: Cambridge University Press, 2001).

M. J. J. Menken, "The Christology of the Fourth Gospel: A Survey of Recent Research," in Marinus de Boer, ed., *From Jesus to John: Essays on Jesus and New Testament Christology in Honour of Marinus de Jonge* (Sheffield: JSOT, 1993), 292–320.

Paul W. Meyer, "'The Father': The Presentation of God in the Fourth Gospel," in R. Alan Culpepper and C. Clifton Black, eds., *Exploring the Gospel of John* (Louisville, KY: Westminster John Knox, 1993), 355–73.

NOTEWORTHY MONOGRAPHS AND COLLECTIONS OF ESSAYS

The collection of essays and monographs is so diverse that the best we can do is identify the major topics. Since Bultmann, the issue of the sources of John, especially the sign source, has enjoyed continuous attention, formerly in Robert Fortna's *The Fourth Gospel and Its Predecessor: From Narrative Source to Present Gospel* (Philadelphia, PA: Fortress Press, 1988) and more recently in Gilbert Van Belle's *The Signs Source in the Fourth Gospel* (Leuven: University Press, 1994). The trial motif has been a regular staple of Johannine scholarship; Anthony E. Harvey's small book *Jesus on Trial* (Atlanta: John Knox, 1976) should be followed up with Andrew T. Lincoln's *Truth on Trial: The Lawsuit Motif in the Fourth Gospel* (Peabody, MA: Hendrickson, 2000) for a more detailed discussion of the motif. New attention is being given to family and kinship in John; Sjef van Tilborg's *Imaginative Love in John* (Leiden: Brill, 1993) nicely complements Jan G. van der Watt's *Family of the King: Dynamics of Metaphor in the Gospel According to John* (Leiden: Brill, 2000). Gender studies of John are appearing, the most comprehensive of which are the two volumes of essays edited by Amy-Jill Levine, *A Feminist Companion to John*, vols. I and II (Sheffield: Sheffield Academic Press, 2003). Among the following, readers can find materials on the Passion, temple, Johannine characters, and eating:

Raymond E. Brown, *The Community of the Beloved Disciple* (New York: Paulist Press, 1979).

Mary L. Coloe, *God Dwells with Us: Temple Symbolism in the Fourth Gospel* (Collegeville, MN: Liturgical Press, 2001).

Colleen M. Conway, *Men and Women in the Fourth Gospel: Gender and Johannine Characterization* (Atlanta: SBL Press, 1999).

John P. Heil, *Blood and Water: The Death and Resurrection of Jesus in John 18–21* (Washington, DC: The Catholic Biblical Association of America, 1995).

Barnabas Lindars, *Essays on John* (Leuven: University Press, 1992).

James McCaffrey, *The House with Many Rooms: The Temple Theme of Jn. 14, 2–3* (Rome: Pontifical Biblical Institute, 1988).

Gail R. O'Day, *Revelation in the Fourth Gospel: Narrative Mode and Theological Claim* (Philadelphia, PA: Fortress Press, 1986).

Fernando F. Segovia, *The Farewell of the Word: The Johannine Call to Abide* (Minneapolis, MN: Fortress Press, 1991).

Jane S. Webster, *Ingesting Jesus: Eating and Drinking in the Gospel of John* (Atlanta: Scholars Press, 2003).

JOURNAL ARTICLES AND CHAPTERS IN COLLECTIONS OF ESSAYS

Harold W. Attridge, "'Don't Be Touching Me': Recent Feminist Scholarship on Mary Magdalene," in Amy Jill Levine, ed., *A Feminist Companion to John,* Volume II (Sheffield: Sheffield Academic Press, 2003), 140–66.

Jouette Bassler, "Mixed Signals: Nicodemus in the Fourth Gospel," *JBL* 108 (1989), 635–46.

"The Galileans: A Neglected Factor in Johannine Research," *CBQ* 43 (1981), 243–57.

Peder Borgen, "Logos Was the True Light," *NovT* 14 (1972), 115–30.

"Bread from Heaven: Aspects of Debates on Expository Method and Form," in his *Logos Was the True Light and Other Essays on John* (Trondheim: Tapir, 1983), 32–46.

David Brakke, "Parables and Plain Speech in the Fourth Gospel and the Apocryphon of James," *JECS* 7 (1999), 187–218.

R. E. Brown, "The Johannine Sacramentary," *New Testament Essays (1968)*, 77–107.

"Incidents That Are Units in the Synoptic Gospels but Dispersed in St. John," *CBQ* 23 (1961), 143–152.

"The Paraclete in the Fourth Gospel," *NTS* 13 (1966), 113–32.

D. A. Carson, "The Function of the Paraclete in John 16:7–11," *JBL* 98 (1979), 547–66.

"Understanding Misunderstandings in the Fourth Gospel," *TynB* 33 (1982), 59–91.

Raymond Collins, "Representative Figures in the Fourth Gospel," *Downside Review* 94 (1976), 26–46, 118–32.

"Mary in the Fourth Gospel: A Decade of Johannine Studies," *Louvain Studies* 3 (1970), 130–36.

"From John to the Beloved Disciple: An Essay on Johannine Characters," *Interpretation* 49 (1995), 359–69.

R. Alan Culpepper, "The Pivot of John's Prologue," *NTS* 27 (1980), 1–31.

Nils A. Dahl, "'Do Not Wonder!' John 5:28–29 and Johannine Eschatology Once More," in Robert T. Fortna and Beverly R. Gaventa, eds., *The Conversation Continues: Studies in Paul and John* (Nashville, TN: Abingdon Press, 1990), 322–36.

J. D. M. Derrett, "The Samaritan Woman's Purity (John 4:5–42)," *EvQ* 60 (1988), 291–98.

C. H. Dodd, "The Prophecy of Caiaphas," *Neotestamentica et Patristica* (Leiden: Brill, 1962), 134–42.

Thomas Dozemann, "Sperma Abraham in John 8 and Related Literature," *CBQ* 42 (1980), 324–58.

Robert Fortna, "Theological Use of Locale in the Fourth Gospel," *ATR* Suppl 3 (1974), 58–95.

Charles H. Giblin, "Suggestion, Negative Response, and Positive Action in St. John's Portrayal of Jesus (2:1–11; 4:46–54; 7:2–14; 11:1–44)," *NTS* 26 (1980), 197–211.

J. Warren Holleran, "Seeing the Light. A Narrative Reading of John 9," *ETL* 69 (1993), 3–26.

L. Jacobs, "'Greater Love Hath No Man . . .' The Jewish Point of View of Self-Sacrifice," *Judaism* 6 (1957), 41–47.

H. L. N. Joubert, "'The Holy One of God' (John 6:69)," *Neotestamentica* 2 (1968), 57–69.

Craig Koester, "'Savior of the World' (John 4:42)," *JBL* 109 (1990), 665–80.

"Messianic Exegesis and the Call of Nathanael (John 1:45–51)," *JSNT* 39 (1990), 23–34.

Robert Kysar, "The Contributions of the Prologue of the Gospel of John to New Testament Christology and Its Historical Setting," *CurTM* 5 (1978), 348–64.

Judith M. Lieu, "The Mother of the Son in the Fourth Gospel," *JBL* 117 (1998), 61–77.

Andrew T. Lincoln, "The Beloved Disciple as Eyewitness and the Fourth Gospel as Witness," *JSNT* 85 (2002), 3–26.

James P. Martin, "History and Eschatology in the Lazarus Narrative, John 11:1–44," *SJTh* 17 (1964), 332–43.

Wayne A. Meeks, "The Son of Man in Johannine Sectarianism," *JBL* 91 (1972), 44–72.

"'Am I a Jew?' – Johannine Christianity and Judaism," in J. Neusner, ed., *Christianity, Judaism and Other Greco-Roman Cults* (Leiden: Brill, 1975), 163–86.

"The Divine Agent and His Counterfeit in Philo and the Fourth Gospel," in E. Schussler Fiorenza, ed., *Aspects of Religious Propaganda in Judaism and Early Christianity* (Notre Dame, IN: University of Notre Dame Press, 1976), 43–67.

"Equal to God," in Robert T. Fortna and Beverly R. Gaventa, eds., *The Conversation Continues: Studies in Paul and John* (Nashville, TN: Abingdon Press, 1990), 301–21.

"The Ethics of the Fourth Evangelist," in R. Alan Culpepper and C. Clifton Black, eds., *Exploring the Gospel of John* (Louisville, KY: Westminster John Knox, 1996), 318–26.

Paul S. Minear, "We Don't Know Where . . . John 20:2," *Interpretation* 30 (1976), 125–39.

Francis J. Moloney, "From Cana to Cana (Jn. 2:1–4:54) and the Fourth Evangelist's Concept of Correct (and Incorrect) Faith," *Salesianum* 40 (1978), 826–45.

"A Sacramental Reading of John 13:1–38," *CBQ* 53 (1991), 237–56.

Jerome H. Neyrey, "Jacob Traditions in the Interpretation of John 4:10–26," *CBQ* 41 (1979), 419–37.

"'My Lord and My God': The Divinity of Jesus in John's Gospel," *SBLSP* (1986), 152–71.

"Jesus the Judge: Forensic Process in John 8, 21–59," *Biblica* 68 (1987), 509–41.

"'I Said: You are Gods': Psalm 82:6 and John 10," *JBL* 108 (1989), 647–63.

"The Footwashing in John 13:6–11: Transformation Ritual or Ceremony?" in L. Michael White and O. Larry Yarbrough, eds., *The Social World of the First Christians: Essays in Honor of Wayne A. Meeks* (Minneapolis, MN: Fortress Press, 1995), 198–213.

"The Trials (Forensic) and Tribulations (Honor Challenges) of Jesus: John 7 in Social Science Perspective," *BTB* 26 (1996), 107–24.

Jerome H. Neyrey and Richard L. Rohrbaugh, "Increase," *CBQ* 63(2001), 476–81.

John Painter, "The Farewell Discourses and the History of Johannine Christianity," *NTS* 27 (1981), 525–43.

"John 9 and the Interpretation of the Fourth Gospel," *JSNT* 28 (1986), 31–61.

"Tradition, History and Interpretation in John 10," in J. Beutler and R. Fortna, eds., *The Shepherd Discourse of John 10 and Its Context* (Cambridge: Cambridge University Press, 1991), 53–74.

Ronald A. Piper, "Satan, Demons and the Absence of Exorcisms in the Fourth Gospel," in David G. Horrell and Christopher Tucker, eds., *Christology: Controversy and Community* (Leiden: Brill, 2000), 253–78.

J. A. T. Robinson, "The Relation of the Prologue to the Gospel of John," *NTS* 9 (1963), 120–29.

Francisco F. Segovia, "Structure, *Tendenz* and *Sitz im Leben* of John 13:31–14:31," *JBL* 104 (1985), 471–93.

"The Theology and Provenance of John 15:1–17," *JBL* 101 (1982), 115–28.

"The Final Farewell of Jesus: A Reading of John 20:30–21:25." *Semeia* 53 (1991), 167–90.

Turid K. Seim, "Roles of Women in the Gospel of John," in Lars Hartman and Birger Olsson, eds., *Aspects on the Johannine Literature* (Uppsala: Almqvist and Wiksells, 1986), 56–73.

D. Moody Smith, "Johannine Christianity: Some Reflections on Its Character and Delineation," *NTS* 21 (1975), 222–48.

Jeffrey L. Staley, "Stumbling in the Dark, Reaching for the Light: Reading Character in John 5 & 9," *Semeia* 53 (1991), 55–80.

M. W. G. Stibbe, "A Tomb with a View: John 11:1–44 in Narrative-Critical Perspective," *NTS* 40 (1994), 38–54.

S. W. Theron, "'HINA OSIN HEN' (That They Be One): A Multifaceted Approach to an Important Thrust in the Prayer of Jesus in John 17," *Neotestamentica* 21 (1987), 77–94.

Sjef van Tilborg, "Ideology and Text: John 15 in the Context of the Farewell Address," in P. J. Hartin and J. H. Petzer, eds., *Text and Interpretation: New Approaches in the Criticism of the New Testament* (Leiden: Brill, 1991), 259–70.

Thomas H. Tobin, "The Prologue of John and Hellenistic Jewish Speculation," *CBQ* 52 (1990), 252–69.

D. Francois Tolmie, "The Characterization of God in the Fourth Gospel," *JSNT* 69 (1998), 57–75.

Linwood Urban and P. Henry, "'Before Abraham Was I AM': Does Philo Explain John 8:56–58?" *Studia Philonica* 6 (1979), 157–93.

S. Voorwinde, "John's Prologue: Beyond Some Impasses of Twentieth-Century Scholarship," *WTS* 64 (2002), 15–44.

William O. Walker, "The Lord's Prayer in Matthew and John," *NTS* 28 (1982), 237–56.

Jan G. van der Watt, "The Composition of the Prologue of John's Gospel: The Historical Jesus Introducing Divine Grace," *WTS* 57 (1995), 311–32.

Herold Weiss, "Foot Washing in the Johannine Community," *NovT* 21 (1979), 298–325.

Catlin H. Williams, "'I Am' or 'I Am He'? Self-Declaratory Pronouncements in the Fourth Gospel and in Rabbinic Tradition," in Robert T. Fortna and Tom Thatcher, eds., *Jesus in the Johannine Tradition* (Louisville, KY: Westminster John Knox, 2001), 343–52.

Ritva H. Williams, "The Mother of Jesus at Cana: A Socio-Scientific Interpretation of John 2:1–12," *CBQ* 59 (1997), 679–92.

Bruce Woll, "The Departure of 'the Way': The First Farewell Discourse in the Gospel of John," *JBL* 99 (1980), 225–39.

III. Commentary

JOHN 1:1–18 – BEGINNING, MIDDLE, AND END

1 In the beginning was the Word, and the Word was with God, and the Word was God.

2 He was in the beginning with God.

3 All things came into being through him, and without him not one thing came into being. What has come into being

4 in him was life, and the life was the light of all people.

5 The light shines in the darkness, and the darkness did not overcome it.

6 There was a man sent from God, whose name was John.

7 He came as a witness to testify to the light, so that all might believe through him.

8 He himself was not the light, but he came to testify to the light.

9 The true light, which enlightens everyone, was coming into the world.

10 He was in the world, and the world came into being through him; yet the world did not know him.

11 He came to what was his own, and his own people did not accept him.

12 But to all who received him, who believed in his name, he gave power to become children of God,

13 who were born, not of blood or of the will of the flesh or of the will of man, but of God.

14 And the Word became flesh and lived among us, and we have seen his glory, the glory as of a father's only son, full of grace and truth.

15 (John testified to him and cried out, "This was he of whom I said, 'He who comes after me ranks ahead of me because he was before me.'")

16 From his fullness we have all received, grace upon grace.

17 The law indeed was given through Moses; grace and truth came through Jesus Christ.

18 No one has ever seen God. It is God the only Son, who is close to the Father's heart, who has made him known.

Alas, All Questions Cannot Be Explored. Of the many scholarly questions typically asked about John 1:1–18, these tend to be the most frequently discussed: (1) "prologue" – what is a prologue?;[1] (2) background and provenance (i.e., wisdom or Genesis allusions);[2] (3) literary or chiastic shape of the prologue; (4) relationship of the prologue to the rest of the Gospel; (5) when was it appended to the Gospel?; and (6) what does it suggest about the interaction of the Johannine group with other Judeans? Only two of these are addressed here: the literary shape of the prologue, and its relationship to the rest of the Gospel.

Prologue: Chiastic Structure. A "chiasm"[3] describes the conscious shaping of a passage according to an "X" shape (the Greek letter "chi" is X-shaped, *chi*asm). In general, a chiasm places parallel words or phrases at the top and bottom of the passage (A & A′) and also includes subsequent parallels (B & B′ and C & C′, etc.), thus signaling beginnings and endings, which frame the intervening communication. Scholars mark the parallels by labeling them as A, B, C and C′, B′, A′, which often draws attention to a central passage, "D," which serves as the focus or climax of the rhetoric. By providing clarity and focus, a chiastic structure draws an audience's attention to significant materials both by means of repetitive parallels and by highlighting the center of the figure, presumably the major thrust of the passage. This common form, moreover, was anticipated by audiences to aid in following the argument or narrative.

As regards the Fourth Gospel, current scholarship regularly identifies John 1:1–18 and other passages in this Gospel as chiasms.[4] The following diagram reflects the common reading of the prologue in chiastic form.

A. 1:1 In the beginning was *the Word*, and *the Word* was with God, and *the Word* was God. 1:2 He was in the beginning with God.

A′. 1:18 No one has ever seen God. It is God the only Son, who is close to the Father's heart, *who has made him known.*

B. 1:3 All things *came into being through him,* and without him *not one thing came into being.*

B′. 1:17 The law indeed was given *through* Moses; grace and truth *came through Jesus Christ.*

---

1   Vernon Robbins, "Prefaces in Greco-Roman Biography and Luke-Acts," *PRS* 6 (1979), 94–108; Loveday Alexander, "Luke's Preface in the Context of Greek Preface Writing," *NovT* 28 (1986), 48–72; and Adele Reinhartz, *The World in the World: The Cosmological Tale of the Fourth Gospel* (Atlanta: Scholars Press, 1992), 18–25.

2   Rudolf Schnackenburg, "Logos Hymnus und johanneischer Prolog," *BZ* 1 (1957), 69–109; C. K. Barrett, *New Testament Essays* (London: SPCK, 1972), 27–48; and more recently, Thomas H. Tobin, "The Prologue of John and Hellenistic Jewish Speculation," *CBQ* 52 (1990), 252–69.

3   The pioneering work on the chiastic interpretation was done by M.-E. Boismard in *St. John's Prologue* (London: Blackfriars, 1957), 76–81; see also R. A. Culpepper, "The Pivot of John's Prologue," *NTS* 27 (1980), 2–7.

4   For an alternative argument that biblical parallelism better explains the dynamic of the prologue, see Francis J. Moloney, *Belief in the Word: Reading John 1–4* (Minneapolis, MN: Fortress Press, 1993), 23–27.

C. 1:3 What has come into being 1:4 in him was *life*, and the *life* was the *light* of all people. 1:5 The *light* shines in the darkness, and the darkness did not overcome it.

C'. 1:16 From his *fullness* we have all received, *grace upon grace.*

D. 1:6 There was a man sent from God, whose name was *John.* 1:7 He came as a *witness* to *testify to the light*, so that all might believe through him. 1:8 He himself was not the light, but he came to *testify to the light.*

D'. 1:15 *John testified* to him and cried out, "This was he of whom I said, 'He who comes after me ranks ahead of me because he was before me.'"

E. 1:9 The true light, which enlightens everyone, was *coming into the world.* 1:10 He *was in the world*, and the world came into being through him; yet the world did not know him.

E'. 1:14 And the *Word became flesh and lived among us*, and we have seen his glory, the glory as of a father's only son, full of grace and truth.

F. 1:11 He came to *what was his own*, and *his own people* did not accept him.

F. 1:13 who were born, *not of blood or of the will of the flesh or of the will of man*, but of God

G. 1:12 But to all *who received him*

G'. 1:12c . . . *who believed in his name*

H. 1:12b He gave power to become *children of God*

Presuming that this chiasm is not merely ornamental but structures the communication, let us now examine the seven pairs of parallels to see what is communicated by each parallel and by their combined message.

A & A' (1:1–2 & 18). The Gospel asserts that God communicates only through Jesus, who is both the *Word* of God (1:1) and who uniquely reveals God to the world (1:18). God's prophets never saw God (1:18; 6:46). Jesus, the unique Word, alone makes God known. Moreover, unique temporal and spatial claims are made for Jesus: As regards time, he is uncreated in the beginning and eternal in the future; as regards space, he begins in heaven, is found on earth, and returns back to God's "heart."[5]

B & B' (1:3 & 17). Both panels stress the mediation of Jesus. All creation, without exception, came into being *through him* (1:3). While conceding that Moses mediated the Law, the Gospel argues that "grace and truth came *through* Jesus Christ" (1:17). Indeed, the author will argue that all heavenly revelations came *through* Jesus to Abraham, Jacob, Isaiah, and even Moses. Just as Jesus alone sees

---

[5] Craig S. Keener, *The Gospel of John: A Commentary* (Peabody, MA: Hendrickson, 2003), 365–74 and 422–26.

God and makes God known (1:18), so is he the unique and superior mediator of all of God's covenantal blessings.[6]

C & C' (1:4–5 & 16). Jesus' premier creative benefactions are "life" and "light," later explained as "eternal life" (6:40, 54–58) and "light of the world" (8:12).[7] Paralleling this benefaction, Jesus bestows "fullness" and his disciples receive "grace upon grace" (1:16) or maximum divine favor.

D & D' (1:6 & 15). The mythical time line we have been following is punctuated by a precise historical moment still in the memory of the audience, namely, the testimony of John the Baptizer.[8] As an authorized speaker ("sent by God"), he testifies rather than calls to repentance and washing. Emphatically we are told that he was *not* the "light" but its witness. The Baptizer's description contrasts him with Jesus: *time* – although he precedes Jesus in chronological time ("who comes after me"), John attests to Jesus' eternal priority ("he was before me"); *relationship to God* – although Jesus was the Word "with God," John is only the messenger "sent by God"; *scope* – whereas "all" things were made by the Word, the messenger brings a word to "all"; *light* – the Word himself is "light," whereas the messenger only testifies "about the light."[9]

E & E' (1:9–10 & 14). Both panels celebrate the Word in our midst, either as Light among us or as "pitching a tent" among us. Yet the honorable Word was shamed and rejected by many. This first mention of hostility in the Gospel heralds a narrative of intense, continuous conflict. This shame of rejection is balanced by the honor given the flesh-and-blood Word, whom his disciples acknowledge. When they "beheld his glory," they acknowledged his role and status as "the unique Son of a Heavenly Father." The schism[10] described here will be repeated throughout the narrative, but it informs the audience that the place where the Word pitched a tent was inherently hostile.

F & F' (1:11 & 13). These panels intensify the schism just mentioned. Balancing "the world did not know him" is the comment that "his own did not accept him." "His own" includes kin and country, who should honor and acknowledge their own (see 4:44). Membership in the clan or family normally occurs by birth ("born of blood"), then by entrance rituals such as circumcision ("born

---

[6] C. S. Keener, *Gospel of John Commentary* (2003), 364–71 and 421–22; see also Ruth B. Edwards, "ΧΑΡΙΝ ΑΝΤΙ ΧΑΡΙΤΟΣ (John 1:16): Grace and the Law in the Johannine Prologue," *JSNT* 32 (1988), 3–15.

[7] C. S. Keener, *Gospel of John Commentary* (2003), 381–87.

[8] Morna Hooker, "John the Baptist and the Johannine Prologue," *NTS* 16 (1970), 354–58.

[9] John Painter, *The Quest for the Messiah: The History, Literature and Theology of the Johannine Community*, 2nd ed. (Nashville, TN: Abingdon Press, 1993), 152–54.

[10] Crowds divided over Jesus become a major narrative event in the Gospel (see 7:43; 9:16 and 10:19).

of the will of the flesh") or by adoption ("born by the will of man").[11] But none of these can achieve the kinship described here, for those who calibrate kinship according to the three modes just mentioned "did not accept him." True "children of God," however, are those who "accept" Jesus and believe in his name, and so are born into God's family. Whereas "his own" serves as an exclusive identification marker (i.e., Israelites), "born . . . of God" functions as an inclusive label, which may apply to anyone.

G & G′ (1:12a & c). Earthly criteria do not assure membership in God's family (v. 11). One must be "born of God," which can only happen when people "receive him [Jesus]" and "believe in his name." As the Word descends into the world (1:4–11), we are repeatedly told that the Light was *not* received, the world did *not* acknowledge him, and "his own" did *not* receive him. Thus the Word appears as an alien in an alien land.[12] However, just the opposite story is told about the ascent of the Word back to God (1:12–18); we hear about those who honor Jesus, are born of God, behold his glory, and receive his fulness and his revelations of the Father. The shame resulting from the rejection of the Word is balanced by the honor received from those who believe in his name and by God, at whose heart he rests.

H (1:12b). The logic of chiastic structure indicates that here is the key, pivotal center and the major idea in the communication. According to rhetorical logic, then, "the word became flesh" is not the center but rather the "giving of power to become children of God."[13] This reading, then, argues that there are two foci in the prologue, one Christological (Word, Light, Unique Son who descends to earth and reascends to heaven) and another related to the Johannine group ("children of God"), which occupies the center of the chiasm.

Prologue and Gospel. When scholars argued that the prologue was a wisdom hymn stitched by the author to the front of the Gospel to make it more acceptable to Hellenistic readers, it was judged to have little relationship to the rest of the Gospel.[14] Now scholars stress the extensive relationship between prologue and Gospel, such that one might say that the prologue is a topic sentence,[15] an

[11] Raymond E. Brown, *The Gospel According to John* (Garden City, NY: Doubleday, 1966), 1.10–13; and Sjef van Tilborg, *Imaginative Love in John* (Leiden: E. J. Brill, 1993), 33–47.

[12] "Alien" is the suggestive term coined by Wayne A. Meeks in his "The Man from Heaven in Johannine Sectarianism," *JBL* 91 (1972), 44–72.

[13] R. Alan Culpepper, "The Pivot of John's Prologue," *NTS* 27 (1980), 2–4.

[14] On reading the prologue this way, see J. A. T. Robinson, "The Relation of the Prologue to the Gospel of St. John," *NTS* 9 (1962), 120–29; Warren Carter, "The Prologue and John's Gospel: Function, Symbol and Definitive Word," *JSNT* 39 (1990), 35–58; and Elizabeth Harris, *Prologue and Gospel. The Theology of the Fourth Evangelist* (Sheffield: Sheffield Academic Press, 1994), esp. 1–25.

[15] We argue that the following passages function as topic statements for subsequent development in which each term or phrase is clarified by Jesus: 1:26–28 vis-à-vis 1:29–34; 3:2 vis-à-vis 3:3–21; 4:10 vis-à-vis 4:7–15; 4:20 vis-à-vis 4:22–24; 5:18 vis-à-vis 5:19–29; 6:31

overture, a summary of what is subsequently developed. I concur with the scholars who argue that the prologue introduces major themes that appear later in the Gospel. In the following pages, I will unpack every verse of the prologue, identifying its major thematic elements, and indicate some places in the Gospel where these themes reappear. I hope that the exposition of the thematic content of the prologue will serve to introduce and set the terms for my reading of the Gospel as a whole.

Word of God and Words of God. In the beginning was the unique Word (1:1), who alone makes God known (1:18; 6:46). Moreover, the Word of God "comes from heaven . . . and testifies to what he has seen and heard. . . . He whom God has sent speaks the words of God" (3:31–34). In his final prayer, Jesus tells God how faithful he has been in revealing God's word: "I have made your name known to those whom you gave me from the world" (17:6, 26). Yet one might also ask who in the Johannine community controls the "words" spoken to it? Who remembers the secret meaning of Scriptures spoken by Jesus (2:19–22)? Who brokers the past meaning of Jesus' words (14:26) and gives "witness to him" (15:26–27)? We must keep in mind, then, three points: the Word, his words, and the custodians and exegetes of his words.[16]

The Word Was "God." In several places, Jesus is accused of being "equal to God" (5:17–18; 10:33). The name "God" will be shown to refer to God's creative power,[17] which Jesus, who is Logos and "God," exercises in 1:1–3. The deity's other name, "Lord," is associated with the second power (i.e., eschatological power). Hence, at the Gospel's ending, when Jesus has demonstrated power over death, he is acclaimed "My Lord and my God."

In Him Was Life. Jesus tells us that God gave him "to have life in himself" (5:26), meaning that Jesus is imperishable or immortal, just as God is. Jesus also tells us that God gave him power to lay down his life and power to take it up (10:17–18). Both of these remarks, we suggest, indicate what the author means when he says, "in him was life."

The Light of All People. At the feast of Tabernacles, Jesus claims that "I am the light of the world" (8:12; see also 9:5). He is light in the sense of illumination

---

vis-à-vis 6:32–59; 8:21–24 vis-à-vis 8:25–30; 14:1–4 vis-à-vis 14:5–21; and 15:1–2 vis-à-vis 15:3–11. On topic statements from Scripture, see Peder Borgen's "Observations on the Targumic Character of the Prologue of John," *NTS* 16 (1970), 288–95; *Bread from Heaven* (Leiden: Brill, 1965); and "Bread from Heaven: Aspects of Debates on Expository Method and Form," in his *Logos Was the True Light* (Trondheim: Tapir, 1983), 32–46.

[16] See Werner H. Kelber, "The Birth of a Beginning: John 1.18," *Semeia* 52 (1990), 120–44.

[17] In John 5:19–29, Jesus will be shown to have God's two powers, which in rabbinic tradition are associated with the two names of Israel's deity. God's creative power is linked with "God" (θεός) because it is linked with τίθημι, meaning "to place, to create." See Jerome H. Neyrey, *An Ideology of Revolt: John's Christology in Social Science Perspective* (Philadelphia: Fortress Press, 1988), 25–29.

and revelation, but he is also light as the shepherd of sheep: "Whoever follows me will never walk in darkness but will have the light of life" (8:12).

The Light Shines in the Darkness. The Word's dwelling here will not be without conflict. This prefigures the later description of a dualistic cosmos in which "light" battles with "darkness." Implicit here is a vision of a world divided into two radical and hostile camps: light or darkness, truth or deception, and life or death. The light–darkness dualism also refers to peoples (3:19–20; 11:9–10), times (9:4–5), and places (12:35–36).

The Light Is Not Received by the Darkness. How odd that light is rejected! What farmer would scorn sunlight for his crops? What sage would spurn illumination? In a world without electricity, what folly to prefer to work and walk in the dark! Yet, the more we learn of people who prefer darkness to light (3:19–21; 12:35–36), the more we understand about the alien character of the world into which Jesus has come.

John Came for Testimony . . . to Bear Witness to the Light. The author tells us repeatedly of John's "testimony" about Jesus (1:19–34) and his pointing of his disciples in Jesus' direction. Later, when Jesus' success provokes envy among John's disciples, he speaks again in Jesus' favor, declaring that Jesus must increase in fame and respect, even at his own expense (3:25–30). Finally, Jesus summons John as his first witness when on trial (5:33–36).

The True Light. Jesus is described as "true light"; that is, the only authentic and trustworthy light. The claim that Jesus is "true" implicitly contrasts him with what is *not* true, or *un*reliable. This will result in a sharp polemic that compares and contrasts Jesus and his heavenly blessings with the earthly state of the synagogue and Temple. Jesus is also "true" bread from heaven (6:32) versus Moses' manna; his judgment is "true," whereas his audience judges according to appearances (8:16); he is the "true" vine, the new national center, in contrast to Israel-as-vine (15:1). The same label sets apart "true" worshipers from those who worship on "this mountain or in Jerusalem" (4:23). "True," then, seems to stand in contrast with what the author considers obsolete, defective, and unreliable.

He Was in the World. "World" has two meanings in the narrative. At first, it is a friendly abode for Jesus' mission: God so loved this world that he sent his son to be its savior (3:16–17; 4:42); because of his signs and wonders, people acclaim Jesus as "the prophet come into this world" (6:14) and the "light of the world" (8:12; 9:5). But as hostility grows against Jesus and his disciples, the world becomes the place of evil, hatred, and death, in which neither Jesus nor his disciples are at home. The world "hates Jesus" but not Jesus' brothers; he is not part of it, but they are (7:7; 15:18–19). Although Jesus will leave this world, he refuses to pray that they be taken from it, so he prays to God to protect them from it (17:14–16). The negative labeling of "this world" metamorphoses into a dualism according to which two worlds are contrasted: this world of hatred and obtuseness versus the true world of Jesus, which is the world above (see 8:23; 12:25; 17:16; 18:36).

The World Knew Him Not. "To know" refers either to special information and identification or acknowledgment and honor. As regards the first meaning, characters such as Nicodemus claim to know certain information: "We know that you are a teacher who has come from God" (3:2). But their "knowledge" is thin and inadequate, and they utterly fail to acknowledge Jesus in any significant way. Other characters who begin "not in the know" progress to "in the know" (see 4:17–26), not just knowledge but acknowledgment. Pharisees, for example, "know that God has spoken to Moses, but as for this man, we do not know where he comes from" (9:29), but the man born blind knows (9:31–33) and shortly acknowledges the Son of Man (9:35–38).

He Came to His Own and His Own People Did Not Accept Him. "His own" refers both to Jesus' immediate kinship group (7:1–7; 19:27), and his clan or people.[18] Inasmuch as 1:13 will argue that blood relationship fails as a criterion for association with Jesus (7:5), it would seem that "his own" looks particularly to Jesus' ethnic relationship with Israel. Later, we are told that, like all prophets, Jesus has no honor among "his own" (4:44). Moreover, from Chapter 5 onward, the Jerusalem elites ceaselessly put Jesus on trial.

But to All Who Received Him, Who Believed in His Name. Jesus' titles become boundary markers separating insiders from outsiders. We find in the Gospel two sets of names given to and used by Jesus. First, John and the original disciples name Jesus as Lamb of God; Messiah, of whom Moses wrote; Son of God; and King of Israel. The Samaritans add to this list by acknowledging him as savior of the world (4:42). The man born blind acknowledges Jesus in a rising chain of titles (9:17, 31–33, 35–38). A second set of names is revealed by Jesus himself: "Son of Man" (1:51; 3:13; 9:35) and the name of God, which Jesus reveals to his disciples, namely "I AM" (17:6, 11–12, 26). At a certain point, the crowds are told that unless they believe that Jesus is "I AM," they will die in their sins (8:24), suggesting that in time a higher Christology was demanded by the group. Not just any name will do.

He Gave Power to Become Children of God. This serves as the functional center of the prologue, the ultimate benefaction achieved in Jesus. Later we learn that those who seek to enter God's kingdom must be "born from above" (3:3, 5). Moreover, not all Israelites are indeed "children of God," whether they claim

---

[18] Rudolf Schnackenburg's *The Gospel According to St. John* (New York: Herder and Herder, 1968), 1.259–60, argues that "his own" includes "homeland, domain or property." The true homeland of the Logos is God (1:1), but in virtue of his creation of the world, Jesus' alternate homeland is this world, even Israel; see Jacob Jervell, "Er kam in sein Eigentum. Zu Joh. 1:11." 10 (1956), 14–27.

God or Abraham as Father (8:33, 41). True children of a father are "chips off the old block" and do what their fathers do; true children of Abraham would do what Abraham did (i.e., receive heavenly messengers). But children of Ishmael, Cain, and Satan do what their fathers did: lie and murder (8:41, 44). But "If God were your Father, you would love me, for I came from God and now I am here" (8:42). Only insiders are called "my brothers" (20:17). People become "children of God" when they accept Jesus as the premier son of God. God draws potential children to Jesus (see 6:36–37, 44, 65). Those who know Jesus know his Father (8:19) and those who see Jesus see the Father (14:9).

The Word Became Flesh and Lived among Us. At first glance, this is improbable and downright scandalous. What sense could anyone make of an immortal figure taking on mortality? And in the world of purity concerns and separation from all evil and corruption, how bizarre to hear of a heavenly being camping in the company of sinners and enemies. Yet, God's broker comes precisely as the agent of illumination, healing, and purification. As "Lamb of God" he takes away the sin of the world (1:35); he feeds the hungry and gives sight to the blind; he prepares a new location for worshiping God in spirit and truth (2:19; 4:20–24). Hence, his presence is a functional one that makes holy what is sinful or common. Yet caution is necessary, for although at the early stages of this Gospel the "world" seemed like a place worthy of God's concern, it quickly became an alien land in which Jesus himself was an alien.[19]

The Glory as of a Father's Only Son. "Glory" means Jesus' worth, honor, and status. On the one hand, God bestows this glory on Jesus (17:5), which is the only honor that Jesus seeks (8:54). On the other hand, Jesus' signs manifest it to his disciples and require acknowledgment of it (2:11). Finally, Jesus' "glory" is oxymoronic because it is attached to his shame, namely his crucifixion (12:23; 13:31). Thus "glory" becomes a divisive thing, for most earthly people seek glory and approval from their peers (5:41, 44), unlike Jesus, who seeks it only from God. They "saw" this glory means that they acknowledged Jesus as Son and agent of God and were not scandalized by the shame of his cross. The term "only"[20] is a classic indicator of honor in epideictic rhetoric.[21]

From His Fullness . . . Grace upon Grace. Although Jesus is not the benefactor (God is), he functions throughout the narrative as the unique mediator, broker,

---

[19] J. H. Neyrey, *Ideology of Revolt* (1988), 100–102; see also W. A. Meeks, "Man from Heaven in Johannine Sectarianism," *JBL* 91 (1972), 50–57, 60–61.

[20] Aristotle, *Rhet.* 2.7.2; Quintilian, *Inst. Orat.* 3.7.16. See Paul Winter, "ΜΟΝΓΕΝΗΣ ΠΑΡΑ ΠΑΤΡΟΣ," *ZRG* 5 (1953), 335–65, and John V. Dahms, "The Johannine Use of Monogenes Reconsidered," *NTS* 29 (1983), 222–32.

[21] Of course, forensic rhetoric is prevalent in all of Jesus' trials, but even it includes attacks and defenses in which honor and shame are the result.

apostle, and agent of God.[22] As a unique broker, he mediates the fullness of God's benefaction and with generosity for he has come that his disciples may have "life in abundance" (10:10), which may mean abundant wine (2:6–10), bread/manna (6:11–13), the bread of life (6:35, 49–51), water (7:37–39), light (8:12; 9:5), and life (10:10; 11:43). Moreover, his healings illustrate the fullness of his power. "Grace" here is the common term used for benefaction in the Hellenistic world.[23] If "grace upon grace" is understood as accumulation,[24] then Jesus functions as a superior broker, whose gifts are endless.[25]

The Law through Moses . . . Grace and Truth through Jesus Christ. This next comparison claims superiority for Jesus vis-à-vis Moses ("law" vs. "grace and truth")[26] and Israel's other patriarchs and prophets. Jesus is greater than Moses because his person and gift are superior. Similarly, Jesus is "greater than our father Jacob" (4:12) because of his water, which slakes thirst, and "greater than our father Abraham" (8:53) because he "is eternally," before Abraham ever "came into being." Jesus, moreover, is not simply superior to the old figures of Israel, he replaces them. He is the new place of worship, as well as the Bread from heaven, which replaces Moses and manna. All who ate Moses' manna died, but all who eat the Bread of Life have eternal life (6:49–50, 58).

No One Has Ever Seen God. Frequently, the author makes exclusive claims for Jesus that describe his unique access to God: no one has ever seen God (1:18; 6:46); no one has ever gone up to heaven, except the one who descended from there (3:13); nor can anyone do the signs Jesus does unless God is with him (3:2). The initial claim ("no one has ever seen God") prepares us for the later argument that neither Abraham in his visions, nor Jacob at Bethel, nor Moses at Sinai, nor Isaiah in the Temple ever saw God. They saw Jesus. This clarifies Jesus' role as unique and exalted mediator: He alone has access to God's words and wisdom.

Pattern of Descent and Ascent. Most scholars plot the movement of the Logos in the prologue as a descent into the world from being "face to face" with God,

---

[22] Peder Borgen, "God's Agent in the Fourth Gospel," in Jacob Neusner, ed., *Religions in Antiquity* (Leiden: Brill, 1968), 137–47; see also George W. Buchanan, "Apostolic Christology," *SBLSP* (1986), 172–82.

[23] Bruce J. Malina, "Patron and Client: The Analogy Behind Synoptic Theology," in his *The Social World of Jesus and the Gospels* (London: Routledge, 1996), 171–73.

[24] R. B. Edwards, "*Charin and Charitos* (John 1:16): Grace and Law in the Johannine Prologue," *JSNT* 32 (1988), 3–7. R. E. Brown's *Gospel According to John* (1966), 1.15–16, provides a survey of possible interpretations of this phrase.

[25] Francis J. Moloney (*Belief in the Word* [1993], 46–47) suggests that we translate this as "unsolicited gift"; this would make sense if framed in a social context of patron–broker–client relations.

[26] Scholars often argue that "grace and truth" correspond to *hesed* and *émet*; see C. H. Dodd, *The Interpretation of the Fourth Gospel* (Cambridge: Cambridge University Press, 1968), 70–78. Elizabeth Harris argues that Jesus is the unique and only source of divine benefaction and hence "truth" means "real" (*Prologue and Gospel* [1994], 65–71).

which is balanced with an ascent back to the heart of the Father. The formal repetition of this same pattern in 13:1–3 confirms the importance of this pattern. Moreover, fragments of the pattern also appear, such as the remarks that only the Son of Man has descended from the heavens (3:13), that the Son of Man will ascend to where he was before (6:62), or the prayer in 17:5 that the Son will resume the glory he had with God before the creation of the world. Throughout the Gospel, much will be made of "whence" Jesus comes and "whither" he goes. True knowledge of these serves as an indicator of insider, elite status, which occurs only when Jesus reveals this information to them (14:1–7; 20:17–18). Outsiders, who claim to know "whence" Jesus comes, argue that he cannot be the Christ because he comes from Galilee or that he cannot be the Bread from heaven because they know his earthly family. Outsiders, moreover, think that "whither" Jesus goes is either his flight to the Diaspora or his suicide (7:35; 8:22). Knowing of his descent and ascent, then, unlocks the mystery of whence he comes and whither he goes.

JOHN 1:19–28 – QUESTIONS AND ANSWERS: THE TESTIMONY OF JOHN

19 This is the testimony given by John when the Jews sent priests and Levites from Jerusalem to ask him. "Who are you?"
20 He confessed and did not deny it, but confessed, "I am not the Messiah."
21 And they asked him, "What then? Are you Elijah?" He said, "I am not." "Are you the prophet?" He answered, "No."
22 Then they said to him, "Who are you? Let us have an answer for those who sent us. What do you say about yourself?"
23 He said, "I am the voice of one crying out in the wilderness, 'Make straight the way of the Lord,'" as the prophet Isaiah said.
24 Now they had been sent from the Pharisees.
25 They asked him, "Why then are you baptizing if you are neither the Messiah, nor Elijah, nor the prophet?"
26 John answered them, "I baptize with water. Among you stands one whom you do not know,
27 the one who is coming after me; I am not worthy to untie the thong of his sandal."
28 This took place in Bethany across the Jordan where John was baptizing.

The Great Testifier. The author shapes his interpretation of John the Baptizer by framing it with an inclusion: "This is the testimony of John" (1:19) and "I have testified that . . . " (1:34); he makes salient now the earlier remark in the prologue that "John came for testimony" (1:7–8). Thus John, while a Baptizer, is transformed into a Witness.[27] Even his response to the interrogation "Why do you baptize if you are not the Christ . . . or Elijah?" (1:25) is metamorphosed into a testimony to Jesus, whom he declares to be "unknown to them," yet so honorable that even John is unworthy to loose his sandal. Unlike Mark and Matthew, this author is ambiguous on whether John baptized Jesus, saying only that "'He on whom you see the Spirit descend and remain is the one who baptizes with the Holy Spirit'" (1:33). Two questions arise: What is the content of John's "testimony"? And what is the rhetorical importance of "testimony"?

John and Jesus. Two aspects of John's testimony are found already in the prologue, namely that he came as a "witness to testify to the light" (1:7–8) and that "This was he of whom I said, 'He who comes after me ranks ahead of me because he was before me'" (1:15). The latter remark is repeated in 1:27: "the one who is coming after me, I am not worthy to untie the thong of his sandal." In time, Jesus comes after John, but his status surpasses that of John, because he existed before John. Thus their relative statuses and roles are clarified so there can be no rivalry between them, as each has a distinct role and an appropriate status. The honorable John was a burning light in which Israel rejoiced (5:35), but he totally served the "light coming into the world" (1:9). Scholars often interpret this delicate adjustment of roles and statuses in terms of a hypothetical conflict between the disciples of John and those of Jesus, which is implied in Acts 18:25 and 19:1–7 and in John 3:22–30.[28]

Most Questions Are Hostile Challenges. John's testimony about Jesus comes in parallel blocks of material, 1:19–28 and 1:30–34. Although both are "testimony," each is directed to a different audience: priests, Levites, and Pharisees; and disciples. The rhetorical form of each differs, as does the content, tone, and context of its delivery. For example, the rhetorical form of the materials in 1:19–23 and 1:24–28 is that of "Question and Answer," as the following diagram indicates:

Questions and Answer with Priests/Levites (1:19–23)	*Question and Answer with Pharisees* (1:24–28)
Q: Who are you?	Q: Why do you baptize if you are not Christ, Elijah, or prophet?
A: I am not the *Christ!*	

---

[27] Some argue that "witness" has two meanings here: judicial (see A. E. Harvey, *Jesus on Trial: A Study of the Fourth Gospel* [Atlanta: John Knox, 1976], 18–32) and confessional (see Walter Wink, *John the Baptist in the Gospel Tradition* [Cambridge: Cambridge University Press, 1968]). See E. Harris, *Prologue and Gospel* (1994), 39–62, for a recent survey of opinions.

[28] Raymond E. Brown, *The Community of the Beloved Disciple: The Life, Loves, and Hates of an Individual Church in New Testament Times* (New York: Paulist Press, 1979), 29–30, 69–71.

Q: Who are you? *Elijah?*

A: I baptize with water, among you stands one whom you do not know, even he who "comes after me," the thong of whose sandal I am not worthy to untie

A: I am not!

Q: A *prophet?*

A: No!

Q: Who then?

A: I am the voice of one crying in the desert: "Prepare the way of the Lord"
(Isa 40:3)

How do we interpret these question–answer exchanges? Are they impartial inquiries for information, challenges to John to which he must respond, or forensic questions, such as occur in judicial proceedings? On the basis of classical rhetoric, we argue that the question–answer exchange here is a hostile challenge to John's role and status. These questions are not requests for information but are intended to expose and belittle John.[29]

A CLOSER LOOK – QUESTIONS AS WEAPONS

In ancient rhetoric, "questions" are more than statements in an interrogatory form, for they provide points for dispute, quarrel, discussion, and the like; they frequently function as topics for debate, controversy, difficulties, quarrels, and puzzles. Questions are only occasionally disinterested quests for information. Quintilian explained the rhetorical purposes of questions as he described the latent hostility that shapes them: "What is more common than to *ask* and *enquire?* For both terms are used indifferently, although the one seems to imply a desire for knowledge and the other a desire to prove something" (*Inst. Orat.* 9.2.6). He distinguished seemingly neutral questions seeking information from aggressive ones, which "desire to prove something" either in attack or defense. He then itemized different types of questions and noted their rhetorical aims. Functions of hostile questions include: to put an audience on the spot, to stump an opponent, to throw odium on the person addressed, to embarrass an opponent, and to provoke indignation (*Inst. Orat.* 9.2.6–11).

Aggressive questions and answers occur also in philosophy. Socrates, for example, asked two types of questions. As a midwife, he asked educating questions to give birth to the truth already existing in the minds of interlocutors. But he also asked hostile questions of sophists to expose their folly

---

[29] See Jerome H. Neyrey, "Questions, *Chreiai*, and Challenges to Honor: The Interface of Rhetoric and Culture in Mark's Gospel," *CBQ* 60 (1998), 657–81.

and pretension. In Plato's *Republic*, one sophist fed up with Socrates' hostile questions put him on the spot: "If you really wish, Socrates, to know what the just is, neither merely ask questions nor criticize for the sake of gaining honor (μηδὲ φιλοτιμοῦ ἐλέγχων) since your acumen has perceived that it is easier to ask questions than to answer them – but do you yourself answer and tell what you say the just is (*Rep.* 1.336C). He accuses Socrates of asking questions "for the sake of gaining honor" or out of weakness ("easier to ask questions than to answer them"). Similarly, in the diatribe, the speaker pelted his audience with questions ("Don't you see?" "Don't you understand?" "Do you not know?"). Also, his interlocutor in turn hurled questions at him, usually drawing a (false) conclusion from what the speaker said to refute him. As Stanley Stowers said, "The diatribe is discourse . . . where the teacher employed the 'Socratic' method of censure and protreptic. The goal of this part of the instruction was not simply to impart knowledge, but to transform students, to point out error and cure it."[30]

Questions from the Prosecution. Why do those in the "center," priests and Levites, come to the "periphery"? They are the people most likely to be threatened by a figure who performs purificatory rites apart from the Temple and who talks about a person whose potential role is higher than theirs. Their questions, then, are hardly an impartial search for knowledge but rather attempts to challenge John: "Who are you?" John's answers, as Quintilian instructs, evade the issue: "I am not the Christ . . . [Elijah?] I am not . . . [A prophet?] I am not." These answers should prove that John is no threat to Jerusalem's Temple elite. But they persist: "Who are you? Let us have an answer for those who sent us. What do you say about yourself?" (1:22). John gives yet another evasive response: "I am the voice of one crying out in the wilderness, 'Make straight the way of the Lord,' as the prophet Isaiah said" (1:23). Minimally, he claims authorization to speak publicly, although the content of his discourse remains veiled. Thus, he evades their questions as one would dodge a weapon.

Asking Questions = "Not in the Know." The hostile nature of these questions can be seen more clearly in the second wave of questioners, who examine John's previous answers and then ask another question: "Why then are you baptizing if you are neither the Messiah, nor Elijah, nor the prophet?" (1:25). He evades the challenge cleverly. Although he baptizes, his real role is to proclaim an unknown person, so he shifts ground: "Among you stands one whom *you do not know*, the one who is coming after me" (1:26–27). Although this must surely refer to Jesus, only an insider would grasp the reference. John has accused Pharisees, who are outsiders, of a terrible evil, namely *not* knowing vital information (". . . whom

---

[30] Stanley K. Stowers, *The Diatribe and Paul's Letter to the Romans* (Chico, CA: Scholars Press, 1981), 76.

you do *not* know"). The author introduces here a pattern that contrasts those "in the know" with those "*not* in the know." And in the sectarian epistemology of this Gospel, "*not* knowing" proves that one is outside the circle of the family of God: ". . . the world knew him not" (1:10). The following figure illustrates how it functions as a sharp criterion for determining insiders from outsiders as well as hard-core insiders from lukewarm insiders.

A CLOSER LOOK – KNOWING AND NOT KNOWING

These data illustrate how the author regularly distinguishes insiders from outsiders according to the pivotal index of whether they "know" or "do not know":

3:2	"We know that you are a teacher from God."
3:10	"You are a teacher of Israel and you do not know this?"
4:22	"You worship what you do not know."
5:13	"He did not know who it was who said . . ."
7:27	"We know where this man comes from; no one knows where the Messiah comes from."
7:28	"So you know me? And you know whence I come?"
8:15	"You do not know whence I have come or whither I am going."
11:2	"I know that whatever you ask of God . . ."
11:49	"You know nothing."
11:50	"You do not know that it is expedient for one man . . ."

JOHN 1:29–34 – "NOT IN THE KNOW" THEN "IN THE KNOW"

29 The next day he saw Jesus coming toward him and declared, "Here is the Lamb of God who takes away the sin of the world!

30 This is he of whom I said, 'After me comes a man who ranks ahead of me because he was before me.'

31 I myself did not know him; but I came baptizing with water for this reason, that he might be revealed to Israel."

32 And John testified, "I saw the Spirit descending from heaven like a dove, and it remained on him.

33 I myself did not know him, but the one who sent me to baptize with water said to me, 'He on whom you see the Spirit descend and remain is the one who baptizes with the Holy Spirit.'

34 And I myself have seen and have testified that this is the Son of God."

I Heard and Testified. As a new audience appears, the hostile questions vanish. John testifies plainly about Jesus to a group of insiders, who are with John to learn, unlike the Jerusalem elites sent to spy on him and challenge him. In place of the hostile questions and evasive answers, John's positive testimony now leads his audience "into the know," unlike the Pharisees, who do "not know." The two previous questionings (1:19–22, 25) are balanced now by parallel, positive testimonies (1:30, 34). In each, two basic elements appear: "This is he. . . . This is the one" and "I did not know him." Although John was once "not in the know," God gave him revelations about Jesus so he became "in the know." Whereas he gave evasive answers to earlier questioners, John shares his knowledge about the worthy one who "comes after me" by publicly identifying Jesus as "The Lamb of God."

A CLOSER LOOK — THE LAMB OF GOD

"Lamb of God" may refer to (1) the King of Israel, a messianic, militant figure,[31] (2) the redemptive work of a figure based on Isaiah 53,[32] (3) the servant who purifies through wisdom,[33] and (4) a victorious lamb who defeats lions and other beasts.[34] At this point in the narrative, if we take the title in relation to later events in the story, we can say something in favor of each interpretation: (1) Jesus is eventually revealed as King of Israel (18:33–37; 19:19–22); (2) he lays down his life for his sheep not as a sheep but as a shepherd (10:11); (3) he baptizes with the Holy Spirit (1:33; 3:22), offering new forms of purification; and (4) in his death, Jesus confronts "the ruler of this world" (14:30), who hates Jesus and his disciples (15:18–19) but whom Jesus boasts of conquering (16:33).[35]

John thus makes Jesus known: "This is he. . . . This is the one." And "this one" is not simply the one "who comes after me" but rather the one "who ranks ahead of me because he existed before me." Although "after" John in chronological time, Jesus is "ahead" of John by virtue of his precedence (i.e., his superior role

---

[31] C. H. Dodd, *Interpretation of the Fourth Gospel* (1968), 230–38.

[32] Stephen Virgulin, "Recent Discussion of the Title 'Lamb of God,'" *Scripture* 13 (1961), 76–78.

[33] Joachim Jeremias, "παῖς θεοῦ," *TDNT* 5(1967), 702–4; M.-E. Boismard, "Le Christ-Agneau-Rédempteur des hommes," *Lumière et Vie* 36 (1958), 97–104.

[34] Charles H. Talbert, *Reading John: A Literary and Theological Commentary on the Fourth Gospel and the Johannine Epistles* (New York:Crossroad, 1992), 81; and Ben Witherington, *John's Wisdom. A Commentary on the Fourth Gospel* (Louisville,KY: Westminster John Knox, 1995), 66.

[35] Bruce Malina and Richard Rohrbaugh, in their *Social Science Commentary on the Gospel of John* (Minneapolis, MN: Fortress Press, 1998), 50–52, present this "Lamb" in terms of ancient astronomy, arguing that Jesus, who is considered a heavenly or sky being by the author, is associated with the heavenly Aries. In 1:51, Jesus tells his disciples that they, too, will soon see a heavenly being, the Son of Man. The Baptizer and the disciples both look into the sky and see a heavenly figure, who is Jesus.

and status) and his temporal superiority to John, who is a mere mortal, whereas Jesus does not come into being nor pass out of existence because he exists in eternal time.

Knowledge Is Everything. How does John know this? Whence comes his knowledge? Why should hearers trust him? While John confessed twice that he was "not in the know" (1:31, 33), God later favored him with a revelation that put him "in the know": "The one who sent me said to me, 'He on whom you see the Spirit descend and remain is the one who baptizes with the Holy Spirit'" (1:33). John sees a vision of the Spirit of God descending and remaining on Jesus, which God then interprets for John to mean that Jesus enjoys God's unique and abiding favor and that he has a premier role as the one who purifies. And so John summarizes the revelation: "I have seen" and "I testify" that "This one" is the Chosen One of God.

Kinds of Testimony. John's testimony functions in two ways: It deflects the hostile challenges of Jerusalem outsiders and makes Jesus known to insiders. Moreover, John tells us five distinct things about himself. First, the purpose of his baptizing was also testimony about Jesus: "I came baptizing . . . that he might be revealed" (1.31) and "The one who sent me to baptize with water said to me, 'He on whom you see the Spirit descend and remain is the one who baptizes with the Holy Spirit'" (1:33). Second, John and his baptism will shrink in importance, for they will be replaced by "the Lamb of God," whose "baptism with the Holy Spirit" (1:33) surpasses John's washing. This shrinking has John's approval (see 3:27–30). Third, John twice declared that "even I did not know him" (1:31, 33), indicating his radical dependence on a special revelation from God to acknowledge Jesus. Fourth, John testifies to Jesus' superiority, for even though he was first on the scene, Jesus "ranks ahead of me because he was before me" (1:30; see also 3:27–30). Fifth, the testimony of John is intentionally progressive. At first we hear his cryptic statement about "the one standing among you whom you do not know" (1:26), the veil over which he removes for the insiders: "This is the Lamb of God" (1:29). It finally becomes clear when John repeats God's revelation that the "Son of God" is "he upon whom the Spirit descends and remains" (1:33).[36] We note, then, progressive revelation whereby even insiders only gradually come to full knowledge and acknowledgment.

John's Later Testimony. In this Gospel, John's role is always that of one who gives testimony about another person. Later, when a controversy erupts between John's and Jesus' disciples, John's disciples remind the Baptizer that he about whom John once bore witness has become immensely successful (3:26). Presumably, this complaint challenges John to defend his honor and thus their honor.

---

[36] "Son of God" does not mean that Jesus is a divine figure, for many people in Israel were thus called; see Jerome H. Neyrey, *The Passion According to Luke* (Mahwah, NJ: Paulist Press, 1985), 168–70. In the Roman Empire, it became a regular title of the emperor; see B. J. Malina and R. L. Rohrbaugh, *Commentary on John* (1998), 52–53.

But John again testifies about his inferior status to Jesus, that he is but the friend of the bridegroom. Second, in 5:33–36, when Jesus is put on trial, he summons John to testify on his behalf. Although in 1:19 and 1:24 the Jerusalem elites once sent agents to John to test him, here Jesus claims that John's testimony was highly acceptable to this court, for "He was a burning and shining lamp, and you were willing to rejoice for a while in his light" (5:33).

JOHN 1:35–51 – PROGRESSIVE REVELATION AND MEMBERSHIP

35 The next day John again was standing with two of his disciples,

36 and as he watched Jesus walk by, he exclaimed, "Look, here is the Lamb of God!"

37 The two disciples heard him say this, and they followed Jesus.

38 When Jesus turned and saw them following, he said to them, "What are you looking for?" They said to him, "Rabbi" (which translated means Teacher), "where are you staying?"

39 He said to them, "Come and see." They came and saw where he was staying, and they remained with him that day. It was about four o'clock in the afternoon.

40 One of the two who heard John speak and followed him was Andrew, Simon Peter's brother.

41 He first found his brother Simon and said to him, "We have found the Messiah" (which is translated Anointed).

42 He brought Simon to Jesus, who looked at him and said, "You are Simon son of John. You are to be called Cephas" (which is translated Peter).

43 The next day Jesus decided to go to Galilee. He found Philip and said to him, "Follow me."

44 Now Philip was from Bethsaida, the city of Andrew and Peter.

45 Philip found Nathanael and said to him, "We have found him about whom Moses in the law and also the prophets wrote, Jesus son of Joseph from Nazareth."

46 Nathanael said to him, "Can anything good come out of Nazareth?" Philip said to him, "Come and see."

47 When Jesus saw Nathanael coming toward him, he said of him, "Here is truly an Israelite in whom there is no deceit!"

48 Nathanael asked him, "Where did you get to know me?" Jesus answered, "I saw you under the fig tree before Philip called you."

49 Nathanael replied, "Rabbi, you are the Son of God! You are the King of Israel!"

50 Jesus answered, "Do you believe because I told you that I saw you under the fig tree? You will see greater things than these."

51 And he said to him, "Very truly, I tell you, you will see heaven opened and the angels of God ascending and descending upon the Son of Man."

The Gossip Network: How Information Spreads.[37] John once more testifies about Jesus, now to two intimate disciples, Andrew and someone else. He names Jesus with the same title he used earlier, "Lamb of God." But something new happens: The two disciples begin to "follow" Jesus, not John. Thus the narrative turns its full attention to Jesus. Then follows an extensive repetition of this catechetical process, which may be summarized in this way: (1) Disciples name Jesus with titles to potential disciples, thus acknowledging his honor; and (2) Jesus himself makes revelations to them of profound significance. The following "closer look" illustrates the recruitment by disciples of relatives and neighbors.

A CLOSER LOOK — HOW GOSSIP FUNCTIONS IN THE GOSPEL

As we become familiar with this Gospel, we notice numerous significant patterns that are evidence of both literary craft and special argument. Because this pattern of "insiders" catechizing others occurs throughout the Gospel, we highlight it here. Jesus himself does not recruit anyone, but "believers" bring would-be disciples to him.

A believer evangelizes someone	John the Baptizer speaks to two disciples 1:35	Andrew found Peter 1:40f	??? found Philip 1:43	Philip found Nathanael 1:45f
Christological title	Behold, the Lamb of God 1:36	Messiah 1:41b	–	The one of whom Moses and the Prophets wrote 1:45b–46
Evangelizer leads recruit to Jesus	They listened and followed 1:37	he led him to Jesus 1:42	–	"Come and see" 1:46b
Jesus sees newcomer and confirms him	Jesus saw them: "Come and see" 1:38–39	Jesus saw him: "You are Cephas" 1:43	. . . said to him: "Follow me" 1:43b	Jesus saw and said: "Here is truly an Israelite in whom there is no deceit!" 1:47
Discipleship sealed	They came, saw, and remained 1:39	–	–	"You will see greater things than these" 1:50

---

[37] On "gossip," see Richard L. Rohrbaugh, "Gossip in the New Testament," in John J. Pilch, ed., *Social-Scientific Models for Interpreting the Bible: Essays by The Context Group in Honor of Bruce J. Malina* (Leiden: Brill, 2001), 239–59. Also see Sian Lewis, *News and Society in the Greek Polis* (Chapel Hill: University of North Carolina Press, 1996); and Robert F. Goodman and Aaron Ben-Ze'ev, eds., *Good Gossip* (Lawrence: University of Kansas Press, 1994).

If one focuses on the titles ascribed to Jesus ("Lamb of God," "Messiah," "the one of whom Moses and the Prophets wrote," and "Son of God and King of Israel"), we are struck by their density and progressive significance. The process illustrates a developing appreciation of Jesus' role and status, which accompanies and illustrates the "insider" status of those who use this language. Outsiders can't or won't speak this way.

Recruitment Not Volunteering. No volunteers ever succeed in becoming disciples, not even the Greeks in 12:20–22, who are warned off by Jesus with his parable of the seed dying (see Luke 9:57–62).[38] Hearing is the only way recruits are made, but not hearing Jesus' voice. We observe a recruitment process in which Jesus does not call any disciple (see Mark 1:16–20) but rather disciples who are already attached to Jesus recruit their siblings and neighbors to "come and see" this Jesus. Jesus might then say a confirming word, as when he gave "Simon, son of John" a new name: "You are Cephas, which means 'Peter'." Similarly, to Nathanael, Jesus reveals that he knew him already under the fig tree and that he is "truly an Israelite in whom there is no deceit" (1:47). Recruits hear disciples and then see Jesus.

Although the full recruitment pattern is found only in 1:35–50, it appears throughout the Gospel in condensed and fragmentary form. For example, the Samaritan woman speaks about Jesus to the villagers, inviting them to "come and see" (4:28–29), and Martha informs Mary that Jesus is outside (11:28). The dynamic of the recruitment process remains the same: Disciples talk to neighbors, siblings talk to siblings, and group members talk to group members. In each case, Jesus is named and heralded in an increasingly sophisticated manner; and Jesus himself continues his own progressive revelation to those who "come and see" (1:50).

Downsizing Peter's Traditional Position. When we compare John with the synoptic accounts of Jesus' relationship with his first disciples, we are struck by how different the Johannine version is. The synoptics narrate that Peter and Andrew were called together and similarly James and John – two pairs of brothers (Matt 4:18–22; Mark 1:16–20) who reside in Capernaum (Mark 1:29) and all of whom are fishermen, a fact withheld from the Johannine audience until 21:2–3. Jesus recruits them himself, saying "Follow me" (Matt 4:19), whereupon they immediately walk away from boats, nets, and family; no conflict of any sort

---

[38] In an honor–shame culture, volunteering was considered as a positive challenge, for it seeks to create a debt in the person accepting the volunteer. Yet that culture demands that we "owe no one anything" (Rom 13:8). See Bruce J. Malina, *The New Testament World: Insights from Cultural Anthropology*, 3rd edition (Louisville, KY: Westminster John Knox, 2001), 33–34; and also Jerome H. Neyrey, *Honor and Shame in the Gospel of Matthew* (Louisville, KY: Westminster John Knox, 1998), 45–46.

is mentioned. No honorific names are given any of them, Peter included;[39] nor is anyone particularly praised.

In contrast, John the Baptizer recruits the first disciple (Andrew), who later recruits Peter; Philip recruits Nathanael. *Jesus himself recruits no one.* Nothing is said about disciples abandoning families and trade or whether this posed any problem. Unlike the positive synoptic reaction, Nathanael challenges the word he heard about "Jesus of Nazareth," rebutting the claim that this figure from a mean village could possibly be the one of whom Moses and the prophets wrote. This constitutes a substantial problem, but our narrative deals with it successfully. While the success of the recruitment means honor for Andrew, Peter, and Philip, the truly praiseworthy figure becomes Nathanael, of whom we shall shortly speak. Peter, then, is not first and has no special position among the first disciples.

Peter, in Second Place. These differences invite explanations that fit the redactional character of this Gospel. If one tracks characters such as Peter throughout the narrative, an interesting pattern emerges. He is recruited second, not first. How unlike the wisdom revealed to Peter at Caesarea Philippi (Matt 16:16–17) is the lukewarm remark in 6:68: "To whom shall we go? You have the words of eternal life." Peter is bypassed in the chain of approach to Jesus in 12:20–21, where the key figures are Philip and Andrew. When Jesus washes Peter's feet, Peter "does not know" what Jesus does (13:4–6). When esoteric knowledge is needed, Peter must consult another disciple physically closer to Jesus (13:23), who later provides Peter with access to the High Priest's house (18:16) and who outruns Peter to the empty tomb (20:4), as well as outclassing him by knowing what the linens mean (20:6–8). Finally, only this Beloved Disciple "recognizes" the Lord and tells Peter that the Master stands on the shore (21:7). These data suggest that Peter is not the most prominent person of this group. He seems never to be favored with revelations and esoteric knowledge.[40]

An Israelite without Guile. Nathanael originally challenges the claims made for Jesus, that Israel's hopes cannot come from Nazareth. This implies that he knows "Moses and the Prophets" well enough to judge Philip's claims as ridiculous. Is he possibly a scholar learned in the Scriptures? Jesus reveals to him unique information, namely that he "saw" Nathanael the previous day when he was "under the fig tree." As is typical of all of the Gospels, Jesus can read hearts and knows what is within them (2:25). He manifests this first by reading Nathanael's heart, thus knowing him as "truly an Israelite without guile." Yet when Jesus says that he "saw" him under the fig tree, this does not mean physical sight. What do we need to know about "fig trees"?

---

[39] See Raymond E. Brown, Karl P. Donfried, and John Reumann, *Peter in the New Testament* (New York: Paulist Press, 1973), 129–68.

[40] Jerome H. Neyrey, *2 Peter, Jude* (New York: Doubleday, 1993), 171–72.

The Fig Tree. Some rabbinic texts imply that "fig tree" was both the locale for and symbol of studying the Scriptures. For example, in *b. Erubin* 54a we read: "R. Higga b. Abba in the name of R. Johannan expounded with reference to the Scriptural text, 'Whoso keepeth the fig tree shall eat the fruit thereof' (Prov 27:18), why were the words of Torah compared to the 'fig tree'? As with the fig tree, the more one searches it the more figs one finds on it, so it is with the Words of Torah; the more one studies them the more relish he finds in them."[41] Many other rabbinic texts[42] make the same equation of fig tree with Torah and searching for figs with study of the same. This material supports the view that Nathanael was a student of the writings of "Moses and the Prophets," so much so that he could employ them against claims for Jesus. But when Jesus tells him that he "saw him under the fig tree," he recants of his earlier reading of the Scriptures and now acclaims Jesus of Nazareth as the improbable "Son of God and King of Israel." How noble, then, is Nathanael's change of mind.

Representative Characters. Many scholars argue that the characters in John are types who represent postures and behaviors, somewhat in the fashion of Theophrastus' characters.[43] Focusing here on Nathanael, we observe that the narrative positions him as the climactic figure in the process of recruitment. He has the most difficulty in acknowledging Jesus, but overcomes it; Jesus praises him, something not done to any previous recruit: "truly an Israelite without guile." And Jesus promises Nathanael a benefit not promised the others (1:50). As a representative character, Nathanael's difficulty in reconciling Jesus with the Scriptures as he formerly knew them serves to compare and contrast him with others in the narrative who do not overcome this difficulty. Later we see his antithesis in those who argue that Jesus cannot be Messiah or prophet because he comes from Galilee (7:26–27, 40–44, 52). Many, then, challenge claims about Jesus from Israel's Scriptures. Still, others "search the Scriptures" (5:39) but fail to find life in them because they cannot acknowledge Jesus. Indeed, if they could read Moses correctly, they would find Jesus, for "Moses wrote of me" (5:46). Thus, in his own right and in contrast with others, Nathanael represents a success story, an insider who overcame great difficulties.

Recruitment and Status-Transformation Rituals. This recruitment process might be described as a status-transformation ritual, which generally consists of four stages: separation, liminality, transformation ritual, and popular acceptance of the new role or status.[44] The recruits in 1:35–51 all separate

---

[41] R. E. Brown, *Gospel According to John* (1966), 1.83; see also C. F. Moule, "A Note on 'under the fig tree' in John 1:48, 50," *JTS* n.s. 5 (1954), 210–11.

[42] *Midr. Qohelet* 5.11.2; *Midr. Song of Songs* 6.2.2.

[43] Raymond Collins, "The Representative Figures in the Fourth Gospel," *Downside Review* 94 (1976), 26–46, 118–32; and J. H. Neyrey, *Ideology of Revolt* (1988), 70–71, 78–79.

[44] See Jerome H. Neyrey, "The Footwashing in John 13:6–11: Transformation Ritual or Ceremony?," in L. Michael White and O. Larry Yarbrough, eds., *The Social World of the First*

themselves from their contexts because they must "*come* and see" and even "remain" in a new location. Some transit and process of enlightenment is presumed as new recruits are mentored and led to Jesus; one even enduring a struggle. All of this represents various aspects of liminality. The transformation from recruit to disciple occurs in each case when Jesus invites them to stay and/or when he proclaims a new name or praises their courage, all of which mark them as true insiders. When they in turn recruit others, they function in their new role as disciple and insider, which is then acknowledged by those recruited.

Toward the Climax. A dramatic shift occurs as this narrative draws to a climactic conclusion. Jesus, silent for most of the recruitment narrative, assumes the role of teacher and revealer. To Nathanael he reveals earthly secrets (1:47–48), and then to all the disciples he proclaims a revelation (1:51). Whereas Jesus promised Nathanael that he would see "greater things" (1:50), to all the recruits he promises that they would see a theophany in the center of the heavens (1:51). Surpassing all previous titles that others ascribe to him, Jesus himself reveals a new, superior one, "Son of Man." The rhetoric of the narrative identifies 1:51 as the climax of an extended process of recruitment and a crescendo of revelations. Readers are referred to the discussion of the title "Son of Man" at 3:13–15.

You Will See What Jacob Saw, I Promise. Jesus promises these elite disciples a vision of the Son of Man in heaven. His remark requires us to compare what Jesus promises here with the vision by Jacob in Genesis 28, upon which Jesus' vision depends. Jacob received a theophany – that is, a revelation of God – at Bethel; he saw a ladder linking heaven and earth, with angels climbing up and down it, and God standing atop the ladder. The ladder functions as a bridge between heaven and earth. But Jesus' remarks, although similar to Jacob's vision, describe a different scene.

John 1:51	*Genesis 28*
1. you will see	1. Jacob saw
2. heavens opened	2. ladder from earth to heaven
3. angels up/down	3. angels up/down
4. on Son of Man	4. on ladder

Minimally, the disciples will be Jacob-like figures, seeing a vision comparable to that of Jacob.[45] But unlike Jacob's vision, there is no ladder in John, earth is not linked to heaven, and nothing is said in John about this earthly place

Christians: Essays in Honor of Wayne A. Meeks (Minneapolis, MN: Fortress Press, 1995), 198–208.

[45] Nils A. Dahl, "The Johannine Church and History," in his *Jesus in the Memory of the Early Church* (Minneapolis, MN: Augsburg, 1976), 112–13.

being the "house of God and gate of heaven." Heaven alone is in view, and it is "opened" so that mortals below may see into it, emphasizing revelation, if not a theophany. The angels, moreover, do not ascend and descend on a nonexistent ladder but stream to the center of the heavens, that is, toward the Son of Man. According to 1:51, we imagine Jesus seated on the throne in heaven's center; to him angels from all directions make their way, presumably to honor him. They will see the Son of Man, who ultimately ascends to take the glory he had with God before the beginning of the world.

Jesus, the Appearing Deity in the Scriptures? This vision inaugurates a pattern that will recur many times in the Gospel. Because we know that "No one has ever seen God" (1:18), no one, not Moses, not Isaiah, not Abraham, and not Jacob, ever saw God! For seeing God is the unique prerogative of Jesus ("Not that anyone has seen the Father except the one who is from God; he has seen the Father," 6:46; see also 1 John 4:12). Then whom did the prophets see? Jesus, the appearing heavenly figure.

A CLOSER LOOK – JESUS, THE APPEARING DEITY OF THE SCRIPTURES

Philo argues that the theophanies in the Bible were not visions of God but revelations by God's Logos or a Power of God. Like John, he accepts that no one can see God (Exod 33:20–23). Nevertheless, Jacob is called "Israel"; that is, "he who sees God" (Gen 32:28–30).[46] Philo also argues that in Genesis 28:12 Jacob saw one of the powers of God (*Somn.* I. 70). And, in another place (Gen 31:13), Jacob learns that the appearing figure is *not* God but "god who appeared to you *in place of God*" (*Somn.* I. 228).[47]

Similarly, Justin Martyr argued that it was not God but another figure who appeared to the Patriarchs. After demonstrating that Jesus appeared to Abraham (*Dial.* 56, 59), to Moses (*Dial.* 56, 59, 60, 120), and to Jacob (*Dial.* 58, 60, 86, 126), Justin concluded: " . . . neither Abraham, nor Isaac, nor Jacob, nor any other man, saw the Father and ineffable Lord of all, but (saw) him who was according to his will his Son, being God, and the Angel because he ministered to his will" (*Dial.* 127). Thus Philo, John, and Justin make a common argument: (1) no one has ever seen God, (2) therefore when the Patriarchs received genuine theophanies (3) they saw the Logos, who is properly called God.

A Problematic Promise. Was the promise fulfilled? How does it relate to the Gospel narrative? First, the prologue established that Jesus is a timeless figure who existed in the past before creation and who later returns to God's heart,

---

[46] See also *Ebr.* 44–45; *Migr.* 201; and *Mut.* 44–45, 81–82.
[47] Jerome H. Neyrey, "The Jacob Allusions in John 1:51," *CBQ* 44 (1982), 592–93

suggesting an eternal future existence (1:18). Thus, the argument that Jacob, Abraham, Moses, and Isaiah saw Jesus in the past is not illogical, for Jesus enjoys an eternal "is"; he was, and was active in, Israel's past and he will be at God's right hand, or "heart," when he returns to God's house. Second, the Gospel does not say that anyone *saw* with earthly eyes the vision described in 1:51. But many were exceptionally enlightened or received special revelations to discern Jesus' heavenliness: for example, Thomas ("My Lord and my God," 20:28). Thus insight, not sight, is the Johannine way to interpret this promise. Whereas in 1:51 Jesus makes a promise of a future revelation, no such vision is literally recorded in the narrative. But what insights about the heavenly Jesus did the insiders receive? Elements of that future "Christophany" include knowledge of his restoration to former glory ("Father, glorify me in your own presence with the glory that I had in your presence before the world existed," 17:5), knowledge that the Son of Man was originally a heavenly being who will return there (3:13–15; 6:62), and accepting Jesus' word that "I am ascending to my Father and your Father, to my God and your God" (20:17). Inasmuch as this Gospel deals with insider knowledge, revelation of special secrets, and unique insights, we interpret 1:51 in this light. The promise is fulfilled in many insights, not just one vision.

JOHN 2:1–12 – THE FIRST SIGN

1 On the third day there was a wedding in Cana of Galilee, and the mother of Jesus was there.

2 Jesus and his disciples had also been invited to the wedding.

3 When the wine gave out, the mother of Jesus said to him, "They have no wine."

4 And Jesus said to her, "Woman, what concern is that to you and to me? My hour has not yet come."

5 His mother said to the servants, "Do whatever he tells you."

6 Now standing there were six stone water jars for the Jewish rites of purification, each holding twenty or thirty gallons.

7 Jesus said to them, "Fill the jars with water." And they filled them up to the brim.

8 He said to them, "Now draw some out, and take it to the chief steward." So they took it.

9 When the steward tasted the water that had become wine, and did not know where it came from (though the servants who had drawn the water knew), the steward called the bridegroom

10 and said to him, "Everyone serves the good wine first, and then the inferior wine after the guests have become drunk. But you have kept the good wine until now."

11 Jesus did this, the first of his signs, in Cana of Galilee, and revealed his glory; and his disciples believed in him.

12 After this he went down to Capernaum with his mother, his brothers, and his disciples; and they remained there a few days.

Telling Time in the Fourth Gospel. The evangelist begins this episode by noting that Jesus appeared in Cana "on the third day." The evangelist uses double-meaning terms and symbolic language, so we suspect that "third day" does not mean mere calendar time.[48] A "first day" included John's testimony in 1:19, followed by three "next days" (1:29, 35, 39) dedicated to recruitment. Each of these "days" implies a longer period than a mere twenty-four hours, for the first disciples "remained with Jesus that day for it was the tenth hour" (1:39), presumably a Sabbath but more likely a period of extended personal relationship, which "remain" symbolizes. The recruitment in 1:39–51, then, indicates a meaningful block of time and spans many calendar days.

A CLOSER LOOK – CALENDAR VERSUS IDEOLOGICAL TIME

The evangelist knows how to "tell time," both *calendar* and *ideological* time.[49] Regarding calendar time, he tells us of "daybreak" (18:28; 20:1; 21:4) and says that a typical day has "twelve hours" (11:9). For rhetorical purposes, he reckons exact calendar time, such that Lazarus was in the tomb for "four days" (11:17); that Jesus enters Jerusalem "six days before Passover" (12:1); that Jesus' resurrection occurred on "the first day of the week" (20:19); or that Jesus' reappearance happened "eight days later" (20:26). The healings in Chapters 5 and 9 would be uneventful had they not happened on a precise day, namely the Sabbath (5:9–10; 9:14). As regards symbolic time, major tableaux in the Gospel occur on feast days, which are calendar markings of time: Passover (2:13; 6:4; 12:1; 13:1; 18:28; 19:14); Tabernacles, especially "the last day of the feast, the great day" (7:37); and Dedication (10:22). These times must first be genuine calendar times before the evangelist can reinterpret them and give them new ideological meaning.

Other times are clearly not calendar times but ideological and relational periods. Take, for example, the frequent remark that Jesus "remained two

---

[48] See Craig R. Koester, *Symbolism in the Fourth Gospel: Meaning, Mystery, Community* (Minneapolis, MN: Fortress Press, 1995), 82, 264, 267; Frédric Manns, *L'Évangile de Jean à la lumière du Judaisme* (Jerusalem: Studium Biblicum Franciscanum, 1991), 248–52, 282–84.

[49] For a social-scientific interpretation of biblical time, see Bruce J. Malina, "Christ and Time: Swiss or Mediterranean," in his *The Social World of Jesus and the Gospels* (London: Routledge, 1996), 179–214. For time according to narrative criticism, see Alan Culpepper, *Anatomy of the Fourth Gospel* (Philadelphia: Fortress Press, 1983), 53–70. For esoteric calibration of time, see K. Hanhart, "'About the tenth hour' ... on Nissan 15 (Jn 1,35–40)," in Marinus de Jonge, ed., *L' Évangile de Jean: Sources, rédaction, théologie* (Leuven: Leuven University Press, 1977), 335–46. See also Margaret Davies, *Rhetoric and Reference in the Fourth Gospel* (Sheffield: JSOT Press, 1992), 44–66.

days" (2:12; 4:40, 43; 11:6). Just as "remaining" is not a spatial category, neither is "two days" a calendar period. Some people "saw my day" (8:56), not a calendar day but a moment of great enlightenment or relationship. Other "days" speak of a noncalendar manifestation of power, "I will raise them on the last day" (6:39, 40, 44, 55; 11:24; 12:48), of revelation, "in that day . . ." (14:20), or of future eras when disciples petition God without a broker (16:23, 26).

Similarly, times of the day mean more than nighttime and daytime, for they serve to distinguish "insiders" from "outsiders."[50] Day (and light) are positive times for "insiders" (9:4, 14; 11:9), when they act boldly in public and all may hear them. Just as Jesus is "the light of the world" (8:12), so, too, do, they work in the light and manifest that their deeds are wrought in God (3:21). But night and darkness are the time of "outsiders" or of those afraid to testify publicly about Jesus (3:2, 19–20; 9:4; 11:10; 13:30; 19:39).

Finally, calendar days are measured in hours, which occasionally serves to make time reckoning more exact, such as "the tenth hour" (1:39; 4:6; 19:14). But in John "hour" is rarely a calendar time marker[51] but rather a statement about ideological interpretations of time. When Jesus declares that "my hour has not yet come" (2:4; 7:30; 8:20; 12:27), this speaks of God's providential orchestration of Jesus' life and Passion and to Jesus' knowledge of this mystery. The frequent remark about the "hour" of Jesus' glorification (12:23; 13:1; 17:1) serves as a marker of Jesus' high status as he begins his return to God and glory. Only insiders know his Passion as "glory" and so are able to "tell time." Third, "hour" refers to the period when bad things will happen to the disciples (16:2, 4, 21, 25, 32); that is, markers of phases of their experience. The fact that Jesus foretells this "hour" indicates that he controls the fate of the disciples and provides an insider interpretation for "telling time."

Therefore, we should not consider "on the third day" as calendrical time. Although it is tempting to imagine the evangelist mapping out a cosmic week as in Genesis 1,[52] the data do not support this. It seems more profitable to interpret "third day" as a transition from times of testimony and recruitment to times of "signs"; that is, a different aspect of Jesus' career. His remark that "my hour has not yet come," then, functions in several ways. First, Jesus, the insider, knows the plans of God, which this "woman," a doubtful insider, does not. Thus knowing

---

[50] On light symbolism, see C. R. Koester, *Symbolism in the Fourth Gospel* (1995), 123–52.

[51] See John Ashton, *Understanding the Fourth Gospel* (Oxford: Clarendon, 1991), 269–70.

[52] See Thomas Barosse, "The Seven Days of the New Creation in St. John's Gospel," *CBQ* 21 (1959), 507–16. For another version of a "7-day week," see Jeffrey Lloyd Staley, *The Print's First Kiss: A Rhetorical Investigation of the Implied Reader in the Fourth Gospel* (Atlanta: Scholars Press, 1988), 74–90.

"the hour"[53] distinguishes persons according to the most important evaluative criterion in the Gospel: *Who* knows *what when?*

Signs and Co-signs. By classifying this story as "the first of his signs" (2:11), the author invites us to consider the form and function of this narrative. First, several miracle stories are actually labeled "first sign" and "second sign" (4:54), which has led many to argue that at some early time a collection of them existed.[54] If there was a "sign source," how many events belonged to it? Were all of them miracles? Most scholars favoring a sign source list seven signs: (1) changing water to wine (2:1–12); (2) healing the official's son (4:46–52); (3) healing the paralytic (5:1–9); (4) the multiplication of loaves (6:1–14); (5) walking on water (6:16–21); (6) giving sight to the blind man (9:1–12); and (7) raising Lazarus (11:17–44, 47). Lazarus' restoration has paramount significance because it occupies the climactic last position, demonstrates Jesus' power over death, and precipitates the plot to kill Jesus. As regards the function of these "signs," they work rhetorically, as do most miracle stories in antiquity: as credentials that the wonderworker enjoys God's favor and has a certain role, such as prophet. In the grammar of honor, they occasion acknowledgment of the power and worth of the healer, and so yield great honor and respect.[55]

Credentials. Luke understands Jesus' miracles precisely as credentials: "Jesus ... A man attested to you by God with deeds of power, wonders, and signs that God did through him among you" (Acts 2:22). In the Q-Source, Jesus responds to the Baptizer's disciple with a summary of his mighty deeds (Matt 11:2–5; Luke 7:18–23), data that should answer their question satisfactorily. Similarly, in John 9, the man born blind first argues "he is a prophet" (9:17) on the basis of Jesus' mighty deed, and later he makes the connection between miracle and God's authorization: "If this man were not from God, he could do nothing"(9:33). In this first sign, Jesus "manifested his glory" (2:11); that is, he made an honor claim, which the disciples acknowledge.

A CLOSER LOOK – SIGNS, WONDERS, AND HONOR

Miracle stories in antiquity were told to bring honor to those who performed them. For example, Josephus relates how an Israelite miracle worker

---

[53] See 7:6, 8, 30; 8:20. "Hour" has many meanings in this Gospel, especially those dealing with the present and a distant time. See R. E. Brown, *Gospel According to John* (1966), 517–18.

[54] See Robert T. Fortna, *The Gospel of Signs: A Reconstruction of the Narrative Source Underlying the Fourth Gospel* (Cambridge: Cambridge University Press, 1970); and more recently, Gilbert van Belle, *The Sign Source in the Fourth Gospel: Historical Survey and Critical Evaluations of the Semeia Hypothesis* (Leuven: Leuven University Press, 1994).

[55] Yet "glory" manifested by Jesus leads his disciples to believe in him (2:11). For a reading of 2:1–11 in terms of "glory" and "honor," see Matthew S. Collins, "The Question of *Doxa*: a Socioliterary Reading of the Wedding of Cana," *BTB* 25 (1995), 100–109.

performed a healing before the emperor Vespasian in order to glorify the healer, God, and Solomon, whose divine wisdom mediates God's power: "The understanding and wisdom of Solomon were clearly revealed, on account of which we have been induced to speak of these things, in order that all men may know the greatness of his nature and how God favoured him, and that no one under the sun may be ignorant of the king's surpassing virtue of every kind" (*Antiquities* 8.47–48). Similarly, this Gospel ends with a formal claim about the rhetorical function of the "signs": "These are written so that you may come to believe that Jesus is the Messiah, the Son of God, and that through believing you may have life in his name" (20:31). The "signs" are meant to enlighten and convince people that Jesus enjoys the unique role of "Messiah, Son of God," thus giving Jesus honor and glory.

Suggestion, Negative Response, Positive Action. Johannine "signs" are more than claims to honor and belief because there seems to be a peculiar conflictual dynamic in three of them. C. H. Giblin's literary examination of four stories plots them as sharing a common sequence of stages: a request to Jesus, his negative response, and then his eventual positive action.[56] When viewed synoptically, the pattern and text appear as follows:

Suggestion:

They have no wine 2:3	Come down and heal my son 4:47	Leave here and go to Judea 7:3–4	He whom you love is ill 11:3

Negative Response:

Woman, what concern is that to me? My hour has not yet come 2:4	Unless you see signs you do not believe 4:48	My time is not yet come; your time is always here. . . . I am not going up 7:6–8	This illness is not unto death. . . . He stayed 11:4–6

Positive Action:

Fill the jars with water! 2:7	Go, your son lives 4:50	then he also went up to the feast 7:10	Let us go into Judea 11:7

But how do we interpret this? First, who speaks this way, to whom, and why? One would think that Jesus' mother (2:3), his brothers (7:3–4), and the "beloved" Lazarus and his sisters (11:3) are insiders, such that Jesus has debts of kinship and friendship with them. Thus, the royal official (4:47) stands apart from these other petitioners. But how difficult it is to know who truly believes and who is a genuine insider in this Gospel; blood relationship to Jesus is *not* a

---

[56] C. H. Giblin, "Suggestion, Negative Response, and Positive Action in St. John's Portrayal of Jesus (2:1–11; 4:46–54; 7:2–14; 11:1–44)," *NTS* 26 (1980), 197–211.

sure qualification for membership (1:13). Second, if Jesus responds negatively at first, why act positively later? In three cases, it seems that neither the initial "time" (surely not calendar time!) nor the "place" is right – for Jesus, that is. Some adjustment in both is needed, which only Jesus can perceive. Third, although one might argue that three of the stories have a humanitarian aspect to them, namely coming to the aid of another, it would seem also that Jesus insists that things happen according to his dictates, timetables, and so forth even if it means that Lazarus dies. The plot must eventually work out that Jesus alone is master of the scene. Because Giblin's literary analysis cannot completely explain Jesus' behavior, we seek clues from the world of anthropology to unlock this material.

Honor versus Being Taken Advantage Of. In the world of honor and shame, all males everywhere and at all times live under the gaze of their peers, knowing what others expect of them and striving to live up to their expectations – all for the purpose of gaining respect. But because the ancients perceived that all the goods of this world, honor included, exist in short and limited supply, all players of this game learn when someone is encroaching on their turf, either challenging them or seeking to take advantage of them.[57] These encroachments are called "challenge–riposte" exchanges, which may be either *positive* (take advantage of, create a debt) or *negative* (harming, diminishing).

All of the Gospels regularly describe Jesus as engaged in negative challenge–riposte exchanges, which in rhetoric are labeled as *responsive chreiai*.[58] Thus, these same episodes can be interpreted either in terms of anthropology (challenge–riposte) or rhetoric *(chreia)*. The typical choreography of a "challenge" contains the following four movements. (1) A sage or prominent person already enjoys a reputation or claims some worth. (2) Others, who sense that the rise of the claimant means their diminishment, fight back by challenging or questioning the sage. (3) Because part of honor is one's ability to defend it, the person challenged must fight back. (4) All such challenges take place in plain view of observers, who determine the winner and honor the victor. But there are other challenges in which someone seeks to take advantage of another (see the comments about "volunteering" at 1:35–51). They seek something from the person approached, but not necessarily his humiliation or injury. Nevertheless, his authority, independence, freedom of action, and assets could be put at risk. *Gifts* come with strings attached: "I give so as to get." Hence a donor expects a return. *Volunteering* encroaches on a person's autonomy because he may not

---

[57] See Jerome H. Neyrey and Richard L. Rohrbaugh, "'He must increase, I must decrease' (John 3:30): Cultural and Social Interpretation," *CBQ* 63 (2001), 468–76; and also Jerome H. Neyrey and Anselm C. Hagedorn, "'It Was Out of Envy that They Handed Jesus Over' (Mark 15:10): The Anatomy of Envy and the Gospel of Mark," *JSNT* 69 (1998), 15–56.

[58] See J. H. Neyrey, "Questions," *CBQ* 60 (1998), 664–70 and 673–76.

want certain people in his faction (Luke 9:57–62; Matt 8:19–22); John's Jesus also responds severely to volunteers (12:24–26). *Compliments*, such as "Good teacher . . . " (Mark 10:17–18), create an expectation of reciprocal praise, which one may not wish to grant. Finally, *requests* put the one petitioned on the spot, for he may not desire any relationship with the client petitioning him or he may have limited resources for the request (Mark 7:25–29; 9:18); how embarrassing, then, it is to be put on the spot and forced to do something one may not want to do.

Herein lies the supplement to Giblin's pattern. In all four cases he identifies, a *request* is made of Jesus. If requests put the person petitioned on the spot, then Jesus is indeed challenged. The quadruple "negative response" serves as Jesus' defense of his honor and independence from coercion. If he subsequently accedes to the request, he does it *on his own terms*: The time and the place are now "right" – for Jesus, that is.[59]

Woman and Mother, but Believer? As with Nathanael, we examine Jesus' mother as a representative character in this drama. Kinship is evident; she is "mother" and the wedding that she, Jesus, and his brothers and disciples attend would likely involve their kin or even a blood relative. Second, although she is identified as "mother," Jesus does not address her by that honorific role but calls her "woman." As Raymond Brown noted, "There is no precedent in Hebrew or, to the best of our knowledge, in Greek, for a son to address his mother thus."[60] Strange, indeed. Two contradictory interpretations have developed to explain this. Some see the role of the mother of Jesus positively widened into a type of new Eve; hence no personal name is needed because only her role counts.[61] Negatively, although other females have names, the mother has no name. Mary, Martha, and Mary Magdalene all enjoy a special relationship with Jesus. Of Martha and Mary, we are told: "Jesus loved Martha and her sister and Lazarus" (11:5); Mary Magdalene, on the other hand, is called by name (20:16–18).[62] Thus Jesus minimizes his mother's role by calling her "woman," which also puts in

---

[59] On the "right time," see Renée Bloch, "Quelque aspects de la figure de Moïse dans la tradition rabbinique," in H. Cazelles, ed., *Moïse, l'homme de l'alliance* (New York: Desclée, 1955), 93–167.

[60] Raymond E. Brown, "The Mother of Jesus in the Gospel of John," in Raymond E. Brown, Karl P. Donfried, Joseph A. Fitzmyer, and John Reumann, eds., *Mary in the New Testament* (Philadelphia: Fortress Press, and New York: Paulist Press, 1978), 188. Yet, in his commentary, *Gospel According to John* (1966), 1.99, Brown insists that "this is not a rebuke, nor an impolite term, not an indication of a lack of affection. . . . It was Jesus' normal, polite way of addressing women (Matt xv 28; Luke xiii 12; John iv 21, viii 10, xx 13)."

[61] R. E. Brown, "The Mother of Jesus in the Gospel of John," in *Mary in the New Testament* (1978), 180–90.

[62] See Margaret Davies, "Named Characters, the Mother of Jesus, and the Beloved Disciple," in her *Rhetoric and Reference in the Fourth Gospel* (1992), 333–40.

doubt her status as a disciple.[63] Third, from the beginning of the Gospel, we have been alerted to contrasting modes of discipleship – mere blood relationships versus birth and adoption by God's power: "He came to what was his own, and his own people did not accept him. But to all who believed in his name, he gave power to become children of God" (1:11–13). Thus "his own" reject him outright or are deficient in discipleship, which includes fellow Israelites (off-spring of Abraham in John 8), "brothers" (7:1–10), and even "mother."[64] The synoptic Gospels likewise repeat this anti-kinship motif.[65] Thus, the mother of Jesus appears to be less than a hard-core believer; rather, she represents kin or blood relationship, which is found wanting here. A blood relative but not a genuine believer, she does not know his "hour." The issue of her relation-ship to Jesus as disciple and believer must wait until her final appearance in 19:25–27.

The Best Is Last. Earlier, we examined how time is told in this gospel, which has a bearing on the temporal sequencing mentioned in 2:10. The steward tells the groom: " . . . the good wine first, and then the inferior. . . . You have kept the good wine until now." This is very surprising, for earlier is always better and later is deficient. Modern readers, however, are socialized by Darwin and evolutionary thinking to think the best is yet to come. But the ancients operated out of a completely different model of time: First came the golden age, then the silver age, then the bronze age, and soon, a model of degeneration. For example, Hesiod employs this degeneration model in describing the races whom the gods made: "A second race thereafter, one far worse, the dwellers in Olympus made, of silver. . . . Then Zeus the father made a third new race of men unlike the silver; these of bronze, from ash-trees, dread and mighty" (*Works and Days*, 127–128 and 143–45). What is recent is suspect; it cannot be as good as its predecessor. When we apply this model to John 2:1–11, Jesus appears as a recent phenomenon,[66] so what good can come from him? Ironically, the issue is not wine but Jesus. The steward, moreover, does "not know" about Jesus or "whence the wine came." But he articulates two major themes that weave their way through the Gospel: "knowing," and particularly knowing "whence" Jesus comes. Although

---

[63] Yet most commentators consider Jesus' remark in 2:4 to be rude; see Raymond Collins, "Mary in the Fourth Gospel: A Decade of Johannine Studies," *Louvain Studies* 3 (1970), 99–142.

[64] Compare this scene with Luke 2:46–49, where Jesus acts contrary to the wishes of his earthly parents but in compliance with those of his heavenly Father. See S. van Tilborg, *Imaginative Love* (1993), 7.

[65] Stephen C. Barton, *Discipleship and Family Ties in Mark and Matthew* (Cambridge: Cambridge University Press, 1994), 67–86, 223; and see S. van Tilborg, *Imaginative Love* (1993), 33–57, 243–45.

[66] Jesus' eternity in the past should be seen in this light; for example, before Abraham came into being, Jesus existed (8:58).

not "in the know" himself, he functions as challenger of the old axiom that what is good comes first and everything later is degenerative. So, he knows something! But the issue is not wine, but Jesus as the "sign" pointing to Jesus: Although "new" in time, like the wine, Jesus is also old because he was before John (1:15, 30).

JOHN 2:13–22 – THE FIRST JERUSALEM APPEARANCE

13 The Passover of the Jews was near, and Jesus went up to Jerusalem.

14 In the temple he found people selling cattle, sheep, and doves, and the money changers seated at their tables.

15 Making a whip of cords, he drove all of them out of the temple, both the sheep and the cattle. He also poured out the coins of the money changers and overturned their tables.

16 He told those who were selling the doves, "Take these things out of here! Stop making my Father's house a marketplace!"

17 His disciples remembered that it was written, "Zeal for your house will consume me."

18 The Jews then said to him, "What sign can you show us for doing this?"

19 Jesus answered them, "Destroy this temple, and in three days I will raise it up."

20 The Jews then said, "This temple has been under construction for forty-six years, and will you raise it up in three days?"

21 But he was speaking of the temple of his body.

22 After he was raised from the dead, his disciples remembered that he had said this; and they believed the scripture and the word that Jesus had spoken.

Challenging the Major Political Shrine.[67] According to the synoptics, the "cleansing of the Temple" occurs at the beginning of Jesus' week in Jerusalem before his crucifixion. Because of its explosive character, Jesus' actions occasion an immediate challenge by the Temple elite, an accusation at his trial (Matt 26:60; Mark 14:58), and mockery on the cross (Matt 27:40; Mark 15:29).[68]

---

[67] On temple as "political shrine," see B. J. Malina and R. L. Rohrbaugh, *Commentary on John* (1998), 77–79.

[68] Richard Bauckham, "Jesus' Demonstration in the Temple," in Barnabas Lindars, ed., *Law and Religion: Essays on the Place of the Law in Israel and Early Christianity* (Cambridge: James Clarke and Co., 1988), 72–89.

How greatly the Fourth Gospel differs from the synoptics.[69] First, the Temple event occurs on Jesus' first of three visits to Jerusalem and is positioned as his inaugural action there. Second, although the author retains the remark about making the Temple "a marketplace," he either did not know or ignores the material about the Temple as a "house of prayer for all the nations" (Matt 21:13; Mark 11:17; Luke 19:46). Moreover, subsequent material in the synoptics on prayer is absent here (see Mark 11:24–25). Because it is Jesus' inaugural appearance in the Temple, we take it as a programmatic event. As we saw concerning 2:10, all things occurring first in a list or sequence generally have thematic and not just temporal importance. Might this event introduce a discussion about worship – *where* to worship, *when* to worship, and *how* to worship? (See 4:20–24.) With this event, Jesus inaugurates a discussion about worship and sacrifice that will end only with his death. Here, when Jesus drives out "sheep and oxen" from the Temple (2:15), he challenges the Temple's system of sacrifices. He charges those who sold sacrificial animals with profaning the Temple by making it a "marketplace" (2:16). But soon we shall see Jesus proposing new rites of membership (3:3–5), new feasts, new benefits prayed for and given at feasts, and new food, both bread and lamb. This episode, then, inaugurates a theme of "replacement" by Jesus in regard to Israel's sacred space, feast days, and sacred objects petitioned.[70]

Reading with Johannine Eyes. The disciples, presumably after Jesus' glorification, remember a Scripture concerning this event that illuminates its secret meaning for those "in the know": "Zeal for your house will consume me" (Ps 69:9). This is, of course, a proof from prophecy, which illustrates how Jesus died according to a providential plan, a motif found especially in chapter 19:24, 28, 36, 37. But it says much more; namely, how Jesus' dedication to reforming the worship of God equals "zeal," not blasphemy. "House" is not to be equated with the Temple but with God's household or family.[71] And "consume me" suggests that such behavior will cause Jesus' death, not unlike the noble shepherd who lays down his life for his sheep. Not only are the key terms here all double meaning, but the context here for Psalm 69:9 is highly ironic. First of all, Jesus *seems* to act like a blasphemer who pollutes the traditional worship of God; thus, in the eyes of the Temple elite he acts sinfully and so cannot be God's agent. But those "in the know" understand his actions differently, for they provide the correct interpretation of the event: According to the psalm cited in 2:18, Jesus is

---

[69] For a detailed exegesis of this passage, see Mary L. Coloe, *God Dwells with Us: Temple Symbolism in the Fourth Gospel* (Collegeville, MN: Liturgical Press, 2001), 65–84; and Alan R. Kerr, *The Temple of Jesus' Body: The Temple Theme in the Gospel of John* (Sheffield: Sheffield Academic Press, 2002), 79–97.

[70] See J. H. Neyrey, *Ideology of Revolt* (1988), 131–37.

[71] Sverre Aalen, "'Reign' and 'House' in the Kingdom of God in the Gospels," *NTS* 8 (1962), 215–40.

not guilty of sin but saintliness, not "blasphemy" against God but "zeal," which is an intense positive interest in something. Moreover, "zeal" is not a quest for one's own glory, for Jesus seeks only God's glory by his actions, in contrast with the personal glory sought by his opponents (5:44; 12:43). Ironically, then, Jesus' distinctive loyalty to God will kill him. "Consume" might mean destruction or death, but because "zeal" "consumes" Jesus, his death is holy and noble.

Double-Meaning Words: An Introduction.[72] In the synoptic version of this episode, Jesus answers a hostile question with a hostile question: "I will ask you a question; answer me, and I will tell you by what authority I do these things" (Mark 11:29). Although John's version begins with a hostile question, "What 'sign' can you show us for doing this?" (2:18), Jesus does not stump his questioners so much as mislead them with double-meaning speech. Jesus states, "Destroy this temple, and in three days I will raise it up" (2:20). First of all, Jesus said "Destroy!" – that is, a command that grammatically makes the interlocutors the agents of the hostile action: "*You* destroy this temple [Jesus]." Thus, they are cast as aggressors, even his murderers (see the comments at 8:44). They miss his point entirely, for they hear Jesus claiming that he will destroy the Jerusalem Temple. Moreover, they understand "temple" to be a building, the shrine of Israel, but he spoke of the "temple of his body." They take "destroy" to mean dismantle, but he means it as "kill," as in crucify. Thus they hear Jesus claiming to do all this, whereas he stated that they, his challengers, will destroy his temple. Worst of all, Jesus' opponents ignore his claim that he will have the last word, the final riposte: "I will raise it up in three days." His opponents, then, miss all the irony and the double meanings, a sign that they are outsiders.

Honor: Challenge and Riposte. Cultural studies of New Testament stories regularly describe exchanges such as 2:18–19 in terms of a social dynamic called challenge and riposte.[73] As noted earlier, it contains four stages: (1) *claim*; (2) *challenge*, based on the honor principle that what one starts one must finish (Luke 14:28–32); (3) *response*; and (4) *success awarded* by the spectators. Jesus' actions in 2:14–16 constitute the "claim," implying that he enjoys a role and status authorizing him to deal with the Temple as he does. A challenge immediately follows from those who stand to lose prestige and wealth as a result of Jesus'

---

[72] On this motif, see D. W. Wead, *The Literary Devices of John's Gospel* (Basel: Reinhardt, 1970); D. A. Carson, "Understanding Misunderstandings in the Fourth Gospel," *TynB* 33 (1982), 61–90; and Earl Richard, "Expressions of Double Meaning and Their Function in the Gospel of John," *NTS* 31 (1985), 96–112.

[73] Bruce J. Malina and Jerome H. Neyrey, "Honor and Shame in Luke-Acts: Pivotal Values of the Mediterranean World," in Jerome H. Neyrey, ed., *The Social World of Luke-Acts: Models for Interpretation* (Peabody, MA: Hendrickson, 1991), 35–38; and Bruce J. Malina, *The New Testament World*, 3rd ed. (Louisville, KY: Westminster John Knox, 2001), 32–36.

action: "What sign can you show us for doing this?" (2:18). Again, their question
does not seek information but rather attacks Jesus once more. He responds to
their challenge and gives them a "sign": "Destroy this temple, and in three days
I will raise it up" (2:19). Misunderstanding what he said, they mock him about
something he did not say: "This temple has been under construction for forty-
six years, and will you raise it up in three days?" (2:20). The disciples eventually
give the public verdict at a time in the future when they comprehend what the
challengers missed: "After he was raised from the dead, his disciples remembered that he had said this; and they believed the scripture and the word that
Jesus had spoken" (2:22). Readers know that although Jesus won this first round
of challenge and riposte, his opponents will return again and again. Readers,
moreover, learn how to classify people from this exchange. Inasmuch as these
people miss the double meanings of Jesus' riposte, the author considers them as
"outsiders" who never learn his secrets and so remain "not in the know." Success
in this Gospel lies in the comprehension by characters and groups of the double
meaning of Jesus' words. Special levels of knowing, then, divide winners from
losers.

JOHN 2:23–25 – JESUS, KNOWER OF ALL SECRETS

23 When he was in Jerusalem during the Passover festival, many believed in his
name because they saw the signs that he was doing.
24 But Jesus on his part would not entrust himself to them, because he knew all
people
25 and needed no one to testify about anyone; for he himself knew what was in
everyone.

When "Place" Is Not "Space." At Cana in Galilee, Jesus' disciples believed in
him because of his sign; but in Jerusalem, when his opponents demand a sign,
discipleship is certainly not in their minds. What do we make of this "Galilee"
versus "Jerusalem" contrast? John interprets space in symbolic and theological
terms, not topological ones.[74] What meaning has the author invested in each
place? Consider the author's use of the term "remain." He tells us that Jesus "was"
in Jerusalem for a few days, but he never "remains" there.[75] Disciples "remain"

---

[74] See Robert T. Fortna, "Theological Use of Locale in the Fourth Gospel," *ATR* Suppl
   3 (1974), 58–95; and Jouette Bassler, "The Galileans: A Neglected Factor in Johannine
   Research," *CBQ* 43 (1981), 243–57.
[75] Rudolf Schnackenburg, *Die Johannesbriefe*, 2nd ed. (Freiburg: Herder, 1963), 105–9.

with Jesus (1:38–39), and he "remains" at Cana (2:12), Samaria (4:40), and Galilee (7:9). Conversely, Jesus urges his disciples to "remain" in the vine (15:4), in Jesus himself (15:5–7) and in his love (15:9–10). Thus, if "remaining" indicates loyalty and adherence to Jesus, then the Gospel tells us that this happens in "Galilee," wherever that might be. But it does not happen in "Jerusalem." Thus we assess these two places not simply as geographical locations but as "classified" places: in "Galilee" Jesus is accepted, gains disciples, and "remains"; in "Judea" he is harassed, put on trial, and killed.[76] In a survey article addressing this issue, Sean Freyne provides, I think, the correct interpretation of "Galilee" and "Jerusalem": "'The Galileans received him' is John's positive evaluation of attitudes towards Jesus within the narrative framework of the gospel (4,45). . . . A Galilean is one who is open to the journey of faith, not one who has already arrived. But [the Galileans] are immediately contrasted with Judeans as the main opponents of Jesus."[77] And because we learn of Judeans in Galilee (6:52), we should not reduce them solely to geography.[78]

Thinking about Space. In the anthropology of space, "territoriality" describes a process whereby peoples first classify a space as sacred/profane, safe/hostile, and the like.[79] Those classifying the space communicate this to others in order to control it: City walls and gates communicate the sense that this urban space is ours, not yours, and so control of access and egress backs up the classification. In John, we observe a classification system, namely "Galilee" and "Judea," although no attempt is made in the Gospel to endorse or prohibit movement of people to or from either space. Unlike in Mark 13:14, Jesus does not urge the disciples to leave Jerusalem, nor does he command them to flee to Galilee for safety.[80] But because "Galilee" and "Judea" identify either friendly or hostile reactions, some classification of places/peoples is made. The author labels each place in terms of some dualism or binary opposite: "love/hate," "friendly/hostile," or

---

[76] This is hardly a new idea. Wayne Meeks stated in his "Galilee and Judea in the Fourth Gospel," *JBL* 85 (1966), 169: "The geographical symbolism of John is not dominated by Jerusalem to the exclusion of Galilee, but it is shaped by the apparently deliberate dialectic between Jerusalem, the place of judgment and rejection, and Galilee and Samaria, the places of acceptance and discipleship." Similarly, see J. Bassler, "The Galileans," *CBQ* 43 (1981), 256–57.

[77] Sean Freyne, "Locality and Doctrine: John and Mark Revisited," in his *Galilee and Gospel* (Tübingen: Mohr Siebeck, 2000), 293.

[78] See John Ashton, "The Identity and Function of the Ἰουδαῖοι in the Fourth Gospel," *NovT* 27 (1985), 40–75.

[79] On "territoriality" and the Fourth Gospel, see Jerome H. Neyrey, "Spaces and Places, Whence and Whither, Homes and Rooms: 'Territoriality' in the Fourth Gospel," *BTB* 32 (2002), 64–74; and his "'Teaching You in Public and from House to House' (Acts 20:20): Unpacking a Cultural Stereotype," *JSNT* 26 (2003), 69–102.

[80] Although John 21 finds the disciples in Galilee, we do not know why they went there; we hear of no command either by Jesus (Mark 14:28) or angels (see Mark 16:7).

"remain/not remain."[81] "Galilee" and "Judea," then, indicate that Jesus and the disciples have friends and foes.[82]

In light of "Jerusalem" as a place of nonfaith and even hostility, we should be very cautious how we interpret the remark in 2:23 that "many believed in his name because they saw the signs that he was doing." Red flags go up. First, "believe in his name" is found also in 1:12 and 3:18, but what "name"? Insiders believe in his role (One sent by God) and his titles ("Messiah," "King of Israel," and "Son of God"). But his name? Second, although an earlier "sign source" functioned as propaganda for Jesus, "sign faith" will shortly become a problematic way of relating to Jesus, for it often fails to lead to loyalty or insight. Jesus does not entrust himself to these "sign believers," suggesting that he perceives a defect in what they acknowledge about himself. Finally, because Jesus knows what is in the hearts of these would-be believers, he does not trust them. Nor should the Gospel's audience.

A Prophet Who Reads Hearts. One aspect of Jesus' remarkable knowledge is his ability to read hearts. It belongs to a prophet to discern the heart and so distinguish exteriors from interiors. The Baptizer manifested this in the Q-Source; when elites from Jerusalem approach him, ostensibly they seek repentance. John saw the truth: "You brood of vipers . . . " (Matt 3:7–10; Luke 3:7–9).[83] Jesus, too, can read hearts, as he discerns criticism in the minds of scribes (Mark 2:8) and hardness in the hearts of the Pharisees (Mark 3:5). John repeatedly tells us that Jesus "knew from the beginning" Judas' character, that "he had a demon" (6:70).[84] All others think that Judas leaves the supper to give alms, but Jesus knows that Judas goes to assemble his enemies (13:27–29). Jesus knows all secrets and can read hearts. Nothing is outside his knowledge and thus his control.

---

[81] Some places in "Galilee," such as Cana, seem friendly and safe, but not the synagogue in Capernaum (6:59); and whereas "Judea" is generally hostile, Bethany is not (11:1 ff.; 12:1–8).

[82] Disciples who go to the local synagogue could be expelled for acknowledging Jesus (9:22; 12:42; 16:1–2) according to the Judean classification of the synagogue in terms of purity and pollution. Thus the synagogue classified its gatherings and exercised control by expelling those claiming to be Jesus' disciples.

[83] The Fourth Gospel does not refer to anyone as "hypocrite," a term common in the synoptics. Yet, in 8:30–58, Jesus unmasks the lie told him by steadily revealing that these "alleged believers" are really sons of Cain and Satan, murderers and liars. See David E. Garland, *The Intention of Matthew 23* (Leiden: Brill, 1979), 96–123; and Ivor W. J. Oakley, "'Hypocrisy' in Matthew," *IBS* 7 (1985), 118–37.

[84] The proper anthropological framework for understanding the disguise of certain people and the power claimed by those who can reveal disguised evil is the sociology of sorcery or witchcraft, of which the entire New Testament is rife. See Bruce J. Malina and Jerome H. Neyrey, *Calling Jesus Names* (Sonoma, CA: Polebridge Press, 1988), 1–32; and also Jerome H. Neyrey, *Paul, in Other Words: A Cultural Reading of His Letters* (Louisville, KY: Westminster John Knox, 1990), 181–206, 207–18.

JOHN 3:1–21 – COMING TO JESUS AT NIGHT

1 Now there was a Pharisee named Nicodemus, a leader of the Jews.

2 He came to Jesus by night and said to him, "Rabbi, we know that you are a teacher who has come from God; for no one can do these signs that you do apart from the presence of God."

3 Jesus answered him, "Very truly, I tell you, no one can see the kingdom of God without being born from above."

4 Nicodemus said to him, "How can anyone be born after having grown old? Can one enter a second time into the mother's womb and be born?"

5 Jesus answered, "Very truly, I tell you, no one can enter the kingdom of God without being born of water and Spirit.

6 What is born of the flesh is flesh, and what is born of the Spirit is spirit.

7 Do not be astonished that I said to you, 'You must be born from above.'

8 The wind blows where it chooses, and you hear the sound of it, but you do not know where it comes from or where it goes. So it is with everyone who is born of the Spirit."

9 Nicodemus said to him, "How can these things be?"

10 Jesus answered him, "Are you a teacher of Israel, and yet you do not understand these things?

11 "Very truly, I tell you, we speak of what we know and testify to what we have seen; yet you do not receive our testimony.

12 If I have told you about earthly things and you do not believe, how can you believe if I tell you about heavenly things?

13 No one has ascended into heaven except the one who descended from heaven, the Son of Man.

14 And just as Moses lifted up the serpent in the wilderness, so must the Son of Man be lifted up,

15 that whoever believes in him may have eternal life.

16 "For God so loved the world that he gave his only Son, so that everyone who believes in him may not perish but may have eternal life.

17 "Indeed, God did not send the Son into the world to condemn the world, but in order that the world might be saved through him.

18 Those who believe in him are not condemned; but those who do not believe are condemned already, because they have not believed in the name of the only Son of God.

19 And this is the judgment, that the light has come into the world, and people loved darkness rather than light because their deeds were evil.

20 For all who do evil hate the light and do not come to the light, so that their deeds may not be exposed.

21 But those who do what is true come to the light, so that it may be clearly seen that their deeds have been done in God."

Setting the Stage. Already this Gospel has conditioned us to certain patterns that greatly influence how we read John 3. In regard to 1:36–51, we learned that the Johannine group recruits others; volunteers are suspect (see footnote 34 in commentary on John 1). Also, we remember that in 2:24–25 Jesus did not trust himself to the people in Jerusalem who allegedly believed in him because of signs, for he knew what was in everyone. This extends also to 3:1–21, when another Jerusalemite comes to him because of signs. The setting of this narrative is very clear. *Where?* Presumably still in Jerusalem, in some unidentified residence. *When?* The calendar day seems less important than the time of day, "by night" (3:2), which is definitely not horological time. True acknowledgment of Jesus occurs in daylight (see 11:9–10); fear, secrecy, and malice occur at night (19:38–39 and 13:30). *Who?* Only Jesus and "a Pharisee named Nicodemus, a leader of the Jews" converse (3:1). *Why?* To learn from Jesus? To teach Jesus? Nicodemus guardedly states: "Rabbi, we know that you are a teacher who has come from God; for no one can do these signs that you do apart from the presence of God." (3:2).[85] What does this mean? Is he a believer? What does he know? Why does he come to Jesus at all, especially at night?

Three formal ways of interpreting this story are available to us: rhetorical analysis, literary patterns, and cultural patterns.

Rhetoric. Nicodemus' remark functions as a topic statement[86] containing five phrases to be sequentially explained: (1) "Rabbi . . . teacher"; (2) "we know"; (3) "come from God"; (4) "no one can do these signs"; and (5) "unless."

Teacher. He who addresses Jesus as a teacher is himself a "teacher of Israel" (3:10). Teachers teach, but when Jesus tries to teach Nicodemus, he utterly fails. Does this reflect on the teacher or the pupil? Jesus continues speaking to Nicodemus, but without results. But "teacher" is too thin a role to describe Jesus, for he is a revealer of heavenly and spiritual things. Thus Jesus should be acknowledged far above Nicodemus' minimalist designation of him as "teacher." In turn, Jesus mocks Nicodemus by addressing him as "a teacher of Israel," but one who knows very little at all (3:10).

Know/Knowledge. Nicodemus boasts of knowledge: "*We know* you are a teacher come from God." But what does he really know? The topics in Nicodemus' opening statement will prove to be misleading and of minimal content: He knows something, but not very much. And by the end of the conversation, he

---

[85] Jouette Bassler, "Mixed Signals: Nicodemus in the Fourth Gospel," *JBL* 108 (1989), 635–46; and David Rensburger, *Johannine Faith and Liberating Community* (Philadelphia: Westminster, 1988), 37–51. See also Marinus de Jonge, "Nicodemus and Jesus: Some Observations on Misunderstanding and Understanding in the Fourth Gospel," in his *Jesus: Stranger from Heaven and Son of God* (Missoula, MT: Scholars Press, 1977), 29–48.

[86] Jerome H. Neyrey, "The Debate in John III: Sectarian Epistemology and Christology," *NovT* 23 (1981), 115–27.

has learned nothing from Jesus' discourse. This is so because Nicodemus, being an earthly, fleshly person, is impervious to the revelations Jesus makes about spiritual and heavenly matters: "If I have told you about earthly things and you do not believe, how can you believe if I tell you about heavenly things?" (3:12). Finally, Jesus scolds him for failing to learn his teaching: "We speak of what we know and testify to what we have seen; yet *you do not receive our testimony*" (3:11). Nicodemus knows little when he arrives and has learned nothing when he leaves.

Come from God. The man born blind understands Jesus as "come from God" in a way that surpasses Nicodemus' remark. He said: "If this man were not from God, he could do nothing" (9:33), thus speaking boldly, during the daylight, and in a context that costs him his place in the community. He accepted Jesus the healer-prophet, so "come from God" for him means acknowledgment of Jesus' agency, authority, and commissioning by God. By comparison, Nicodemus' remark is thin, imprecise, even evasive. Jesus himself reveals what "come from God" means when he says, "No one has ascended into heaven except the one who descended from heaven, the Son of Man" (3:13). Thus, Nicodemus' understanding of Jesus as "come from God" is empty, and by 3:13–14 he is proved to be incapable of knowing anything else.

These Signs. How does Nicodemus understand Jesus' "signs"? In 2:18 some adversaries aggressively demand from Jesus a "sign" to affirm his credentials and authorization (see Mark 11:28). Yet the signs at Cana (2:1–12) and Capernaum (4:54) enlighten and lead to loyalty. Although Nicodemus seems to make some connection between "sign" and Jesus' credentials as God's agent, Jesus examines him carefully, just as he scrutinized those who earlier claimed to believe because of the signs he worked (2:23). Nicodemus is only able to name Jesus as "teacher," a low-level role, not "prophet" or "Messiah." Although signs can occasion discipleship (2:12; 4:53), Nicodemus never acclaims Jesus as anything but a "teacher." In fact, Jesus eventually rebukes him for unbelief: "You *do not receive our testimony*. I have told you about earthly things and *you do not believe*" (3:11–12). Jesus' signs teach Nicodemus nothing.

Unless. Nicodemus is the first character to use the term "unless": ". . . unless God was with him." But Jesus counters with his own "unless" remarks, which state his nonnegotiable criteria for discipleship: "*Unless* one is born from above, one cannot see the kingdom of God" (3:3). When Nicodemus mocks Jesus about this, Jesus states another "unless": "*Unless* one is born of water and Spirit, one cannot enter the kingdom of God" (3:5). Simply put, Jesus parodies Nicodemus' "unless" by turning the expression into a criterion for true disciples. Nicodemus has no comprehension of Jesus' two "unless" statements, which suggests that he does not know much of anything and so readers question his initial "unless" remark as an empty claim.

Therefore, the narrator presents us with this first instance of a rhetorical pattern that will occur often in the Gospel, namely a topic statement with subsequent development that only insiders know or accept. Here Nicodemus acclaims Jesus as teacher but learns nothing from him; he boasts of knowledge but proves impervious to Jesus' discourse. His understanding of Jesus is shallow compared with what Jesus reveals of himself. He comes and leaves as an outsider.

Literary Pattern: Statement–Misunderstanding–Clarification. This literary pattern[87] weaves through 3:1–15 and occurs often in the Gospel.[88] Because it, too, deals with knowledge and understanding, it confirms the pattern of topic statement and development just seen. In essence, Jesus makes a *statement*, which is *misunderstood* and prompts him to *speak further*. This form functions in two ways. When Jesus engages in catechetical instruction, he tolerates initial misunderstanding in order to produce an enlightened climax (e.g., the Samaritan woman). But at other times Jesus' speech distances people and proves their incapacity to comprehend him (e.g., 8:21–58). After Nicodemus' claim to knowledge, Jesus makes a *statement:* "No one can see the kingdom of God without being born from above" (3:3). Nicodemus *misunderstands:* "How can anyone be born after having grown old? Can one enter a second time into the mother's womb and be born?" (3:4). He misinterprets the Johannine double meaning of "born" as second physical birth, not birth "from above." When he mocks Jesus, his ridicule suggests that his misunderstanding is complete. Yet Jesus *speaks again*, embroidering his earlier remark: "No one can enter the kingdom of God without being born of water and Spirit" (3:5). But Nicodemus is not in any way enlightened; on the contrary, he appears to be utterly obtuse.

Inadequate Epistemology. Why does Nicodemus *misunderstand?* Jesus expounds a theory of knowledge that explains why some are "in the know" and others are not.[89] The world, he tells us, may be divided in two: Some are "born" of "flesh" and others of "spirit." Is Nicodemus capable of understanding this? Normally one would expect Jesus' next remark to be a *clarification* of what was *misunderstood.* But not here, for Jesus increases the level of complexity for understanding "spirit" with double-speak about spirit/wind: "The wind (spirit) blows where it chooses. . . . *You do not know* where it comes from or where it goes" (3:8). Nicodemus' *misunderstanding* deepens when Jesus chides him for not knowing key items: "You *do not know* its origin (whence) or destiny (whither)."[90] He who once addressed Jesus in a clear declarative sentence

---

[87] Marinus de Jonge, "Nicodemus and Jesus," in *Jesus: Stranger* (1977), 337–59; D. A. Carson, "Understanding Misunderstanding in the Fourth Gospel," *TynB* 33 (1982), 61–91.

[88] For a survey of this pattern, see Jerome H. Neyrey, "The Sociology of Secrecy and the Fourth Gospel," in Fernando Segovia, ed., *What Is John? Volume II: Literary and Social Readings of the Fourth Gospel* (Atlanta: Scholars Press, 1998), 107–8.

[89] See J. H. Neyrey, " The Debate in John III," *NovT* 23 (1981), 118–22.

[90] See. J. H. Neyrey, "Territoriality," *BTB* 32 (2002), 66–68.

(3:2) is now reduced to questions: "How can this happen?" (3:9). Recall that earlier Nicodemus' question mocked Jesus (3:4), but not here, for his question signals a complete failure to learn from Jesus the teacher. Jesus certainly does not interpret the question here as a request for information but as the last challenge, and so he responds in kind: "Are you a teacher of Israel, and yet you *do not know* these things?" (3:10). Nothing Jesus can say will clarify the matter or enlighten Nicodemus because he is "flesh," who does not even know matters of flesh and earth. "If I have told you about earthly things and you do not believe, how can you believe if I tell you about heavenly things?" (3:12). Misunderstanding remains; clarification is not possible. Nicodemus, born only of the flesh, has a hopelessly inadequate epistemology for accessing Jesus.

Cultural Pattern: Challenge and Riposte.[91] Nicodemus' first statement to Jesus seems like a *claim*. A "ruler" of the Judeans claims knowledge of Jesus the "teacher" and presents himself as a fellow teacher: "*We know* that you are a teacher who has come from God" (3:2). *First Challenge* Jesus tests this claim to see just what knowledge this teacher has by responding: "No one can see the kingdom of God without being born from above" (3:3). *Riposte* Nicodemus' question seeks not to learn knowledge but to mock Jesus: "How can anyone be born after having grown old? Can one enter a second time into the mother's womb and be born?" (3:4). He ridicules Jesus' teaching by reducing it to literal absurdness. In response, Jesus makes a *second challenge* by repeating his teaching with a few new twists: "No one can enter the kingdom of God without being born of water and Spirit" (3:5). Part of Jesus' challenge to Nicodemus consists of a sustained exposition of his nature as "flesh," not "spirit," and his consequent inability to understand heavenly things (3:6–8). *Riposte*: Nicodemus' final question exudes none of the challenging mockery of the earlier one but functions as his total capitulation on the issue of understanding. He is hopelessly "not in the know." How minimalist his earlier claim turns out to be. Jesus then completes his *challenge* first by turning Nicodemus' earlier mockery back on him, "Are you a teacher of Israel, and yet you *do not understand* these things?" (3:10), and then by utterly dismissing him with the accusation of "not receiving our testimony" (3:11). Thus this dynamic pattern presents a contest between two teachers, rather like a fencing match: challenge and riposte; challenge and riposte.

Unless. In 3:3 and 3:5 the author introduces his audience to a pattern that occurs regularly in the narrative. A radical demand ("Unless . . .") is made that some action be done or some confession be made; failure to do so results in catastrophe.

---

[91] See Jerome H. Neyrey, "The Trials (Forensic) and Tribulations (Honor Challenges) of Jesus: John 7 in Social Science Perspective," *BTB* 26 (1996), 119–22.

3:3	"*Unless* one is born anew, he cannot see the kingdom of God."
3:5	*Unless* one is born of water and the spirit, he cannot enter the "kingdom of God."
3:27	"*Unless* it is given from heaven, one cannot receive anything."
6:53	"*Unless* you eat the flesh of the Son of Man and drink his blood, you have no life in you."
8:24	"*Unless* you believe that 'I AM,' you will die in your sins."
12:24	"*Unless* a grain of wheat falls into the earth and dies, it remains alone."
13:8	"*Unless* I wash you, you have no part in me."
15:4	"As the branch cannot bear fruit by itself, *unless* it abides in the vine, neither can you, *unless* you abide in me."[92]

The NRSV translation used in this commentary translates the Greek term *ei me* as "without" ("*without* being born"), which mutes the rhetorical force of the demand here and in the other examples cited earlier. In each instance, some status transformation is demanded of would-be disciples, either being "born again," "eating the flesh of the Son of Man," "believing that 'I AM,'" or "falling into the ground and dying." The transformation in 3:3 and 3:5 refers to some entrance ritual. Although baptism is not explicitly mentioned, it is a likely referent (see "born of water and the Spirit"; and see also 3:22, 26). The "birth" here is effected by God, for it is achieved "from above" and not, as Nicodemus thinks, "again."[93] One should cross reference this with the proclamation in 1:12–13 that some receive power "to become children of God, who were born, not of blood or of the will of the flesh or of the will of man, but of God" (1:12–13). But if one is "born from above," one will "see" the kingdom, "enter it," and understand all the revelations that Jesus speaks. There is no other way.

No One.... Jesus makes an exclusive statement: "No one has ascended into heaven except the one who descended from heaven, the Son of Man" (3:13); "no one," not Moses, Elijah, or anyone credited with making a heavenly journey to receive revelation. The pattern here claims more than "greater than" did. "Greater than" Moses (1:17), Jacob (4:12), and Abraham (8:53) implies a comparison on this or that point. But twice the evangelist claims that "no one" (but Jesus) does such-and-such (1:18; 3:13), and because the exclusive claim appears often in the Gospel, we should examine it more closely.

---

[92] J. H. Neyrey, *Ideology of Revolt* (1988), 41–42, 143–44; and his "Footwashing," in *Social World of the First Christians* (1995), 202–3.

[93] Ben Witherington III, in his "Waters of Birth: John 3.5 and 1 John 5.6–8," *NTS* 35 (1989), 155–60, cites rabbinic material to argue that the born "of water" and the Holy Spirit refers to the birth of a child as it emerges through the birth canal and through its amniotic "waters." Regardless of whether "born of water and the Holy Spirit" refers to a physical birth or baptism, it is an entrance rite.

1 :18   "*No one* has ever seen God. It is God the only Son, who is close to the
          Father's heart, who has made him known."
3:13   "*No one* has ascended into heaven except the one who descended from
          heaven, the Son of Man."
6:44   "*No one* can come to me unless drawn by the Father who sent me."
6:65   "*No one* can come to me unless it is granted by the Father."
14:6   "*No one* comes to the Father except through me."

The uses of this in 6:44 and 6:65 function to discriminate insiders from outsiders:
Whoever accepts Jesus has been "drawn" by God or "granted" this benefaction by
the Father – thus they are favorites of God, select objects of God's benefaction.[94]
In contrast, all of the other uses of this rhetorical pattern serve to sharpen Jesus'
claims to uniqueness: No one but Jesus has seen God, and no one but he has
descended and then reascended; only through him can mortals approach God.
If "no one" else can do these things, then Jesus is acclaimed as "unique" and
thus greatly to be honored.

A CLOSER LOOK — UNIQUENESS IN THE RHETORIC OF PRAISE

From Aristotle on, we can track a rhetorical commonplace on "uniqueness";[95]
that is, instruction on how to amplify praise because of singularity:

[In epideictic] one should also use many kinds of amplification, for example if the
subject [of praise] is the *only* (μόνος) one or the *first* (πρῶτος) or *one of a few* (μετ'
ὀλίγων) or the one who *most* (μάλιστα) has done something; for all these things are
honorable. (*Rhet.* 1.9.38 emphasis added; see also *Rhet.* 2.7.2)

This norm prospered in the rhetoric of Cicero (*De Orat.* 2.85.347) and Quintilian (*Inst. Orat.* 3.7.16) and became codified in the rhetorical handbooks
used to educate second-level students. Thus Aelius Theon writes:

Praiseworthy actions are also those occurring in a timely manner, and if one acted
alone (μόνος), or *first* (πρῶτος), or when *no one acted* (οὐδείς), or *more than others*
(μᾶλλον τῶν ἄλλων), or with a *few* (μετ' ὀλίγων), or *beyond one's age* (ὑπέρ ἡλικίαν),
or *exceeding expectation* (παρά ἐλπίδα), or with hard work, or what was done most
easily and quickly. (*Progymnasmata* 9.35–38)[96]

---

[94] On the particularistic character of ancient benefaction, see Richard Saller, "Patronage
and Friendship in Early Imperial Rome: Drawing the Distinction," in Andrew Wallace-
Hadrill, ed., *Patronage in Ancient Society* (London: Routledge, 1990), 52–53. See also Bruce
J. Malina, "Patron and Client: The Analogy behind Synoptic Theology," in his *The Social
World of Jesus and the Gospels* (London: Routledge, 1996), 143–78.

[95] See Jerome H. Neyrey, "Uniqueness: 'First,' 'Only,' 'One of a Few,' and 'No One Else' –
Rhetoric, and the Doxologies in 1 Timothy," *Biblica.* 86 (2005), 59–89.

[96] James R. Butts, *The "Progymnasmata" of Theon: A New Text with Translation and Commentary* (unpublished dissertation, Claremont Graduate School, 1987), 470–71.

But uniqueness is also a rhetorical marker for the deity as in 2 Maccabees
1:24–25:

> O Lord, Lord God, creator of all things,
> Who art awe-inspiring and strong and just and merciful,
> Who alone (μόνος) art King and art kind,
> Who alone (μόνος) art bountiful,
> Who alone (μόνος) art just and almighty and eternal.

Occasionally in the synoptic Gospels, we find the same grounds for praise of
God: "But of that day and hour, *no one* (οὐδεὶς) knows, not even the angels
in heaven, nor the Son, but the Father *only* (μόνος)" (Matt 24:36). And when
Jesus forgave a man his sins, critics saw this as encroaching on God's uniqueness: "Who can forgive sins but God *alone?*" (εἰ μὴ εἷς ὁ θεός, Mark 2:7).

Son of Man. The meaning of the title "Son of Man"[97] here differs from that
found in the synoptic Gospels, where it basically describes a figure who was
rejected on earth by men but vindicated in heaven by God (Mark 8:31; 9:31; 10:33;
14:62). Our author, however, sees the Son of Man as first descending from heaven
and returning there, thus reinforcing the heavenly status of Jesus articulated in
1:1–18 and 13:1–3. This title, we suggest, contains a large measure of the content
and argument of the Gospel. First, like other examples of "uniqueness" in the
Gospel (1:18; 6:46), Jesus alone has descended and ascended.[98] Second, this
compares Jesus with others, a rhetorical figure called a "synkrisis." It has close
parallels with one found in Israelite midrash: "R. Jose says: Behold it says: 'The
heavens are the heavens of the Lord, but the earth hath he given to the children
of men' (Ps 115:16). Neither Moses nor Elijah ever went up to heaven, nor did
the Glory ever come down to death."[99] While this remark argues that no one
or no thing ever descended or ascended, it argues that there was an intramural
debate in Israel precisely about the heavenly ascents of Moses, Elijah, and others.
Third, although the technical terms "whence" and "whither" are not used here,
the answer to those questions about Jesus most assuredly is given here in the
mention of descent ("whence") and ascent ("whither"; see 3:13–14; 6:62). Fourth,
the title contains elements of conflict and vindication, which are couched in the
double-meaning term "lift." In time, we learn that "lift" means both lifted high
on the cross (shame) and lifted in glory back to God (honor) (8:28; 12:23, 34;
13:31). Nicodemus, who cannot fathom double-meaning terms such as "born
again" and "born of water and spirit," would never grasp the complexity of "lift."

---

[97] W. A. Meeks, "The Man from Heaven in Johannine Sectarianism," *JBL* 91 (1972), 44–72;
Peder Borgen, "The Son of Man Saying in John 3:13–14," in his *Philo, John and Paul*
(Atlanta: Scholars Press, 1987), 110–12.

[98] C. H. Talbert, *Reading John* (1992), 265–84.

[99] *Mekilta de Rabbi Ishmael*, trans Jonathan Z. Lauterbach (Philadelphia: Jewish Publication
Society of America, 1976), 2.224, as cited in C. H. Talbert, *Reading John* (1992), 101.

Finally, Son of Man refers to some "heavenly" aspect of Jesus – his authority (5:27), his benefaction (6:27), or his heavenly status (1:51).

As You Judge, So You Are Judged. For the first time in this Gospel, we encounter the motifs of judge and judgment.[100] The primary judgment is the forensic process that begins in 5:17 and continues to Jesus' death. His judges may be Jerusalem elites or others who pass negative judgment on him. But this judgment is tenuous and even perilous, for most opponents judge Jesus according to the flesh; that is, according to appearances. Thus, in 3:18–21 we learn that there are two types of judges: those who believe in Jesus and those who do not. The critical issue is whether these judges judge justly. The evangelist now judges the judges.[101] As in the case of Daniel and the two elders, the evil judgment made in regard to Susanna turned back on them, and they suffered the sentence originally destined for Susanna. One's judgment can backfire and become one's ruin. Thus the narrator distinguishes believers, who judge rightly and so are not condemned, from unbelievers, who judge wrongly and so are condemned. Neither God nor Jesus renders this judgment (3:16–17), but only the person who encounters Jesus. Can we know who these people are? Those who love darkness and whose deeds are evil do not come to the light (i.e., accept Jesus) and so are judged. In contrast, those who know what is true and whose deeds are known by God, to say nothing of the public arena, come to the light. Readers do well to remember this motif of judgment and judge, which will play a significant role in the coming public trials of Jesus.

JOHN 3:22–30 – HE MUST INCREASE, I MUST DECREASE

22 After this Jesus and his disciples went into the Judean countryside, and he spent some time there with them and baptized.

23 John also was baptizing at Aenon near Salim because water was abundant there; and people kept coming and were being baptized.

24 John, of course, had not yet been thrown into prison.

25 Now a discussion about purification arose between John's disciples and a Jew.

26 They came to John and said to him, "Rabbi, the one who was with you across the Jordan, to whom you testified, here he is baptizing, and all are going to him."

27 John answered, "No one can receive anything except what has been given from heaven.

---

[100] C. H. Dodd, *Interpretation of the Fourth Gospel* (1968), 208–12; see also Andrew T. Lincoln, *Truth on Trial: The Lawsuit Motif in the Fourth Gospel* (Peabody, MA: Hendrickson, 2000), 65–72.

[101] Matthew 7:1–2 is useful here. On the one hand, one ought not judge; on the other, if one judges, one is liable to the same judgment rendered against another: "Do not judge, so that you may not be judged. For with the judgment you make you will be judged, and the measure you give will be the measure you get."

28 You yourselves are my witnesses that I said, 'I am not the Messiah, but I have been sent ahead of him.'
29 He who has the bride is the bridegroom. The friend of the bridegroom, who stands and hears him, rejoices greatly at the bridegroom's voice. For this reason my joy has been fulfilled.
30 He must increase, but I must decrease."

Envy in Antiquity. Whereas the NRSV translates the phrase as "a 'discussion' about purification" (3:25), the Greek term ζητησις also means "controversy" or "dispute."[102] The issue is envy, for the nub of the complaint of John's disciples is that "all are going to him [Jesus]" (3:26; see 11:48). Evidently they expect John to join their indignation, because all of them, including John, are diminished because of Jesus' success. Surprisingly, John deflects this challenge to Jesus and delivers the appropriate riposte to his disciples. To make cultural sense of this "controversy," we need to know more about the perception of "limited good" in antiquity and the inevitable consequence of envy that arises from it.

A CLOSER LOOK – LIMITED GOOD AND ENVY

"Limited good" is a matter of social perception that characterizes the ancient world. George Foster defines "limited good" in this way:

> Peasants view their social, economic, and natural universes – their total environment – as one in which all of the desired things in life such as land, wealth, health, friendship and love, manliness and honor, respect and status, power and influence, security and safety, exist in finite quantity and are always in short supply. . . . There is no way directly within peasant power to increase the available quantities."[103]

In other words, the world and everything in it are like a zero-sum game: There is only so much to go around. For someone to increase in any dimension, others must decrease. In consequence, Foster continues: "Any advantage achieved by one individual or family is seen as a loss to others, and the person who makes what the Western world lauds as 'progress' is viewed as a threat to the stability of the entire community."[104] Inevitably, those who perceive that they are losing in any way must and will rise up to challenge those who are increasing. Hence envy is born.

Foster's modern theory can be illustrated at great length in the ancient world. Native illustrations of these perceptions make plausible the reading of John in this light. First, an extensive collection of illustrations of "limited good" perception in antiquity can be found in the study by Neyrey and

---

[102] See H. Greeven, "ζητησις," *TDNT* 2.756–57; *BDAG* (1964), 339.
[103] George M. Foster, "Peasant Society and the Image of Limited Good," *American Anthropologist* 67 (1965), 296.
[104] George M. Foster, "The Anatomy of Envy: A Study in Symbolic Behavior," *Current Anthropology* 13 (1972), 165–202 at 169.

> Rohrbaugh.[105] In one instance, Plutarch observes how listeners are loath to react positively to speakers: "As though commendation were money, he feels that he is robbing himself of every bit that he bestows on another" (*On Listening to Lectures* 44B). Fronto writes this advice to Marcus Aurelius: "Set yourself to uproot and utterly stamp out one vice of mutual envy and jealousy among your friends, that they may not, when you have shown attention or done a favor to another, *think that this is so much taken from or lost to themselves*" (*The Correspondence of Marcus Cornelius Fronto* 4.1).

Second, envy, a frequent topic of ancient Greek and Christian authors,[106] was traditionally defined as "a certain kind of distress at apparent success on the part of one's peers in attaining the good things that have been mentioned, not that a person may get anything for himself but because of those who have it" (Aristotle, *Rhet.* 2.10.1).[107]

The disciples of John view Jesus' success in terms of limited good. If "all are going to him," then none are coming to them; if fame and honor accrue to Jesus, then they must be losing the same. By complaining to John, they seek to enlist him in their envious reaction to Jesus. Thus far, the pattern of limited good/envy is operating normally. John, too, perceives the situation in terms of limited good: Jesus indeed gains and John loses. But he is not injured by this, and he calls an end to the game of envy that the disciples began.

Each of John's remarks deflates the injurious perceptions that so trouble his disciples. First, he states that Jesus' achievement is not his own. No one, not even Jesus, has anything but "what is given him from above" (v. 27). Thus in the key of honor and shame, God has ascribed success and honor to Jesus; how foolish of mortals to disagree with God (Acts 5:39). John therefore does not share his disciples' perception of a controversy because Jesus' status and fame are God-given. Second, John reminds his disciples of his own earlier testimony to Jesus (3:28; see 1:19–23), thus indicating that his role has always been to herald and acknowledge Jesus' precedence. He acts as Jesus' premier promoter, whose task it is to see that Jesus increases. Third, John describes his relationship to Jesus as the close "friend" who "rejoices greatly at the groom's voice" (v.29). To be sure, groom and "friend" are not rivals; nor does the "friend" lose anything if the groom is happy. Whereas John's disciples see only loss in Jesus' growing success, John sees "fullness of joy" at Jesus' fame. Finally, John makes one of

---

[105] J. H. Neyrey and R. L. Rohrbaugh, "He Must Increase, I Must Decrease," *CBQ* 63 (2001), 468–76.

[106] See Plutarch, *On Envy and Hate*, Dio Chrysostom, *Orations* 67, 68; Stobaeus, *Ecl.* 3.38; 1 Clem. 4; Gregory of Nyssa, *Life of Moses*, 2.256–59 (*S.C.* 1, 282–284), *Or. cat.* 6 (*P.G.* 45.28–29), and *De beat.* 7 (*P.G.* 44.1285–88); Cyprian, "Jealousy and Envy" (*CCSL* 3A); and Basil, "Concerning Envy" (*P.G.* 31.372–86).

[107] Cicero calls envy "distress incurred by reason of a neighbor's prosperity" (*Tusc. Disp.* 4.8.17); Basil defines it as "pain caused by a neighbor's prosperity" ("Concerning Envy," *PG* 31.377–41).

the most countercultural statements in the New Testament: "He [Jesus] must increase, but I must decrease" (v. 30). He sees what they see, but he is not moved to envy as they are. In fact, he praises Jesus all the more.

This episode of limited good/envy is not the only one in this Gospel. Later, because of Jesus' fame from raising Lazarus, certain chief priests and Pharisees grind their teeth at Jesus' success (11:46–48). They perceive that if "every one believes in him," then they will plummet in status and respect. They respond in envy and so plot to kill Jesus (11:50). All of the accusations that Jesus "makes himself" this or that deserve to be considered in this light: They perceive that Jesus promotes himself, at the expense of God ("makes himself equal to God," 5:18; 10:33; "makes himself the Son of God," 19:7), Caesar ("makes himself a king," 19:12), or the leaders of Israel (6:53). Hence his attackers attempt to cut him back down to size.[108]

JOHN 3:31–36 – SUMMARY AND CONCLUSION

31 The one who comes from above is above all; the one who is of the earth belongs to the earth and speaks about earthly things. The one who comes from heaven is above all.

32 He testifies to what he has seen and heard, yet no one accepts his testimony.

33 Whoever has accepted his testimony has certified this, that God is true.

34 He whom God has sent speaks the words of God, for he gives the Spirit without measure.

35 The Father loves the Son and has placed all things in his hands.

36 Whoever believes in the Son has eternal life; whoever disobeys the Son will not see life, but must endure God's wrath.

Who Is Speaking? This material regularly gives interpreters heartburn, for they cannot decide who is speaking and therefore what relationship it has to 3:1–21. Some argue that the Baptizer is speaking because there is no indication of a change of place, time, and speaker after 3:30. Others suggest that Jesus speaks, concluding his remarks to Nicodemus. Finally, might the author be speaking?[109] So, let us ask other questions and approach the passage from a different direction.

---

[108] Limited good and envy explain Mark's comment that Pilate perceived that the elites of Jerusalem handed Jesus over "out of envy" (Mark 15:10). Similarly, see the reaction of Jesus' own disciples to a successful exorcist (Mark 9:38–41) and the reaction of Jesus' townsfolk to him (Mark 6:1–6).

[109] See R. E. Brown, *Gospel According to John* (1966), 1.159–60; C. K. Barrett, *The Gospel According to St. John* (Philadelphia: Westminster, 1978), 224; and Rudolf Schnackenburg, "Die 'situationsgelösten' Redestücke in Jon 3," *ZNW* 49 (1958), 88–99.

Once More, with Feeling. If scholars do not agree on the speaker of 3:31–36, they strongly agree that there is a decided link between materials in 3:1–21 and 3:31–36. First, *"from above,"* the term Nicodemus misunderstood as "again," now recurs as a description of Jesus, who "comes from above" (3:3, 7, 31). Second, Jesus is the "one who *came down from heaven"* (3:13, 31), and thus he is more than a "teacher come from God." Third, just as Jesus earlier contrasted *flesh with spirit* (3:6) and *earthly with heavenly* knowledge (3:12), the speaker contrasts those from above with those of earth, who speak earthly things (3:31). Fourth, Jesus *"testifies"* to what he has heard and seen (3:11, 32), testimony that neither Nicodemus (3:11) nor those addressed in 3:32 accept. Fifth, Jesus, the *"Son"* whom *"God sent"* (3:17), is the same figure as *"he whom God has sent"* to speak God's words (3:34). Sixth, *"Spirit"* functions in 3:5–8 both as the agent of "birth" or status transformation and as a symbol of "windy" knowledge accessible to few. But spirit seems to be used in a different sense in that Jesus "gives the Spirit without measure" (3:34). This is the same term, but now its meaning surpasses new birth and has to do with enlightenment. Finally, *final fates* are described in 3:19–21: Those in darkness are judged but those in light are saved. Similarly, in 3:36 virtue is contrasted with vice and linked with the respective reward or punishment of each.

How, then, do we interpret this? Inasmuch as the rhetorical consideration of 3:1–21 consisted of a topic statement (3:2), each term of which is then examined, discussed, and qualified, we should consider 3:31–36 as the discourse's peroration or conclusion. In regard to this rhetorical part of a discourse, Cicero states that it contains a summary, which may be achieved by "touching on each single point and so running briefly over all the arguments" (*De Inventione* 1.52.98). The seven items noted in 3:31–36 pick up most of the pivotal remarks in Jesus' statements to Nicodemus. But they are not simply repeated, instead being stated to arouse "indignation" against those who "do not accept our testimony" or who are impervious to the discourse (*De Inventione* 1.53.101–54.105). Thus, praise is awarded to those who grasp Jesus' words (3:36a) but blame and scorn to those who do not (3:36b).

JOHN 4:1–3 – BRIDGE TO SAMARIA

1 Now when Jesus learned that the Pharisees had heard, "Jesus is making and baptizing more disciples than John"
2 – although it was not Jesus himself but his disciples who baptized –
3 he left Judea and started back to Galilee.

Setting a New Stage: Where? Jesus leaves Jerusalem, travels down to the Jordan, and then proceeds north to Samaria. *When?* Whereas Nicodemus came "at night," the Samaritan woman meets Jesus at noon. We know enough not to take references to place and time literally but to read them in terms of John's symbolic world.[110] *What?* Although 3:22–30 claims that Jesus baptized, this is qualified in 4:1–2; nevertheless, "water" links 3:5 and 4:1–2 with the discourse in 4:7–15. *Who?* When we compare 3:1–21 with 4:4–26, we see them as intentionally contrasted episodes. First, whereas Jesus is "Teacher" in Jerusalem, he is "Messiah" in Samaria. Second, although Nicodemus stalled in the pattern of statement–misunderstanding–clarification, not so the Samaritan woman. And if Nicodemus could not grasp the double meaning of water and spirit of which Jesus spoke, the Samaritan woman positively seeks his water. Finally, the best reading of Chapters 3 and 4 occurs when they are radically compared and contrasted:

Nicodemus	Samaritan Woman
at night	at noon
Israelite	Samaritan
teacher	housewife
male	female
impervious to learning	progressive learning
Jesus = "Teacher"	Jesus = "Prophet" and "Messiah"

JOHN 4:4–26 – WHAT'S WRONG WITH THIS PICTURE?

4 But he had to go through Samaria.

5 So he came to a Samaritan city called Sychar, near the plot of ground that Jacob had given to his son Joseph.

6 Jacob's well was there, and Jesus, tired out by his journey, was sitting by the well. It was about noon.

7 A Samaritan woman came to draw water, and Jesus said to her, "Give me a drink."

8 (His disciples had gone to the city to buy food.)

9 The Samaritan woman said to him, "How is it that you, a Jew, ask a drink of me, a woman of Samaria?" (Jews do not share things in common with Samaritans.)

10 Jesus answered her, "If you knew the gift of God, and who it is that is saying to you, 'Give me a drink,' you would have asked him, and he would have given you living water."

11 The woman said to him, "Sir, you have no bucket, and the well is deep. Where do you get that living water?

12 Are you greater than our ancestor Jacob, who gave us the well, and with his sons and his flocks drank from it?"

---

[110] For more on "telling time," see Norman Walker, "The Reckoning of Hours in the Fourth Gospel," *NovT* 4 (1960), 69–73.

13 Jesus said to her, "Everyone who drinks of this water will be thirsty again,

14 but those who drink of the water that I will give them will never be thirsty. The water that I will give will become in them a spring of water gushing up to eternal life."

15 The woman said to him, "Sir, give me this water, so that I may never be thirsty or have to keep coming here to draw water."

16 Jesus said to her, "Go, call your husband, and come back."

17 The woman answered him, "I have no husband." Jesus said to her, "You are right in saying, 'I have no husband';

18 for you have had five husbands, and the one you have now is not your husband. What you have said is true!"

19 The woman said to him, "Sir, I see that you are a prophet.

20 Our ancestors worshiped on this mountain, but you say that the place where people must worship is in Jerusalem."

21 Jesus said to her, "Woman, believe me, the hour is coming when you will worship the Father neither on this mountain nor in Jerusalem.

22 You worship what you do not know; we worship what we know, for salvation is from the Jews.

23 But the hour is coming, and is now here, when the true worshipers will worship the Father in spirit and truth, for the Father seeks such as these to worship him.

24 God is spirit, and those who worship him must worship in spirit and truth."

25 The woman said to him, "I know that Messiah is coming" (who is called Christ). "When he comes, he will proclaim all things to us."

26 Jesus said to her, "I am he, the one who is speaking to you."

From "Not in the Know" to "In the Know." The story of the enlightenment of the Samaritan woman consists of two scenes. In the first (4:7–15), she regularly misunderstands Jesus, and the grammatical form of her speech is that of questioning. But in the second (4:16–26), she speaks declarative sentences and understands Jesus all too clearly. Thus, the story narrates her transformation from a Samaritan outsider who knows little and misunderstands much to that of a privileged insider who comes to know important secrets and revelations. Each half, moreover, is built around a typical Johannine topic statement, which is subsequently developed term by term.

Scene One (4:7–15). The topic statement in 4:7, "(You) give me a drink," consists of four terms subsequently developed to convey special Johannine information. The first term is "*You.*" Because it is in the imperative mood, the verb "give" contains the subject "you," which is the first item in the topic to be developed: "The Samaritan woman said to him, 'How is it that *you, a Jew,* ask a drink of *me, a woman of Samaria*?' (Jews do not share things in common with Samaritans)" (4:9). Jesus requests water from her, and thus "you" seems neutral here. But when she responds to Jesus using "you," she articulates a radical distance between Judeans and Samaritans. Her use distances Jesus. Readers see another meaning of the Samaritan woman in Jesus' "you." She is female, an outsider, a prohibited person, and a person of dubious reputation. The second term is "*Give.*" This functions here as a double-meaning word. The woman ignores Jesus' request, "Give me a drink" (v. 9), for which Jesus declares that she lacks something important, namely a *gift* from God: "If you knew the *gift of God . . .*" (v. 10). Jesus states that were she *gifted*, "you would have asked him, and he would have *given* you living water." Ultimately, when she is transformed from giver to receiver of water, she will ask him (a male) and he will do the bizarre thing of giving water to her (a female). Thus she will experience a status role reversal, in which she asks (commands?) males to do female tasks. The third term is "*Me.*" As one would expect, knowledge plays a significant role in this conversation. Jesus knows all; at the start, however, the Samaritan woman knows nothing. She does not yet know the knowledge that counts, namely Jesus' identity, role, and status: "If you knew the gift of God and who it is that is saying to you . . ." (4:10). According to 4:11, Jesus' remark seems to produce scant enlightenment, but then the Samaritan woman asks, "Are you greater than our ancestor Jacob?" (4:12). Yes, as a matter of fact, Jesus is "greater than" Jacob, Abraham (8:53), Moses (1:17), and all the ancestors, although she does not know this. But gradually the woman begins to learn "*who* it is that asks you 'Give me a drink.'" The fourth term is "*Drink/Water.*" Although the entire conversation is about *drink* and *water*, the meaning of *water* metamorphoses from the liquid from the well that will slake Jesus' thirst to the substance that Jesus himself gives, which will cause those who drink it never to thirst. Far from being the fluid deep down in the well, the *water* Jesus gives "will become in them a spring of water gushing up to eternal life" (4:14). *Drink*, of course, first refers to swallowing *water* drawn from the well but then is transformed into coming to know Jesus and thereby coming to have a spring that automatically gushes life. This scene climaxes in 4:15, where the topic statement is repeated, but now with dramatic changes:

v. 7	(You)	give	me	to drink
v. 15	Sir (you)	give	me	this water.

This Samaritan woman is indeed coming to know the gift of God and who it is who said "Give me a drink" because she eventually asks Jesus to give her this water. Mission accomplished.

Statement–Misunderstanding–Clarification. We observed in 3:1–21 a Johannine pattern whereby Jesus states something that is misunderstood, which prompts a clarification. The same pattern structures the conversation with the Samaritan woman in 4:7–15 and will recur again in the discourse with the disciples in 4:31–38:

Statement	4:7	4:10	4:32
Misunderstanding	4:9	4:11–12	4:33
Clarification	4:10	4:13–14	4:34–38

The dynamic here turns on double-meaning words ("give," "drink," and "water"), the meaning of which only slowly dawns on the Samaritan woman. But unlike nighttime Nicodemus, who stalled from the start, the noonday woman is successfully catechized and transformed from one "not in the know" to one who "knows the gift of God." Sometimes this pattern serves successfully to catechize someone and lead them "into the know," as is the case here, but in other instances, such as those of Nicodemus (3:3–11) and the Jerusalem crowds (7:12–52), the pattern seems intended to prove that the hearers do not hear Jesus and do not grasp his double meanings, thus remaining outsiders.

A CLOSER LOOK – GREATER THAN OUR FATHER JACOB?

When the Samaritan woman compares Jesus with the Great Patriarchs, the audience presumably has knowledge of Jacob from Scriptures, midrash, or legend. We can compare Jesus with Jacob in four ways: the well; courtships at wells; worship; and "Jacob" as "supplanter."

Well. The legend about Jacob's well says that on occasion water automatically surged to its top and overflowed: "Five miracles were wrought for our father Jacob at the time that he went forth from Beersheba. . . . The fourth sign: the well overflowed and rose to the edge of it, and continued to overflow all the time he was in Haran."[111] Jesus remarks that whoever drinks his water has a "spring of water welling up," not just occasionally but forever. In this regard to "wells," Jesus is "greater than Jacob."

Courtships at Wells. Scripture narrates three scenes of males and females meeting at wells (Gen 24:10–49; 29:4–14; Exod 2:15–22); and the *Protoevangelium of James* (11.1) records another. In these scenes, men or their agents meet prospective brides. Because the key element of a worthy wife is virginity or sexual exclusivity, the narratives all insist that the social intercourse at the well be strictly in accord with cultural customs. Females are shy and defensive of their virtue, speak respectfully to males, and obey when commanded. They then seek the shelter of the "private" world as soon as possible. But the Samaritan woman is hardly "sexually exclusive," not with five husbands and still another male in her life. Her appearance at noon independent of the company of other women suggests an outcast. Even Jesus' disciples raise their eyebrows at her presence with him (4:27). But Jesus is not taking a bride as did Jacob.

---

[111] *Tg. Yer.I* and *Tg. Neof.* Gen 28:10.

Worship. When Jacob awoke from his dream in Genesis 28, he exclaimed "Surely the LORD is in this place – and I did not know it!" (28:16). Samaritan traditions that supported worship on Mount Gerizim interpreted Jacob's vision as referring to that mountain.[112] And according to Genesis 33:19–20, Jacob built an altar at Shechem.[113] This Jacob material seems to stand behind the woman's question about the right place to worship and Jesus' dismissal of "Jerusalem and this mountain" (4:20–24). Jesus will prove "greater than our father Jacob" in his knowledge of where and how to worship God.

Supplanter. According to Genesis 25:26, Jacob's name means "to grab by the heel" or "to supplant"; Jacob is so proficient at being "Jacob" that he supplants Esau at birth (25:26), birthright (25:34), and blessing (27:36). Philo makes much of Jacob and assigns him the sobriquet "the Supplanter."[114] Clearly, then, Jesus out-"Jacobs" Jacob, for he surpasses him in well, water, and unique knowledge of where and how to worship God.

Scene Two (4:16–26). The second scene at the well contrasts with the first. No longer is the Samaritan woman led through the process of statement–misunderstanding–clarification. No longer does she question Jesus or misunderstand his double-meaning statements. Now she speaks declarative sentences. Her enlightenment continues, as she moves rapidly to remarkable revelations. Paralleling Jesus' command to her in 4:7 ("Give me . . ."), he now orders her, "Go, call your husband, and come back" (4:16). Whereas earlier she challenged Jesus' remark, she now answers him "truly": "I have no husband." Although this is not the whole truth (she hides the fact that she has had five husbands), she understands clearly what Jesus said – for a change. For this Jesus twice commends her: "*You are right* in saying, 'I have no husband'. . . . *What you have said is true!*" (4:17–18). Jesus praises very few people, but he praises her twice here. It may not seem like a great revelation when Jesus tells the woman her sexual history, but it so impresses her that she repeats this "revelation" to numerous people (4:29, 39). Recall that Jesus can read hearts (2:23–25) and that no secrets are withheld from him; he knows what kind of person she is. The woman then makes an acknowledgment of Jesus that ranks her alongside many Johannine heroes: She "sees" that Jesus is a prophet (4:19; see 9:17 but also 7:40, 51). Having conceded that, she puts Jesus' prophetic status to the test as she engages

---

[112] See John Macdonald, *The Theology of the Samaritans* (Philadelphia: Westminster, 1964), 328–33; Josephus, *Ant.* 18.85–87; Hans Kippenberg, *Garizim und Synagoge* (Berlin: de Gruyter, 1971), 258–59.

[113] Judean traditions likewise interpreted Genesis 28 as indicating the correct place to worship, albeit Jerusalem's temple. See Jerome H. Neyrey, "Jacob Traditions and the Interpretation of John 4:10–26," *CBQ* 41 (1979), 427–29.

[114] See *Cher.* 67; *Leg. All.* 1.61; 2.89; 3.15, 93, 180; *Mut.* 81; *Somn.* 1.171.

Jesus in a contest over worship, the stuff about which prophets were most qualified.

Challenge and Riposte. In the grammar of challenge/riposte exchanges, Jesus made a *claim* by exposing the secrets about the Samaritan woman's life. She in turn *challenges* his prophetic knowledge by confronting him with a controversial matter – where to worship: "Our ancestors worshiped on this mountain, but you say that the place where people must worship is in Jerusalem" (4:20). Again her remark challenges Jesus by putting him on the spot. If Jesus responds, he will inevitably anger some group. But his *riposte* boldly denies her challenge: "Woman, the hour is coming when you will worship the Father neither on this mountain nor in Jerusalem" (4:21). Reading this as a challenge and riposte exchange helps us to make sense of Jesus' own counterchallenge to the woman: "You worship *what you do not know*: we worship what *we know*" (4:22). Jesus, then, still holds the high cards, for he "knows" but she "does not know." The contest takes one more turn as the woman *challenges* Jesus with her knowledge: "*I know* that Messiah is coming (who is called Christ). When he comes, he will proclaim all things to us" (4:25); that is, he will put us "in the know" about all things. This "Messiah," then, will presumably have better knowledge than the prophet with whom she speaks. But Jesus delivers a final *riposte*, which silences her: "I am he, the one who is speaking to you" (4:26). Although only the Samaritan woman and Jesus play a game of challenge and riposte, he does not shame her and send her away in defeat. On the contrary, he rewards her with a revelation of great importance. This is not how the vanquished are treated in typical challenge/riposte exchanges (see 3:3–10).

Topic Statement Again. A second way of reading 4:16–26 parallels the structures seen in 4:7–15, namely a topic sentence and subsequent development of key terms in it. We consider the woman's statement as a topic statement, "Our ancestors worshiped on this mountain, but you say that the place where people must worship is in Jerusalem" (4:20), which contains four terms soon to be given Jesus' unique interpretation: "*the place*" (this mountain, Jerusalem); "*worshipers*" (ancestors, you; Samaritans/Jews); "*worship*"; and "*must*" (i.e., What does God require?). The woman states this as a challenge; thus, contrast and competition are built into the statement. Who is correct?

"The Place." Jesus cancels the issue of "*place*" for "neither on this mountain nor in Jerusalem" will you worship. There is no fixed space where God wishes to be worshiped.[115]

---

[115] On the classification of space as "fixed sacred" or "fluid sacred" space, see J. H. Neyrey, "Territoriality," *BTB* 32 (2002), 62–66; and Bruce J. Malina, *Christian Origins and Cultural Anthropology: Practical Models for Biblical Interpretation* (Atlanta: John Knox Press, 1986), 31–38.

Worshipers. Jesus taunts the Samaritan woman with an Israelite claim: "You worship what you do not know; we worship what we know" (4:22). Yet both Samaritan and Judean ancestors who made claims to fixed sacred spaces and sacrificial systems of worship were in error. "Salvation from the Judeans" hardly refers to Jerusalem's Temple and cult but most likely in this context to Jesus himself, born and raised as an Israelite. Person, not place or system, seems to be the thrust of the remark. So, prior to this moment, no "worshipers" got it right – another absolute claim by Jesus.

"Worship." How will true worshipers *worship*? ". . . in spirit and truth . . . God is spirit, and those who worship him must worship in spirit and truth" (4:23–24). As stated, there is no fixed space (i.e., temple), no system of sacrifice. We shall see in John 14–17 that Johannine worship is exclusively verbal: either speech directed to God in prayer and confession or speech from God to the Johannine group in homilies, judgments, prophecies, and the like. Thus, worship is not material or sacrificial: It is inspired and mediated by "the spirit of truth."

"Must." As God's agent, Jesus declares what God requires in this matter: "True worshipers will worship the Father in spirit and truth, for the *Father seeks such as these* to worship him" (4:23). Because God is spirit, those who worship him "*must worship* in spirit and truth" (4:24). Thus, the topic statement made in 4:20 is replaced word by word by Jesus' remarks on worship:

| 4:20 | where (place) | does God want | worshipers | to worship? |
| 4:21–24 | neither here/there | God wants | true worshipers | in spirit/truth! |

Admittedly, we do not receive the full Johannine discourse on worship. But this exchange constitutes remarkable information given to a most unlikely person, thus giving the Samaritan woman high status.

Representative Character. Readers are often attracted to the Samaritan woman because of the way she spars with Jesus and speaks boldly to him. Her significance, however, rests in the fact that she finally receives one of the great benefactions of the Gospel: Jesus' revelation about true worship of God and about himself as Messiah. What she hears, then, surpasses what she says. As with most Johannine persons, we consider her a "representative" character.[116] She is an *ethnic outsider*, with whom all commerce by Judeans was prohibited (4:9), but like Gentile females in other Gospels, Jesus purposely ignores the social significance of this category (see Matt 15:21–28). She is *unclean*: Popular legends argued that Samaritan women are always unclean,[117] but Jesus wishes to drink from her vessel and he offers her a drink in turn, thus erasing "clean/unclean"

---

[116] R. Collins, "The Representative Figures in the Fourth Gospel," *Downside Review* 94 (1976), 37–40; J. H. Neyrey, "What's Wrong With This Picture?" *BTB* 24 (1994), 86–88.

[117] David Daube, "Jesus and the Samaritan Woman: The Meaning of Συνχράομαι," *JBL* 69 (1950), 137–47; see also J. Duncan M. Derrett, "The Samaritan Woman's Purity (John 4:4–52)," *EvQ* 60 (1988), 291–98.

as a meaningful classification. She is *shameless*: The cultural world of the Gospel highly valued female sexual exclusivity, the core of a female's virtue and worth. Thus a female with five husbands and a current companion not her spouse mocks this criterion; hardly virtuous, she is instead a *sinner*, an *adulteress*, a *shameless person.*[118] But as in other Gospels, Jesus befriended courtesans.[119] Another stereotype transcended! She is *female*: Gender conventions in antiquity would never have expected a female to be alone in public at noon, nor to converse with males not related to her by kinship.[120] Unlike Nicodemus, who encountered Jesus at night and never understood a thing Jesus said, this woman meets Jesus at high noon and is incrementally enlightened. Thus, society's gender expectations of her are trumped by Jesus' exchange with her. As a representative character, then, she represents the ultimate outsider, whom Jesus transforms into an informed insider. As noted, she is best appreciated as the antithesis of Nicodemus.

JOHN 4:16, 27–30 – AN APOSTLE? PUBLIC VOICE?

16 Jesus said to her, "Go, call your husband, and come back."
27 Just then his disciples came. They were astonished that he was speaking with a woman, but no one said, "What do you want?" or, "Why are you speaking with her?"
28 Then the woman left her water jar and went back to the city. She said to the people,
29 "Come and see a man who told me everything I have ever done! He cannot be the Messiah, can he?"
30 They left the city and were on their way to him.

Disobedient? Although Jesus told her "Go, call your husband," she did not comply (Mark 1:45; 5:19–20). But is this a Johannine irony or double-meaning action? If the gender expectations of females were such that they should not be speaking with non–kinship-related males and certainly not in public, this woman compounds the problem not only by not obeying Jesus' formal command but by going to *all the men* in the village. Leaving her water jar at the well,

---

[118] See Luise Schottroff, "The Samaritan Woman and the Notion of Sexuality in the Fourth Gospel," in Fernando Segovia, ed., *What Is John? Volume 2* (Atlanta: Scholars Press, 1998), 157–67; and Jane S. Webster, "Transcending Alterity: Strange Woman to Samaritan Woman," in Amy-Jill Levine, ed., *A Feminist Companion to John: Volume 1* (Sheffield: Sheffield Academic Press, 2003), 126–42.

[119] Kathleen E. Corley, "Were Women around Jesus Really Prostitutes? Women in the Context of Greco-Roman Meals," *SBLSP* (1989), 487–521; and her *Private Women, Public Meals: Social Conflict in the Synoptic Tradition* (Peabody, MA: Hendrickson, 1993), 152–58.

[120] See J. H. Neyrey, "What's Wrong With This Picture?" *BTB* 32 (2002), 77–82.

she did not go to her house but to the public square of her village, where males generally gathered and where she talked to them about her latest encounter with a man. She rehearses with those in the village square the fact that Jesus knew her sexual history: ". . . a man who told me everything I have ever done!" (4:17–18, 29, 39). Surely the evangelist approves of her actions.

Special Role? Status? Does the Samaritan woman have a special role and/or status? When Jesus tells the "brethren," "As the Father has sent me, so I send you" (17:18), they enjoy a recognized role, *apostles*. For they are expected to travel from village to village and will enjoy public voice all of their lives, as they speak an authorized message. Moreover, they have duties and rights in regard to their role: a duty to fulfill the mission and a right to respect, if not support. The Samaritan woman does not enjoy this type of role. Jesus only sent her to Sychar and then only to "your husband," not to any other part of Samaria nor to other peoples. She will not move from village to village, nor will she proclaim an authorized message. In fact, the grammatical form of her speech to the men of Sychar is a question, not a declaration: "He cannot be the Messiah, can he?" And as we saw, her "message" to them is all about a man who revealed her sexual history (4:29, 39). Finally, as significant as it is that she invites others to "come and see," her importance in the process is short-lived, for they shortly dismiss her, saying: "It is no longer because of what you said that we believe, for we have heard for ourselves, and we know that this is truly the Savior of the world" (4:42). Thus, although she enjoys high status because of Jesus' revelations to her, the data do not support modern claims that she enjoys a formal role, certainly not that of an "apostle."

Gossip Network. The Samaritan woman is another example of the gossip network[121] whereby disciples spread news about Jesus to others (11:3, 28; 12:21–22; 20:24). News spreads informally in "gossip networks," a technical anthropological term that describes the spread of information in a low-media world.[122] Spreading news does not seem to entail any *formal role*; there emerges no recognized system of rights and duties characteristic of "roles." Anyone can be a conduit of information about any topic. The woman spreads the "gossip" about Jesus.[123] But she went to only one place, her village. Once she spreads the news, her place in the network ceases, just as it does for others who "gossip" about Jesus, such as the healed leper (Mark 1:45) and the Gadarene demonic

---

[121] For a fresh reading of John 4 in terms of "gossip," see B. J. Malina and R. L. Rohrbaugh, *Commentary on John* (1998), 103–4.

[122] See R. L. Rohrbaugh, "Gossip in the New Testament," in *Models for Interpreting the Bible* (2001), 239–59; Deborah Jones, "Gossip: Notes on Women's Oral Culture," *Women's Studies International Quarterly* 3 (1980), 193–98; Don Handelman, "Gossip in Encounters: The Transmission of Information in a Bounded Social Setting," *Man* 8 (1973), 210-17; Pieter J. J. Botha, "Paul and Gossip: A Social Mechanism in Early Christian Communities," *Neotestamentica* 32 (1998), 267–88; and S. Lewis, *News and Society* (1996).

[123] We note that the men of Samaria describe what the woman says as "chatter" (*lalia*), which seems to be derogatory.

(Mark 5:20). A person with good gossip might enjoy high status, but not a formal role.

JOHN 4:31–38 – INSTRUCTING THE DISCIPLES ON THEIR ROLE AS APOSTLES

27 Just then his disciples came. They were astonished that he was speaking with a woman, but no one said, "What do you want?" or, "Why are you speaking with her?" . . .

31 Meanwhile the disciples were urging him, "Rabbi, eat something."

32 But he said to them, "I have food to eat that you do not know about."

33 So the disciples said to one another, "Surely no one has brought him something to eat?"

34 Jesus said to them, "My food is to do the will of him who sent me and to complete his work.

35 Do you not say, 'Four months more, then comes the harvest'? But I tell you, look around you, and see how the fields are ripe for harvesting.

36 The reaper is already receiving wages and is gathering fruit for eternal life, so that sower and reaper may rejoice together.

37 For here the saying holds true, 'One sows and another reaps.'

38 I sent you to reap that for which you did not labor. Others have labored, and you have entered into their labor."

Eating, Not Drinking. Balancing the woman who gave Jesus water to drink, his disciples bring him food to eat: "Rabbi, eat" (4:31). Like hers, their encounter with Jesus is structured according to the pattern of statement–misunderstanding–clarification. Jesus states, "I have food to eat that you do not know about" (4:32), which they misunderstand: "Surely no one has brought him something to eat?" (4:33). Jesus proceeds to clarify his statement: "My food is to do the will of him who sent me and to complete his work" (4:34). Just as with "water" earlier, "food" here functions as a typical Johannine double-meaning term. Like most such things in this Gospel, its literal or earthly understanding clashes with Jesus' spiritual meaning of it. The dynamic of the story, then, is to bring the disciples to that knowledge, comparable to the way Jesus catechized the woman.

Apostle: A Formal Role. Jesus' remark about "the will of him who sent me" means that he has a *formal role*, which is to enlighten others and reveal secrets. All of the remarks in 4:35–38 are stitched together in terms of agriculture – namely sowing, reaping, gathering fruits and harvesting – by which process "bread" to eat is produced. Interpreting them literally would be a misunderstanding, for here the verbs refer to group formation, such that sowing equals preaching the word and reaping and harvesting equals transforming people who enter the group. This resembles the agricultural processes found in the parables of Mark 4 and Matthew 13, except that in place of Jesus' own sowing of the kingdom of God, the disciples in John 4:31–38 are the official apostles who spread the Gospel about Jesus.

Field of Sowing/Harvest. This agricultural metaphor for group formation would be simple and transparent except for the remark that "I sent you to reap that for which you did not labor. Others have labored, and you have entered into their labor" (4:38). Who preempted them in this work? Options are limited:[124] an earlier Samaritan recruitment; John's disciples preaching at Aenon near Salin (see 3:23); or followers from other Jesus groups (Acts 8). What seems momentous is the fact that these disciples were not first in Samaria. Being the first or founder was a mark of singular honor, as Paul never tired of telling his churches. He was "father" to the Corinthians (1 Cor 4:15), the one who planted (1 Cor 3:6), and the architect who laid the foundation (1 Cor 3:10).[125] Encroaching on another's turf would surely be an honor challenge, but Jesus authorizes it here. If Jesus is "greater than Jacob," who was a consummate supplanter, then it might be that these disciples will imitate their Supplanter by engaging in a recruitment where others have plowed and sowed.

JOHN 4:39–42 – STAGES IN BELIEF

39 Many Samaritans from that city believed in him because of the woman's testimony, "He told me everything I have ever done."
40 So when the Samaritans came to him, they asked him to stay with them; and he stayed there two days.
41 And many more believed because of his word.
42 They said to the woman, "It is no longer because of what you said that we believe, for we have heard for ourselves, and we know that this is truly the Savior of the world."

From Revelation to Acknowledgment. Just as the story of the Samaritan woman contained two features (growth in insight and gradual acknowledgment of Jesus), so, too, in 4:38–42 the men of Samaria come to acknowledge Jesus in an extraordinary way. This resembles the process of recruitment in John 1, where disciples recruited others to "come and see" and then acknowledged

---

[124] See R. E. Brown, *Community of the Beloved Disciple* (1979), 22–23, 35–40; and J. A. T. Robinson, "The 'Others' of John 4.38," *Studia Evangelica* 1 (1959), 510–15.

[125] Paul, who considered Corinth his turf, became furious when others crossed into it; he boasted that he had never encroached on another's turf (2 Cor 10:14–16; Rom 15:20; 1 Cor 3:10–15). See Jerome H. Neyrey, "Seduced in Corinth: More Witchcraft Accusations," in his *Paul, in Other Words* (1990), 210.

Jesus in virtue of their own experience. Whereas the woman hesitantly names Jesus "the Christ," the men boldly and expansively confess him as "Savior" of the world. Parallel to the way disciples acknowledged Jesus with increasingly elevated titles in 1:36–51, the titles given Jesus in John 4 illustrate a continual growth in knowledge about and acknowledgment of Jesus: v. 9 "a Judean"; v. 11 "Sir"; v. 12 "greater than our father Jacob"; v. 19 "a prophet"; v. 25 "Messiah/Christ"; v. 26 "I am the messiah"; and v. 42 "Savior of the World." The final acknowledgment of Jesus goes well beyond what could possibly be announced by the woman, so it represents a true climax in the story. Initially Jesus merely stops for drink and food before continuing; but we are later told that he "remained for two days" (4:40), indicating a most welcome reception and acknowledgment by insiders.

Savior of the World. "Savior," a general term for a benefactor,[126] might be a local, imperial,[127] or celestial being. As a benefactor, a "savior" might rescue from dangers, wars, and illnesses; protect and preserve the polis and its citizens; inaugurate a golden age; and benefit others.[128] The benefaction in Samaria consists of unique revelation. When the Samaritans acclaim Jesus as "Savior *of the world*," this picks up the erasure of ethnic boundaries illustrated in the story (4:9), as well as the negation of Mount Gerizim and Jerusalem as fixed sacred spaces (4:23–24).

JOHN 4:43–52 – THE SECOND SIGN

43 When the two days were over, he went from that place to Galilee
44 (for Jesus himself had testified that a prophet has no honor in the prophet's own country).
45 When he came to Galilee, the Galileans welcomed him, since they had seen all that he had done in Jerusalem at the festival; for they too had gone to the festival.
46 Then he came again to Cana in Galilee where he had changed the water into wine. Now there was a royal official whose son lay ill in Capernaum.

---

[126] Paul Wendland, "Σωτήρ," *ZNW* 5 (1904), 335–53; Georg Fohrer, "σωτήρ," *TDNT* 7.1003–23; and F. F. Bruce, "'Our God and Saviour': A Recurring Biblical Pattern," in S. G. B. Brandon, ed., *The Savior God* (Manchester: Manchester University Press, 1963), 51–66.

[127] Cities and senates declared kings and emperors "Saviors"; and monarchs began to describe themselves as "savior of the world" (Nero) and "world-rescuer" (Hadrian). See Adolf Deissmann, *Light from the Ancient East* (Grand Rapids, MI: Baker, 1965), 363–64.

[128] Arthur Darby Nock's "Soter and Euergetes," in his *Essays on Religion and the Ancient World* (Cambridge, MA: Harvard University Press, 1972), 2.721, summarized the ways in which the gods acted as saviors: "Zeus as father of men and gods was strong to aid; Artemis protected women in childbirth; Athena guarded the Acropolis."

47 When he heard that Jesus had come from Judea to Galilee, he went and begged him to come down and heal his son, for he was at the point of death.

48 Then Jesus said to him, "Unless you see signs and wonders you will not believe."

49 The official said to him, "Sir, come down before my little boy dies."

50 Jesus said to him, "Go; your son will live." The man believed the word that Jesus spoke to him and started on his way.

51 As he was going down, his slaves met him and told him that his child was alive.

52 So he asked them the hour when he began to recover, and they said to him, "Yesterday at one in the afternoon the fever left him."

53 The father realized that this was the hour when Jesus had said to him. "Your son will live." So he himself believed, along with his whole household.

54 Now this was the second sign that Jesus did after coming from Judea to Galilee.

Signs and Precarious Faith. Signs, because they are Jesus' credentials, work only when people make the same kind of logical link as did the man born blind: "If this man were not from God he could do nothing" (9:33). But people also want benefaction of some sort, without acknowledging Jesus' role or status (see 6:26). This episode illustrates the fluctuating value of signs. At first Jesus rejects the request, disvaluing a faith that needs earthly props. But just as Jesus led the Samaritan woman and the people of her town to faith (4:42), so here he is able to evoke in the official a correct and honorable acknowledgment of himself. The result is that his request is finally granted and he and his whole household "believed" in Jesus.[129]

Challenge and Riposte. As the narrative progresses, we will see negative challenges mounted against Jesus by rivals who seek to discredit him. Recalling the commentary on 2:1–11, we recognize positive challenges that are not hostile but that put one on the spot, such as volunteering, gift giving, paying compliments, and making requests.[130] As did the "woman" in 2:1–10, the official requests something of Jesus, which he may interpret as taking advantage of himself (Mark 7:25–27). As we see frequently in this Gospel, Jesus first rejects the request/challenge but negotiates how the petitioner might show him greater respect or reach a higher level of faith.[131] The end result is that Jesus takes complete control of the situation and responds to the request. Thus he is not taken advantage of and so his honor is maintained.

---

[129] On "telling time" in 4:52, see B. P. Robinson, "The Meaning and Significance of 'The Seventh Hour' in John 4:52," in E. A. Livingstone, ed., *Studia Biblica 1978* (Sheffield: University of Sheffield Press, 1980), 255–63.

[130] For more on "positive challenges," see the commentary on 2:1–12. See also B. J. Malina and J. H. Neyrey, "Honor and Shame in Luke-Acts," in *Social World of Luke-Acts* (1991), 49–52; and B. J. Malina, *New Testament World* (2001), 33–35.

[131] C. H. Giblin, "Suggestion," *NTS* 26 (1980), 197–211.

JOHN 5:1–16 – A HEALING BECOMES A CONTROVERSY

1 After this there was a festival of the Jews, and Jesus went up to Jerusalem.

2 Now in Jerusalem by the Sheep Gate there is a pool, called in Hebrew Beth-zatha, which has five porticoes.

3 In these lay many invalids – blind, lame, and paralyzed.

5 One man was there who had been ill for thirty-eight years.

6 When Jesus saw him lying there and knew that he had been there a long time, he said to him, "Do you want to be made well?"

7 The sick man answered him, "Sir, I have no one to put me into the pool when the water is stirred up; and while I am making my way, someone else steps down ahead of me."

8 Jesus said to him, "Stand up, take your mat and walk."

9 At once the man was made well, and he took up his mat and began to walk. Now that day was a sabbath.

10 So the Jews said to the man who had been cured, "It is the sabbath; it is not lawful for you to carry your mat."

11 But he answered them, "The man who made me well said to me, 'Take up your mat and walk.'"

12 They asked him, "Who is the man who said to you, 'Take it up and walk'?"

13 Now the man who had been healed did not know who it was, for Jesus had disappeared in the crowd that was there.

14 Later Jesus found him in the temple and said to him, "See, you have been made well! Do not sin any more, so that nothing worse happens to you."

15 The man went away and told the Jews that it was Jesus who had made him well.

16 Therefore the Jews started persecuting Jesus, because he was doing such things on the sabbath.

Where? Although the narrator told us in 4:3 that Jesus was returning to Galilee, now Jesus abruptly reappears in Jerusalem (5:1) and will shortly return to Galilee (6:1). We had best not read this literally but rather as symbolic geography, inasmuch as "Jerusalem" refers to the place where Jesus is rejected and "Galilee" to where he is accepted.[132]

Who? The story opens at a pool where many "unwhole" people are gathered (invalids – blind, lame, and paralyzed), but switches to the Temple, where observant Judeans confront the invalid man (5:10–13). These places correspond to the persons in them; at the pool are people who are unwhole and thus unclean, but in the Temple, all persons must be whole and clean. The healed man, then,

---

[132] J. Bassler, "The Galileans," *CBQ* 43 (1981), 243–57; J. H. Neyrey, "Territoriality," *BTB* 32 (2002), 63–64.

moved from a state of unwholeness to one of wholeness as he moved from the pool to the Temple. But observant Pharisees in the Temple criticize the man made whole for carrying his mat on the Sabbath, and thus they stand in judgment first of the man and then of Jesus. Significantly, Jesus' benefaction occurs apart from the holy shrine, even as his dialogue with the unclean Samaritan woman described worship not located in fixed sacred space.

When? The author locates the story on "a feast," which we cannot identify.[133] Although Jesus will return for the feasts of Tabernacles, Dedication, and Passover, the only significant thing about this feast is that it was the Sabbath, which colors the evaluation of the healed man and Jesus' actions.

Water, Water Everywhere. Water has played a significant role thus far in the narrative, from John's washing (1:28), to the water poured into stone jars for purification (2:7–10), to birth by water and spirit to enter God's kingdom (3:5), to the baptizing with water by both Jesus' and John's disciples (3:22–30), to Jesus' pause at a well in Samaria where he promises wells of living water springing up (4:7–15), and now to a pool near the Sheep Gate, where a paralyzed man lies (5:2). In all instances, water accompanies or causes a status-transformation ritual. Sinners become holy again, ordinary folk are born by baptism, and outsiders become insiders by virtue of Jesus' water. Thus one would expect the water in the pool to signal a transition, which it does. However, the transition here is merely from unwhole to whole, not from outsider to insider.[134]

Typical Miracle Story. Many label this narrative of an invalid made "whole" (5:1–9) as the third "sign" in a collection of seven. It reads like a typical miracle story found in both Hellenistic sources and the synoptic Gospels. Such stories typically contain five elements: *confrontation, severity of disease, cure,* sometimes with *materia medica* (such as roots or spittle), *proof* of healing, and *honor* to the healer. On many occasions, we read of a *confrontation* between a healer and an ill person because the dominant taxonomy of what causes illness in the ancient world was spirit aggression;[135] thus "confrontation" suggests that the healer grapples with or makes war on the spirit causing harm (see Mark 5:1–7). The more *severe* the disease, the greater the glory of the healer or the healer's patron (see Luke 7:16; 17:18). It is often the case that the *healing* is done by means of some sort of *materia medica*, such as roots, herbs, and ointments.[136] Not infrequently the healer devises some sort of *proof* of the healing. The aim and function of such proofs of healings in antiquity was the *praise and honor*

---

[133] Yet Aileen Guilding's *The Fourth Gospel and Jewish Worship* (Oxford: Clarendon, 1960), 69–91, argues that the "feast" in 5:1 is the feast of the New Year.

[134] See L. Th. Witkamp, "The Use of Traditions in John 5.1–18," *JSNT* 25 (1985), 19–47.

[135] John J. Pilch, *Healing in the New Testament: Insights from Medical and Mediterranean Anthropology* (Minneapolis, MN: Fortress Press, 2000), 80–82, 103–6.

[136] Jesus occasionally uses spittle as a type of *materia medica* (see John 9:6; Mark 7:33, 8:23).

accorded the healer. Unlike in the synoptics, no demons afflict people in this Gospel,[137] so no confrontation is mentioned in John 5. The severity of the illness, however, is noted, in that the man "had been ill for thirty-eight years" (5:5).[138] Rather than healing with the spittle and mud rubbed on the blind man's eyes (9:6), Jesus heals with a word: "Stand up, take your mat and walk" (5:8). The proof is demonstrated when the healed man walks (5:9), especially in the Temple. Finally, although this healing should bring respect and honor to Jesus (see Mark 1:28, 45; Luke 7:16–17), it instead precipitates a controversy that seeks to shame him (5:15). Nevertheless, the story formally contains the elements of a typical healing story.

A CLOSER LOOK – TYPICAL FORM OF A MIRACLE

Gospel authors often narrate the miracles of Jesus using many, if not all, of the elements found in typical miracle stories found in the Greco-Roman world. We gain great insight into John 5 if we know just what ancient miracle stories look like. Consider this example, in which the Judean apologist Josephus honors Solomon as the source of Israelite wisdom used to impress the Roman elites:

And God granted him (Solomon) knowledge of the art used against demons for the benefit and healing of men. He also composed incantations by which illnesses are relieved, and left behind forms of exorcisms with which those possessed by demons drive them out, never to return. And this kind of cure is of very great power among us to this day, for I have seen a certain Eleazar, a countryman of mine, in the presence of Vespasian, his sons, tribunes and a number of other soldiers, free men possessed by demons [*confrontation*], and this was the manner of the cure: he put to the nose of the possessed man a ring which had under its seal one of the roots prescribed by Solomon [*cure: materia medica*], and then, as the man smelled it, drew out the demons through his nostrils, and when the man at once fell down, adjured the demon never to come back into him, speaking Solomon's name and reciting the incantations which he had composed. Then, wishing to convince the bystanders and prove to them that he had this power [*proof*], Eleazar placed a cup or foot-basin full of water a little way off and commanded the demon, as it went out of the man, to overturn it and make known to the spectators that he had left the man. And when this was done, the understanding and wisdom of Solomon were clearly revealed,[139] on account of

---

137 See Ronald A. Piper, "Satan, Demons and the Absence of Exorcisms in the Fourth Gospel," in his *Christology, Controversy, and Community* (Leiden: Brill, 2000), 253–78.

138 Similarly, in 9:1 the man was born blind, and in 11:39 Lazarus is dead and already four days in the tomb. "Severity of illness," then, is a regular factor in Johannine healings.

139 In the synoptic Gospels, Jesus is often called "Son of David," which Dennis Duling argues refers to Jesus the miracle worker as actually "Son of Solomon, Son of David." See his "Solomon, Exorcism, and the Son of David," *HTR* 68 (1975), 235–52; "The Therapeutic Son of David," *NTS* 24 (1978), 392–410; and "The Eleazar Miracle and Solomon's Magical Wisdom in Flavius Josephus' *Antiquitates Judaicae* 8.42–48," *HTR* 78 (1985), 1–25.

which we have been induced to speak of these things, in order that all men may know the greatness of his nature and how God favoured him, and that no one under the sun may be ignorant of the king's surpassing virtue of every kind [*honor and praise*]." (Josephus, *Ant.* 8.45–48; see also Lucian, *Lover of Lies* 16).

Miracle Becomes Controversy. The healing becomes a controversy when observant Judeans label the man's carrying of his mat as a Sabbath violation: "It is not lawful for you to carry your mat" (5:10). He denies responsibility and shifts the blame to Jesus: "The man who made me well said to me, 'Take up your mat and walk'" (5:11). But the identity of the person responsible is unknown. For, when questioned about Jesus, the invalid does not know who his healer is (5:13). He will, of course, learn the identity of the man who healed him, that it was Jesus, and so return with this "testimony" to his accusers: "He told the Jews that it was Jesus who had made him well" (5:15). As a result, they "started prosecuting Jesus, because he was doing such things on the sabbath" (5:16).[140]

Representative Character. In many ways, this man parodies previous Johannine characters. First, he begins the story "not in the know," for he cannot tell his accusers that Jesus healed him; he later comes "into the know" when Jesus finds him. But this contrasts with all other transitions we have previously seen: The man does not become a believer or a disciple of Jesus. His "knowledge" of Jesus is minimal and material (a mere name, "Jesus"); it contains no faith in Jesus' role, nor does it lead to a relationship with him.[141] Second, when the disciples in 1:35ff. and the Samaritan woman in 4:28–30 "tell" others about Jesus, they are recruiting on his behalf. But this man acts differently, for he aids and abets Jesus' enemies; he recruits no one. Third, Jesus "finds" him in the Temple (5:14). Normally in this Gospel "finding" describes recruitment (1:41, 43, 45) and even Jesus' confirmation of a recruit's faithfulness (9:35). But here Jesus' "finding" of this man has nothing whatever to do with discipleship but issues a warning: "Do not sin any more, so that nothing worse happens to you" (5:14). Might his "sin" be that he does not come to faith and in fact testifies against Jesus? Thus many elements of the process of outsiders becoming insiders are present, but

---

[140] Synoptic miracles often metamorphose into controversies (Mark 2:1–12; 3:1–6; Luke 13:10–17); this miracle remains controversial throughout the Fourth Gospel (7:22–23; see also 9:13–17).

[141] It has been suggested that this man behaves like the parents of the man born blind, who are afraid to say anything positive about Jesus lest they be expelled from the synagogue (9:22; 12:42). See J. Louis Martyn, *The Gospel of John in Christian History* (New York: Paulist Press, 1978), 90–121.

they seem to be parodied. Therefore, as a representative character, the healed man symbolizes people with minimal knowledge who are impervious to who Jesus is and the significance of what he does. Seeing, he does not comprehend; hearing, he does not understand.[142]

JOHN 5:17–29 – THE ENEMIES REALLY GET ANGRY

17 But Jesus answered them, "My Father is still working, and I also am working."
18 For this reason the Jews were seeking all the more to kill him, because he was not only breaking the sabbath, but was also calling God his own Father, thereby making himself equal to God.
19 Jesus said to them, "Very truly, I tell you, the Son can do nothing on his own, but only what he sees the Father doing; for whatever the Father does, the Son does likewise.
20 The Father loves the Son and shows him all that he himself is doing; and he will show him greater works than these, so that you will be astonished.
21 Indeed, just as the Father raises the dead and gives them life, so also the Son gives life to whomever he wishes.
22 The Father judges no one but has given all judgment to the Son,
23 so that all may honor the Son just as they honor the Father. Anyone who does not honor the Son does not honor the Father who sent him.
24 Very truly, I tell you, anyone who hears my word and believes him who sent me has eternal life, and does not come under judgment, but has passed from death to life.
25 "Very truly, I tell you, the hour is coming, and is now here, when the dead will hear the voice of the Son of God, and those who hear will live.
26 For just as the Father has life in himself, so he has granted the Son also to have life in himself;
27 and he has given him authority to execute judgment, because he is the Son of Man.
28 Do not be astonished at this; for the hour is coming when all who are in their graves will hear his voice
29 and will come out – those who have done good, to the resurrection of life, and those who have done evil, to the resurrection of condemnation.

---

[142] Yet others argue for a more positive interpretation of the man. Precisely because of his anonymity, readers are said to be drawn to him and identify with him. See D. R. Beck, "The Narrative Function of Anonymity in Fourth Gospel Characterization," *Semeia* 63 (1993), 143–58.

Two Trials: Two Charges and Two Defenses. As a result of his healing on the Sabbath, Jesus is accused of sinfulness for breaking the law (5:16). But Jesus' remark in 5:17, while justifying his sabbath actions, takes the crisis to a new level: "My Father is still working, and I also am working." His judges interpret this as claiming much more than authority to transcend sabbath observance, for they see it as the ultimate sin: "For this reason the Jews were seeking all the more to kill him, because he was not only breaking the sabbath, but was also calling God his own Father, thereby making himself equal to God" (5:18). When these two different charges are carefully compared and contrasted, we can discern that two distinctive forensic processes are being narrated:[143]

Old Charge (5:16)	*New Charge (5:18)*
sinful action:	blasphemy:
violation of sabbath	he makes himself equal to God
Sentence: public shaming	*Sentence:* death
Old Defense (5:30–47)	*New Defense (5:19–29)*
series of witnesses	careful explanation
testifying to Jesus'	of how Jesus truly is
obedience and sinlessness	"equal to God"

When contrasted in this way, we see two distinct charges, which warrant two different punishments and, as we will shortly see, call for two different defenses on Jesus' part. We have, then, a sign that metamorphosed into a controversy, which belongs to an early period of the history of the Johannine group. The charge that Jesus makes himself equal to God, however, represents a later development in the Gospel and has been inserted into this narrative to highlight how it, too, is treated as an abomination by outsiders but is proudly defended by insiders. The forensic controversy over sabbath transgression is the older, whereas the process over blasphemy has a more recent history.[144]

Not "Makes Himself." The evangelist distinguishes two elements in the new charge, one of which is false and should be rejected but the other is true and requires careful exposition. The new charge reads: (1) he makes himself (2) equal to God. The first element is utterly false: Jesus does *not* make himself anything, although opponents of Jesus persistently make this charge:

---

[143] J. H. Neyrey, *Ideology of Revolt* (1988), 10–21.

[144] Most commentators distinguish 5:17–30 from 5:31–47 but infrequently relate these materials to the two different forensic charges made in 5:16–18. See G. Beasley-Murray, *John*, 2nd ed. (Nashville, TN: Thomas Nelson, 1990), 75–77; and Francis J. Moloney, *Shadows and Signs: Reading John 5–12* (Minneapolis, MN: Fortress Press, 1996), 10–28.

5:18	"*. . . making himself* equal to God."
8:53	"Who do you *make yourself* to be?"
10:33	"You, though only a human being, are *making yourself* God."
19:7	"He ought to die because he *made himself* to be the Son of God."
19:12	"Everyone who *makes himself* a king sets himself against the emperor."

This charge not only implies that Jesus acts as an ambitious person seeking honor and glory, but worse, he is stealing this glory from the glorious persons of the world, Caesar and God. Honor and glory are limited goods, and if Jesus were to acquire them, others must lose them.[145] Caesar executes such upstarts; God destroys such vainglorious fools. So, the evangelist labors to show that this part of the charge is utterly false: Jesus does not make himself anything, for God makes him what he is.

Ascribed, Not Achieved Honor. Responding to the charge that "he makes himself," Jesus disowns acting independently of God, much less contrary to God's law, for "of himself the Son can do nothing" (5:19). Rather he does "what he sees the Father doing," and God gives him whatever honor and power he enjoys:

5:20	"The Father *loves* the Son and *shows* him all that he does."
5:22	"The Father judges no one, but *has given* all judgment to the Son."
5:26	"As the Father has life in himself, so he *has given* the Son to have life in himself."
5:27	". . . and *has given* him authority to execute judgment."

Thus, Jesus does not suffer from ambition,[146] nor has he taken any actions that encroach on God's sovereignty. On the contrary, God has made him who he is and endowed him with the powers he enjoys. The first part of the charge, then, is utterly false.

But "Equal to God"? What of the second element in the charge in 5:18, "equal to God"? In what sense is this true? How do we explain it? The defense in 5:21–29 provides ample argument for "equality."[147]

---

[145] Readers are referred back to the discussion of limited good and honor in 3:21–30.

[146] On the prevalence of "ambition" in antiquity, see A. C. Hagedorn and J. H. Neyrey, "'It Was Out of Envy that They Handed Jesus Over,'" *JSNT* 69 (1998), 15–56, esp. 34–36.

[147] Wayne Meeks's "Equal to God," in Robert Fortna and Beverly Gaventa, eds., *The Conversation Continues: Studies in Paul & John in Honor of J. Louis Martyn* (Nashville, TN: Abingdon, 1990), 309–21, asks three questions on John 5:18. First, what did Jesus' accusers understand by "equal to God"? Second, what did the Johannine disciples understand by it? And third, how could Jesus' disciples make themselves so odious by proclaiming this declaration?

5:19	"Whatever the Father does, the Son does likewise."
5:20	"The Father shows him all that he himself is doing."
5:21	"As the Father raises the dead and gives them life, so the Son gives life."
5:22	"The Father judges no one but has given all judgment to the Son."
5:23	"All must honor the Son just as they honor the Father."
5:26	"As the Father has life in himself, so he has granted the Son to have life in himself."
5:27	"He has given him authority to execute judgment."

"Equality" is based on the full range of actions Jesus does, including the respect and honor he is owed (5:23). Most importantly, God gives Jesus the greatest of God's powers, namely the eschatological power to raise the dead, judge them, and requite them. All of this, moreover, is God's grant or gift to Jesus.

"Equal" = God's Two Powers. Although there are many items attributed to Jesus in 5:19–29, the ancients would recognize them and reduce them to God's two powers.[148] If raising the dead, judging, and having life in oneself refer to God's eschatological power itemized in 5:21–29, what power is credited to Jesus in 5:19–20? It refers neither to executive leadership nor eschatological power but to God's creative power, which is already applied to Jesus in 1:1–5. In 5:17, Jesus claimed that "My Father is still working, and I also am working." Although this statement functions as a defense for *not* resting on the Sabbath, it implies that God did not stop creating on the seventh day but continued working.[149] In regard to his healing in 5:1–9, Jesus defends himself by claiming two things: (1) God continues to work on the Sabbath and hence Jesus is imitating God's continued creative work by his healing on the Sabbath; and (2) God shows him all that he does, empowering him for works of creation and providence. Thus all of God's deeds of creation/providence Jesus likewise does.[150] Jesus' opponents in the narrative understand his words in the second sense, namely as a claim to divine power, for we are told that on the basis of these words they no longer persecuted him for Sabbath violation but for the blasphemy of claiming God's creative power (5:18). Thus "equality" with God, which is fiercely defended, consists of God's donation of two basic powers to Jesus: creative and eschatological.

---

[148] C. H. Dodd's *Interpretation of the Fourth Gospel* (1968), 322–23, argued that two powers are alluded to, but Dodd described them inaccurately as "to give life" and "to judge."

[149] As early as Philo, it was argued that despite Genesis 1, God continued to work on the Sabbath in the sense of maintaining creation; see Philo *Cher.* 88–89; *Leg. All.* 1.5; later midrash was not offended by this (see *Gen. R.* 11.10 and *Ex. R.* 30.6).

[150] J. H. Neyrey, *Ideology of Revolt* (1988), 18–22.

A CLOSER LOOK – GOD'S TWO POWERS AND GOD'S TWO NAMES

Two Powers. All theology in antiquity, Greek and Judean, dealt with God's *operations* in the world, summarized as creative/providential and executive. Philo expresses this most clearly in his exposition of God's *two powers*: the *creative power* (δύναμις ποιετική) and the *executive power* (δύναμις βασιλική).[151] Through the δύναμις ποιετική God "creates and operates the world," and by the δύναμις βασιλική God "rules over what has come into being" (*Q. Ex.* 4.2). For Philo, then, these two powers express all of God's actions and operations in the world. The δύναμις ποιετική is described in terms of "goodness," "mercy," and "beneficence," as well as creation; alternatively, the δύναμις βασιλική is "authority," "legislation," and "punishment," as well as governance. When the high priest Simon prays, he is identifying God as having both powers: "Lord, Lord, king of the heavens and sovereign of all creation. . . . You, the creator of all things and the governor of all, are a just Ruler and you judge those who have done anything in insolence" (3 Macc 3:2–3). The two powers are joined as the primary mode of addressing God: "creator of all . . . governor of all" (see also 2 Macc 7:28–29).[152]

Names and Powers. In Philo and the Rabbis, the two powers of God are often associated, respectively, with God's two names.[153] For Philo, the beneficent, creative power (δύναμις ποιετική) is called Θεός, or "God," and the royal, judicial power (δύναμις βασιλική) is called Κύριος, or "Lord." For example, in explaining the cherubim (Exod 25:18), Philo identifies the two powers of the Deity and names them accordingly: "I should myself say that they (the Cherubim) are allegorically representations of the two most August and highest potencies (δυνάμεις) of Him that is, the creative and the kingly. His δύναμις ποιετική is called *God* (Θεός), because through it He placed and made and ordered this universe, and the δύναμις βασιλική is called *Lord* (Κύριος), being that with which He governs what has come into being and rules it steadfastly with justice" (*Mos.* 2.99; see *Q. Ex.* 2.68; *Plant.* 86–87; *Abr.* 124–125; *Somn.* 1.160, 163; *Fuga* 101).

---

[151] See *Leg. All.* II.68; *Cher.* 27–28; *Sac.* 59; *Plant.* 86–87; *Heres* 166; *Fuga* 95, 100; *Somn.* 1.159–163; *Abr.* 124–125; *Mos.* II.99; *Spec.* 1.307; *All. Leg.* 4 & 6; and *Q. Ex.* II.62, 64–66, 68. See also Harry Wolfson, *Philo* (Cambridge, MA: Harvard University Press, 1948), I. 218–25.

[152] In describing the "faith of Abraham," Paul claims that Abraham acknowledged God's two powers: "Abraham believed in God . . . who gives life to the dead and calls into existence the things that do not exist" (Rom 4:17).

[153] See Alan Segal and Nils Dahl, "Philo and the Rabbis on the Names of God," *JSJ* 9 (1978), 1–28; see also A. Marmorstein, "Philo and the Names of God," *JQR* 22 (1931–32), 295–306.

God's Powers and Names in John. In the prologue, where Jesus is credited with *creative power*, he is called Θεός, or "God" (1:1–3). In 5:1–16, the focus is initially on Jesus' creative "working," in which context Jesus is alleged to be "equal to God" (5:18). Θεός/"God," then, is the appropriate name for Jesus when he exercises creative power. Κύριος, however, is more difficult to deal with, for while Jesus is often acclaimed *kyrios* in John, this title is constantly open to the minimalist interpretation of "sir" or "master." There is, however, one climactic confession in the Gospel in which Jesus is acclaimed "My Lord (Κύριος) and my God (Θεός)" (20:28). Surely at this point *Kyrios* should be treated as a cultic title, its full force acclaiming Jesus as a divine figure. But what is intended by acclaiming Jesus as *Kyrios* after his resurrection? Is his exercise of a certain power implied and acknowledged? Creative power is not only claimed but demonstrated (1:1–18; 5:1–9, 19–20), and so Jesus is rightly called "God"/Θεος.

A CLOSER LOOK – JESUS: "GOD," "EQUAL TO GOD," "I AM"

The Fourth Gospel is the most explicit Gospel in giving content to the Christian claims that Jesus is a heavenly, divine figure. A defense is given to the claim "equal to God" in 5:18 by showing as we have just seen that Jesus has God's two basic powers, creative and eschatological. Possession of these powers implies that Jesus was "in the beginning" and returns to God, expressing "eternity," a characteristic only of a true deity.[154] He is thereby rightly called "God" and "Lord." His eternity is also expressed in his appropriation of the name "I AM," which we will see in the commentary in 8:24, 8:28, and 8:58 refers to his continuous existence. Abraham came into being and died, in contrast to Jesus. It is also argued that because "no one has ever seen God," Abraham and the patriarchs saw someone, namely the appearing Jesus; thus his antiquity is affirmed as well as his continued role of giving knowledge, revelations, and manifestations. Thus, the Fourth Gospel is willing to acknowledge Jesus' heavenly and divine character, always giving specific content to the declaration, content that would be readily understood by a Judean audience.[155]

Topic Statement and Development. Eschatological power is initially only claimed in 5:21–29, and its demonstration remains the task of the rest of the Gospel, especially the next several chapters. As is characteristic of the Fourth Gospel, a sentence or statement is frequently made that serves as the

---

[154] See Jerome H. Neyrey, "'Without Beginning of Days or End of Life' (Hebrews 7:3): Topos for a True Deity," *CBQ* 53 (1991), 439–55.

[155] See Jerome H. Neyrey, "'My Lord and My God': The Divinity of Jesus in John's Gospel," *SBLSP* (1986), 152–71.

text, topic, or agenda of subsequent discussion. Verses 5:18, 21–29 are just such a topic statement. The following chart lists the seven items contained in 5:18–29, which are subsequently explained and illustrated in Chapters 6, 8, 10, and 11.

Eschatological Power	John 6	John 8	John 10	John 11
1. *Equal to God:* ". . . making himself equal to God" (5:18)	–	–	10:30, 33	–
2. *Son gives life:* "Just as the Father raises the dead and gives them life, so also the Son gives life to whomever he wishes." (5:21)	6:27, 33, 47–50, 54, 57, 58	8:51	10:28	11:25a
3. *Judgment:* "The Father . . . has given all judgment to the Son" (5:22); "He has given him authority to execute judgment, because he is the Son of Man." (5:27)	–	8:21–30	10:26	–
4. *Equal honor:* "All honor the Son just as they honor the Father. Who does not honor the Son does not honor the Father." (5:23)	–	the name "I AM"	(10:31, 39)	11:4
5. *The dead hear and live:* "The dead will hear the voice of the Son of God, and those who hear will live." (5:25)	–	–	(10:3–5)	11:43–44
6. *Life in himself:* "Just as the Father has life in himself, so he has granted the Son also to have life in himself." (5:26)	6:51	8:24, 28, 58	10:17–18, 34–36	11:25a
7. *Resurrection and life:* "All who are in their graves will hear his voice and come out – those who have done good, to the resurrection of life, and those who have done evil, to the resurrection of condemnation." (5:28–29)[156]	6:40, 44, 54	–	–	11:25–26

---

[156] Nils A. Dahl, in his "'Do Not Wonder!' John 5:28–29 and Johannine Eschatology Once More," in Robert T. Fortna and Beverly R. Gaventa, eds., *The Conversation Continues: Studies in Paul & John in Honor of J. Louis Martyn* (Nashville, TN: Abingdon, 1990), 322–36, argues in regard to 5:28–29 that these remarks support statements about present eschatology, not corrections to it.

JOHN 5:30–47 – DEFENSE FOR THE FIRST CHARGE: LAWBREAKING

30 "I can do nothing on my own. As I hear, I judge; and my judgment is just, because I seek to do not my own will but the will of him who sent me.

31 If I testify about myself, my testimony is not true.

32 There is another who testifies on my behalf, and I know that his testimony to me is true.

33 You sent messengers to John, and he testified to the truth.

34 Not that I accept such human testimony, but I say these things so that you may be saved.

35 He was a burning and shining lamp, and you were willing to rejoice for a while in his light.

36 But I have a testimony greater than John's. The works that the Father has given me to complete, the very works that I am doing, testify on my behalf that the Father has sent me.

37 And the Father who sent me has himself testified on my behalf. You have never heard his voice or seen his form,

38 and you do not have his word abiding in you, because you do not believe him whom he has sent.

39 You search the scriptures because you think that in them you have eternal life; and it is they that testify on my behalf.

40 Yet you refuse to come to me to have life.

41 I do not accept glory from human beings.

42 But I know that you do not have the love of God in you.

43 I have come in my Father's name, and you do not accept me; if another comes in his own name, you will accept him.

44 How can you believe when you accept glory from one another and do not seek the glory that comes from the one who alone is God?

45 Do not think that I will accuse you before the Father; your accuser is Moses, on whom you have set your hope.

46 If you believed Moses, you would believe me, for he wrote about me.

47 But if you do not believe what he wrote, how will you believe what I say?"

Judean Forensic Process. A typical Judean trial contains five elements: a charge of evildoing; witnesses for or against the accused; judges who are elders; the verdict; and the sentence.[157] In the case of Susanna, witnesses accuse her of adultery; her trial occurred in the midst of "the people," who convicted her and

---

[157] A. E. Harvey, *Jesus on Trial* (Atlanta: John Knox, 1976), 46–66. See also J. D. M. Derrett, "Law in the New Testament: The Parable of the Unjust Judge," *NTS* 18 (1971), 178–91; and Jerome H. Neyrey, "Jesus the Judge: Forensic Process in John 8, 21–59," *Biblica* 68 (1987), 509–18.

then sentenced her to death. The heart of this process is the witnesses, whom Daniel proves to be false witnesses. Eventually, Susanna's verdict is overturned and the false witnesses suffer the fate to which Susanna was sentenced. In John 5, the man whom Jesus healed *testifies* that Jesus told him to carry his mat on the sabbath (5:16). Thus Jesus is *accused* of *lawbreaking* before the "*court*" of "*Judeans.*" His *defense* against this charge consists of a battery of *witnesses*, all noble, wise, and acceptable to this court (5:30–47).[158] Thus the original version of this episode included a *deed* (5:1–13), the *witness* against Jesus (5:15), the *charge* of Sabbath violation (5:16), and *witnesses* called for the defense (5:30–47). As with Susanna's trial, strange things happen, such as the judges being exposed for judging unjustly. Thus the trial may be turned upside down, and the accused becomes the accuser and the judges themselves are judged.

How Do You Plead? Not Guilty! The court charges Jesus with sinfulness, for he did not keep one of the sacred commands of Israel's law, forgoing "work" on the Sabbath. He pleads "not guilty" because he acted not on his own authority but in obedience to the authority of God. In fact, his action on the Sabbath is a virtuous, holy action: "My judgment is just, because I seek to do not my own will but the will of him who sent me" (5:30). Hence, he is no maverick, but an observant and obedient person; he is not a sinner, but a holy person. But we do not just take his word for it; we listen to what witnesses say on his behalf.[159]

Witnesses for the Defense. The essence of trials in Israelite and Greco-Roman antiquity rested on the testimony of witnesses for or against the accused. What counted was the word of honorable, noble people known by the court. Moreover, the testimony of a person speaking on his own behalf has little standing in the court. Furthermore, two or more witnesses are needed (see John 8:17–18; Deut 19:15; *m. Ket.* 2.9). Jesus now calls five witnesses to testify on his behalf.

1. *John, the Perpetual Witness* (5:33–36). He enjoys good standing in this court because it once sent to John for testimony (1:19–28; see 1:6–8, 15) and accepted his word: "He was a burning and shining lamp, and you were willing to rejoice for a while in his light" (5:35). John, then, is a witness that both the accused and the court accept. He testified to Jesus' holiness and authorization by God (1:32–34). But Jesus has "a testimony greater than John's" (5:36).

2. *Actions Speak Louder than Words* (5:36). Jesus' second witness is the "works" God gave him to do: "The very works that I am doing, testify on my behalf that the Father has sent me." The man born blind articulated this argument when he was examined because of Jesus' sign performed on the Sabbath: "We know that

---

158 A. E. Harvey's remarks about the character of witnesses bears noting: "Whose word can we trust? If a citizen who enjoyed the respect of society solemnly affirmed that something was the case, this is all one could ask for. If two or three such citizens gave identical evidence (and stood up to cross-examination), this was sufficient even to condemn a man to death. . . . The all-important question was the character of the witnesses" (*Jesus on Trial* [1976], 20). Compare Acts 4:13.

159 See J. H. Neyrey, *Ideology of Revolt* (1988), 10–15.

God does not listen to sinners, but he does listen to one who worships him and obeys his will. If this man were not from God, he could do nothing" (9:31–33). His works, then, are precisely his credentials that he is God's agent (see 3:2; 9:30–33).

3. *The Best Possible Witness* (5:37–38). "The Father who sent me has himself testified on my behalf." Obviously, this "Father" is God, whose knowledge of the human heart is perfect and whose judgment is true. Hence, the most honorable possible witness testifies on Jesus' behalf. Clearly, then, Jesus is not a disobedient or nonobservant sinner as charged, but holy in the paramount way holiness was assessed: total faithfulness and obedience to God.[160] Where does one find God's testimony? His works, as noted, but also the Scriptures. Yet many people are unable to read them correctly, for even to find, much less understand, God's testimony in the Scriptures depends on how one knows. (Recall from 3:6, 12 that Nicodemus reasoned in an earthly, not spiritual and heavenly, manner.)

The trial of Jesus now becomes the trial of his judges. When Jesus says about them "You do not have his word abiding in you, because you do not believe him whom he has sent" (5:38), he accuses his judges of a terrible sin: The court neither has God's word nor does it believe in God. The accused now accuses his accusers. They, the arbiters of Israel's religion, are sinners and evildoers. And it gets worse: "You have *never* heard his voice or seen his form" (5:37). While this may be read as a denial that Moses and Israel saw God at Sinai ("no one has ever seen God," 1:18; 6:46), it likewise charges Jesus' accusers with being utterly deaf to God's word, in whatever form it comes. They, then, are the disobedient sinners, not Jesus.

4. *Israel's Sacred Writings* (5:39). Judaism, a religion of the Book, lives and dies on its understanding of the Scriptures. Hence, Jesus notes the pious practice "You search the scriptures because you think that in them you have eternal life," but with what bias? Earlier, Nathanael mocked the testimony that a peasant from Nazareth could be the one of whom Moses and the prophets wrote (1:45–46). Later, in another trial in the Temple, we hear of a divided judgment about Jesus on the basis of the Scriptures (7:40–43), a debate that ends with a hardened judgment: "Search and you will see that no prophet is to arise from Galilee" (7:51). Nathanael was gifted to acknowledge Jesus, but very few others who search the Scriptures find the truth about Jesus. Hence, this, too, can be construed as a judgment on Jesus' judges. They cannot understand their own Scriptures.

5. *And Then There Was Moses* (5:46–47). The last witness for the defense is Israel's most reliable figure, Moses. Of him Jesus claims: "If you believed Moses, you would believe me, for he wrote about me" (5:46). No biblical book or passage of a book is cited, but if Moses was considered the author of the Pentateuch,

---

[160] See James M. Reese, "Obedience (Submission)," in John J. Pilch and Bruce J. Malina, eds., *Handbook of Biblical Social Values* (Peabody, MA: Hendrickson, 1998), 142–43.

then this part of the Scripture is in view. But why don't Jesus' accusers find him attested to in the Scriptures? The reason is the same as expressed in 5:37–38, namely hardness of heart and blindness: "But if you do not believe what he wrote, how will you believe what I say?" (5:47). The tables are turned and the accusers are now accused.

To What Do These Witnesses Testify? They do not support the defense of Jesus in 5:19–29 that he is "equal to God." No witnesses were called in that defense because no witnesses can testify to that, only God. But in 5:30–47 the witnesses Jesus cites function in his defense against the charge of being a sinner and lawbreaker made in 5:16. Five acceptable, high-status witnesses attest to Jesus' agency from God and his holiness even in his signs: He is a saint, not a sinner.

The Tables Are Turned. As noted, trials can be turned upside down;[161] the accused becomes the accuser and the judges are judged – which is what happens in 5:31–47. Jesus is not the sinful person; his accusers are. When Jesus said "I know that you do not have the love of God in you" (5:42), he accuses them of grave sinfulness, especially because they are the leaders and guardians of Israel's faith. He offers *proof* of their sinfulness: "I have come in my Father's name, and you do not accept me" (5:43). Not to receive a king's agent is to insult the king because according to the ancient, widespread principle of agency, "an agent is like the one who sent him" and "the agent of the ruler is like the ruler himself."[162] Indeed, "How can you believe when you seek not God's glory but your own"? (5:44). Although Moses acted as advocate for Israel before God,[163] Jesus claims that the advocate will become a witness for the prosecution. "Do not think that I will accuse you before the Father; your accuser is Moses, on whom you have set your hope" (5:45). *Judge:* Either they will judge themselves (3:19–20), or Jesus, who was credited in 5:22–29 with authority and power to judge, will judge his judges. But the judges are now being judged. If Jesus is correct when he says that "you do not have the love of God within you" (5:42) and that "you do not have his word abiding in you" (5:38), the accusing judges are guilty. *Sentence:* Although their aim in searching the Scriptures is to find "eternal life" (5:39), these sinners fail to find it; they instead will find eternal death.

---

[161] Urban C. Von Wahlde, "The Witnesses to Jesus in John 5:31–40 and Belief in the Fourth Gospel," *CBQ* 43 (1981), 385–404.

[162] P. Borgen, "God's Agent," in *Religions in Antiquity* (1968), 138–44; see also A. E. Harvey, "Christ as Agent," in L. D. Hurst and N. T. Wright, eds., *The Glory of Christ in the New Testament* (Oxford: Clarendon Press, 1987), 239–50.

[163] According to Exodus 32:11–14 and Numbers 14:13–19, Moses functioned as Israel's defender before God, a tradition found widely in Philo, Josephus, Qumran, and the midrashim. See Wayne A. Meeks, *The Prophet King: Moses Traditions and Johannine Christology* (Leiden: Brill, 1967), 118, 125, 137, 159–61, 200–204, 254–56.

JOHN 6:1–15 – ANOTHER SIGN: BREAD AT PASSOVER

1 After this Jesus went to the other side of the Sea of Galilee, also called the Sea of Tiberias.

2 A large crowd kept following him, because they saw the signs that he was doing for the sick.

3 Jesus went up the mountain and sat down there with his disciples.

4 Now the Passover, the festival of the Jews, was near.

5 When he looked up and saw a large crowd coming toward him, Jesus said to Philip, "Where are we to buy bread for these people to eat?"

6 He said this to test him, for he himself knew what he was going to do.

7 Philip answered him, "Six months' wages would not buy enough bread for each of them to get a little."

8 One of his disciples, Andrew, Simon Peter's brother, said to him,

9 "There is a boy here who has five barley loaves and two fish. But what are they among so many people?"

10 Jesus said, "Make the people sit down." Now there was a great deal of grass in the place; so they sat down, about five thousand in all.

11 Then Jesus took the loaves, and when he had given thanks, he distributed them to those who were seated; so also the fish, as much as they wanted.

12 When they were satisfied, he told his disciples, "Gather up the fragments left over, so that nothing may be lost."

13 So they gathered them up, and from the fragments of the five barley loaves, left by those who had eaten, they filled twelve baskets.

14 When the people saw the sign that he had done, they began to say, "This is indeed the prophet who is to come into the world."

15 When Jesus realized that they were about to come and take him by force to make him king, he withdrew again to the mountain by himself.

When? Where? Who? The time notation is obviously important, as the narrative moves from the indeterminate "feast of the Jews" (5:1) to "Passover, the feast of the Jews" (6:4). The notice of Passover (the second of three in the Gospel) urges the audience to think of Moses, manna, and the Exodus as relevant background for the current events. Hence Passover is not just calendar time but symbolic time. *Where?* The scene shifts from Jerusalem to "the other side of the Sea of Galilee." But other contrasts of place occur: Whereas we first find Jesus on land, sitting on "the mountain" (6:3), after the multiplication of loaves (6:4–15), he and his disciples are on the sea (6:16–21).[164] *Who?* Finally, Jesus and his disciples meet a crowd on the mountain (6:1–15) and in the synagogue at

---

[164] For a closer reading of the narrative elements in 6:1–21, see L. Th. Witkamp, "Some Specific Johannine Features in John 6:1–21," *JSNT* 40 (1990), 43–60.

Capernaum. The relocation of Jesus from high to low, dry to wet to dry, and stable to turbulent allows the narrator to show Jesus in masterful control in all venues.

John and Traditional Miracles. Whereas in the synoptics Jesus multiplied loaves, scholars cannot agree whether John's narrative depends on them or is an independent account.[165] All four Gospels similarly tell of meager resources (five loaves), which feed thousands; an oasis of grass in a semiarid place; Jesus' command that the disciples feed the crowd; the typical benediction by Jesus over the food ("took . . . blessed . . . broke . . . gave"); fragments gathered into twelve baskets; and Jesus walking on the turbulent sea to the disciples. Dependent or not, the author has nevertheless edited a distinctive story that metamorphoses into something more than a feeding miracle. First, unlike the synoptics, John's account locates the event at Passover, a feast of breads (6:4). Second, he notes that Jesus' "signs" trigger the crowds to follow Jesus (6:2), "signs" that we already know prove to be ambiguous or inadequate reasons for discipleship (2:23–25; 3:2; 5:1–15). Third, John's choreography reverses that of the synoptics. Here Jesus asks the disciples about feeding the crowds, whereas in the synoptics they come to Jesus and ask him to send the crowds away. Fourth, whereas in the synoptics Jesus commands the disciples "you give them something to eat" and they distribute the foods, here Jesus distributes the foods: "Jesus took the loaves . . . distributed them to those who were seated" (6:11). Thus Jesus completely controls the scene, from the time he sees the crowds to his command to gather the fragments. Fifth, in the synoptic version, no disciple is named or stands out, but here Philip declares the situation impossible (6:7) and Andrew comments on the meagerness of their resources (five loaves and two fish, 6:9). Sixth, in the synoptics, Jesus himself orderly dismisses the crowds, but John's version climaxes in chaos. Those who saw this "sign" acclaim Jesus as "a prophet," less a name that honors Jesus and more an opportunistic acclamation of him. For the crowds come to take Jesus by force and make him king (6:15), a gesture that ironically seems to honor Jesus even as it seeks to exercise power over him. The Johannine Jesus will never stand for such challenges.[166] Thus the major thrust of this view of John 6:1–16 focuses on the absolute control by Jesus of his situation. Jesus commands every aspect of it, either testing his disciples, distributing the foods himself, commanding the collection of the fragments, or refusing to be manipulated by the crowds. This "sign" produces nothing but many filled bellies, a fact not lost on Jesus (6:26).

Form of the Feeding. The multiplication of loaves, although not a healing miracle (5:1–9), nevertheless contains several formal elements previously identified

---

[165] On the similarities and differences between John's account and the synoptic accounts, see R. E. Brown, *Gospel According to John* (1966), 1.236–50. Erwin Johnston's "The John Version of the Feeding of the Five Thousand – An Independent Tradition?" *NTS* 8 (1962), 151–54, argues that the differences in the Johannine account point to an independent tradition that has strong claims to historicity.

[166] See C. H. Giblin, "Suggestion," *NTS* 26 (1980), 197–211. See the use of Giblin's article at 2:1–12.

as part of a typical miracle story. In place of "severity of disease," we hear of an impossible situation: massive crowds descending on Jesus. These are so large that Jesus asks "Where are we to buy bread for these people to eat?" (6:6). Moreover, two disciples articulate the severity of the problem for the reader. Philip notes that "Six months' wages would not buy enough bread for each of them to get a little" (6:7), which, of course, the disciples do not have anyway. Andrew indicates how severe the situation is when he mocks their meager resources: five loaves and two fish for five thousand people (6:9). Yes, the situation is severe. Second, in place of the "proof" of a healing, we learn that not only did all "eat their fill" but that a substantial surplus remained, namely twelve baskets of fragments (6:12–13). Thus a "severe" problem is solved, "proof" of which is given in the impressive surplus.

JOHN 6:16–21 – MYSTERIOUS PRESENCE

16 When evening came, his disciples went down to the sea,
17 got into a boat, and started across the sea to Capernaum. It was now dark, and Jesus had not yet come to them.
18 The sea became rough because a strong wind was blowing.
19 When they had rowed about three or four miles, they saw Jesus walking on the sea and coming near the boat, and they were terrified.
20 But he said to them, "It is I; do not be afraid."
21 Then they wanted to take him into the boat, and immediately the boat reached the land toward which they were going.

An Old Sea Story. All four Gospels narrate this story, and in such a way that two elements are emphasized, namely separation and reunion. First, Jesus and the disciples are dramatically separated, with Jesus alone on a mountain and the disciples in a boat on the sea. Yet they are mysteriously reunited hours later when Jesus intentionally comes to them, collapsing distance and difficulty. The storm so prominent in Mark and Matthew is reduced here to "a strong wind" (6:18), which reduces emphasis on this as a miracle of power but accentuates it as Jesus' reunion with the disciples.[167] More than the synoptics, John portrays the event as a theophany – that is, the revelation of a heavenly figure ("they were frightened") – not the "ghost" mentioned in Mark and Matthew. Unlike the synoptic accounts, the disciples are mute here, so that Jesus alone speaks: "It is I; do not be afraid" (6:20). It may be a small point, but in John "they wanted to

---

[167] Charles H. Giblin's "The Miraculous Crossing of the Sea (John 6:16–21)," *NTS* 29 (1983), 96–103, argues that this episode is not a sea rescue narrative, and so we should consider other functions, such as uniting disciples and master after separation. "Going away" and "coming back" are strong motifs also in John 14–16.

receive him into the boat" (6:21), "receive" being the same verb used in 1:12–13 to describe how some few became disciples. Thus we observe a reunion, not just a passing meeting. Hence, the union of master and disciple stands out as the key element, not the calming of a spirit-induced storm.

"I AM" or "I Am He"? Jesus speaks a word to the disciples that transforms them from "terrified" to "glad." He says *"ego eimi,"* which might be translated as "It's me" or "I AM." In the first case, he is not a ghost, as we find in the synoptic versions (Mark 6:49; Matt 14:26); he is "Jesus," and so "It's me" makes good sense. But later in the Gospel Jesus will use "I AM" as a distinct name that God gives him (John 8:24, 28, 58), which is not the evident meaning of Jesus' "It's me (*ego eimi*)" in 6:20.[168] Yet, given the author's penchant for double-meaning words and for terms that can be understood in both fleshly and spiritual modes, we should retain some flexibility in reading "It's me" or "I AM."[169] In this case, the elite inner circle of disciples alone would understand the reference and agree with it.

Mysterious Presence. Mark's narrative of the loaves and the walking on water are explicitly joined by the remark that "They did not understand about the loaves, but their hearts were hardened" (6:52). If the disciples understood the "loaves," then they would understand Jesus' mysterious presence with them. Shall we say "loaves" mean [Eucharistic] presence of Jesus? By sculpting the walking on the water as a manifestation of mysterious presence with the inner-circle disciples, the evangelist strongly suggests such a meaning, appreciated only by the elite insiders.

JOHN 6:22–29 – CHIPPING AWAY AT AMBIGUITY

22 The next day the crowd that had stayed on the other side of the sea saw that there had been only one boat there. They also saw that Jesus had not gotten into the boat with his disciples, but that his disciples had gone away alone.
23 Then some boats from Tiberias came near the place where they had eaten the bread after the Lord had given thanks.

---

[168] Some read 6:20 as "pure identification" and not as a revelatory formula; see C. K. Barrett, *Gospel According to St. John* (1978), 281. Others see it as a "borderline" case. See R. E. Brown, *Gospel According to John* (1966), 252; and John P. Heil, *Jesus Walking on the Sea: Meaning and Gospel Functions of Matt 14:22–33, Mark 6:45–52 and John 6:15b–21* (Rome: Biblical Institute Press, 1981), 79–80.
[169] On the double meaning of "I AM," see Catrin H. Williams, "'I Am' or 'I Am He'? Self-Declaratory Pronouncements in the Fourth Gospel and in Rabbinic Tradition," in Robert T. Fortna and Tom Thatcher, eds., *Jesus in the Johannine Tradition* (Louisville, KY: Westminster John Knox, 2001), 343–52. See similarly David M. Ball, *'I Am' in John's Gospel: Literary Function, Background and Theological Implications* (Sheffield: Sheffield Academic Press, 1996), 181–85, 255–57.

24 So when the crowd saw that neither Jesus nor his disciples were there, they themselves got into the boats and went to Capernaum looking for Jesus.

25 When they found him on the other side of the sea, they said to him, "Rabbi, when did you come here?"

26 Jesus answered them, "Very truly, I tell you, you are looking for me, not because you saw signs, but because you ate your fill of the loaves.

27 Do not work for the food that perishes, but for the food that endures for eternal life, which the Son of Man will give you. For it is on him that God the Father has set his seal."

28 Then they said to him, "What must we do to perform the works of God?"

29 Jesus answered them, "This is the work of God, that you believe in him whom he has sent."

Who Are These People? Why Does Jesus Treat Them This Way? By now, readers have learned to be suspicious of claims by others and have come to know that something is inadequate in the relationship of people who follow Jesus because of "signs" (6:2, 14). The crowd that earlier saw the multiplication of loaves now comes in search of Jesus, or so it seems. But is this an honest quest for him? From what we saw in 6:14–15, the crowd relates to him in a shameful and opportunistic manner. Although it *seems* laudable to "seek" Jesus,[170] "seeking" is one of those troublesome double-meaning words. Positively, it can mean seeking Jesus to become his disciple (1:39); praised are they who "seek" the will of God or the glory of God (5:30, 44). Mary, who "seeks" the body of Jesus, will find it (20:15). Negatively, many people "seek" Jesus; that is, to arrest him (7:30), stone him (10:39; 11:8), and kill him (7:1; 18:4–8). True, the Gospels tell us that "those who seek will find" (Matt 7:7; Luke 11:9), which at first seems to be the meaning of "seek" in 6:25. But this crowd is shrouded in ambiguity. Of them Jesus will shortly reveal, "You will seek me and you will not find me" (7:34, 36). Why, then, is Jesus treating these people in this manner?

Ambiguity. Readers know that Jesus has been made "judge" and has all judgment (5:22, 27). In ancient trials, the judge's chief action was to evaluate the testimony of witnesses about some matter. Moreover, we know that Jesus can read hearts and knows what is in them (2:25), something he manifested first with Nicodemus and then with the Samaritan woman; he knows who can be catechized and who cannot. Now a crowd "seeks" him, and their loyalty to Jesus is at best questionable because of their "sign" faith, their attempt to control Jesus, and now their search for material benefit. Are they genuine disciples? At

---

[170] Yet John Painter's *Quest for the Messiah* (1993), 177–79, 267–70, labels John 6 and many other episodes in the Fourth Gospel as "Quest Stories." In this he softens the sharpness of traditional pronouncement stories; hence "seeking" Jesus is a positive and praiseworthy action.

the end of the chapter, we will be told that "Jesus knew from the first who were the ones that did not believe, and who was the one that would betray him" (6:65). Jesus, then, even at the start of this story, fully knows what kind of people these are who seek him, but the reader does not. So we watch Jesus remove the veil of ambiguity by provoking them to speak and act in order to reveal the quality of their discipleship.

Witnesses under Fire. The forensic sharpness of the dialogue is best grasped when we read the exchange in terms of the dynamic of challenge and riposte (see the commentary on 3:2–12). The crowd that finds Jesus asks a *question*: "Rabbi, when did you come here?" (6:25). Remember that questions generally serve as aggressive, hostile weapons; moreover, when compared with labels just used by this group ("prophet" and "king"), "Rabbi" is a colorless and deflated title for Jesus (see Nicodemus' "Rabbi" in 3:2). This might imply that they are true disciples, who have "sought" and "found" Jesus and who acclaim him "Teacher," thus claiming some relationship with him. But Jesus *challenges* their claim by revealing the motives of their hearts (and stomachs): "You are looking for me . . . because you ate your fill of the loaves" (6:26). If they are disciples, then Jesus exhorts them to act like true disciples: "Do not work for the food that perishes, but for the food that endures for eternal life, which the Son of Man will give you. For it is on him that God the Father has set his seal" (6:27). First, there is a "food" that is not material and does not perish – this is what they should seek (see "water" in 4:13–14). Second, this food comes from "the Son of Man," whom God has authorized (who is no mere "Rabbi"). These claimants whom Jesus challenges offer the weakest of *ripostes*: "What must we do to perform the works of God?" (6:28). Again a question, but one that ignores what Jesus has just said about true "food" given by God's "sealed" agent. Their question in any other context might merit favorable consideration, but not here and now. Hence Jesus *challenges* them once more, in part answering them but forcing the issue of whether they can possibly be his disciples: "This is the work of God, that you believe in him whom he has sent" (6:29). Yes, he picks up their request to know what it is to "do the works of God," but he answers it with the same type of material that they have just ignored in 6:27–28, namely acknowledgment of Jesus as the Son of Man, who is "sealed" by God and "whom He has sent." Because they stand mute, we know that Jesus has revealed the ambiguity of their character and their claims. Their misunderstanding of his statements only confirms how similar they are to those of Nicodemus in 3:3–12 – earthly, unable to understand heavenly things, knowing Jesus only on the most superficial level. Their "seeking," then, is shallow and even duplicitous. They can never be disciples.

Representative Characters. Although we do not know this crowd completely, we know thus far that their faith in Jesus is shallow and insincere because it is not even "sign faith" but a search for material benefaction (6:25–26, see also v.15). As long as Jesus feeds them loaves of bread, they are loyal, but when he speaks of the

Bread of Life (6:30–59), they prove to be pseudo-believers. The episode will end with many of these same people walking away (6:60–65), a rejection balanced by the fragile loyalty of the disciples (6:66–71).[171] They may "seek" him and travel to find him, but they cannot in any meaningful sense be called his "disciples."

JOHN 6:30–58 – HE GAVE THEM BREAD FROM HEAVEN TO EAT

30 So they said to him, "What sign are you going to give us then, so that we may see it and believe you? What work are you performing?

31 Our ancestors ate the manna in the wilderness; as it is written, 'He gave them bread from heaven to eat.'"

32 Then Jesus said to them, "Very truly, I tell you, it was not Moses who gave you the bread from heaven, but it is my Father who gives you the true bread from heaven.

33 For the bread of God is that which comes down from heaven and gives life to the world."

34 They said to him, "Sir, give us this bread always."

35 Jesus said to them, "I am the bread of life. Whoever comes to me will never be hungry, and whoever believes in me will never be thirsty.

36 But I said to you that you have seen me and yet do not believe.

37 Everything that the Father gives me will come to me, and anyone who comes to me I will never drive away;

38 for I have come down from heaven, not to do my own will, but the will of him who sent me.

39 And this is the will of him who sent me, that I should lose nothing of all that he has given me, but raise it up on the last day.

40 This is indeed the will of my Father, that all who see the Son and believe in him may have eternal life; and I will raise them up on the last day."

41 Then the Jews began to complain about him because he said, "I am the bread that came down from heaven."

42 They were saying, "Is not this Jesus, the son of Joseph, whose father and mother we know? How can he now say, 'I have come down from heaven'?"

43 Jesus answered them, "Do not complain among yourselves.

44 No one can come to me unless drawn by the Father who sent me; and I will raise that person up on the last day.

45 It is written in the prophets, 'And they shall all be taught by God.' Everyone who has heard and learned from the Father comes to me.

46 Not that anyone has seen the Father except the one who is from God; he has seen the Father.

---

171 See Peder Borgen, "John 6: Tradition, Interpretation and Composition," in Martinus de Boer, ed., *From Jesus to John: Essays on Jesus and New Testament Christology in Honour of Marinus de Jonge* (Sheffield: JSOT Press, 1993), 268–91.

47 Very truly, I tell you, whoever believes has eternal life.

48 I am the bread of life.

49 Your ancestors ate the manna in the wilderness, and they died.

50 This is the bread that comes down from heaven, so that one may eat of it and not die.

51 I am the living bread that came down from heaven. Whoever eats of this bread will live forever; and the bread that I will give for the life of the world is my flesh."

52 The Jews then disputed among themselves, saying, "How can this man give us his flesh to eat?"

53 So Jesus said to them, "Very truly, I tell you, unless you eat the flesh of the Son of Man and drink his blood, you have no life in you.

54 Those who eat my flesh and drink my blood have eternal life, and I will raise them up on the last day;

55 for my flesh is true food and my blood is true drink.

56 Those who eat my flesh and drink my blood abide in me, and I in them.

57 Just as the living Father sent me, and I live because of the Father, so whoever eats me will live because of me.

58 This is the bread that came down from heaven, not like that which your ancestors ate, and they died. But the one who eats this bread will live forever."

Conflict Continued. The *challenge/riposte* exchange observed in 6:26–29 continues, with the "seekers" now putting Jesus on the spot by demanding a sign: "What sign are you going to give us, then, so that we may see it and believe you? What work are you performing? (6:30; see also 2:18). Their remark again challenges Jesus by means of a hostile question that makes improper demands of him.[172] Similarly, the *challenge* here demands that before they believe in Jesus, he must satisfy their demands and pass their test. Just as this crowd sought "with force to make him king," now they seek to force Jesus to do what they want. Never in this Gospel does such a thing succeed; on the contrary, when challenged in this way, Jesus makes a "negative response" to a request until he becomes the in-charge, focal person who is not manipulated or taken for granted. Yet, the crowd is not finished challenging him, for they next make claims for the worth of Moses, manna, and the Exodus. The challenge, then, inaugurates a comparison between Passover matters and Jesus' actions. Comparisons functioned aggressively in antiquity to elevate one person or thing over another.[173] Hence, the crowd claims that their bread is superior to that of Jesus when they cite the Scripture, "He gave them bread from heaven to eat" (6:31). Jesus, of course, must respond.

---

[172] In the synoptic Gospels, Jesus labels those seeking signs as a "wicked and adulterous generation" (see Matt 12:38–39; 16:4; Mark 8:11–12; Luke 11:29).

[173] See Peter Marshall, *Enmity at Corinth: Social Conventions in Paul's Relations with the Corinthians* (Tübingen: Mohr, 1987), 53–55, 259–393; and David H. J. Larmour, "Making Parallels: *Synkrisis* and Plutarch's 'Themistocles and Camillus,'" *ANRW* II. 33.6., 4154–4200.

Topic Statement and Development. Peder Borgen argues that 6:31 is a Scriptural text that is treated in a midrashic manner in the rest of the discourse.[174] He identifies Exodus 16 as the source of the text[175] for three reasons. (1) Typically, homiletic traditions take a text from the Pentateuch and supplement it with a subordinate quotation from the Prophets or the Writings (Isa 54:13 in John 6:45). (2) Exodus 16:15 provides a solid basis for the philological exegesis of the text (6:31) in the next two verses. (3) Only Exodus 16 provides a context that includes both the words about the bread in John 6:31, 32–51 and the "murmuring" in 6:41–43.[176] Arguing that 6:31–59 should be taken as a *homily*, Borgen then itemizes the typical midrashic way of arguing in it, such as (1) "contrast" ("not . . . but"); (2) "philological exegesis" ("not 'gave' but 'gives'"; "not 'Moses' but 'my Father'"; read "you" not "them"); and (3) "supplemental qualification" ("the 'true' bread").[177] Although Borgen established the rules for reading this discourse in terms of midrashic argumentation and development, his assertion that 6:31–59 is a "homily" is much debated.[178]

As we have seen, Johannine dialogues are frequently structured in terms of a topic statement followed by development of each item. The topic statement here contains six items (6:31), each subsequently interpreted in a manner unique to the ideology of the Johannine community. As with Nicodemus (3:2), the crowds deliver the topic statement that embodies their claim: "He gave them bread from heaven to eat" (6:31). It contains six terms to be debated in the following discourse: "he," "gave," "them," "bread," "from heaven," and "to eat." Jesus immediately *challenges* this *claim*:

	1	2	3	4	5	6
Claim:	He	gave	them	bread	from heaven	to eat
Challenge:	It was not Moses who	gave	you	the bread	from heaven,	
	but it is my Father who	gives	you	the true bread	from heaven	

---

[174] Peder Borgen, *Bread from Heaven: An Exegetical Study of the Concept of Manna in the Gospel of John and the Writings of Philo* (Leiden: Brill, 1965), 59–98; and his "Observations on the Midrashic Character of John 6," *ZNW* 54 (1963), 232–40.

[175] Other scholars argue that Psalm 78:24 is the better source for 6:32. See M. J. Menken, "The Provenance and Meaning of the Old Testament Quotation of John 6:31," *NovT* 30 (1988), 39–56; and G. Geiger, "Aufruf an Rückkehre: Zum Sinn des Zitats von Ps 78,24b in Joh 6,31," *Biblica* 65 (1984), 449–64.

[176] P. Borgen, *Bread from Heaven* (1965), 40–42.

[177] P. Borgen, *Bread from Heaven* (1965), 61–68.

[178] Peder Borgen, "Bread from Heaven: Aspects of Debates on Expository Method and Form," in his *Philo, John and Paul: New Perspectives on Judaism and Early Christianity* (Atlanta: Scholars Press, 1987), 131–44. See also Lawrence Wills, "The Form of the Sermon in Hellenistic Judaism and Early Christianity," *HTR* 77 (1984), 277–99; and C. Clifton Black, "The Rhetorical Form of the Hellenistic Jewish and Early Christian Sermon: A Response to Lawrence Wills," *HTR* 81 (1988), 1–18.

The rhetoric of the discourse oscillates between *claim* and *challenge*, indicating a polemical, hostile event. Thus honor is also at stake, a limited good, over which the dramatis personae will battle. After challenging their claim, Jesus develops his interpretation of each of the six terms in the statement, giving each a sectarian meaning that separates disciples from the synagogue. He does not develop them in the order we find them in 6:31, but the development nevertheless is systematic and clear.

"Bread." The first term developed is "bread": "For the bread of God is that which comes down from heaven and gives life to the world." . . . "Sir, give us this bread always." . . . "I am the bread of life. Whoever comes to me will never be hungry . . . never be thirsty" (6:33–35; see also 4:14–15). Jesus' initial remark about the "bread of God which comes down from heaven" contains ambiguity, for it could just as easily be understood as manna in the desert for literal-minded people. But when Jesus claims that "*I am* the bread of life," all ambiguity vanishes. Whether "bread" is a metaphor for teaching or an edible substance, Jesus is exclusively identified with it. "Bread," therefore, means Jesus himself. As with all "I am + predicate" statements in the Gospel, something is affirmed (Jesus is the only, unique item) and something denied (manna is *not*).

"Them." The crowds claimed that "he gave *them* bread from heaven," referring to Moses' benefaction to Israel's ancestors in the past. But Jesus interprets "them" as "you," his present audience, not past ancestors. This also brings the issue of faith or acknowledgment to the fore, which can only occur in the here-and-now: "But I said to 'you' that 'you' have seen me and yet do not believe. Everything that the Father gives me will come to me" (6:36–37). Yet, "them" is even more narrowly defined: not ancestors or current audience ("you") but "believers." God only gives faithful people the bread of life. Hence, if "they" are not coming to Jesus, it must be because God is not giving them to him. "Drive away" is another Johannine double-meaning word, for it is not Jesus who drives anyone away but rather the synagogue that drives away Jesus' disciples (9:22; 12:42; 16:1–2). God would give "you" bread, but because "you" challenge his agent, "you" do not receive his bread.

"He" (Not Moses, but My Father). Jesus counters that "he" in their scriptural claim is "not Moses but my Father who gives you the true bread" (6:32). Moreover, this "he" is the one whose will Jesus has come to do: " . . . not to do my own will, but the will of him who sent me." Thus the true "He" (i.e., "My Father") wills that "Bread" (i.e., Jesus) come down and give life. But to whom? "This is indeed the will of my Father, that all who see the Son and believe in him may have eternal life" (6:40). The will of "my Father," then, is that Jesus be honored and acknowledged (see 5:24; 6:29), which has been the will of God from the Gospel's beginning (1:12–13; see also 17:3). Thereby people become

"children of God," who then becomes "Father" to them. "My Father," then, is the sole patron and benefactor; Moses was but an intermediary.

"From Heaven or from Nazareth." When they "murmur," John's audience reenacts Israel's hostile challenge to Moses and/or God (Exod 16:2, 8; Num 11:1; Ps 78:21–22). "Murmuring" begins this part of the discourse (6:41) and concludes it (6:43), thus bracketing the challenging and ridiculing of Jesus' claim that he has "come down from heaven" (6:33). The crowd mocks Jesus' own words: "Is not this Jesus, the son of Joseph, whose father and mother we know? How can he now say, 'I have come down from heaven'?" (6:42).[179] Their challenge has two parts: "my Father," heavenly or earthly?; and "from heaven," descending from or merely authorized by heaven? Like Nicodemus, who could only understand Jesus' words in a material, literal fashion, this crowd concludes that "my Father" must refer to the only father of Jesus that they know of, his earthly one, "son of Joseph whose father we know" (6:42), an undistinguished peasant. But whence comes Jesus? From a material, earthly family? Only insiders know Jesus' true "whence," that he descends from God's heart, and so they know the secret that "from heaven" means just that. At the feast of Booths, we will observe a clever debate over "whence" Jesus comes and "whither" he goes (7:27–28); indeed the Gospel has already toyed with the double meaning of these terms (2:9; 3:8)[180] and told the audience the truth about Jesus' heavenliness (1:1–18; 3:13). The crowd's mockery signals that they are most assuredly not disciples but hostile outsiders.

"Not Gave, but Gives." Earlier Jesus corrected the crowd's claim that "[Moses] gave." For in truth, "my Father in heaven 'gives' you true bread." Moreover, God's giving is a present event ("gives"), not a past one ("gave"). Those who understand Johannine time recognize the importance of Jesus' telling of present time. Then the author plays with multiple meanings of the word "give": The bread of God "gives" life to the world (6:33); "All whom the Father 'gives' me come to me (6:37); and Jesus will lose nothing of all that God "has given" him (6:39). Thus "gives" describes both God's benefaction and the recruitment of others for Jesus.

In 6:44–46, we find a fuller discussion of "gives," but in terms of God's election of Jesus' disciples. How does one become a disciple? "No one can come to

---

[179] Encomia and *bioi* in antiquity begin by noting gender, generation, and geography; noble people necessarily come from noble *poleis* (not Nazareth) and from noble families and parents (not peasant laborers), but, of course, the crowd does not know that Jesus' geography is the heavenly world and that God is his Father. See B. J. Malina and J. H. Neyrey, *Portraits of Paul* (1996), 19–34; and J. H. Neyrey, *Honor and Shame* (1998), 90–105.

[180] See J. H. Neyrey, "Territoriality," *BTB* 32 (2002), 66–68.

me unless *drawn by the Father*" (6:44). Moreover, divine enlightenment alone qualifies one for discipleship: "Everyone who has heard and learned from the Father comes to me" (6:45). Thus, if some do not hear and do not learn what Jesus is saying, then they are not being taught by God and so are not "drawn" by the Father or "given" anything. God's "giving" is centered in Jesus, for he alone knows God: "Not that anyone has seen the Father except the one who is from God; he has seen the Father" (6:46; see also 1:18; 3:13). Thus access to God's "giving" is exclusively through Jesus.

"To Eat" (First Meaning: "Believe"). Just as "drink" had a double meaning in the discourse in Samaria (4:10–15), as did "food" in the conversation with the disciples (4:31–34), so, too, "eat" has multiple meanings. When Jesus repeats that he is the "bread of life" (6:48; see also 6:35), the "living bread" (6:51) that one must "eat" (6:50) to have life, "eating" means "believing." "Whoever *believes* has eternal life" (6:47) balances "whoever *eats* of this living bread will live forever" (6:51). Just as "seeing is believing," so, too, is "eating."

Some interpreters liken Jesus, the Logos of God, to Lady Wisdom, who prepares a banquet to feed her followers (see Prov 9:1–9 and Sir 24:19–22). In this context, "bread" means teaching or wisdom, and "eat" means learning or study. So in 6:47–51 one might understand the discourse to be a matter of correct teaching, which would give insight into the contrast made in 6:49–50. "Your ancestors ate the manna in the wilderness, and they died. This is the bread that comes down from heaven, so that one may eat of it and not die." Moses has been associated in 1:17 with law or Torah, in 3:14 with salvation, in 5:45–46 with Scripture, and in 6:31 with bread, but this Gospel claims that Moses' gift is inferior to that of Jesus. Jesus sees, knows, and reveals what Moses did not know and so did not reveal. If "bread" can be teaching, then "eating" means believing.

"To Eat" (Second Meaning: "to consume food"). Jesus makes a bold statement, "The bread that I will give for the life of the world is my flesh" (6:51), which is partly misunderstood. The crowd challenges Jesus' claim and mocks him: "How can this man give us his flesh to eat?" (6:52). In the ears of those who thus far did not hear Jesus' words at all, misheard them, or mocked them, his remark sounds like a terrible uncleanness, namely consuming human flesh. But, as usual, that would be a fatal misunderstanding of Jesus' demand. He reasserts that food and drink will truly be ingested, which should be interpreted as consumption of eucharistic foods. Thus, we understand that the author now speaks of genuine food that is consumed: "for my flesh is true food and my blood is true drink" (6:55). But it is not literal flesh and blood of which Jesus speaks but substances that nevertheless are both chewed and drunk, as are bread and wine at a meal.

Jesus next demands that disciples participate in this group ritual action: "Unless you eat the flesh of the Son of Man and drink his blood, you have no life in you" (6:53). The term "unless" contains a demand, paralleling other "unless" statements used regarding birth from above and by water (3:3, 5), special belief (8:24), washing by Jesus (13:8), and abiding in the vine (15:4). In these "unless" demands, one is either transformed in status or confirmed in membership.[181] Meals, especially sacred or sacrificial ones, confirm one's membership in a certain group as well as one's role and status there.[182] The ceremonial function of consuming sacred foods is best explained when Jesus declares a kind of indwelling: "Those who eat my flesh and drink my blood abide in me, and I in them. Just as the living Father sent me, and I live because of the Father, so whoever eats me will live because of me" (6:56–57). We saw earlier that "abide" does not refer to geographical space but to membership in the circle of the disciples. Thus those who consume the eucharistic foods "abide in Jesus" and he "abides in them." "Having life" and "living" likewise refer to relationships: Jesus is the "living bread" and "those who eat my flesh and drink my blood have eternal life." Again in terms of the symbolic meaning of foods, "you are what you eat." Hence, if one consumes life, then one has life and becomes life. The relationship aspect of this ceremonial eating is emphasized by Jesus' claim of eternal loyalty to his consuming disciples: "I will raise them up on the last day" (6:54).[183]

In conclusion, we see that the rhetorical character of the conversation in 6:31–59 is one of claim, challenge, and riposte. Comparison and contrast serve as the rhythm of the argument. "It was not Moses who gave you the bread from heaven, but it is my Father who gives you the true bread from heaven" (6:32). Similarly, "breads" are contrasted, which lead either to death or to life (6:49–50). Finally, the contest ends with another contrast: "This is the bread that came down from heaven, not like that which your ancestors ate, and they died. But the one who eats this bread will live forever" (6:58). If the Gospel audience was confused about the true nature of the crowds who "sought" and "found" Jesus earlier, the drama now reveals how far they are from discipleship; they reject what Jesus says and mock him. They are positioned in the story to side with Moses, the ancestors, and the bread that led to death.

Spiritual or Sacramental Food? Eating and drinking are ritual actions, so one wonders if and to what extent the author speaks of "sacraments." Two questions

---

181 Jerome H. Neyrey, "Footwashing" in *Social World of the First Christians* (1995), 202–6.
182 Jerome H. Neyrey, "Ceremonies in Luke-Acts: The Case of Meals and Table-Fellowship," in his *The Social World of Luke-Acts* (Peabody, MA: Hendrickson, 1991), 362–63, 374–75.
183 One of the best recent treatments of "flesh and blood" is that of Maarten J. Menken, "John 6:51–58: Eucharist or Christology," in R. Alan Culpepper, ed., *Critical Readings of John 6* (Leiden: Brill, 1997), 189–201.

will guide this inquiry: (1) *What* is being talked about? and (2) *When* might 6:51–58 be taken as a ceremony?

A CLOSER LOOK – "SACRAMENTS"

"Sacramentum" was the oath of loyalty taken by Roman soldiers to the emperor but became the designation of rites and ceremonies in the early Western church. Scholarship on the Fourth Gospel might be said to split into two camps, the pro-sacramentalists and the anti-sacramentalists.[184] The former group contains scholars who either find numerous examples of many sacraments or who accept basically two, namely baptism and Eucharist, which occur with some frequency in the Gospel. In general, these scholars are comfortable with a highly symbolic view of the Gospel, naturally appreciating the double meanings of Johannine words and gestures and thus not taking John on the literal level as Nicodemus did. In contrast, scholars such as Rudolf Bultmann[185] argued that the Gospel was anti-sacramental. Although he admitted 3:5, 6:51–58, and 19:34, he claimed that these were added to the Gospel much later by a church redactor who thus tried to make the Gospel conform to the others and their practices. This last point has had the greatest influence because it invites consideration of the Gospel as a developing document whose editors were at various times either non-sacramental or pro-sacramental. The issue thus becomes when was it pro- and when anti-sacramental.[186]

What? John knows of two basic rites, a status-transformation entrance ritual (3:3–5, 22) and a ceremony confirming one's belonging, both of them eating events (see chapters 6 and 13). But it was not until centuries later that these were labeled "sacraments." The earliest Christians had no theological terminology to label their transformation rituals or ceremonies, although they clearly knew of such rites. Jesus and his disciples practiced "baptism"; that is, an entrance ritual that replaced the covenant entrance rite of circumcision (Matt 28:19; John 3:22; 4:1–2). They also celebrated a sacred meal rooted in Jesus' practice (1 Cor 11:24; Mark 14:22–25), which replaced the Passover meal. Transformations and ceremonies yes, but not "sacraments."[187]

---

[184] See Raymond E. Brown, "The Johannine Sacramentary," in his *New Testament Essays* (Milwaukee, WI: Bruce, 1965), 51–76.

[185] Rudolf Bultmann, *Theology of the New Testament* (London: SCM Press, 1955), 2.70–92.

[186] For a survey of this, see Francis J. Moloney, "When Is John Talking about Sacraments?" *AusBR* 30 (1982), 10–33.

[187] Some scholars suggest a maximal list of possible sacraments, including matrimony (2:1–12); anointing of the sick (12:1–8); penance (20:23); baptism (1:31–33; 4:1–15; 5:1–9; 6:22–24; 7:38; 9:1–12; 13:5–11); Eucharist (2:1–12; 4:31–34; 6:1–58; 15:1–11; 21:9–14); and baptism and Eucharist (19:34); see R. E. Brown, *New Testament Essays* (1965), 75–76.

When? All agree that this Gospel went through stages of development, including a time when ceremonies and transformations were valued and practiced and a time when they were not; the argument focuses on the chronological order of these stages.

Ideological Development. Bultmann accepted three "sacramental" passages in the earliest stages of the Gospel (3:5; 6:51 c–58; 19:34), but he assessed the mature Gospel as anti-sacramental. If, he claims, other ritual practices show up in the latest stages of the Gospel's development, these function to suppress or discipline the earlier phenomena of personalized illumination. Others have argued that material rituals were part of an anti-docetic program that sought to undermine the utterly heavenly view of Jesus and discipleship.[188]

Historical Development. Raymond Brown and others offer a more historical and less ideological sketch of the Gospel's development and link the value or disvalue of rituals to the conflict between disciples and synagogue from which the group exited.[189]

Church Conditioning. Still others seem to stand on positions developed in later church history (i.e., evangelical vs. catholic),[190] thus attacking or defending sacraments. Let us read on, for the Gospel offers data for consideration.

JOHN 6:59–65 – TURNING AWAY, DROPPING OUT

59 He said these things while he was teaching in the synagogue at Capernaum.
60 When many of his disciples heard it, they said, "This teaching is difficult; who can accept it?"
61 But Jesus, being aware that his disciples were complaining about it, said to them, "Does this offend you?
62 Then what if you were to see the Son of Man ascending to where he was before?
63 It is the spirit that gives life; the flesh is useless. The words that I have spoken to you are spirit and life.
64 But among you there are some who do not believe." For Jesus knew from the first who were the ones that did not believe, and who was the one that would betray him.

---

[188] Oscar Cullmann, *The Johannine Circle* (Philadelphia: Westminster, 1976); and E. C. Hoskyns, *The Fourth Gospel* (London: Faber and Faber, 1950).
[189] R. E. Brown, *Community of the Beloved Disciple* (1979), 25–92. See also Kikuo Matsunaga, "Is John's Gospel Anti-Sacramental? A New Solution in the Light of the Evangelist's Milieu," *NTS* 27 (1981), 516–24.
[190] James D. G. Dunn, "John VI – A Eucharistic Discourse?" *NTS* 17 (1971), 328–38; and G. H. C. MacGregor, "The Eucharist in the Fourth Gospel," *NTS* 9 (1962), 111–19.

65 And he said, "For this reason I have told you that no one can come to me unless it is granted by the Father."

Crisis. The previous challenge/riposte exchange took place in a "synagogue at Capernaum" (6:59), a traditional place of worship and study. In addition to members of the synagogue, some of "his disciples" eventually reject Jesus' claims and teaching. In what seems to be a pun on the "bread" motif, they say, "this teaching is 'stale'" and therefore hard to chew and eat (6:60). This hardly surprises Jesus, because he reads hearts and knows what is in a person (2:23–25). Hence the narrator tells us that he was "aware that his disciples were complaining" (6:61) and knew that "among you there are some who do not believe" (6:64). His acute knowledge of dropouts and traitors serves an important apologetic function in the narrative because nothing happens that Jesus does not already know, plan for, and voluntarily accept. "For Jesus knew from the first who were the ones that did not believe, and who was the one that would betray him" (6:65). Even in a crisis,[191] he is totally in charge.

Dropouts. The narrator labels the people in 6:60 as "disciples," which implies that they had some previous relationship with Jesus, which includes acknowledgment of his role and status, acceptance of his teaching, and possibly shared meals. They would seem to have fulfilled a host of "unless" demands for status transformation and ceremonial confirmation of that status. But they leave abruptly, which creates a particular crisis. If indeed they were "born from above" and "ate the living bread," then they had "entered the kingdom of God" and now "have life in themselves . . . and will live forever." But when they "drop out" of the group, can their status transformation and the ceremonial confirmation have genuinely achieved the functions claimed for them? Can anyone trust the "unless" demands as firm criteria for true membership?[192]

Stock Crash. If dropouts cause a crisis in the reliability of the "unless" demands of Jesus, the result is like a crash in our financial markets. What worth, if any, can now be attached to "birth from above" or "eating the flesh of the Son of Man"? Now Jesus tells them: "It is the spirit that gives life; the flesh is useless. The words that I have spoken to you are spirit and life" (6:63). This unqualified and

---

[191] Readers are referred to a study of the various crises faced by the Johannine community as reflected in John 6; see Paul N. Anderson, "The *Sitz im Leben* of the Johannine Bread of Life Discourse and Its Evolving Context," in R. Alan Culpepper, ed., *Critical Readings of John 6* (Leiden: Brill, 1997) 24–50.

[192] On the phenomenon of "ambiguity," see Jerome H. Neyrey, "Deception, Ambiguity, and Revelation: Matthew's Judgmental Scenes in Social-Science Perspective," in Alan Avery-Peck, Daniel Harrington, and Jacob Neusner, eds., *When Judaism and Christianity Began* (Leiden: Brill, 2004), 199–230; and his "The Sociology of Secrecy and the Fourth Gospel," in Fernando Segovia, ed., *What Is John? Volume II: Literary and Social Readings of the Fourth Gospel* (Atlanta: Scholars Press, 1998), 96–109.

absolute devaluation of material things ("the flesh is useless") covers the "signs" that have become problematic for faith as well as the rites and ceremonies that transform and confirm membership. In contrast, only "spirit gives life," which is a gift from heaven bestowed by God on select people (see 6:37, 44–46). This "spirit," moreover, is not attached to any rite but linked with special knowledge and teaching: "The words that I have spoken to you are spirit and life" (6:63). Those "disciples," then, who did not accept Jesus' words, lacked spirit and life; it does not matter if they accepted "unless" demands, for they were never drawn by God to become true disciples. With the crash in worth of rituals and ceremonies, a new currency emerges that only a few elite can access.

What Is the Value in Jesus' Becoming Flesh? Earlier in the narrative, Jesus pitched his tent among us and "became flesh" (1:14). His various "signs" gave value and worth to simple things such as water (2:7–10; 4:7–14). As long as the narrative was open to recruitment and disciple-making, the coming of Jesus into the world meant salvation for it (3:16). The earth and material things were places and things worthy of Jesus' attention. But in 6:60–65, even as we learn of the collapsing value of signs, transformation rituals, and ceremonies that give value to material things, Jesus raises the bar about his person and performance: "Does this offend you? Then what if you were to see the Son of Man ascending to where he was before?" (6:62).[193] If his teaching thus far was offensive or "stale," how much more will be the proclamation that this Son of Man will return whence he came, namely the heart of the Father (1:18). Jesus says that this material world is filled with nonperceiving, hostile people; as a spiritual, heavenly person he is not at home here but frustrated with its obtuseness. He is an alien in an alien land. What, then, of the success of him who pitched his tent here? As the prologue said, "his own received him not." Now alleged disciples prove that, despite all contact with Jesus, they do not believe. Criteria for authentic membership must be found elsewhere.

JOHN 6:66–71 – SCHISM, INTERNAL CHAOS

66 Because of this many of his disciples turned back and no longer went about with him.

67 So Jesus asked the twelve, "Do you also wish to go away?"

68 Simon Peter answered him, "Lord, to whom can we go? You have the words of eternal life.

69 We have come to believe and know that you are the Holy One of God."

---

[193] This "ascent," of course, belongs with the "descent" of the bread come down from heaven. See W. A. Meeks, "The Man from Heaven in Johannine Sectarianism," *JBL* 91 (1972), 59.

70 Jesus answered them, "Did I not choose you, the twelve? Yet one of you is a devil."

71 He was speaking of Judas son of Simon Iscariot, for he, though one of the twelve, was going to betray him.

Schism. Often the evangelist tells us that the crowds discussing and evaluating Jesus experienced a "schism"; that is, were "divided" (7:43; 9:16; 10:19). By their particular stand toward Jesus and his teaching, some come into the light, whereas others turn away from it. Thus the Gospel describes them as judging themselves (3:17–21). The judgment they render is the judgment they will receive. No other Gospel describes so many "schisms" about Jesus, which suggests that great emphasis is placed on public acknowledgment of Jesus as a criterion for elite membership. Remember, those who come to Jesus at night (3:1–2) are ambiguous, if not weak, characters.

Challenge and Riposte to the End. The rhetoric here suggests continued challenging, even with the seemingly loyal disciples. Jesus questions them, which we generally accept as a challenging mode of speech. He is not searching for information because the author tells us that Jesus "knew from the first who were the ones that did not believe, and who was the one that would betray him" (6:64). The question serves another, very aggressive purpose: "Do you also wish to go away?" (6:67). Peter answers Jesus' question with a question, "Lord, to whom can we go? You have the words of eternal life" (6:68), thus fending off Jesus' challenge. Jesus responds with another question, "Did I not choose you, the twelve? Yet one of you is a devil" (6:70), this time challenging the disguised traitor with knowledge of his malice (6:71). No response from Judas is recorded, and thus the challenge goes unanswered. The point is that whereas some "disciples" dropped out of Jesus' company and walked away, thus shaming him (6:60–65) so Jesus aggressively confronts the remainder with a test of loyalty (6:66–71). The circle of disciples, then, is stricken with rejection, lukewarmness, and deception. The mode of discourse is painfully one of challenge and riposte.

Caesarea Philippi? The synoptics describe how Peter delivers a rich confession of Jesus' honor, role, and status at Caesarea Philippi, which indicates the highwater mark of Jesus' successful recruitment in Galilee (Mark 8:27–30; Matt 16:13–20; Luke 9:18–21). Matthew's version even states that Peter received a unique heavenly revelation as the basis for his remark (Matt 16:16). Peter, who speaks for the group, first reports the favorable evaluation by the crowds that Jesus is a prophet, but then speaks about Jesus as did no one else in Matthew, honoring Jesus as "the Christ (of God)." This Gospel locates the current episode in the synagogue at Capernaum, not the Hellenistic city of Caesarea Philippi; the context here is not the synoptic high-water mark of success but a hostile mitosis of the group, dropouts walking away while the loyalty of the rest is tested. So

Peter's remarks here seem lukewarm and unenthusiastic: "We have come to believe and know that you are the Holy One of God" (6:69).

Holy One of God. If not acknowledgment that Jesus is "the Christ," what does "Holy One of God" mean? Basically, Peter admits that Jesus is God's agent, for the background of "holy one" in the Scriptures refers to a person consecrated to God; that is, "set apart" for holy tasks.[194] Peter's remark seems pale when compared with designation of Jesus as "prophet" and "king" in 6:14–15. Moreover, it is far from the mark set by Jesus when he spoke of himself as "Son of Man," who descends from heaven (3:13) and reascends there (6:62). Similarly, Peter's remark that Jesus has "words of eternal life," although echoing what Jesus said in 6:63, does not express itself in a confession or in loyalty. It acknowledges Jesus as the agent of God who is consecrated (6:27; 10:36), but by no means recognizes Jesus' role and status any higher than Nicodemus' statement in 3:2.

Peter. In the grammar of "representative characters," how should we think about Peter?[195] This is but the second time that he stands out from the pack. When recruited, he was not the first to attach himself to Jesus; rather, his brother Andrew brought him to Jesus (1:40). Because chronology in antiquity gave greater importance to what was first in time, it seems like a slight for Peter to be called second. Moreover, Andrew seems to play a larger role than Peter in the narrative: in the multiplication of the foods (6:8) and as the mediator who brings "the Greeks" to Jesus in 12:22. Peter, of course, shows up badly when his feet are washed, "not knowing" what Jesus is doing and rebuffing his master (13:4–9). We pass over in silence his boast of loyalty to Jesus and subsequent denial of him (13:36–38; 18:17–18, 25–27). He is slower than the elite Beloved Disciple, both in running to the tomb and then in grasping its meaning. Even when fishing, he does not recognize Jesus (21:4) and needs to be told it is he. In this pattern of character development, Peter represents a disciple who is unenlightened and cowardly; surprisingly, in a narrative where such people are regularly dismissed as inadequate, Peter remains to be groomed by Jesus to be a noble shepherd, even if not a wise one.[196]

---

[194] R. E. Brown, *Gospel According to John* (1966), 1.298. On agency, see W. R. Domeris, "The Confession of Peter According to John 6:69," *TynB* 44 (1993), 155–67. However, H. L. N. Joubert, "'The Holy One of God' (John 6:69)," *Neotestamentica* 2 (1968), 57–69, argues for an exalted meaning to this title that includes King, Son of Man, Suffering Servant, and Son of God.

[195] On Peter as a representative or symbolic character, see Raymond F. Collins, "The Representative Figures of the Fourth Gospel – II," *Downside Review* 95 (1976), 126–29. See also A. H. Maynard, "The Role of Peter in the Fourth Gospel," *NTS* 30 (1984), 531–47; and Colleen M. Conway, *Men and Women in the Fourth Gospel: Gender and Johannine Characters* (Atlanta: Scholars Press, 1999), 163–77.

[196] See P. N. Anderson, "*Sitz im Leben*," in *Critical Readings of John 6* (1997), 50–57.

JOHN 7:1–9 – SO MUCH FOR BLOOD RELATIVES!

1 After this Jesus went about in Galilee. He did not wish to go about in Judea because the Jews were looking for an opportunity to kill him.

2 Now the Jewish festival of Booths was near.

3 So his brothers said to him, "Leave here and go to Judea so that your disciples also may see the works you are doing;

4 for no one who wants to be widely known acts in secret. If you do these things, show yourself to the world."

5 (For not even his brothers believed in him.)

6 Jesus said to them, "My time has not yet come, but your time is always here.

7 The world cannot hate you, but it hates me because I testify against it that its works are evil.

8 Go to the festival yourselves. I am not going to this festival, for my time has not yet fully come."

9 After saying this, he remained in Galilee.

Where? When? and Why? We hear that, "After this, Jesus went about in Galilee; he would not go about in Judea, because the Jews sought to kill him" (7:1). Thus we link this with the forensic controversy during an unnamed feast in John 5. Despite putting Jesus on trial then, his adversaries could not come to a verdict or a sentence. That trial, then, resurfaces when Jesus returns to Jerusalem on the occasion of the pilgrimage feast of Booths.[197] *When?* The events of Chapters 7 and 8 occur during the feast of Booths, which comprises a seven-day festival with a climactic final day. *Why?* After "the feast of Booths" was announced (7:2–3), the brothers of Jesus urged him, "Leave here and go to Judea." Why? To gain fame and glory, especially their own.

The Feast and the Narrative: Days of the Feast. After Jesus refuses to participate in the feast (7:3–9), he misses the opening festivities. But he makes a grand entrance in the Temple "about the middle of the feast" (7:14), and hostilities begin that endure through "the last day of the feast, the great day" (7:37). The narrative glue, then, is the chronological sequence of the events of the feast of Booths.[198]

---

[197] On the link between John 5 and 7, see R. E. Brown, *Gospel According to John* (1966), 1.307; J. Louis Martyn, *History and Tradition in the Fourth Gospel*, 2nd ed. (Nashville, TN: Abingdon Press, 1979), 68–74; and U. C. Von Wahlde, "The Witnesses to Jesus in Jn 5:31–40 and Belief in the Fourth Gospel," *CBQ* 43 (1981), 385–404.

[198] Harold W. Attridge, "Thematic Development and Source Elaboration in John 7:1–36," *CBQ* 42 (1980), 160–70.

Events of the Feast. Symbolic elements of the feast highlight aspects of the Johannine narrative. Because it is a harvest festival, ritual elements in the feast pertain to the basic necessities of agricultural communities: a prayer for early and late rains (water) and for sunlight (light).[199] Apropos of these, *m. Sukkah* describes "the Water libation," in which a large golden flagon was filled at the Siloam spring and brought to the Temple for libations (4.9). Similarly it tells of giant golden candlesticks that burned during the festival (5.1), whose wicks were made of discarded priestly garments (5.3). These elements of water and light are alluded to when Jesus later promises on the last day of the feast *new water* ("If any one thirsts, let him come to me and drink," 7:37) and when he claims to be the *prayed-for light* ("I am the light of the world; who follows me . . . will have the light of life" (8:12).[200] The narrative presents Jesus making claims to replace the national benefactions prayed for at that time.[201] Yet the conflict here is not about claims of replacement but about old matters left unsettled on a previous feast, namely healing on the Sabbath (5:10, 18; 7:21–23).

First Mother, Now Brothers. One would think that the strongest bonds of loyalty and affection in antiquity were to be found in the family and kinship circles. But not so in this Gospel, which began with a radically different view.[202] The task of God and Jesus is to "give power to become children of God" (1:12). Thus "kinship" ties are not created by virtue of blood relationship or membership in the clan of Abraham (8:33) but by "receiving him . . . believing in his name"; that is, a different type of relationship with Jesus. "Children of God," we are told, are born "not of blood or of the will of the flesh or of the will of man, but of God" (1:13). Hence, when the narrator tells us that "not even his brothers believed in him" (7:5), as representative characters they are positioned at the fringe of Jesus' web of relationships, hostile even to Jesus' own interests. Blood is not thicker than living water.

Warmup for the Main Event. In two previous instances, Charles Giblin focused our attention on a narrative pattern: suggestion, negative reaction, and positive action.[203] The brothers urge Jesus to go to the feast (7:3–4), a suggestion that he categorically rejects (7:7–9). Yet he eventually travels to the feast (7:10). This pattern can be sharpened by interpreting the exchange in terms of the

---

199   Eduard König, "Tabernacles, Feast of," in Joseph Jacobs, ed., *The Jewish Encyclopedia: A Guide to Its Contents, an Aid to Its Use* (New York, Funk and Wagnalls, 1906), 11.660–61; and Louis Jacobs, "Sukkot," *Encyclopedia Judaica*, vol. 15 (Jerusalem: Macmillan, 1971), 499–500; see also R. E. Brown, *Gospel According to John* (1966), 1.326–29.

200   Hakan Ulfgard, *Feast and Future: Revelation 7:9–17 and the Feast of Tabernacles* (Stockholm: Almqvist and Wiksells, 1989), 117–18; and C. H. Talbert, *Reading John* (1992), 148–49.

201   On the motif of Jesus' "replacement" of Israelite worship, see J. H. Neyrey, *Ideology of Revolt* (1988), 131–37, 158–59.

202   See S. van Tilborg, *Imaginative Love* (1993), 13–17.

203   C. H. Giblin, "Suggestion," *NTS* 26 (1980), 206–8.

challenge/riposte model we have used thus far. The brothers make a positive *challenge* to Jesus: They want Jesus to attend the feast in order to increase his fame and public standing.[204] Thus they urge him to act in "public," where honor and respect are earned. But their suggestion functions as a *challenge* because its true focus is their benefit, not that of Jesus. In short, they are manipulating him, a clear challenge to his autonomy. Jesus *responds* by affirming spatial and temporal differences between them. With regard to space, although they are brothers, kinship ties are now meaningless. In fact, Jesus and his brothers belong to two different worlds. The world does not hate them but hates him because they belong to that world, not his. Moreover, they operate on different time: "My time has not yet come, but your time is always here" (7:6). The brothers fall silent, indicating that Jesus' reading of them in 7:6–7 was correct. Jesus knows that they are not believers (7:5; see also 2:23–25) but kin of questionable loyalty who seek to take advantage of him.

JOHN 7:10–24 – THE TRIAL RESUMES: VERDICT AND SENTENCE

10 But after his brothers had gone to the festival, then he also went, not publicly but as it were in secret.

11 The Jews were looking for him at the festival and saying, "Where is he?"

12 And there was considerable complaining about him among the crowds. While some were saying, "He is a good man," others were saying, "No, he is deceiving the crowd."

13 Yet no one would speak openly about him for fear of the Jews.

14 About the middle of the festival Jesus went up into the temple and began to teach.

15 The Jews were astonished at it, saying, "How does this man have such learning, when he has never been taught?"

16 Then Jesus answered them, "My teaching is not mine but his who sent me.

17 Anyone who resolves to do the will of God will know whether the teaching is from God or whether I am speaking on my own.

18 Those who speak on their own seek their own glory; but the one who seeks the glory of him who sent him is true, and there is nothing false in him.

19 "Did not Moses give you the law? Yet none of you keeps the law. Why are you looking for an opportunity to kill me?"

20 The crowd answered, "You have a demon! Who is trying to kill you?"

---

[204] Whereas John's disciples saw themselves losing honor when John decreased, the brothers of Jesus seek to gain respect and honor if Jesus increases. If one member of the family gained success, all in the family shared.

21 Jesus answered them, "I performed one work and all of you are astonished.

22 Moses gave you circumcision (it is, of course, not from Moses, but from the patriarchs), and you circumcise a man on the sabbath.

23 If a man receives circumcision on the sabbath in order that the law of Moses may not be broken, are you angry with me because I healed a man's whole body on the sabbath?

24 Do not judge by appearances, but judge with right judgment."

In Public or in Secret. Earlier, Jesus' brothers argued that honorable people do not work in secret but in public (7:4), but when Jesus goes to the feast, he is initially not in public but in secret (7:10).[205] About the middle of the feast, however, Jesus steps back into the public arena and teaches provocatively in the Temple (7:14). Does it matter if disciples or Jesus act "in secret" or "in private"? Earlier, the evangelist contrasted Nicodemus, who came to Jesus in private at night (3:2; 19:39), with the Samaritan woman, whom Jesus encountered at high noon in public (4:7). Disciples who publicly acknowledge Jesus are liable to shaming (9:22; 12:42); hence, many hide their thoughts and guard their speech "in secret." Jesus, however, models the ideal behavior. When on trial before Annas, he describes his public behavior: "I have spoken openly to the world; I have always taught in synagogues and in the temple. . . . I have said nothing in secret" (18:20). His speech, like that of true disciples, is public and "open."

Public Voice. Not everybody enjoyed "voice" in the ancient world: Children did not lecture adults, nor slaves their masters. Women had limited public voice in the governments of Greco-Roman cities. Even males did not enjoy full public "voice": Their speech and opinions were of no significance if they had no social significance. This has bearing on how we understand the remark about Jesus, "How does this man have such learning, when he has never been taught?" (7:15).[206] Who authorized Jesus or taught him?[207] And if he has no Torah pedigree, why is he speaking at all? Jesus in fact enjoys "voice," but why?

Unlike Paul, Jesus did not study under a celebrated rabbi (Acts 22:3) but is located socially with the uneducated disciples dismissed by the Sanhedrin (Acts 4:13). Yet Jesus is authorized to speak and act by an eminent person,

---

[205] On "public" and "private," see J. H. Neyrey, "Territoriality," *BTB* 32 (2002), 64–65; and his "'Teaching You in Public and from House to House' (Acts 20:20): Unpacking a Cultural Stereotype," *JSNT* 26 (2003), 69–102.

[206] Richard L. Rohrbaugh, "Legitimating Sonship – A Test of Honour: A Social-Scientific Study of Luke 4:1–30," in Philip F. Esler, ed., *Modelling Early Christianity: Social-Scientific Studies of the New Testament in Its Context* (London: Routledge, 1995), 192–95. On Paul's public voice, see J. H. Neyrey, "'Teaching You in Public and from House to House,'" *JSNT* 26 (2003), 99–101.

[207] In the encomium, students learned to honor someone on the basis of "nurture and training" (Josephus, *Life* 8–12). See J. H. Neyrey, *Honor and Shame* (1998), 102–4.

which should be sufficient warrant for his "voice." God sent him, consecrated him to this work, and told him what to say. He is, in short, God's agent and Word.[208] The evangelist states time and again that "God sent him into the world" (3:17). God, moreover, provided credentials for his "voice," namely "the works" that Jesus does (5:36–37; 9:31–33). God's purpose in making Jesus his "apostle" was precisely that he have "voice" and so speak the words of God: "He whom God has sent speaks the words of God" (3:34; 8:42). Thus, when Jesus speaks, he does not speak alone, for the one who sent him speaks, too (5:31; 7:16).

The Trial of Jesus Continues. Scholars recognize that the process against Jesus in John 5 resumes in John 7.[209] The accusation of Sabbath violation (5:10, 16) remains the primary *charge* against Jesus (7:21–23). A "*court*" that tried him (5:18) still seeks to kill him (7:1, 19). As the narrative unfolds, the following aspects of forensic proceedings appear: *arrest* (7:32, 44, 45); *charges* (7:21–23 and 12, 47); and *testimony*, either for the defense (7:15–24, 51) or for the prosecution (25–27), all of which issues in a *verdict* and a *sentence* (see 11:49–53). In addition, we hear debate about the standing of Jesus as witness in this court (7:15), the true criteria of judgment (7:24), and the "law" requiring the accused to have a hearing and not be judged in absentia (7:50). If all trials are also trials of the judges, who is being judged if the legal process is corrupt? It is clear that others judge Jesus (5:16–18; 7:14–24; 8:12–19; 10:22–38). But Jesus also judges them by the authority God gave him to judge (5:22, 27; 8:15) and to conduct trials (8:31–58). More and more the Gospel tells us that the judges of Jesus judge unjustly and so are on trial themselves. All of this forensic material unfolds in six scenes where supporters and opponents render formal and informal judgments of Jesus.[210]

The First Scene (7:10–13). The narrator intends that we link the group controlling the action when the feast was first announced ("the Jews sought to kill Jesus," 7:1) with those appearing when Jesus appears on the scene: "The Jews sought him at the feast, saying 'Where is he?'" (7:11). "Seek" is another of those pesky double-meaning words. Although it occasionally means friendly association with Jesus (1:38–39), in this context it means a hostile assault on him.[211]

---

[208] P. Borgen, "God's Agent," in *Religions in Antiquity* (1968), 137–48; George W. Buchanan, "Apostolic Christology," *SBLSP* (1986), 172–82; A. E. Harvey, "Christ as Agent," in L. D. Hurst and N. T. Wright, eds., *The Glory of Christ in the New Testament* (Oxford: Clarendon Press, 1987), 239–50.

[209] J. Duncan M. Derrett, "Law in the New Testament: The Parable of the Unjust Judge," *NTS* 18 (1971), 178–191; his "Law and Society in Jesus' World," *ANRW* (1982) II.25.1., 477–564; and his "Circumcision and Perfection: A Johannine Equation," *EvQ* 63 (1991), 211–24.

[210] On the forensic shape of John 7, see J. H. Neyrey, "Trials and Tribulations," *BTB* 26 (1996), 109–16.

[211] On double-meaning terms, see D. A. Carson, "Understanding Misunderstandings in the Fourth Gospel," *TynB* 33 (1982), 59–91; Earl Richard, "Expressions of Double Meaning and Their Function in the Gospel of John," *NTS* 31 (1985), 96–112; and J. H. Neyrey, "Secrecy" in *What Is John?* (1998), 94–96.

The announcement that some are "seeking" Jesus (7:11) presents an ominous hint that the subsequent events in Jerusalem could result in Jesus' arrest and execution, as indeed they eventually will (8:59; 10:39; 11:45–53). The narrative audience knows that this public "seeking" means a judgment against Jesus, "For fear of 'the Jews' no one spoke openly of him'" (7:13).

There was "considerable complaining" about him (7:12), a translation that masks the biblical term "murmuring," which identified hostile outsiders earlier (6:41, 43, 61). But the crowd's testimony is "divided": Some say "He is a good man," whereas others insist that "He leads the people astray" (7:12).[212] Judges are judging Jesus; witnesses are testifying for and against him. The testimony that they render about Jesus allows the Johannine audience to stand in judgment of them. They who judge Jesus innocent judge justly, but they who judge him to be a deceiver judge unjustly. They judge according to appearances. As one judges, so is one judged (Matt 7:2).[213]

The Second Scene (7:14, 24). While Jesus remains in private (7:10), he cannot be arrested. But when he appears in the Temple (7:14), a trial immediately ensues (see 10:22). Some accuse him of "deceiving the crowd" (7:12); others question his right to speak (7:15).[214] From a forensic point of view, these remarks function as *charges* against Jesus by calling into question his status as a valid teacher. In effect, he appears as a self-made imposter, who vainly claims special status (i.e., as one who "makes himself" something, 5:18).

Inasmuch as Jesus has been charged with "leading the people astray" (7:12), his remarks in 7:16–24 function as a defense against this charge, and with appropriate testimony from the honorable person who sent Jesus to speak. He testifies first that indeed he has "schooling" from a learned and powerful authority: "My teaching is not mine, but his who sent me" (7:16). As proof of this, he continues: "If any man's will is to do His will, he will know whether my teaching is from God or whether I am speaking on my own authority" (7:17). Thus, if Jesus' judges were obedient to his Sender, they would know whether he speaks truly of and for the Sender. Thus Jesus denies that he is a self-made imposter, for his argument rests on the legal principle accepted even by this court: "Those who speak on their own authority, seek their own glory; but he who seeks the glory of him who sent him is true, and in him there is no falsehood" (7:18; see also 8:12–13). A second reading of this scene reveals that the court itself is on trial. Jesus accuses his own accusers of failing to keep the law of Moses: "Did not Moses give you the law? Yet none of you keeps the law.

---

[212] See J. L. Martyn, *History and Tradition* (1979), 73–81.

[213] See Hans Peter Rüger, "Mit welchem Maß ihr meßt, wird euch gemessen werden," *ZNW* 60 (1969), 174–82.

[214] On the importance of famous and noble teachers in the rhetoric of antiquity, see B. J. Malina and J. H. Neyrey, *Portraits of Paul* (1996), 27–28, 41–43.

Why are you looking for an opportunity to kill me?" Presumably he is speaking of circumcision on the sabbath (see 7:22–23), but this may cryptically refer to other aspects of Moses' law, such as just judgment (see 7:25; 8:15; Deut 19:15–21) or the prohibitions against murder and lying. Why murder and lying? In the continuation of this trial in John 8, Jesus will accuse his hearers of both murder *and* lying: "You are from your father the devil, and you choose to do your father's desires. He was a *murderer* from the beginning and does not stand in the truth, because there is no truth in him. When he *lies*, he speaks according to his own nature, for he is a *liar* and the father of lies" (8:44).[215] This has bearing on how we should read the next exchange, in 7:19–20. Jesus raises both issues, *murder* and *lying*. First, he asks "Why do you seek to kill me?" (v. 19), an accusation of *murder*. The defense is to *lie*: "Who is seeking to kill you?" (v. 20; see also 5:18). The audience knows that this is a *lie* because the evangelist already told us that people were in fact trying to *murder* Jesus: "Jesus would not go about in Judea because the Jews sought to kill him" (7:1). The crowds in Jerusalem, moreover, know that murder is afoot: "Is not this the man whom they seek to kill?" (7:25). *Murder* and *lying*, therefore, truly characterize these judges of Jesus, despite what they say. Thus, in 7:19 Jesus mounts the counter-charge of murder and lying, which he will finally prove in 8:44 when he exposes certain people as offspring of the devil, who is both murderer and liar *from the beginning*.

Most readers link Jesus' remarks in 7:19 with the healing on the Sabbath, which occasioned the formal charge against Jesus earlier (5:10–17). This explains Jesus' remark in 7:21–23 that "I performed one work, and all of you are astonished. I did one deed, and you all marvel at it" (7:21). Whereas Jesus offered no formal defense then to the charge of Sabbath violation, he now compares what he did on the Sabbath with Moses' command to circumcise on the eighth day (7:22–23).[216] His defense uses the standard argument of *qal wayyomer* or a fortiori reasoning.[217] If Jesus is guilty for healing on the Sabbath, then so are they for circumcising on the Sabbath. Thus Jesus' judges judge hypocritically: If they harm a very small bodily organ in order to make the body "whole" for covenant membership, how can they object to Jesus making a man "whole" as well? Jesus turns this hypocrisy into an accusation of false judgment when he commands his judges to judge justly: "Do not judge by appearances, but judge with right

---

[215] On the devil as both murderer and liar, see Jerome H. Neyrey, "Jesus the Judge: Forensic Process in John 8:21–59," *Biblica* 68 (1987), 525–28.

[216] To fulfill certain commands, observant Judeans often had to calculate how these actions overrode other requirements of the Law. See C. S. Keener, *Gospel of John* (2003), 1.716–18.

[217] D. A. Carson, "Jesus and the Sabbath in the Four Gospels," in his *From Sabbath to Lord's Day: A Biblical, Historical and Theological Investigation* (Grand Rapids, MI: Zondervan, 1982), 66–67, 82.

judgment" (7:24). Accordingly, Jesus acts in the role of a judge who judges the local judges.

JOHN 7:25–36 – THE TRIAL CONTINUES

25 Now some of the people of Jerusalem were saying, "Is not this the man whom they are trying to kill?

26 And here he is, speaking openly, but they say nothing to him! Can it be that the authorities really know that this is the Messiah?

27 Yet we know where this man is from; but when the Messiah comes, no one will know where he is from."

28 Then Jesus cried out as he was teaching in the temple, "You know me, and you know where I am from. I have not come on my own. But the one who sent me is true, and you do not know him.

29 I know him, because I am from him, and he sent me."

30 Then they tried to arrest him, but no one laid hands on him, because his hour had not yet come.

31 Yet many in the crowd believed in him and were saying, "When the Messiah comes, will he do more signs than this man has done?"

32 The Pharisees heard the crowd muttering such things about him, and the chief priests and Pharisees sent temple police to arrest him.

33 Jesus then said, "I will be with you a little while longer, and then I am going to him who sent me.

34 You will search for me, but you will not find me; and where I am, you cannot come."

35 The Jews said to one another, "Where does this man intend to go that we will not find him? Does he intend to go to the Dispersion among the Greeks and teach the Greeks?

36 What does he mean by saying, 'You will search for me and you will not find me' and 'Where I am, you cannot come'?"

The Third Scene (7:25–30). The narrative audience shifts from Temple elite to "the people of Jerusalem," who constitute one more voice in the divided crowd described in 7:12–13. Although we were told that "for fear of the Jews no one spoke openly of him" (7:13) – that is, favorably about him – now these "people of Jerusalem" appear to be speaking openly about Jesus. But what role do they play in the grand forensic process against Jesus? Their testimony about Jesus supports the prosecution, not the defense. They are aware of the forensic proceeding against Jesus: they know the *judges* ("the authorities"), the *charges* ("the [false] Christ"), and the *verdict and sentence* ("seek to kill him"). Their remarks do not acknowledge Jesus' role, for they voice a hostile question, "Can this be the Messiah?" They immediately answer it in such a way as to *testify against* Jesus: "Yet we know where this man is from; but when the Messiah comes, no one will know where he is from" (7:27).[218]

Rhetorical Importance of "Origins." As we saw in the Introduction, the ancients universally considered a person's "origins" as significant grounds for ascribing respect and honor: Noble parents and ancestors beget noble off-spring, and noble people spring from noble cities or locations. Rhetorical theorists from Aristotle to Quintilian formally explain the importance of "origins":

The good birth of an individual implies that both parents are free citizens, and that, as in the case of the state, the founders of the line have been notable for virtue or wealth or something else which is highly prized, and that many distinguished persons belong to the family. (Aristotle, *Rhet.* 1.5.5)[219]

Besides, the authors of the *progymnasmata*,[220] exercises for second-level students, all include directives for composers to pay attention to "origins":

Aelius Theon	Aphthonius	Quintilian
ethnic affiliation (ἔθνος)	ethnic affiliation (ἔθνος)	ethnic affiliation (*gens, natio*)
nation/city-state (πόλις)	home locale (πατρίς)	country (*patria*)
government (πολιτεία)	ancestors (πρόγονοι)	ancestors (*maiores*)
	fathers (πατέρες)	parents (*parentes*)

In the Greco-Roman world, a person's origins greatly determined his worth and honor. But the demand that the Messiah's origins be *unknown* is strange indeed.

The Tables Are Turned. When Jesus rebuts his accusers' remarks, he and they are reversing roles, with Jesus, the accused, becoming the judge, while his judges become the accused. He judges them on the basis of a self-evident legal demand

---

[218] Marinus de Jonge, "Jewish Expectations about the 'Messiah' According to the Fourth Gospel," in his *Jesus: Stranger from Heaven and Son of God* (Missoula, MT: Scholars Press, 1977), 85–92.

[219] On the rhetorical importance of knowing a person's origins in order to evaluate the person, see B. J. Malina and J. H. Neyrey, *Portraits of Paul* (1996), 23–26, 113–25; and J. H. Neyrey, *Honor and Shame* (1998), 90–102.

[220] The basic *progymnasmata* used in this study are: Aelius Theon of Alexandria (Spengel II. 112.20–115.10; see James R. Butts, *The Progymnasmata of Theon: A New Text with Translation and Commentary* [unpublished dissertation, Claremont, 1986]); Menander Rhetor (see D. A. Russell and N. G. Wilson, *Menander Rhetor* [Oxford: Clarendon Press, 1981]); Aphthonius of Ephesus (Spengel II. 42.20–44.19; see Ray Nadeau, "The Progymnasmata of Aphthonius in Translation," *Speech Monographs* 19 [1952], 264–285); and Quintilian, *Inst.* 3.7.10–18.

that judges should judge rightly and not according to appearances (7:24). Jesus' attack plays with a phrase about "knowing" Jesus. Having claimed to "know Jesus," they are shown *not* to know him as "insiders" do. Jesus remarks with heavy irony, "So you know me and you know where I come from?" when they claim to know whence Jesus comes, either from Galilee (7:41, 52) or from peasant parents in Nazareth (6:42). They are "judging according to appearances," bearing "false" testimony about Jesus. They are, then, *lying* about Jesus, which will lead to *murder*.

Knowing and Acknowledgment. Genuine knowledge of Jesus means acknowledging the one who has authorized and sent him: "I have not come on my own accord; he who sent me is true, and him *you do not know*" (7:29). As Jesus did with the accusation in 7:19, he now issues a *countercharge* to those who accuse him. They "do not know" God, so they "do not know" the one whom God sent. This is no lapse of information or fallible ignorance, that special remedial education will repair. Not in the Fourth Gospel! *Not to know* comprises a serious charge by Jesus (8:47, 55). Failure to know certain things merits a terrible sentence (see 8:24).

Seeking (to Kill) Jesus. This segment of the trial climaxes in an attempt to "arrest him" (v. 30), a translation that masks the double-meaning word "to seek" (7:1, 19, 25, 34, 36); it might mean "seek" the association of or "seek" to kill. The evangelist, then, links this "court" with others who have judged that Jesus is a false prophet or messiah.

The Fourth Scene (7:32–36). The elites hear the crowds "murmuring" against Jesus (7:32) and co-opt this in support of their verdict; therefore, they send Temple retainers to seize Jesus. Meanwhile Jesus continues to speak boldly in public. But in 7:33–34 he does not defend himself against charges as in 7:14–23, nor does he scrutinize the false testimony of hostile witnesses as in 7:25–29. He speaks both on his own behalf and in accusation of his accusers. His forensic role has metamorphosed from accused defendant to accusing judge. His statement contains three elements that require close examination: (1) "I shall be with you a little longer, and then I go to him who sent me"; (2) "You will seek me and you will not find me"; and (3) "Where I am you cannot come" (7:33–34).

We notice the signature literary pattern in which Jesus makes a *statement* that is *misunderstood* and this often leads to a *clarification*.[221] When Jesus speaks (7:33–34), his hearers completely misunderstand him (7:35–36). But here he offers no clarification, a highly significant change in the pattern. As we have seen, this pattern functions in two ways. In most instances, it describes the

---

[221] Herbert Leroy, *Rätsel und Missverständnis* (Bonn: Peter Hanstein, 1968), 45–47, 53–67; J. H. Neyrey, "Secrecy," in *What Is John?* (1998), 99–101.

process of outsiders becoming insiders as they move from "not in the know" about Jesus to insight and acknowledgment of him. Yet occasionally it serves to prove that Jesus' interlocutors are hopeless outsiders; that is, people who do not and cannot understand Jesus' revelation. Hence it functions forensically to prove that certain people cannot hear his voice because they are not his sheep (3:1–12; 10:24–27; 18:37–38). And the fact that Jesus offers no *clarification* is further evidence that he judges those who *misunderstand* him to be hopelessly obtuse and irrevocably fixed in evil.[222]

Misunderstanding? What is ignored or misunderstood by the hearers? Because Jesus earlier accused them of murder and lying, let us not presume their good faith and candor now.

Jesus' Statement (7:33–34)	*Their Misunderstanding (7:35–36)*
1. I shall be with you a little longer and then I go to him who sent me.	1. Where does this man intend to go that we shall not find him? Does he intend to go to the Dispersion among the Greeks and teach the Greeks?
2. You will seek me and you will not find me;	2. What does he mean by "You will seek me and you will not find me"?
3. Where I am you cannot come	3. and "Where I am you cannot come"?

How significant it is that this "court" utterly ignores Jesus' remark about "going to him who sent me" (7:33), just as others in this extended trial ignore all of Jesus' testimony about God, who sent him (7:16–18, 28). Because Jesus acts as God's agent, it is utterly shameful for his judges and critics to ignore this part of his testimony (see 9:31–33). But by doing so his hearers prove Jesus' main point – namely that they *do not acknowledge God*, which is the ultimate sin. Hence, only those who acknowledge God correctly will judge Jesus correctly; how terrible then *not to know God* or the one whom God has sent. This has been the constant accusation against them: "He who sent me is true and *him you do not know*" (7:28; see 8:19, 47, 55). Jesus' accusation that his judges "do not know God" testifies to their radical sinfulness.

Whence? Whither? We saw in 7:27 that outsiders regularly "judge by appearances" and so misunderstand *whence* Jesus comes (see also 7:41–42, 52) and *whither* he goes. Our narrator tells us repeatedly that Jesus comes from heaven and from God, his true "*whence*," and that he goes back to God and to "heaven," his true "*whither*" (1:1–18; 13:1–3; 17:5). Outsiders such as Nicodemus

---

[222] This resembles the anti-language observed in 3:1–15; see Richard L. Rohrbaugh, "What's the Matter with Nicodemus? A Social Science Perspective on John 3:1–21," in Holly E. Hearon, ed., *Distant Voices Drawing Near: Essays in Honor of Antoinette Clark Wire* (Collegeville, MN: The Liturgical Press), 145–58.

cannot understand whence wind comes and whither it goes (3:8). If he cannot understand earthly things, he will never grasp heavenly ones (3:12), such as Jesus' descent from heaven (whence) and his ascension there (whither) (3:13). Similarly, Jesus' judges either do not know "whence are you?" (19:9) or think they know (6:41–42; 7:27, 41–42, 52). In 7:33–36, the audience does not attend to whence Jesus comes and utterly fails to grasp whither he goes. Here they think that he will leave Judea and go among the Dispersion (7:35), but in 8:22 they think that he will commit suicide.

Seeking. Jesus' judges claim not to know what Jesus means by "you will seek me," but is that true? Consider the statements in John 7 about people "seeking" Jesus:

"The Jews *sought* to kill him." (7:1)	"Is this the man whom they *seek* to kill"? (7:25)
"The Jews *sought* him at the feast." (7:11)	"They *sought* to arrest him." (7:30)
"Why do you *seek* to kill me?" (7:19)	"You will *seek* me and you will not find me." (7:34)
"Who *seeks* to kill you"? (7:20)	"What does he mean by 'You will *seek* me'"? (7:36)

"Seeking" Jesus, then, means either "seeking to arrest" him or "seeking to kill" him. In John 7, "seeking" is tantamount to murder. This audience is either obtuse as to the public controversy over Jesus or lying when it says that it does not know what Jesus means about "seeking" him. Jesus will shortly expose many of his audience to be sons of the devil, who is both *liar* and *murderer* from the beginning (8:44). Hence, we should take the crowd's question in 7:35–36 as a *lie* about *murder*. They are "seeking" Jesus to arrest and kill him, but now they are lying about it.

Finding. If "seeking" is a double-meaning word, what about "finding"? Like other double-meaning terms, it enjoys a wide range of meanings. It can positively describe others gaining benefit by finding Jesus or bringing others to him (1:41, 43, 45). Similarly, Jesus himself "found" the man born blind, who was cast out of the synagogue for testimony on Jesus' behalf (9:35). But in the case of the man healed at the pool, it has a negative connotation, as Jesus "found" him and commanded him not to sin again (5:14). Because this man then identified Jesus to his enemies, no discipleship comes from this "finding." Pilate twice does *not* "find" any cause to execute Jesus (18:38; 19:4). Still, none of these meanings fits John 7. Rather, what Jesus says is that "you will *not find* me," which we take to mean his accusers' impotence in arresting and killing him, at least now. Indeed, the officers sent to arrest him (7:32) return empty-handed (7:45). Because his hour has not come, even those who try to arrest him cannot (8:20).

JOHN 7:37–39 – THE LIBATION ON THE LAST DAY OF THE FEAST

37 On the last day of the festival, the great day, while Jesus was standing there, he cried out, "Let anyone who is thirsty come to me,
38 and let the one who believes in me drink. As the scripture has said, 'Out of the believer's heart shall flow rivers of living water.'"
39 Now he said this about the Spirit, which believers in him were to receive; for as yet there was no Spirit, because Jesus was not yet glorified.

The Fifth Scene (7:37–39). This episode, although clearly part of the feast of Booths, is unlike the rest of John 7 in that it has nothing to do with the continuous forensic process against Jesus. Recall that Booths focused on two petitions for the success of next year's agriculture: water (the early and late rains) and light. At the climax of the feast, Jesus claims to be the true source of water, a claim that goes unchallenged. It has to do with Spirit, which would be given only later. Jesus claims to replace this essential element of the celebration of Booths, just as "birth" by spirit replaces circumcision as entry rite (3:3–5) and Bread from heaven replaces manna at Passover (6:1–12).

Whose "Heart"? Debate on this remains inconclusive.[223] Early Christians interpreted Jesus' remark to mean that Jesus himself is the source of the water.[224] In support, the author will soon describe how from the pierced heart of the crucified Jesus blood and water flowed, certainly good things for the disciple (19:34). Moreover, the evangelist says that as Jesus died, "he gave up his spirit" (19:30). In the double-meaning world of the Fourth Gospel, this might be read by "insiders" as a reference to the Spirit that, according to the aside in 7:39, was later to be given by Jesus. However, a second interpretation argues that the believing disciple will be enriched with a river of water that brings eternal life; hence, it is out of the believer's heart that this river flows. Internal evidence for this comes from Jesus' remark on water to the Samaritan woman: "Those who drink of the water that I will give them will never be thirsty. The water that I will give will become in them a spring of water gushing up to eternal life" (4:14).[225]

---

[223] For a summary of the critical issues, see Gary M. Burge, *The Anointed Community: The Holy Spirit in the Johannine Tradition* (Grand Rapids, MI: Eerdmans, 1987), 88–93; Francis J. Moloney, *Signs and Shadows* (Minneapolis, MN: Fortress Press, 1996), 84–88.

[224] Hugo Rahner's "'Flumina de ventri Christi': Die Patristiche Auglegung von Joh 7:37–38," *Biblica* 22 (1941), 269–302, cited evidence from Eastern and Western authors on this point. M.-E. Boismard's "De son ventre couleront de fleuves d'eau," *RB* 65 (1958), 523–46, expanded Rahner's research to include material from Tertullian, Irenaeus, Cyprian, and Ephrem to confirm this early, widespread interpretation of John 7:38.

[225] Raymond E. Brown's "The Gospel of Thomas and St. John's Gospel," *NTS* 9 (1962), 162, notes a parallel to 7:38 in the Gospel of Thomas that supports the reading that the river flows up from inside the believer.

In each case, a believer comes to Jesus to drink, with the result that a "spring of water" gushes up or a "river" flows up within those who drink. The ultimate source, of course, is Jesus, but "springs" and "rivers" flow out of the believer.

A Johannine Aside. We regularly find footnotes or asides inserted into the discourses. As we have learned, what one knows serves as an index of status within the Johannine group. Insiders in general are given asides and footnotes about a variety of matters, such as the translation of certain Semitic terms into Greek (1:38, 41, 42; 4:25; 5:2; 9:7; 19:13, 17; 20:16);[226] and information about times and places (6:4; 7:2; 9:14; 10:22–23; 11:17), customs (4:9; 19:40), and the identification of persons (6:71; 7:50; 11:2; 18:10, 14, 40; 19:38–39). Some asides contain knowledge of the thoughts and actions of people, such as the recollections of the disciples (2:22; 12:16), explanations of actions or situations (2:9; 4:2; 7:5, 39; 11:51; 12:6; 19:36–37; 21:19), and indications of what Jesus knows (2:24–25; 6:6; 13:1, 3). The narrator also gives special information about himself to this select audience (1:14b; 19:35; 21:24–25); on one occasion he corrects a popular error (21:22–23). The aside in 7:39 reminds us of how cryptic Jesus' remark was; no one at the time could possibly understand it because it refers to a distant phenomenon. Thus 7:39 stands parallel to other remarks of Jesus that are not comprehended at the time he speaks them but are understood after his death and resurrection (2:21–22) and that depend on Jesus' establishment of the Paraclete as his interpreter (14:26; 15:26).

JOHN 7:40–44 – NEW TESTIMONY ABOUT JESUS

40 When they heard these words, some in the crowd said, "This is really the prophet."
41 Others said, "This is the Messiah." But some asked, "Surely the Messiah does not come from Galilee, does he?
42 Has not the scripture said that the Messiah is descended from David and comes from Bethlehem, the village where David lived?"
43 So there was a division in the crowd because of him.
44 Some of them wanted to arrest him, but no one laid hands on him.

The Sixth Scene (7:40–44). The forensic process continues with people judging "these words" of Jesus. As we saw earlier in 7:10–13, once more we find a "schism," a divided judgment. First we find positive acknowledgment that Jesus is "the

---

[226] J. J. O'Rourke, "Asides in the Gospel of Jesus," *NovT* 21 (1979), 210–19; M. C. Tenney, "The Footnotes of John's Gospel," *BSac* 117 (1960), 350–64; J. H. Neyrey, "Secrecy," in *What Is John?* (1998), 87–88; and T. Thatcher, "A New Look at Asides in the Fourth Gospel," *BSac* 151 (1994), 428–39.

prophet" and "the Messiah." Then we find negative testimony: "The Messiah does not come from Galilee."

Origins Again. We have seen that in an encomium ancient authors sought to amplify a person's honor in reference to geography (place/polis) and generation (family/clan). Once more we see a judgment about Jesus based on his origins: place of origin (Galilee, not Bethlehem) and ancestry (not descended of David). Jesus' enemies locate him in terms of some earthly place because they are ignorant of his true origins, his genuine "whence." But the "insiders" know that Jesus is from the most noble of all places, heaven; and they know that he is the unique son of the most noble person in the cosmos, God. According to "origins," then, Jesus should enjoy the highest honor rating and the most noble pedigree.[227]

Prophet Christ. Thus far, the author has told us who is *not* the prophet or the Christ, namely John the Baptizer (1:20–21, 25; 3:28). Conversely, various characters in the narrative acclaim Jesus as "prophet" (4:19; 6:14; 7:40; and 9:17) and "Messiah" (1:41; 4:25, 29; 11:27; 20:31). Whereas no one comes to grief by labeling Jesus a "prophet," such is not the case with "Messiah," for, as we learn later, a ruling has been given that anyone who acknowledges Jesus as "Messiah" will be expelled from the synagogue (9:22; see also 12:42). Curious, then, is the public debate over these two titles in 7:40–44. What is conveyed by each title? "Prophet" describes Jesus by virtue of works of power (6:14; 9:17), as well as revelation of secrets (4:19). "Messiah" suggests royal power ("descended of David") and might well be taken as a synonym for "king" in this Gospel. Hence, "Messiah" is by far the more dangerous label according to the Jerusalem elite and the Romans.

JOHN 7:45–52 – THE PROSECUTION RESTS

45 Then the temple police went back to the chief priests and Pharisees, who asked them, "Why did you not arrest him?"
46 The police answered, "Never has anyone spoken like this!"
47 Then the Pharisees replied, "Surely you have not been deceived too, have you?
48 Has any one of the authorities or of the Pharisees believed in him?
49 But this crowd, which does not know the law – they are accursed."
50 Nicodemus, who had gone to Jesus before, and who was one of them, asked,
51 "Our law does not judge people without first giving them a hearing to find out what they are doing, does it?"
52 They replied, "Surely you are not also from Galilee, are you? Search and you will see that no prophet is to arise from Galilee."

---

[227] Wayne A. Meeks, "Galilee and Judea in the Fourth Gospel," *JBL* 85 (1963), 159–69.

Yes, a Deceiver! When the police sent to arrest Jesus return empty-handed and in praise of him, the Jerusalem elite seize on this as proof that Jesus is a deceiver: "He leads the people astray" (7:12). Although we do not know what Jesus said to them, his speech won them over: "Never has anyone spoken like this!" This might refer to his expertise in the forensic process under way.

The Seventh Scene. Because police were sent to "arrest" Jesus, the presumption is that he had been tried and found guilty. Now the trial is reopened because the accused escaped and new witnesses speak on his behalf, both the police sent to arrest him and Nicodemus. We noted earlier that the social status of a witness greatly determined his reliability in court.[228] The judges, "chief priests and Pharisees," testify against Jesus; they enjoy very high status in Jerusalem. But in this court certain people with no status or standing are dismissed out of hand: "This crowd, which does not know the law – they are accursed" (7:49). The police, who are the retainers of the elites, have a higher social standing based on their service of the elite. Although of moderate social standing, their remarks here are dismissed by their superiors. Finally, another witness speaks, not so much on behalf of Jesus as about correct legal process. Nicodemus, that ambiguous figure[229] who came to Jesus at night (3:1–2), speaks up, which might be considered heroic and so win him a place in the inner circle of disciples. Yet he does not testify on behalf of Jesus but insists on a principle of the law: "Our law does not judge people without first giving them a hearing to find out what they are doing, does it?" (7:51).[230] The elites dismiss his intervention in the trial.

Origins Once More. It was argued in 7:41–42 that Jesus came from Galilee and so could not be the Messiah, who as a descendant of David must come from Bethlehem. So much for "Messiah"! Now the title of "prophet" is debated on the same terms. Prophets simply do not come from low-status places such as Galilee (7:52). Thus, on the basis of origins, Jesus cannot be a person of status or significance. This, of course, is another example of earthly or fleshly thinking; those who think such thoughts "judge by appearances" and not in truth. This judgment, then, is false, and such judges are themselves judged.

---

[228] Paul R. Swarney, "Social Status and Social Behaviour as Criteria in Judicial Proceedings in the Late Republic," in Baruch Halpern and Deborah Hobson, eds., *Law, Politics and Society in the Ancient Mediterranean World* (Sheffield: Sheffield Academic Press, 1993), 137–55.

[229] Jouette M. Bassler, "Mixed Signals," *JBL* 108 (1989), 635–46; see also Marinus de Jonge, "Nicodemus and Jesus: Some Observations on Misunderstanding and Understanding in the Fourth Gospel," in his *Jesus: Stranger from Heaven and Son of God* (Missoula, MT: Scholars Press, 1977), 29–47.

[230] Severino Pancaro's "The Metamorphosis of a Legal Principle in the Fourth Gospel: A Closer Look at Jn 7, 51," *Biblica* 53 (1972), 340–61, notes the double element in Nicodemus' "law": both hearing and seeing. His observation links these two verbs and the Johannine argument that revelation comes both in word (hearing) and work (seeing what is done).

JOHN 7:53–8:11 – A JUDICIOUS JUDGMENT

53 Then each of them went home,

1 while Jesus went to the Mount of Olives.

2 Early in the morning he came again to the temple. All the people came to him and he sat down and began to teach them.

3 The scribes and the Pharisees brought a woman who had been caught in adultery; and making her stand before all of them,

4 they said to him, "Teacher, this woman was caught in the very act of committing adultery.

5 Now in the law Moses commanded us to stone such women. Now what do you say?"

6 They said this to test him, so that they might have some charge to bring against him. Jesus bent down and wrote with his finger on the ground.

7 When they kept on questioning him, he straightened up and said to them, "Let anyone among you who is without sin be the first to throw a stone at her."

8 And once again he bent down and wrote on the ground.

9 When they heard it, they went away, one by one, beginning with the elders; and Jesus was left alone with the woman standing before him.

10 Jesus straightened up and said to her, "Woman, where are they? Has no one condemned you?"

11 She said, "No one, sir." And Jesus said, "Neither do I condemn you. Go your way, and from now on do not sin again."

In Fine Print. Readers will find this episode in fine print in their copies of the Gospel, indicating the scholarly judgment that it is nonauthentic; that is, not part of the original Gospel. The reasons for this are cogent. First, it is absent from most of the early manuscripts; second, it uses non-Johannine language (e.g., "scribes" appears only here); third, it is closer in argument and tone to synoptic stories (i.e., the dilemma presented here resembles the "tribute to Caesar" issue in Mark 12:13–15). Finally, the drama of the feast of Booths is interrupted by this story; it is an unwelcome insert.[231]

Jesus and Sinners. John heralded Jesus as "the Lamb of God who takes away the sin of the world" (1:29), but little more is said about sins after that. Jesus' final remark to the man healed at the pool of Bethzatha was "Sin no more that nothing worse befall you" (5:14), implying that his illness was related to his sinfulness. Just the opposite is said about the man born blind: Sin has nothing

---

[231] See John Paul Heil, "The Story of Jesus and the Adulteress (John 7, 53–8, 11) Reconsidered," *Biblica* 72 (1991), 182–91; and Allison A. Trites, "The Woman Taken in Adultery," *BSac* 131 (1974), 137–46.

to do with his illness. The point is that this Gospel is not initially concerned with behavior. The category of "sin" rather is attached to matters of belief (8:21–31; 16:9). The greater sin is to hand Jesus over (19:11). Most of this "sin" is found in outsiders, not insiders. Although the Risen Jesus empowers the disciples to forgive sins, this surely refers only to sins within the group (20:21–23). Thus, this narrative seems egregious for it presents issues of which the evangelist is not interested until the end of the Gospel.

Watching Jesus Fight. Typically the narrative is choreographed in terms of a challenge/ riposte exchange. The Israelite leaders present Jesus with an obvious case but put him on the spot to make a judgment: "They said this to test him, so that they might have some charge to bring against him" (8:6). Unlike the Jesus of the Fourth Gospel, he does not speak; rather, he doodles in the sand. The leaders consider his silence a concession that he is stumped, so they press on. Jesus stands up, faces them, and says: "Let anyone among you who is without sin be the first to throw a stone at her" (8:7). With that he stoops and continues doodling – a stunning riposte, for he sidesteps their question and puts them on the spot. The proof that Jesus won is that they silently depart. Unlike in most Johannine challenge/riposte exchanges, Jesus then stands and faces the woman. Although her accusers have left, they did not stop accusing her but only stopped seeking a judgment. Jesus, too, does not accuse her, rescuing her from being a pawn in the challenge/riposte exchange.

JOHN 8:12–20 – THE TRIAL THAT NEVER ENDS

12 Again Jesus spoke to them, saying, "I am the light of the world. Whoever follows me will never walk in darkness but will have the light of life."
13 Then the Pharisees said to him, "You are testifying on your own behalf; your testimony is not valid."
14 Jesus answered, "Even if I testify on my own behalf, my testimony is valid because I know where I have come from and where I am going, but you do not know where I come from or where I am going.
15 You judge by human standards; I judge no one.
16 Yet even if I do judge, my judgment is valid; for it is not I alone who judge, but I and the Father who sent me.
17 In your law it is written that the testimony of two witnesses is valid.
18 I testify on my own behalf, and the Father who sent me testifies on my behalf."
19 Then they said to him, "Where is your Father?" Jesus answered, "You know neither me nor my Father. If you knew me, you would know my Father also."
20 He spoke these words while he was teaching in the treasury of the temple, but no one arrested him, because his hour had not yet come.

Continuation of Booths. The story narrated here occurs during the feast of Booths, in which petitioners prayed for water/rains and light/sunlight. In addition to Jesus' claim to provide rivers of water (i.e., "rain"), he declares himself to be the "light of the world." Similarly, the forensic proceedings that structured the narrative in John 7 continue here. Thus nothing has changed, and the trial of Jesus continues. During Booths four immense candlesticks burned in the Court of the Women (*m. Sukkoth* 5.2–4); Jesus claims to be their replacement, namely "the light of the world." This "light" refers to Jesus' revelation of heavenly secrets (see 1:18).[232]

Challenge/Riposte. One may profitably read this narrative in terms of several challenge/riposte exchanges. First, *claim* ("I am the light of the world," 8:12), *challenge* ("Your testimony is not valid," 8:13), and *riposte* ("My testimony is valid," 8:14). Then again *claim* ("My judgment is valid," 8:16), *challenge* ("Where is your father?" 8:19a), and *riposte* ("You know neither me nor my Father," 8:19b). This exchange resembles a fencing match: thrust and parry, lunge and retreat. What matters is who speaks first and who has the last word, both of which in this case belong to Jesus. He makes the claim that precipitates the conflict, and his last word reduces his opponents to silence. In terms of argumentative honor, Jesus succeeds masterfully.

The Eighth Scene: Does He or Doesn't He Judge (8:12–20). One may read this exchange in terms of forensic process, which illuminates its complexities and makes a narrative link with John 7 that much clearer.[233] Jesus' claim to be the "light of the world" is also *testimony* (i.e., he does not lead the people astray but enlightens them). The "court," which just sought to arrest and kill Jesus (7:1, 19, 25, 32), rejects his testimony based on an Israelite custom: "You are testifying on your own behalf; your testimony is not valid" (8:13; see *m. Kethuboth* 2:9). The accused counters by explaining why his testimony is valid: "My testimony is valid because I know where I have come from and where I am going" (8:14). This knowledge makes Jesus superior to his accusers, who totally lack this. Listeners of this Gospel must wait until 8:17–18 to learn that Jesus has two witnesses, himself and "the Father who sent me." Jesus next accuses his accusers and judges his judges: "You do not know where I come from or where I am going. You judge by human standards" (8:14b–15). They "do not know" vital information, which we saw earlier means that they lack Jesus' revelation. Moreover, as Jesus argued in 7:24, they judge falsely because they judge according to appearances and so pervert justice. Having said "I judge no one," Jesus begins to act in the role of judge: "If I do judge, my judgment is valid; for it is not I alone who judge, but I and the Father who sent me" (8:16). The issue of the validity of Jesus' testimony

---

232 R. E. Brown, in *The Gospel According to John* (1966), 1.340, argues the case that "light" stands for reformed Torah.

233 Some commentators see no evidence of a forensic process in John 8, and others even dismiss it; see F. J. Moloney, *Signs and Shadows* (1996), 94–96.

returns, with him arguing that there is more than one witness before this court on Jesus' behalf: "I testify on my own behalf, and the Father who sent me testifies on my behalf" (8:18; see Deut 17:6; 19:15). But how can the court summon this second witness? "Where is your Father?" In response, Jesus judges them guilty of sin: "You know neither me nor my Father. If you knew me, you would know my Father also" (8:19). He has the last word in this the eighth scene of the forensic proceedings occurring during the Feast of Booths. He acts more and more as judge; his speech contains serious accusations against his judges. Verdicts on both sides are maturing, but there is yet no arrest or sentence.

JOHN 8:21–30 – TWO DIFFERENT WORLDS

21 Again he said to them, "I am going away, and you will search for me, but you will die in your sin. Where I am going, you cannot come."
22 Then the Jews said, "Is he going to kill himself? Is that what he means by saying, 'Where I am going, you cannot come'?"
23 He said to them, "You are from below, I am from above; you are of this world, I am not of this world.
24 I told you that you would die in your sins, for you will die in your sins unless you believe that I am he."
25 They said to him, "Who are you?" Jesus said to them, "Why do I speak to you at all?
26 I have much to say about you and much to condemn; but the one who sent me is true, and I declare to the world what I have heard from him."
27 They did not understand that he was speaking to them about the Father.
28 So Jesus said, "When you have lifted up the Son of Man, then you will realize that I am he, and that I do nothing on my own, but I speak these things as the Father instructed me.
29 And the one who sent me is with me; he has not left me alone, for I always do what is pleasing to him."
30 As he was saying these things, many believed in him.

Topic and Development. As in the case of 3:2, 5:18, and 6:31, the evangelist makes a topic statement that is then developed point by point. In this case, the topic is 8:21, which is developed in 8:22–28. The development, moreover, stands in chiastic relationship to the topic, as the following diagram illustrates.

Topic
A. "I am *going away* and you will search for me,
B. but *you will die in your sin.*
C. *Where I am going, you cannot come.*" (8:21)

Development

C'. "Is that what he means by saying, '*Where I am going, you cannot come*'"? (8:22)

B'. "*You will die in your sins* unless you believe that I am he." (8:24)

A'. "When you have *lifted up* the Son of Man, you will realize . . . " (8:28)

References to Jesus' death frame the passage ("go away" . . . "lift up"); and Jesus twice pronounces a sentence of death on his audience ("You will die in your sins"). Moreover, Jesus and the audience belong to two different worlds; hence "where I am going, you cannot come." The holy are separated from the sinful, as are the heavenly from the earthly.

The Ninth Scene: Jesus Judges (8:21–30). This trial does not resemble previous scenes in which the judges judge unjustly and so bring judgment upon themselves. On the contrary, this part of the forensic process takes a new turn as the roles of all the various dramatis personae change. Jesus acts as judge. Although he claimed that "I judge no one" (8:15), now he announces, "I have much to say about you and much to judge" (8:26). His former judges now become the accused. Jesus proclaims a law for which failure to comply warrants a death sentence: "You will die in your sins unless you believe that I AM" (8:24). What do the accused have to say for themselves? Is there testimony on their behalf? The "unless" demand resembles previous ones, such as that spoken to Nicodemus (3:3, 5) and the synagogue crowd at Capernaum (6:53). Unless some action is taken, one shuts oneself out of God's kingdom and so lacks life. Here, a confession is demanded that if not given means that the accused "will die in their sins." Only a judge can make such a law, prescribe a sanction, and enforce it.

What Do You Say for Yourselves? How do the accused respond? What do they say for themselves? Throughout this extended trial, Jesus has been calling them "liars" and "murderers," so no matter what they say, the audience will scrutinize their words and behavior, particularly by tracing the familiar rhetorical pattern of *statement–misunderstanding–clarification*. Whereas the pattern may function to enlighten some, here it serves to expose the deception of a sinful crowd lying about their discipleship. Thus it functions negatively to expose and judge the enemies of Jesus. Are they ignorant or lying when they claim not to know what Jesus means in 8:21, the same statement he made in 7:34? They understand that "I go away" means death but shift the blame on Jesus himself by interpreting it as suicide (8:22). Earlier they shifted blame from themselves by conveniently interpreting "I go away" (7:34) as Jesus' departure for the Dispersion (7:36). But in both 7:34 and now in 8:21 Jesus asserts that "you will seek for me," which we saw means "seek to kill" (7:1, 19–20, 25). Thus we argue that they do not "misunderstand" Jesus so much as dissemble about his charges. They are *lying* about their efforts to *murder* Jesus. The remainder of this chapter dramatizes how

Jesus exposes their lying testimony that they are "believers" (8:30),[234] eventually proving that this audience is the offspring of the archetypal murderer and liar, the devil (8:43).

They bypass an element in Jesus' remark in 8:21 ("You will die in your sins") as they plead "not guilty" to this. But when Jesus repeats it in 8:24, he indicates that one could avoid "dying in one's sins" by a bold confession: "unless you believe that I AM." "Believe" means acknowledgment, loyalty, and respect,[235] which have not characterized the conversations that earlier ended in his attempted "arrest" (7:30, 32, 45; 8:20). Moreover, the audience seems deaf to Jesus' remark about "believing that I AM" when they ask "Who are you?" (8:25). This crowd already rejected the claim that Jesus was either prophet or Messiah. If they consider those titles unacceptable for Jesus, they are surely not ready to acknowledge the cryptic "I AM." But are they just ignorant? Or are they liars?

From Above, From Below. There are five redundant ways to read Jesus' remark, "You are from below, I am from above; you are of this world, I am not of this world" (8:23). First, this crisp judgment serves as a forensic evaluation of character. Second, we know that being "from above" means not only that Jesus was sent by the One who is above but that he has descended from above into this world (3:13). This allies him with God, the Holy One, blessed be He, and speaks to his heavenly character. Third, the dualisms here contrast "above" with "below" and "not of this world" with "this world." They parallel the "heaven" versus "earth" contrast in Nicodemus' knowledge (3:6–11) and the "spirit" versus "flesh" antithesis in 6:63. All worth, value, and holiness are found in "above" and "not of this world," whereas belonging to "this world" and being "from below" mean obtuseness and wickedness. Fourth, we know what importance the ancients put on one's "origins," whether place of origin or parents and ancestors.[236] Jesus, "from above" and "not of this world," then, enjoys illustrious origins, namely from heaven and from a heavenly Father. Those addressed, however, are truly base, originating "from below" and "of this world." In the forensic world, testimony from such base people has little or no worth; this judgment, then, strikes at the credibility of those who speak in 8:22, 8:25, and 8:29. Fifth, we appreciate how important it has been to know the correct "whence" and "whither" of Jesus. In 8:21 Jesus clarifies "whither" to mean his death and

---

[234] Not only does Jesus practice secrecy, but his opponents do also. See J. H. Neyrey, "Secrecy," in *What Is John?* (1998), 79–109.

[235] Although "believe" may contain specific confessional content, it generally means group attachment and solidarity. Both meanings are in play here. See Bruce J. Malina, "Faith/Faithfulness," in John J. Pilch and Bruce J. Malina, eds., *Handbook of Biblical Social Values* (Peabody, MA; Hendrickson, 1998), 72–79.

[236] Nathanael and the Jerusalem elites find fault with Jesus' place of origin (1:46; 7:41–42, 52); others reduce Jesus' status because his parents were of mean status (6:41–42). See the commentary on "origins" at 7:25–30.

return to God; in 8:23, he declares that his "whence" is the heavenly world. But only genuine insiders acknowledge Jesus' heavenly origins and destiny. Thus those whom Jesus addresses here lack more than knowledge, namely light and life.

Irony. Twice the author employs irony in Jesus' declaration of his forthcoming death. First, when Jesus says "I go away" (8:21), his opponents strangely claim that he talks of his suicide (8:22; see 2 Sam 17:23; Josephus, *Wars* 3.375). The irony[237] lies in the fact that, while "death" is clearly understood by both parties, the proponents of suicide not only "seek to kill" Jesus but will eventually finish their task. Second, Jesus declares, "When you have lifted up the Son of Man, then you will realize that I am he" (8:28). As all know, "lift up" is one of the classic Johannine double-meaning terms, suggesting both the lifting up of the crucified Jesus and the enthronement of the King. If "lift up" means "death," then the special name "I AM" means "life."[238] Thus, by taking the life of the one who has life in himself (5:26), the murderers will occasion the manifestation of Jesus as eternally existing in the future. His murderers, then, will cause the very opposite of what they seek.

Knowing about Jesus' "Father." In 8:26–29, Jesus makes a series of statements about his Father: "The one who sent me is true, and I declare to the world what I have heard from him" (8:26); "I speak these things as the Father instructed me" (8:28); "The one who sent me is with me; he has not left me alone" (8:29a); and "I always do what is pleasing to him" (8:29b). As expected, those addressed "did not understand that he was speaking to them about the Father" (8:27). They do not lack information but rather withhold acknowledgment of the Father's son and agent, a serious evil. His "whence" is not so much a place as a person. And if Jesus speaks what he is instructed to say, then his appropriation of the power expressed in "I AM" is legitimate, however shocking to his audience it may be (17:6, 11–12, 26).

"Many Believed in Him." Is this not interesting? The people who seek to arrest and kill Jesus now "believe in him"? The people Jesus accused of a crime worthy of death now claim that they have not broken his law. Now we are told that "many believed in him" (8:30). Caution! What do they believe? Is not this "belief" just

---

237 Paul Duke, *Irony in the Fourth Gospel* (Atlanta: John Knox, 1985), 113–14.
238 Catrin H. Williams's " 'I Am' or 'I Am He' "? in Robert T. Fortna and Tom Thatcher, eds., *Jesus and the Johannine Tradition* (Louisville, KY: Westminster John Knox, 2001), 343–52, distinguishes two meanings of "I am": the identification formula of any speaker ("I am he," 4:26; 6:20; 9:9) and God's self-identification ("I AM"). See also David Mark Ball, *"I Am" in John's Gospel* (Sheffield: Sheffield Academic Press, 1996), 188–98.

too convenient in the face of their judge and his stern law? Are they telling the truth?[239] Recall 2:23–25.

JOHN 8:31–37 – ABRAHAM TESTIFIES AGAINST HIS SONS

31 Then Jesus said to the Jews who had believed in him, "If you continue in my word, you are truly my disciples;
32 and you will know the truth, and the truth will make you free."
33 They answered him, "We are descendants of Abraham and have never been slaves to anyone. What do you mean by saying, 'You will be made free'?"
34 Jesus answered them, "Very truly, I tell you, everyone who commits sin is a slave to sin.
35 The slave does not have a permanent place in the household; the son has a place there forever.
36 So if the Son makes you free, you will be free indeed.
37 I know that you are descendants of Abraham; yet you look for an opportunity to kill me, because there is no place in you for my word.

How Does a Judge Judge? From Daniel we learn that judges were responsible for verifying or falsifying the testimony of witnesses.[240] The testimony from the crowd that they believe in Jesus (8:30) comes from murderers and liars and so must be carefully examined. The roles now played by Jesus and these alleged believers differ from those in 7:14–36 and 8:12–20 in that Jesus himself performs the judicial scrutiny of their testimony, indicating that he is now judge and they are the accused (see 8:26).

Chiastic Shape of the First Test (8:31–37). This first interchange between judge and accused is elegantly crafted in chiastic shape, as the following diagram indicates:

A. If you *remain in my word* (32a)
B. You will know the truth and the truth will set you *free.* (32b)
C. We are the *Seed of Abraham.* (33a)
D. We have never been *slaves.* (33b)

---

[239] Scholars who reject the interpretation of these "believers" as liars (8:30) alternatively call them former believers. See C. H. Dodd, "Behind a Johannine Dialogue," in his *More New Testament Studies* (Manchester: Manchester University Press, 1968), 42–46.
[240] In Roman law, the technical term for the judge's scrutiny of testimony is *cognitio.* See A. N. Sherwin-White, *Roman Society and Roman Law in the New Testament* (Oxford: Oxford University Press, 1963), 1–23; see also J. H. Neyrey, "Jesus the Judge," *Biblica* 68 (1987), 509–11.

D'. Everyone who does sin is a *slave* of sin; the *slave* does not *remain* in the house forever; but the son *remains* forever. (34–35)

C'. I know that you are *Seed of Abraham*, but you seek to kill me. (37a, b)

B'. If the Son makes you *free*, you will be truly *free*. (36)

A'. My *word finds no rest in you*. (37c)

The literary craft, moreover, highlights important elements in the argument. Jesus begins with a conditional remark, "*If* you remain in my word...,"[241] but concludes with a declarative judgment: "My word finds no rest in you." "Remaining" is also part of the middle section, where it is argued that "the slave" (Ishmael) does not remain in the house of Father Abraham. Some "remain" and some do not, which balances the argument that while Jesus' words remain in some they do not in these people. Therefore, by virtue of the discourse, the judge judges against those who claimed to be disciples by proving that in fact they do not believe in him.

Abraham, First Installment. References to "seed of Abraham," "free son" and "slave son," and "remain in the house" have much to do with the argument here, but to appreciate them we must resurrect parts of the Abraham story that are in the background here: Abraham had two sons, Isaac and Ishmael; Isaac, born of a free woman, was free, but Ishmael, born of a slave woman, was a slave;[242] while Isaac "remained" in his father's house, Ishmael was sent away; and legend has it that Ishmael tried to kill Isaac, which links those to whom Jesus says "you seek to kill me" with Ishmael.[243] Thus, the primary issues are: "Who is the heir"? "Who is the legitimate son"? Which son of Abraham are these alleged believers?

Statement–Lie–Clarification. Jesus makes a *statement*: "If you continue in my word, you are truly my disciples" (8:31a). He says more: A true disciple "will know the truth, and the truth will make you free" (8:31b). The audience does not so much misunderstand this as *dissimulate* and lie. By saying "We are descendants of Abraham and have never been slaves to anyone" (8:33), they claim high status as sons of Abraham, something all Israelites could claim.[244] But they dissemble

---

[241] "Remain" speaks to loyalty and affiliation (see 15:4–10). See J. Heise, *Bleiben* (Tübingen: J. C. B. Mohr [Paul Siebeck], 1967).

[242] Many ignore the association in 8:33–38 of "free" with Isaac and "slave" with Ishmael. R. E. Brown's *The Gospel According to John* (1966), 1.362–64, links this with the allegory about Sarah and Hagar in Galatians 4:21–32.

[243] Galatians 4:29 states that Ishmael was cast out for "persecuting him who was born according to the spirit." For midrash on this, see J. Louis Martyn, *Galatians* (New York: Doubleday, 1997), 444; and J. H. Neyrey, "Jesus the Judge," *Biblica* 68 (1987), 522–23.

[244] Controversy over Abraham's offspring belongs to the polemic about blood relatives (1:12–13; 2:1–6; 7:1–10). On descent and ethnic purity in Israel, see Joachim Jeremias, *Jerusalem in the Time of Jesus* (Philadelphia: Fortress Press, 1969), 271–302; and Thomas B. Dozeman, "*Sperma Abraham* in John 8 and Related Literature: Cosmology and Judgment," *CBQ* 42 (1980), 342–57.

by claiming to be offspring of Isaac, the free son who remained, whereas in fact they stem from Ishmael, the slave son who was expelled. Jesus *clarifies* that although they may indeed be "offspring of Abraham," they are exposed as coming from the line of Ishmael, the slave son, because they seek to kill Jesus (8:37).

At This Point in the Trial. . . . After this first scrutiny of the crowd's testimony, by 8:37 we know that they are guilty of lying. Their claim to believe is a lie. Jesus laid down the criterion for a true believer, namely "to remain in my word," but he then proved that "my word finds no place in you." Inasmuch as the premier charges against this audience were "lying" and "murder," Jesus has caught them in a lie when they try to pass themselves off as the offspring of Abraham by Isaac. And he openly accuses them of murder: "You seek to kill me" (8:37; see also 8:40, 44, 59). Lying is proven; murder remains to be shown. The trial could end now with a guilty verdict, but it continues with three more tests.

JOHN 8:38–40 – ABRAHAM AND CHIPS OFF THE OLD BLOCK

38 I declare what I have seen in the Father's presence; as for you, you should do what you have heard from the Father.
39 They answered him, "Abraham is our father." Jesus said to them, "If you were Abraham's children, you would be doing what Abraham did,
40 but now you are trying to kill me, a man who has told you the truth that I heard from God. This is not what Abraham did.

Chiastic Structure. The evangelist has crafted the argument in 8:38–40 in a chiasm similar to that observed in 8:31–38. The beginning and ending both deal with "do . . . what your father did," at first referring to the devil's ancestry of the pseudo-believers and then to Abraham. Two more different "fathers" cannot be found. The middle pair (B & B′) have to do with criteria for determining true children of Abraham; after all, he had two sons, Isaac and Ishmael.

> A. I declare what I have seen in *my Father's* presence; you do what you have heard from *your Father*. (8:38)
> B. *Abraham* is *our father*. (8:39a)
> B′. If you were *Abraham's children*, you would be doing *what Abraham did*. (8:39b)
> A′. But now you are trying to kill me. This is *not* what *Abraham did*. (8:40)

A true son of Abraham will prove to be a chip off the old block by imitating his father, who offered hospitality to strangers from heaven; false sons "try to kill me."

Abraham in Legend Again. The story of Abraham narrates a number of things whereby he achieved legendary honor, such as receiving theophanies from God, an expansive new homeland, the promise of many sons, hospitality to heavenly messengers, and sacrificing Isaac. The author has in view here only Abraham's hospitality to the heavenly messengers (Gen 18).[245] Sons imitate their fathers, and so true sons of Abraham do what their father did;[246] no true son would seek to kill heavenly messengers as these people are doing.

The Second Test (8:38–40). In this second scrutiny of their testimony, Jesus traps them in a lie. They claim honor, credibility, and status by descent: "Abraham is our father." Jesus challenges this and unveils the lie they are telling. Proof that they are not sons of Abraham by the free son, Isaac, rests on the fact that they do not act like this son. In addition to lying, they are also charged once more with murder: "You are trying to kill me." The judge, then, mercilessly exposes the duplicity of their testimony.

JOHN 8:41–44 – FATHERS EVERYWHERE: GOD, ABRAHAM, AND THE DEVIL

41 "You are indeed doing what your father does." They said to him, "We are not illegitimate children; we have one father, God himself."
42 Jesus said to them, "If God were your Father, you would love me, for I came from God and now I am here. I did not come on my own, but he sent me.
43 Why do you not understand what I say? It is because you cannot accept my word.
44 You are from your father the devil, and you choose to do your father's desires. He was a murderer from the beginning and does not stand in the truth, because there is no truth in him. When he lies, he speaks according to his own nature, for he is a liar and the father of lies.

---

[245] On the praise of Abraham's hospitality, see Philo, *Abr.* 107, 114–16, 132, 167; Josephus, *Ant.* 1.196; 1 Clement 10:6–8; and T. Abraham 17.

[246] C. H. Talbert's *Reading John* (1992), 156, cites the Mishnah illustrating how sons represent their fathers in what they do: "He in whom are these three things is of the disciples of Abraham our father; but [he in whom are] three other things is of the disciples of Balaam the wicked. A good eye and humble spirit and a lowly soul – are of the disciples of Abraham our father. An evil eye, a haughty spirit, and a proud soul – are of the disciples of Balaam the wicked" (*Mishnah Aboth* 5.19).

Chiastic Structure Again. After arguing that Abraham cannot be their father, Jesus exposes their true paternity and its shame and stigma. He begins by accusing them of being chips off the old block, but not of Father Abraham, and ends by unveiling the fact that their father is the devil. In the middle part (B & B′), the accused claim as their father the most noble and holy person in the world, a lie that demands exposure. Jesus proves that they cannot have God as their Father because they do not love God's son or listen to God when he speaks through this agent.

A. You are indeed doing what *your father does.* (8:41 a)
B. We are not illegitimate children; we have *one father, God himself.* (8:41 b)
B′. If *God were your Father,* you would love me, for I came from God. I did not come on my own, but he sent me. (8:42–43)
A′. You are from your father the devil, and you choose to do *your father's* desires. He was a *murderer* from the beginning. When he *lies,* he speaks according to his own nature, for he is a *liar* and the *father of lies.* (8:44)

Origins. In antiquity, identity and honor came both from one's place of origin and from one's parents or ancestors. The origins of these pseudo-believers have been unveiled layer by layer: Are they sons of Abraham? Yes, but via the son Ishmael. Are they sons of Abraham? No, for they do not do what their father did. Then are they sons of God, who is the Father? No!: "You are from your father the devil!" And they imitate their father in terms of his characteristic actions: murder and lying.

Devils and Demons Everywhere. Jesus accuses his opponents of being sons of the devil (8:44); and they return the compliment in 8:48 and 8:52. Two questions arise. (1) Is this a serious accusation? (2) What effect is this accusation supposed to have? Anthropological studies classify this as a witchcraft or sorcery accusation, which occurs frequently in the New Testament:[247]

1. *Others accuse Jesus of demon possession*

    Mark 3:23–30; Matthew 12:22–37; Luke 11:14–23
    John 7:20; 8:48, 52; 10:20

2. *Jesus accuses others of demon possession*

    Judas (John 6:70; see also Luke 22:3; John 13:2, 27);
    Peter (Mark 8:33)
    Others (John 8:44; Matt 12:43–44; Luke 11:24–26; Matt 13:38–39)

---

[247] See Jerome H. Neyrey, "Bewitched in Galatia: Paul in Cultural Anthropology," *CBQ* 50 (1988), 73.

3. *Paul accuses others of demon possession*

    "Superlative Apostles" (2 Cor 11:3, 13–15)
    Judaizing preachers (Gal 3:1; 1:8)
    Elymas the Magician (Acts 13:8–11)

4. *John the Baptizer is accused of demon possession*

    Matthew 11:18; Luke 7:33

5. *"Secessionists" who left the group are accused*

    1 John 2:18, 22; 3:8–10; 4:1–3; 2 John 7

In general, this type of labeling argues that some person is evil but disguised; outwardly he appears normal or respectable, but inwardly he is filled with evil and seeks to harm others in the village.[248] This "witch," then, has these characteristics: a corrupt inside (deviant, sinner), a deceiving exterior (hypocrite), attacks either by poison or soul sucking (poison = heresy; soul sucking = stealing faith or leading astray). This accusation is generally made in a social situation of intense and disorderly competition, where authority is weak and techniques for resolving these tensions are underdeveloped. It functions to label a rival as a person inimical to group values and norms and so turn public opinion against this person. If successful, the "witch" will be forced to withdraw from the competition either by weight of popular opinion (i.e., expulsion) or by voluntary choice to flee. In 8:44, 8:48, and 8:52, both competitors accuse each other of being "witches"; that is, of having a dissembling appearance that masks a perverse and deadly interior. Throughout Booths, Jesus has been in conflict with the Jerusalem elites over his role and status as prophet and Messiah. Their strategy was to brand Jesus as a sinner and a deceiver, hoping to discredit him and chase him from the scene. He in turn accuses them of evildoing, both lying and murder; his strategy is to expose their true nature, which is that of "sons of the Devil." Like many witchcraft-accusation contests, this one proves inconclusive; no one has the power to force the other off the stage, so as the competition continues, the hostilities grow more intense.

Lying: An Ancient Pastime. Why do people tell lies? John Pilch, in his survey of the sociology of lying, reveals two kinds of lies: lies of defense and lies of attack.[249] People tell "lies of defense" for many reasons: to conceal failure, intentional or unintentional; to avoid quarrels; and to aid kin and friends. Conversely, people

---

[248] See B. J. Malina and J. H. Neyrey, *Calling Jesus Names* (1988), 20–30; J. H. Neyrey, *Paul, in Other Words* (1990), 198–206, 213–17.

[249] John J. Pilch, "Lying and Deceit in the Letters to the Seven Churches: Perspectives from Cultural Anthropology," *BTB* 22 (1992), 126–34; and his "Secrecy in the Mediterranean World: An Anthropological Perspective," *BTB* 24 (1994), 151–57.

tell "lies of attack" for these reasons: to harm another by false testimony; to achieve material gain; and to stir up mischief and confuse authorities. The lies told by Jesus' accusers in John 8 are of several kinds: defensive lies to avoid Jesus' judgment rendered in 8:23; defensive lies to cover up their "seeking to kill" Jesus; defensive lies to cover up their origins as sons of the Father of Lies; and lies of attack in which a witch disguises itself as good in order to attack and destroy others.

JOHN 8:45–58 – NEW CLAIMS ABOUT ABRAHAM

45 But because I tell the truth, you do not believe me.

46 Which of you convicts me of sin? If I tell the truth, why do you not believe me?

47 Whoever is from God hears the words of God. The reason you do not hear them is that you are not from God."

48 The Jews answered him, "Are we not right in saying that you are a Samaritan and have a demon?"

49 Jesus answered, "I do not have a demon; but I honor my Father, and you dishonor me.

50 Yet I do not seek my own glory; there is one who seeks it and he is the judge.

51 Very truly, I tell you, whoever keeps my word will never see death."

52 The Jews said to him, "Now we know that you have a demon. Abraham died, and so did the prophets; yet you say, 'Whoever keeps my word will never taste death.'

53 Are you greater than our father Abraham, who died? The prophets also died. Who do you claim to be?"

54 Jesus answered, "If I glorify myself, my glory is nothing. It is my Father who glorifies me, he of whom you say, 'He is our God,'

55 though you do not know him. But I know him; if I would say that I do not know him, I would be a liar like you. But I do know him and I keep his word.

56 Your ancestor Abraham rejoiced that he would see my day; he saw it and was glad."

57 Then the Jews said to him, "You are not yet fifty years old, and have you seen Abraham?"

58 Jesus said to them, "Very truly, I tell you, before Abraham was, I am."

59 So they picked up stones to throw at him, but Jesus hid himself and went out of the temple.

Change in Rhetoric. The author no longer shapes the argument as a chiasm but as two parallel challenge/riposte exchanges. Moreover, although one still finds "misunderstandings" of Jesus' statements, they are not failures of understanding as are found in Jesus' discourses with Nicodemus and the Samaritan woman but naked mockery of Jesus' words and challenges to his claims.

First Exchange	Second Exchange
A. You have *a demon*. (v. 48)	A'. Now we know that you have *a demon*. (v. 52b)
B. I do not have a demon. *I do not seek my own glory*; there is *one who seeks it* and who judges. (vv. 49–50)	B'. If I glorify myself, *my glory is nothing*; it is my Father who *glorifies me*, whom you say is your God. (v. 54)
C. Whoever *keeps my word* will never see death [forever]. (v. 51)	C'. You have not known him. . . . I know him and *I keep his word*. (v. 55)
D. *Abraham died*, and the prophets (v. 52)	D'. *Abraham* your Father rejoiced that he was to *see my day*; he saw it and was glad. (v.56)
E. Are you *greater than* our Father *Abraham*, who died. . . . Who do you claim to be? (v. 53)	E'. Before *Abraham* came into being, *I AM*. (v. 58)

Both exchanges begin with an accusation of demonic possession (A & A') against which Jesus appeals to God, who glorifies him (B & B'), thus refuting their judgment about him. In both, Jesus makes new claims: "keeping so-and-so's words" has powerful results, either "not seeing death" or "knowing" God (C & C'). Both claims utilize the figure of Abraham (D & D'), first as an argument against Jesus but later by him to claim heavenly status (E & E').

Claim, Challenge, and Riposte. To give greater precision to the dialogue here, we plot it out in terms of the ubiquitous conflict exchange found in the Gospels.

First Cycle (8:44–49). Jesus' forensic charge in 8:44 functions as his *claim* against the audience. Inasmuch as he accused them of demon possession in 8:44, they *challenge* him by returning the compliment in 8:48. His *riposte* in 8:49 rebuts the challenge by asserting that he honors "his father," while they dishonor him and thus his father, who of course is God.

Second Cycle (8:51–55). Jesus makes a new *claim*, the wording of which we must carefully remember: "Whoever keeps my word will never see death." *Challenge.* The opponents mock this by citing "proof" that Jesus is wrong: "Abraham died, and so did the prophets; yet you say, 'Whoever keeps my word will never taste death'" (8:52–53). What did Jesus say and how did they (not) hear him?

    Jesus: "Whoever keeps my word will never *see* death."
    Crowd: "Whoever keeps my word will never *taste* death."

"See" death or "taste" death? What's the difference?[250] The crowd's error concerning Jesus' words is courtroom evidence that they do not "keep my words." According to Johannine anthropology, this crowd cannot understand the spiritual meaning of his words because it is "from below" and "of this world" (8:23). Hence, Jesus' earlier accusation is proved now by the crowd's substitution of "see" with "taste." The crowd now questions Jesus,[251] not asking for information but *challenging* and ridiculing him: "Are you greater than our father Abraham?" Jesus' *riposte* cuts two ways. In apology to their challenge, "Who do you claim to be?" Jesus states that he is what his Father has made him: "It is my Father who glorifies me, he of whom you say, 'He is our God'" (8:54). More aggressively, Jesus "knows" God who is Father – that is, he honors him (8:49) – but they "do not know him" because they dishonor his agent (5:23). Finally, Jesus contrasts himself with the crowd to argue that if Jesus lied and said that he did not know God, he would be like them, a liar. But his testimony about God in 8:31–58 proves that he knows about God and acknowledges his sovereignty. The proof is that Jesus "keeps his word."

Third Cycle (8:56–58). The remarks in 8:54–55 skirted the question about Abraham, who died, but Jesus now returns with a remarkable *claim*: "Abraham rejoiced that he would see my day; he saw it and was glad." *Challenge*. Again the crowds fail to hear Jesus' words correctly, and on the basis of their obtuseness they try to respond to his challenge. Whereas Jesus said that "Abraham . . . *saw it* and was glad," the crowds hear "You are not yet fifty years old, and *have you seen* Abraham"? They mock the claim that "you" have seen Abraham when what Jesus said was "he" (Abraham) saw my day.[252] His word, then, does not remain in them (8:31); because they do not keep his word, they are liable to death (8:51). Out of their own mouths they are convicted. *Riposte*. The duel concludes with Jesus scoring the perfect touch by silencing his opponents. He responds to their question of age and duration with the ultimate comparison with Abraham: "Before Abraham came into being, I AM" (8:58).

I AM: "Having Life in Himself." The key to 8:58 is our recognition of two forms of existence. All mortals come into existence and die; they are created in

---

[250] See Bruce D. Chilton, "'Not to Taste Death': A Jewish, Christian and Gnostic Usage," in E. A. Livingstone, ed., *Studia Biblica 1978* (Sheffield: JSOT Press, 1980), 29–36.

[251] Recall that questions most frequently are hostile weapons used to embarrass and ridicule someone; see the comments on 3:3–10 and literature cited there.

[252] Most interpret "saw my day" as a revelation to Abraham of the future day of the Messiah. See Rudolf Schnackenburg, *The Gospel According to St. John* (New York: Crossroad, 1982), 221–22. We link it to "what Abraham did" (8:39), which means his reception of heavenly messengers. See Linwood Urban and Patrick Henry, "'Before Abraham Was I Am': Does Philo Explain John 8:56–58?" *Studia Philonica* 6 (1979–80), 166–87.

the past and perish in the future. But God, the immortal one, has no beginning or ending; God is uncreated and imperishable.[253] God eternally "is." And this, too, the author claims for Jesus. We learned that an aspect of Jesus' equality with God was the power to "have life in himself" just as God does (5:26). Later, Jesus will tell us that he has power to lay down his life and power to take it up again (10:17–18), which precludes his corruption or the end of his existence. "Having life in himself" looks to the future, such that Jesus shares God's future imperishability. Here, in 8:58, the claim is made that this "life in himself" extends into the past, such that, unlike Abraham, Jesus did not "come into being" but always "was" or, more accurately, always "is."[254]

JOHN 9:1–12 – ANOTHER SIGN: FROM DARKNESS TO LIGHT

1 As he walked along, he saw a man blind from birth.

2 His disciples asked him, "Rabbi, who sinned, this man or his parents, that he was born blind?"

3 Jesus answered, "Neither this man nor his parents sinned; he was born blind so that God's works might be revealed in him.

4 We must work the works of him who sent me while it is day; night is coming when no one can work.

5 As long as I am in the world, I am the light of the world."

6 When he had said this, he spat on the ground and made mud with the saliva and spread the mud on the man's eyes,

7 saying to him, "Go, wash in the pool of Siloam" (which means Sent). Then he went and washed and came back able to see.

8 The neighbors and those who had seen him before as a beggar began to ask, "Is this not the man who used to sit and beg?"

9 Some were saying, "It is he." Others were saying, "No, but it is someone like him." He kept saying, "I am the man."

---

[253] The ancients developed a topos on true deities (versus divinized mortals) that argued that they are uncreated in the past and imperishable in the future. See Jerome H. Neyrey, "'Without Beginning of Days or End of Life' (Hebrews 7:3): Topos for a True Deity," *CBQ* 53 (1991), 440–50.

[254] Many scholars focus their attention not on the eternal existence Jesus claims but only on his use of the divine name, "I AM"; see R. E. Brown, *Gospel According to John* (1966), 1.366–68 and 533–38. Others concede that it confirms the claim for his pre-existence; see Edwin D. Freed, "Who or What Was Before Abraham in John 8:58?" *JSNT* 17 (1983), 52–59.

10 But they kept asking him, "Then how were your eyes opened?"
11 He answered, "The man called Jesus made mud, spread it on my eyes, and said to me, 'Go to Siloam and wash.' Then I went and washed and received my sight."
12 They said to him, "Where is he?" He said, "I do not know."

When? Where? And Who? The feast of Booths seemingly ended when Jesus "hid himself and exited the temple" (8:58). But many argue that the events in John 9 are a part of this feast. They point out how Jesus' remark "I am the light of the world" (9:5) parallels the same statement in 8:12 and how "light" was one of the two chief benefits prayed for during the feast.[255] *Where?* Jesus is still in Jerusalem, for he sends the blind man to the local pool called Siloam. *Who?* Still on stage are Jesus and his accusers, the Pharisees. But a new character appears, a man born blind. Unlike his parents and others intimidated by the threat of expulsion from the synagogue for acknowledging Jesus (9:22, 34), the blind man comes to serve as Jesus' expert witness. The process against Jesus described during Booths is reopened, but with Jesus absent.

Haven't We Seen This Before? The parallels between the healing of the lame man in John 5 and the man born blind in John 9 are regularly noted by commentators.[256] The following comparison serves us in several ways. It points out how both healing miracles follow the form of a typical miracle story (severity of disease, cure, proof, honor). But it also shows by way of contrast the differences between them, namely that while the healing process did not make a disciple of the man at the Sheep Gate pool, it most certainly did with the man sent to the Siloam pool; the blind man was blessed with sight and insight. His bold public speech on behalf of Jesus leads him to be "cast out," a mark of an elite disciple.

The Lame Man 5:1–17	*How Similar?*	*The Man Born Blind 9:1–34*
1. ". . . a feast in Jerusalem, by the Sheep Gate, a pool . . . Sabbath"	When: Sabbath Where: a pool	1. In Jerusalem . . . a pool called Siloam . . . Sabbath
2. Jesus' initiative; no request	Jesus in control	2. Jesus' initiative; no request
3. Sin appears to be cause of illness (5:14)	Relation of sin to illness	3. "Who sinned, this man or his parents, that he was born blind"? (9:2) Sin rejected as cause

---

[255] See J. J. Menken, *Numerical Literary Techniques in John: The Fourth Evangelist's Use of Numbers of Words and Syllables* (Leiden: Brill, 1985), 190. Some locate this right after Booths; see G. R. Beasley-Murray, *John* (1999), 153.
[256] See Jeffrey L. Staley, "Stumbling in the Dark, Reaching for the Light: Reading Character in John 5 and 9," *Semeia* 53 (1991), 64–65.

4. "One man . . . had been ill for thirty-eight years" (5:5)	Severity of the disease	4. "a man blind from birth" (9:1)
5. Cure by word alone: "Rise, take up your mat and walk." (5:8)	Cure: by command or use of *materia medica*	5. Cure by word and deed: "He spat, made clay, anointed the man's eyes and said: 'Go'." (9:6)
6. Proof of cure: "The man was healed, took up his mat and walked." (5:9)	Proof	6. Proof of cure: "He went and washed and came back seeing." (9:7)
7. Sabbath violation: "It is the Sabbath; it is not lawful for you to carry your mat." (5:10)	Done on the Sabbath	7. "Now it was the Sabbath day when Jesus made the mud and opened his eyes." (9:13)
8. Interrogation of the healed man: "Who is it that said to you, 'Take it up and walk'"? (5:12)	Forensic Process Begun	8. Interrogation of the man born blind: "The Pharisees began to ask him how he had received his sight." (9:15–16)
9. The man does not know who Jesus is or where he is (5:13)	Where is the Sabbath breaker	9. "Where is he?" "I do not know." (9:12)
10. Jesus "finds" him: "Jesus found him in the temple." (5:14): no discipleship	Finding? Finding as recruitment; finding as in finding fault with	10. "When Jesus heard that they had driven him out . . .": recruitment
11. The man eventually knew only the name of the man who healed him, "Jesus." (5:15)	What do those cured say about their healer?	11. The man born blind declares Jesus a "prophet" (9:17), authorized agent of God (9:30–33), and Son of Man (9:35–38).
12. Jesus works as his Father works. (5:17)	Authorization	12. Jesus must do the works of the one who sent him. (9:4)

Representative Characters. Although the two healings are alike, they differ significantly in terms of the characters healed and the honor that accrues to Jesus. The crippled man's illness was related to sinfulness (5:14), whereas Jesus denies that sin had anything to do with the blindness of the man he heals (9:2–3).[257] The crippled man *did not know* the name of his healer (5:13), but the blind man *knew* that "a man named Jesus made clay, anointed my eyes and said, 'Go to Siloam'" (9:11). *Not* knowing and knowing are significant character labels in the Gospel. When the crippled man informed the authorities that Jesus commanded him

---

[257] See R. Collins, "The Representative Figures in the Fourth Gospel," *Downside Review* 94 (1976), 26–46, 118–32; Staley, "Stumbling in the Dark," *Semeia* 53 (1991), 55–58, 64–69.

to carry his mat on the Sabbath (5:15), he was not honoring Jesus or singing his praises, but the man born blind speaks positively and boldly on Jesus' behalf, thus signaling that he is becoming an ideal insider.[258] Both men experience status-transformation rituals. Whereas the crippled man changes status from lame beggar to whole person, the man born blind becomes not only sighted but also an enlightened disciple. If his parents are afraid to speak on Jesus' behalf (9:22), he is not (9:31–33). Typical signs should conclude with acknowledgment of Jesus' role and status (2:12; 7:31; 20:30), which is what happens in the healing of the man born blind. Not so the crippled man, who saw no sign, received no enlightenment, and accorded no honor to Jesus.

A Sign. "Signs" function to glorify the role and status of the healer, which in this case means acknowledgment of Jesus as "prophet" (9:17) and "agent of God" (9:30–33).[259] The man born blind first sees and then sees enough to acknowledge his cure as a sign. Appropriately, Jesus made two remarks earlier that describe the event's function as a "sign": " . . . that God's works might be *revealed* in him" (9:3) and "We must work the works of him *who sent me*" (9:4). This healing, then, has to do with "revealing" and credentials-for-agency, the normal functions of signs. Moreover, although phrased abstractly, the contents of 9:3–4 will be metamorphosed into a forensic argument by the healed man, who in 9:31–33 will draw the obvious conclusions that the sign was supposed to signify.

JOHN 9:13–17 – FORENSIC PROCEEDINGS YET AGAIN

13 They brought to the Pharisees the man who had formerly been blind.

14 Now it was a Sabbath day when Jesus made the mud and opened his eyes.

15 Then the Pharisees also began to ask him how he had received his sight. He said to them, "He put mud on my eyes. Then I washed, and now I see."

16 Some of the Pharisees said, "This man is not from God, for he does not observe the Sabbath." But others said, "How can a man who is a sinner perform such signs?" And they were divided.

17 So they said again to the blind man, "What do you say about him? It was your eyes he opened." He said, "He is a prophet."

---

[258] See P. Duke, *Irony in the Fourth Gospel* (1985), 117–26.

[259] In addition to reading 9:1–7 as a typical "sign," some interpret it symbolically; see Bruce Grigsby, "Washing in the Pool of Siloam: A Thematic Anticipation of the Johannine Cross," *NovT* 27 (1985), 227–35.

The Trial That Never Ends. Once the author tells us that Jesus healed on the Sabbath (9:14), a forensic process begins, just as happened in 5:10–16. The *charge*, Sabbath violation; the *judges*, "the Pharisees"; the *accused*, Jesus, absent from the scene; and the *chief witness*, the man born blind,[260] who testifies on Jesus' behalf. Various neighbors and parents testify as well.[261] The process unfolds in four scenes.

Scene One (9:8–12). At the start, two issues need to be determined: the identity of the man healed and a record of what happened to him. About the first, neighbors and relatives voice conflicting opinions: "The neighbors and those who had seen him before as a beggar began to ask, 'Is this not the man who used to sit and beg?' Some said 'Yes,' others 'No,' and still others 'No, but someone like him' (9:8–9).[262] The man himself settles this issue: "He kept saying, 'I am the man'" (9:9b). But what happened? "How were your eyes opened?" (9:10). In regard to the second point, now that it is established that this man is the correct person, he rehearses the record of events, always testifying about Jesus. When asked "Where is he?" he tells the truth: "I do not know" (9:12). Often in this Gospel, being "not in the know" stigmatizes a character; not so here, for as the following trial will dramatize, the man will gradually move into "the know," acknowledge Jesus, and even receive a revelation.

Scene Two (9:13–17). The *court* formally assembles when "they brought to the Pharisees the man who had formerly been blind" (9:13). *Wrongdoing* comes to light: "It was a Sabbath day when Jesus made the mud and opened his eyes" (9:14). When questioned, the man born blind *testifies* truthfully to what happened. But the court dismisses his testimony because he is a beggar, a person of no status whatsoever (see Acts 4:13). But the court's *judgment* is divided, some arguing that "This man is not from God, for he does not observe the Sabbath," whereas others maintain just the opposite: "How can a man who is a sinner perform such signs?" When they return to the man born blind for further *testimony* to the character of Jesus, he testifies: "He is a prophet" (9:17). The trial comes to an abrupt halt.

---

[260] J. Louis Martyn's *History and Theology in the Fourth Gospel* (1979), 27–29, argues that there are other characters in the story who are not seen, namely certain Johannine disciples who behave with the same courage as the blind man. This is their story, too.

[261] On the forensic character of John 9, see Martin Asiedu-Peprah, *Johannine Sabbath Conflicts as Juridical Controversy* (Tübingen: Mohr Siebeck, 2001), 120–50; and A. T. Lincoln, *Truth on Trial* (2000), 96–105.

[262] This is another instance of the Johannine motif of "schism" or divided judgments; see 7:12, 41–43; 9:16; 10:17–21; and 11:36–37.

JOHN 9:18–23 – THE TRIAL CONTINUES

18 The Jews did not believe that he had been blind and had received his sight until they called the parents of the man who had received his sight

19 and asked them, "Is this your son, who you say was born blind? How then does he now see?"

20 His parents answered, "We know that this is our son, and that he was born blind;

21 but we do not know how it is that now he sees, nor do we know who opened his eyes. Ask him; he is of age. He will speak for himself."

22 His parents said this because they were afraid of the Jews; for the Jews had already agreed that anyone who confessed Jesus to be the Messiah would be put out of the synagogue.

23 Therefore his parents said, "He is of age; ask him."

Scene Three (9:18–23). It belongs to courts and judges to scrutinize testimony. This court is dissatisfied with the testimony of the man born blind because they do not believe he was in fact born blind, so they summon the only *witnesses* who can verify this, namely his parents. They question the parents on two points: "Is this your son, who was born blind?" and "How then does he now see?" Like other questions we have studied in this Gospel, these are by no means simple requests for information but challenges to the son and to Jesus, who healed him. Moreover, these carry with them threats, such that the parents "feared the Jews." The parents answer the first question affirmatively, "Yes, he is our son," but evade the second. Are they lying?[263] They claim not to know "how he now sees" and "who opened his eyes" (9:21). Are readers to suppose that they knew nothing of the news spread about in 9:8–12 in which the son explained "how" and "who"? Are they the last persons to learn of the great fortune of their blind son, once reduced to begging? The narrator tells us in an aside that they are lying: "His parents said this because they were afraid of the Jews; for the Jews had already agreed that anyone who confessed Jesus to be the Messiah would be put out of the synagogue" (9:22). They tell a defensive lie, but what is worse, they abandon their son to the court: "Ask him; he is of age. He will speak for himself" (9:21).

---

[263] John J. Pilch's "Lying and Deceit in the Letters to the Seven Churches: Perspectives from Cultural Anthropology," *BTB* 22 (1992), 126–35, distinguishes two types of lies: defensive (to protect oneself from exposure or harm) and offensive (to attack others). Lies are also told to gain honor and increase reputation. See Michael Gilsenan, "Lying, Honor, and Contraditction," in Bruce Kapherer, ed., *Transaction and Meaning: Directions in the Anthropology of Exchange and Symbolic Behavior* (Philadelphia: Institute for the Study of Human Issues, 1976), 191–219; and J. H. Neyrey, "Secrecy," in *What Is John?* (1998), 83–85, 107). See John 7:1–10; 8:44, 55; and 9:21–22.

JOHN 9:24–34 – TRIED IN ABSENTIA

24 So for the second time they called the man who had been blind, and they said to him, "Give glory to God! We know that this man is a sinner."
25 He answered, "I do not know whether he is a sinner. One thing I do know, that though I was blind, now I see."
26 They said to him, "What did he do to you? How did he open your eyes?"
27 He answered them, "I have told you already, and you would not listen. Why do you want to hear it again? Do you also want to become his disciples?"
28 Then they reviled him, saying, "You are his disciple, but we are disciples of Moses.
29 We know that God has spoken to Moses, but as for this man, we do not know where he comes from."
30 The man answered, "Here is an astonishing thing! You do not know where he comes from, and yet he opened my eyes.
31 We know that God does not listen to sinners, but he does listen to one who worships him and obeys his will. ˙
32 Never since the world began has it been heard that anyone opened the eyes of a person born blind.
33 If this man were not from God, he could do nothing."
34 They answered him, "You were born entirely in sins, and are you trying to teach us?" And they drove him out.

Scene Four (9:24–34). For the second time, the judges confront the man born blind, who now metamorphoses into a savvy witness. First, they pronounce *judgment* not on this man but on Jesus, who has never appeared before this court: "Give glory to God! This man is a sinner" (9:24).[264] How strange a judgment, which is supported only by the making of mud on the Sabbath.[265] But whereas the judges "know" Jesus' status as a sinner, the man effectively denies it – I do not know whether he is a sinner" – another schism. They then demand more *testimony*; nothing new, but the same information already given them several times (9:26, see also vv. 11, 15). The man mocks their demand to hear his testimony once more because they did not accept it previously: "I have told you already, and you would not listen" (9:27a). How ironic that the man born blind came to see Jesus' role ("prophet," 9:17). They, not the man born blind, are defective in sight; he "told" them but they would not "listen." He speaks sarcastically to the court, mocking their demand to hear the same old testimony: "Why do you

---

[264] Readers should remember what Nicodemus said about judgments in absentia: "Our law does not judge people without first giving them a hearing to find out what they are doing, does it?" (7:51). For the Gospel audience, this suffices to show the wrongness of this trial.
[265] Commentators cite *m. Shabbath* 7.2 as illustrative of how Judeans understood "work"; see R. E. Brown, *Gospel According to John* (1966), 1.208.

want to hear it again? Do you also want to become his disciples?" (9:27b) – another aggressive, sarcastic question.

Whose Disciple? Their remark, "We are disciples of Moses. We know that God has spoken to Moses" (9:28), is ambiguous. In an earlier process, Jesus, the accused, testified that this very Moses "wrote of me" (5:46) and that he "will be your accuser" for failing to listen to Jesus. Thus the *judges* are lying and cannot be disciples of Moses; otherwise they would acquit and acknowledge Jesus. Moreover, their evidence against Jesus is bogus: "We do not know where he comes from" (9:29). From Nicodemus on, this question serves to distinguish insiders from outsiders (3:2; 6:41–42; 7:27–28, 41–42, 52). Is this another lie? The man born blind then delivers the most logical, coherent *testimony* on Jesus' behalf, which refutes the arguments of the judges. He starts with a fact: "He opened my eyes." Then he argues for Jesus' close relationship to God, refuting the judgment rendered in 9:24. Not sinners but only saints have access to God's power: "God does not listen to sinners, but he does listen to one who worships him and obeys his will" (9:31). Moreover, Jesus' action is unique in human history, which elevates it beyond the power of human beings (9:32). Third, in *testifying* about Jesus, he makes the only *right judgment*: "If this man were not from God, he could do nothing" (9:33). But the judges once more judge unjustly ("You were born entirely in sins") and sentence him unfairly ("They drove him out").

Representative Characters. We are now able to sort out three groups of characters in this episode in terms of their reaction to Jesus. First are the Pharisees, who know nothing to begin with and even after expert eyewitness testimony refuse to know anything. They have heard a "gospel" about Jesus and been instructed in the logic of Jesus' signs, but to no avail. They are permanent outsiders. Then we have the parents of the man born blind, who although less reprehensible than the Pharisees, are far from authentic discipleship because they lack courage to acknowledge Jesus publicly and so lie about what they know. They eventually abandon their son to the court. Finally, in the course of the narrative, the man born blind matures into an insightful, courageous person who boldly and publicly speaks about Jesus and even suffers public humiliation because of him. He becomes, then, an ideal hero for the group, both in growth of knowledge and public witnessing.

JOHN 9:35–41 – THE BLIND MAN'S COMPLETE TRANSFORMATION

35 Jesus heard that they had driven him out, and when he found him, he said, "Do you believe in the Son of Man?"
36 He answered, "And who is he, sir? Tell me, so that I may believe in him."

37 Jesus said to him, "You have seen him, and the one speaking with you is he."

38 He said, "Lord, I believe." And he worshiped him.

39 Jesus said, "I came into this world for judgment so that those who do not see may see, and those who do see may become blind."

40 Some of the Pharisees near him heard this and said to him, "Surely we are not blind, are we?"

41 Jesus said to them, "If you were blind, you would not have sin. But now that you say, 'We see,' your sin remains."

Transformation. Rites of status transformation generally have four stages: separation, a liminal stage, rite of passage, and acknowledgment of new status. In regard to the man born blind, we learn that his status transformation began when Jesus *separated* him from the world of beggars and infirm people (9:1–6) and dispatched him to the "Sent Place" (Siloam). With his new sight, he enters a *liminal period* in which he is schooled to be an ideal disciple. Liminal periods are generally times of learning, discipline, and endurance of hardships, which for the man born blind are focused in the extended forensic process narrated in 9:8–33. His maltreatment as a deviant in the eyes of the inquisitors is genuine training as an apprentice disciple. He gains great insight into Jesus, becomes adept at reasoning like an insider, and boldly testifies on Jesus' behalf. As a result, he experiences a genuine *rite of passage* out of the synagogue and into the circle of Jesus' disciples (9:34). His new role is that of an ideal insider who sees, knows, and publicly confesses Jesus. As regards *acknowledgment* of his new status, whereas those who expel him label him a deviant, Jesus "finds" him and confirms him as an insider. The transformation, then, from blindness and "not knowing" to a genuine Christophany is complete: "You have seen him, the one speaking with you is he" (9:37).

A CLOSER LOOK – EXCOMMUNICATION

Groups in antiquity regularly make and maintain boundaries. Once boundaries were made to ensure identity or purity or orthodoxy, guardians acted to label others as dangerous to the rest of the group and to urge their expulsion.[266] In Acts, Paul regularly speaks in synagogues, only to have guardians there expel him from the synagogue (Acts 13:45, 50; 14:5, 19).

---

[266] On excommunication in antiquity, see D. R. A. Hare, *The Theme of Jewish Persecution of Christians in the Gospel According to St. Matthew* (Cambridge: Cambridge University Press, 1967); Göran Forkman, *The Limits of Religious Community* (Lund: Gleerup, 1972); and J. Louis Martyn, *History and Theology in the Fourth Gospel* (1979), 24–64.

Sometimes citizens accuse Paul of political deviance (17:5; 18:12) and drive him from the city. The Gospels describe members of the house of Israel expelling disciples of Jesus from the synagogue (Luke 6:22), which is the situation described in John 9:22; 12:42; and 16:2. Even Christians expelled others (Matt 18:15–18; 1 Cor 5:1–7; 2 Thess 3:14–15; Titus 3:10–11).

Qumran provides the best example of this practice:

> If there is a man among them who lies in matters of property, he shall be separated from the midst of the Purification of the Many for one year. And whoever answers his fellow disrespectfully, or speaks (to him) impatiently [or (whoever) metes] out justice with his own hand, shall be punished for one year [and be separated]. [And] whoever makes mention whatever of the name of the Being venerated above all other venerated beings, [shall be put to death]. But if he has blasphemed from fright, or under the blow of distress, or for any other reason whatever while reading the Book or pronouncing the Blessings, he shall be separated and shall return no more to the Council of the Community. And if he speaks irritably against one of the priests, he shall be punished for one year and set apart by himself from the Purification of the Many. And the man who insults his fellow unjustly (and) knowingly shall be punished for one year and separated. (1 QS 6.25–7.4)

Scene Five (9:35–41). This episode concludes the lengthy forensic process dramatized in John 9. Present are the accused (Jesus), the witness (the man born blind), and the judges. The story begins after the court sentenced the man born blind to be expelled from the synagogue. Jesus appears to this faithful witness to vindicate him by canceling the guilty verdict against him and by elevating him to the status of a true insider. Now he is completely transformed from blind to sighted (9:1–7) and from "not knowing" (9:12) to fully enlightened (9:36–38). Yet a *court* is still in session, with Jesus now in the role of judge: "I came into this world for judgment" (9:39). This resumes the claim he made earlier: "I have much to say about you and much to condemn" (8:26). This is hardly the self-judgment described in 3:17–21 but relates to the claim of eschatological power made in the trial in John 5. Jesus claimed that God gave him authority to judge, precisely because he is the Son of Man: "He [God] has given him authority to execute judgment, because he is the Son of Man" (5:27). Indeed, in 9:35–37 Jesus reveals himself as such. He judges justly on behalf of the man born blind, acquitting him of their guilty judgment; he then judges justly those judges who unjustly judged both the man born blind and himself. The criterion for judgment is one of reversal of status: those who do not see, see (i.e., the blind man has many-layered sight); and those who see, become blind (i.e., those who claim to know or who suppress the truth). Jesus the judge issues the final verdict: "Your sin remains." This trial is now over; the one unjustly condemned is vindicated, whereas the unjust judges are in turn judged.

JOHN 10:1–6 – THE REVEALER SPEAKS IN RIDDLES

1 Anyone who does not enter the sheepfold by the gate but climbs in by another way is a thief and a bandit.

2 The one who enters by the gate is the shepherd of the sheep.

3 The gatekeeper opens the gate for him, and the sheep hear his voice. He calls his own sheep by name and leads them out.

4 When he has brought out all his own, he goes ahead of them, and the sheep follow him because they know his voice.

5 They will not follow a stranger, but they will run from him because they do not know the voice of strangers."

6 Jesus used this figure of speech with them, but they did not understand what he was saying to them.

Why Is the Revealer Speaking Obscurely? Jesus regularly acts as the Revealer of God's word (1:18), but at the same time he speaks double-meaning words that many invariably misunderstand, as well as an anti-language that is intended to confuse outsiders. Moreover, all characters keep secrets from one another; some wander in a world of ambiguity, tell lies, and practice deception.[267] Now Jesus tells a series of allegories that are far from obvious: the thief and the shepherd (10:1–6), the door (10:7–10), and the noble shepherd versus the hireling (10:11–16). How are these related? What experiences of the audience might they reflect? And why are they here at this point in the narrative?

Parables or Allegories? A *paroimia* can be translated either as "proverb" or "parable" (Sir 39:3; 47:17); thus it is not direct speech but communication by way of simile or metaphor.[268] Scholarship on parables in the synoptic Gospels argues that they typically make only one point of importance, which provokes surprise or shock by forcing the audience into a kind of reversal of values or expectations. But parables are not entirely accessible to all, only to the in group (John 16:25, 29–30; see also Mark 4:10–13).[269] Understanding them marks one as a genuine, even elite, insider. In contrast, allegories present a story or scene with many points, which creates a comparison or set of binary opposites (true/false; noble/base; "in" / "out"). These function not by means of surprise and shock but more in terms of exhortation. For example, all know the "parable of the sower," who foolishly wastes three of four seeds as he sows yet finally gets it right. This "fool," however, becomes wise when the audience is shocked to realize that Jesus

---

[267] See J. H. Neyrey, "Secrecy," in *What Is John?* (1998), 87–107.

[268] See Kim E. Dewey's "*PAROIMIAI* in the Gospel of John," *Semeia* 17 (1980), 81–99, which focuses primarily on *paroimiai* as proverbs.

[269] See Joel Marcus, "The Parable Theory," in his *The Mystery of the Kingdom of God* (Atlanta: Scholars Press, 1986), 89–123.

speaks of God (Mark 4:3–9). But we also know the allegory of the soils, where soil types correspond to types of hearers. Once the emphasis is shifted to the soil, the parable of the sower is metamorphosed into an allegory exhorting hearers to be good soil. We suggest that the materials in 10:1–16 are allegories, not parables. Are they exoteric, addressed to the crowds, or esoteric, spoken to insiders?

Decoding the Allegory. Two characters are contrasted here, a "thief-bandit" and "the shepherd." They differ in terms of their mode of entry into the "sheep-fold" and the recognition of their voices. First, the thief-bandit climbs into the sheepfold surreptitiously, not through the gate, whereas the shepherd speaks to the gatekeeper, who opens the gate to him, thereby acknowledging his right to be there. Second, this shepherd "calls his sheep by name," and they follow him because they "know his voice" – not so the thief. Thus the author conducts in 10:1–5 a rhetorical comparison, labeling one shepherd legitimate but all others illegitimate.[270] Curiously, the Greek text says that he not only "leads them out" but also "casts them out," which might well be an ironic play on words of the fate of the man born blind, who was just "cast out" of the synagogue (9:34). Nevertheless, he goes before them and the sheep follow him. There is nothing parabolic here; all is as Jesus' peasant audience would expect. The shepherd benefits the flock.

To What Does Any of This Refer? To interpret this allegory, let us draw parallels to this material in other places in the Gospel. (1) The narrative context is that of Jesus' rebuke of the Pharisees at the end of Chapter 9. The only group that listens to him are members of the Johannine circle. Some of these he even calls by name, such as "Lazarus" and "Mary." (2) Like the sheep, some disciples are in fact "cast out," as was the man born blind (9:34), which suggests an apology for the brutal experience of some disciples (16:1–2). (3) Jesus "goes before them" (14:2, 3, 6), for he precedes the disciples in terms of the cross, death, and vindication. (4) The antithesis of the shepherd is likely the Jerusalem elite, especially the Pharisees, who are here denied authorization and legitimacy.[271] (5) Finally, Jesus' critics prove that they are not part of his flock because they do not recognize his voice: "But they did not understand what he was saying to them" (10:6).

---

[270] Some argue that the sheep entrusted to the Messiah are attacked by false messiahs, others see a challenge to Israel's gatekeepers, whether they are ready to open to the Messiah, and finally others argue that Jesus lacks demonstrable authorization, save for the sheep who follow. See J. A. T. Robinson, "The Parable of John 10:1–5," *ZNW* 46 (1955), 233–40.

[271] Some argue that here true shepherds are juxtaposed with false ones. John Painter describes this as "characteristic of a sect, which justifies its rejection and lack of recognition by those outside in such terms"; see his "Tradition, History and Interpretation in John 10," in Johannes Beutler, S. J., and Robert T. Fortna, eds., *The Shepherd Discourse of John 10 and Its Context* (Cambridge: Cambridge University Press, 1990), 60.

JOHN 10:7–10 – THE "DOOR" OF THE SHEEPFOLD AND OF THE KINGDOM

7 So again Jesus said to them, "Very truly, I tell you, I am the gate for the sheep.
8 All who came before me are thieves and bandits; but the sheep did not listen to them.
9 I am the gate. Whoever enters by me will be saved, and will come in and go out and find pasture.
10 The thief comes only to steal and kill and destroy. I came that they may have life, and have it abundantly.

Relationship of 10:1–6 and 7–10. The previous allegory contrasted authorized shepherds with unauthorized ones by virtue of the way they enter the sheepfold. That same contrast continues when the "thief" preys on the sheep and kills them, whereas the true shepherd brings them abundant life. Those who came before Jesus are "all thieves and bandits,"[272] whereas he brings them "salvation" and pasture. As in the previous allegory, these two shepherds relate to flocks of sheep. The sheep did not listen to the thieves and bandits or recognize their voices. But the sheep obviously recognize Jesus' voice and are attached to him: They "enter by me" and they "come in and go out and find pasture."

Who Says What to Whom and Why? Again, turning to parallels in this Gospel, we note that Jesus often functions as a mediating figure, just as the door does. But this door is not always open, for some cannot follow Jesus where he is going (8:21–22) and others will follow later (13:33). Still others, moreover, must be drawn by the Father to come through this door (6:44, 65). Yet no one can come to the Father except "through me," the official door (14:6).[273] Note also that those who "kill and destroy" refer to those who plot to cast the disciples out of the synagogue and even kill them (16:1–2) and that "thief" suggests only one person in the Gospel, Judas: "For he was a thief; he kept the common purse and used to steal what was put into it" (12:6). Finally, eternal life and abundant life are the blessings that Jesus constantly bestows on those who acknowledge him. Thus, we find in 10:7–10 an apologetic for the negative experiences of the Jesus group. Jesus may be speaking to the Judeans but for the community. The author's audience, then, are "insiders," not "outsiders."[274]

---

[272] Some scholars argue that the bandits and thieves refer to the host of "bandits, prophets, and messiahs" who peopled early first-century Israel; see Richard A. Horsley and John S. Hanson, *Bandits, Prophets, and Messiahs: Popular Movements in the Time of Jesus* (New York: Seabury-Winston, 1985).

[273] The best commentary on the significance of "door" is still that of Joachim Jeremias, "θύρα," *TDNT* 3.173–78.

[274] John Painter sees this aimed at would-be followers in the synagogue who are exhorted that only by facing excommunication and entering the Johannine group will they find

JOHN 10:11–18 – THE "NOBLE" SHEPHERD

11 I am the good shepherd. The good shepherd lays down his life for the sheep.

12 The hired hand, who is not the shepherd and does not own the sheep, sees the wolf coming and leaves the sheep and runs away – and the wolf snatches them and scatters them.

13 The hired hand runs away because a hired hand does not care for the sheep.

14 I am the good shepherd. I know my own and my own know me,

15 just as the Father knows me and I know the Father. And I lay down my life for the sheep.

16 I have other sheep that do not belong to this fold. I must bring them also, and they will listen to my voice. So there will be one flock, one shepherd.

17 For this reason the Father loves me, because I lay down my life in order to take it up again.

18 No one takes it from me, but I lay it down of my own accord. I have power to lay it down, and I have power to take it up again. I have received this command from my Father."

"Good" or "Noble" Shepherd? The adjective qualifying "shepherd" in 10:11 and 10:15 is not "good" but "noble."[275] The Greek *kalos* ("noble") belongs in the cultural world of honor and shame but *agathos* ("good") in the realm of virtue, where "good" is contrasted with "evil." Because the "nobleness" of the shepherd is linked with his death (10:11),[276] we turn to Greek rhetoric on "noble death" to discover how and why a death was labeled "noble."[277]

A CLOSER LOOK – NOBLE DEATH IN JOHN 10:11–18

Ancient Funeral Orations and "Noble" Death. Ancient funeral orations praised the death of military heroes according to the following canons.[278]

---

life; 12:24–26 may illustrate this. See J. Painter, "Tradition, History and Interpretation in John 10," in *Shepherd Discourse* (1990), 62.

[275] The adjective *kalos* is interpreted as "noble" (D. A. Carson, *Gospel According to John* [1991], 386), "ideal" (R. E. Brown, *Gospel According to John* [1966], 386, 395–96), or "true" (George R. Beasley-Murray, *John* [Waco, TX: Word Books, 1987], 170).

[276] See J. H. Neyrey, "Noble Shepherd," *JBL* 120 (2001), 267–80.

[277] See David Seeley, *The Noble Death: Graeco-Roman Martyrology and Paul's Concept of Salvation* (Sheffield: JSOT Press, 1990); and Arthur J. Droge and James D. Tabor, *A Noble Death: Suicide and Martyrdom among Christians and Jews in Antiquity* (San Francisco: Harper, 1992). Droge and Tabor focus on suicide, and Seeley on vicarious expiation in Paul. See also Jan Willem van Henten and Friedrich Avemarie, *Martyrdom and Noble Death* (London: Routledge, 2002), 9–41.

[278] See John E. Ziolkowski, *Thucydides and the Tradition of Funeral Speeches at Athens* (Salem, NH: Ayer, 1981); and Nicole Loraux, *The Invention of Athens: The Funeral Oration in the Classical City* (Cambridge, MA: Harvard University Press, 1986).

1. *Beneficial death.* Hyperides touts the gift of freedom given Athens and Greece by its fallen soldiers: "Their courage in arms . . . reveals them as the *authors of many benefits* conferred upon their country and the rest of Greece" (*Funeral Speech* 9).[279]

2. *Justice.* Athens's heroes displayed justice toward the polis in their deaths.[280] Civic memorials, then, focused on the justice that sought to "preserve ancestral customs and institutions and the established laws" (Pseudo-Aristotle, *Virtues and Vices* 5.2–3).

3. *Voluntary death.* Athenian orators expressed the *voluntary character* of death in two ways. Fallen soldiers were said first to "*prefer* noble death to a life of servitude" and second to "*choose*" their death. Pericles' oration over the war dead contains both aspects of "voluntary" death. As regards the first, "[W]hen the moment of combat came, *thinking it better* to defend themselves and suffer death rather than to yield and save their lives, they fled from the shameful word of dishonour. . . . In the brief instant ordained by fate, at the crowning moment not of fear but glory, they passed away" (Thucydides, *History* 2.43.4). Second, Thucydides tells us simply that the soldiers chose their fate: ". . . deeming the punishment of the foe to be more desirable than these things [wealth, escape] . . . they *chose* . . ." (Thucydides, *History* 2.42.4). Because their death was voluntary, they were not victims.[281]

4. *Unvanquished in death.* Although warriors perish, they die noble deaths because in the logic of honor they are judged undefeated or they have conquered their foes by dying (see Heb 2:14). Lycurgus writes: "*Unconquered* they fell at their posts in the defense of freedom, and if I may use a paradox but one which conveys the truth, they *triumphed* in their death" (*Against Leocrates* 48–49).

5. *Posthumous honors.* Ancient cities honored their dead with games and monuments. The funeral orations themselves were one such honor, which honored the dead with a public funeral and later by annual remembrance of their deaths, a type of immortality.

Jesus, the "Noble" Shepherd. The evangelist twice labels the shepherd "noble" and links nobility with the shepherd's death, which benefits others. In light of

---

[279] Hyperides says that Athens's soldiers "sacrificed their lives that others might live well" (*Funeral Speech* 26); see Thucydides, *History* 2.42.3; Plato, *Menexenus* 237a, 242a–b, 246; and Demosthenes, *Oration* 38 8, 23 and *Funeral Speech* 60 8, 10, 29.

[280] Justice referred to one's obligations to four groups of persons: "First among the claims of righteousness are our duties to the gods, then our duties to the spirits, then those to country and parents, then those to the departed"(Pseudo-Aristotle, *Virtues and Vices* 5.2–3).

[281] See Demosthenes, *Funeral Speech* 19.18 192, 207–8.

Greek funeral oratory on "noble death," we will examine John 10:11–18 to see how the Johannine argument reflects the Hellenistic rhetorical commonplace.[282]

Shepherd versus Hireling. When we hear that the "noble" shepherd lays down his life for his sheep but that the "hireling" flees from the wolf (10:11–12), we are reminded of the comparisons employed in the rhetoric of praise noted earlier: manly courage versus cowardice; fight versus flight; death versus life; and honor/glory versus shame/disgrace. The contrast between the noble shepherd and the hireling goes as follows. The noble shepherd displays courage, chooses to fight the enemy, and thus dies on behalf of the flock. He earns, therefore, the praise of being "noble."In comparison, the cowardly hireling flees from the conflict; by choosing to save his own life, he earns only contempt and disgrace.

"Knowing" and Justice. The shepherd is "noble" because he "knows his own" sheep (10:14). "Knowing" refers to the virtue of justice. In the "noble death" tradition, two virtues are praiseworthy: courage[283] and justice. In 10:11–18, two aspects of justice are in view: piety to God and fair dealing toward the disciples/sheep. The hireling has no duty to the sheep; they are not his (10:13). He is not in any way obligated in justice to face the wolf on their behalf; the owner should, but not the hireling.[284] When the shepherd proclaims that he "knows his sheep," he owns them and assumes responsibility for them (10:14–15). Thus "knowing" conveys a sense of relationship and responsibility rather than esoteric information.[285] The shepherd's duty to the sheep is expressed in the declaration that "I lay down my life for my sheep" (10:15).

Love and Obedience as Justice. The justice of the Noble Shepherd points also to his Father, who is God. Paralleling the remark about the reciprocal "knowing" between shepherd and sheep, the shepherd declares a similar relationship with the Father: "The Father knows me and I know the Father" (10:15).[286] The Father's relationship to Jesus is further developed when he says, "For this reason my Father loves me, because I lay down my life in order to take it up again"

---

[282] J. H. Neyrey, "Noble Shepherd," *JBL* 120 (2001), 281–88.

[283] Athenian funeral orators praise the courage of the fallen; see Thucydides, *Histories* 2.42; Isocrates, *Evagoras* 29, 42–44; Plato, *Menexenus* 237–246; and Hyperides, *Funeral Speech* 8–19.

[284] A shepherd was by no means honorable; see J. Jeremias, *Jerusalem in the Time of Jesus* (1969), 303–12. A hireling is worse because he works at the pleasure of another and for a wage.

[285] R. E. Brown, in *The Gospel According to John* (1966), 1.396, links 10:14 with 10:3–5: "Hence 'knowledge' means acknowledging someone or accepting a relationship; the sheep manifest their relationship to the shepherd because they 'hear his voice, he calls them by name ... and the sheep follow him because they know his voice.'"

[286] John Ashton, in his *The Understanding of the Fourth Gospel* (Oxford: Clarendon Press, 1992), 328, states: "The Father's 'knowing' the Son is in the Old Testament and Judaic tradition of election, while knowing on the Son's part means acknowledgment: the Son accepts the Father's revelation and his will."

(10:17). In ancient virtue theory, "love" is a part of justice.[287] New Testament "love" basically refers to relationships or social glue that hold persons together, especially kin.[288] The Father's "love," moreover, suggests his pride in Jesus. But in terms of a noble death, the Father's "love" of Jesus is expressed in Jesus' statements that he both lays down his life (10:11, 15) and takes it back (10:17–18). Whereas "nobility" and "lay down my life" belong to the topos on noble death, the second part, "in order that I may take it again," seems obscure. Although prophets raised the dead on occasion, no one has actively "taken his own life back again." We are "mortals" (i.e., those who die), which distinguishes us from God, the "immortal." Has Jesus crossed a boundary line here? For a mere mortal to claim such is both ludicrous and blasphemous. How may Jesus' remarks be seen as honorable? Jesus claims authorization from his God: "I have received this command from my Father" (10:18). A son who obeys his father honors him; he fulfills the basic justice that offspring owe their parents. Moreover, sons who obey their fathers show justice to them and similarly honor them.

Voluntary Death and Not a Victim. Jesus articulates the voluntary character of his death in 10:17–18. He states again that *he* lays down *his own* life; thus he chooses his death and dies willingly.[289] But Jesus says more: "No one takes it from me." He is not a victim, nor is he mastered by anyone. Thus he dies *unvanquished* and *unconquered*, which are marks of a noble death. Furthermore, Jesus claims to have "power" to lay down his life and to take it back. People with "power" control their destiny; they accomplish what they set out to do. This suggests, then, that Jesus ranks very high on the scale of people who do difficult deeds and who are masters of their fate.

Posthumous Honors and/or Immortality. Whereas Greek political life conveyed a kind of immortality by annual remembrance and by enduring monuments, Jesus enjoys a genuine imperishability in the future: "I have power to take it [my life] again" (10:17–18). God, who loves him and commands him, honors Jesus with this power and imperishability. Moreover, Jesus is the only person with this power; no one else has it. Whereas resurrection in the New Testament typically has some note of divine vindication of Jesus (Acts 2:24, 36; 3:14–15; 4:10–11), in John, Jesus has life in himself (5:26); his "lifting" up means the manifestation that he is "I AM," who is imperishable in the future.

---

[287] On "justice" and "love": "Piety to the gods consists of two elements: being *god-loved* (*theophilotes*) and *god-loving* (*philotheotes*). The former means being loved by the gods and receiving many blessings from them, the latter consists of loving the gods and having a relationship of friendship with them" (*Menander Rhetor* 1.361.17–25).

[288] See Bruce J. Malina, "Love," in John J. Pilch and Bruce J. Malina, eds., *A Handbook of Biblical Social Values* (Peabody, MA: Hendrickson, 1998), 110–14.

[289] In regard to the voluntary character of a noble death in 10:17–18, some scholars turn to examples from the Scriptures such as David facing both the bear and the lion in 1 Samuel 17:34–35; see R. E. Brown, *Gospel According to John* (1966), 1.398. Alas, the Hellenistic world is nowhere in view.

What, then, does consideration of John 10:11–18 in the light of the rhetorical tradition of a "noble death" tell us? There seems to be a close affinity on the following points:

Rhetorical Tradition about "Noble Death"	John's Discourse on the Noble Shepherd
1. Death benefited others, especially fellow citizens.	1. Death benefited the sheep, who enjoy a special relationship with the shepherd.
2. Contrast between courage/cowardice, fight/flight, death/life, and honor/shame	2. Contrast between shepherd/hireling: courage/cowardice, fight/flight, death/life, honor/shame
3. Manly courage displayed by soldiers who fight and die	3. Manly courage displayed by the shepherd who battles the wolf and dies
4. Voluntary death is praised.	4. Voluntary death claimed: "I lay it down of my own accord."
5. Unconquered in death; victory in dying nobly	5. Not a victim: "No one takes it from me."
6. Posthumous honors: speeches, tombs, games	6. Posthumous honors: power to take his life back
7. Justice and noble death: Soldiers uphold the honor of their families and serve the interests of the fatherland; duties served = justice.	7. Justice and noble death: The shepherd manifests loyalty to his sheep and his Father/God. He has a command from God; duties served = justice.

Who Says What to Whom and Why? Obviously, this refers to Jesus and functions as a miniature passion apologetic: He is the "noble" shepherd, and his virtues and his voluntary, beneficial death are praised. But he is compared with a "hireling," who may be either an insider or outsider. Peter acts as a hireling, denies "knowing" Jesus, and flees (18:17, 25–27). He cowardly chooses life by lying and flight rather than choosing death with loyalty. Noble insiders are defined as those who boldly face danger, excommunication, and even death, or whose "knowledge" and "love" of the group remains steadfast. The man born blind would be a good illustration of this type of character. Yet some scholars identify the "hireling" as a type of synagogue leader, who is judged according to prophetic criticisms directed against Israel's bad shepherds.[290]

JOHN 10:19–21 – COMING WITH A SWORD TO CAUSE DIVISION

19 Again the Jews were divided because of these words.
20 Many of them were saying, "He has a demon and is out of his mind. Why listen to him?"

---

[290] F. J. Moloney, *Signs and Shadows* (1996), 136–37. The actions of others against Jesus and his disciples include acting like wolves, and attacking the disciples (16:1–2) and scattering them (16:32).

21 Others were saying, "These are not the words of one who has a demon. Can a demon open the eyes of the blind?"

Challenge and Riposte. Jesus' discourse in 10:1–18 constitutes the *claim* here, which some inevitably *challenge*. Yet the very fact that some publicly defend Jesus identifies them as acting heroically according to the standards of the group (see 9:22, 31–34). Because it is the crowd that is divided, there can be no *verdict* and so no success in the contest and no award of honor.

Judgment. In forensic terms, the court has heard the testimony of the "noble" shepherd and must judge if it is true or not. In this case, the judges are divided, some condemning Jesus and others affirming him. As such, this judgment continues the public debate about Jesus and the relentless "division" of judgments about him (7:12, 25–27, 40–41; 9:8–9, 16; 12:29). Some accuse Jesus of "having a demon," which we saw constitutes an accusation of witchcraft. The remark that "he is out of his mind" seems to be another form of accusation of demon possession. This judgment, then, links the present crowd with the lying people of John 8, who were themselves sons of the devil – liars and murderers. Moreover, by urging others not to listen to Jesus, they demonstrate that they do not hear his voice; nor are they called by name or come through the gate. Others, however, declare, "These are not the words of one who has a demon. Can a demon open the eyes of the blind?" They demonstrate that in some sense they hear the shepherd and "know" him and are loyal to him. And by alluding to the argument of the man born blind (9:31–33), they are thereby associated with that heroic figure who was bold in defense of Jesus.

JOHN 10:22–33 – TELL US PLAINLY: WHO ARE YOU?

22 At that time the festival of the Dedication took place in Jerusalem. It was winter,
23 and Jesus was walking in the temple, in the portico of Solomon.
24 So the Jews gathered around him and said to him, "How long will you keep us in suspense? If you are the Messiah, tell us plainly."
25 Jesus answered, "I have told you, and you do not believe. The works that I do in my Father's name testify to me;
26 but you do not believe, because you do not belong to my sheep.
27 My sheep hear my voice. I know them, and they follow me.
28 I give them eternal life, and they will never perish. No one will snatch them out of my hand.
29 What my Father has given me is greater than all else, and no one can snatch it out of the Father's hand.
30 The Father and I are one."
31 The Jews took up stones again to stone him.
32 Jesus replied, "I have shown you many good works from the Father. For which of these are you going to stone me?"

33 The Jews answered, "It is not for a good work that we are going to stone you, but for blasphemy, because you, though only a human being, are making yourself God."

Forensic Process and the Anatomy of 10:22–39. After an absence of several months, Jesus comes back to alien territory for the winter feast of Dedication.[291] We argue that the extended exchange occurring in 10:22–39 is best understood in terms of the anatomy of a trial, a dynamic that occurs again and again. The "portico of Solomon" serves as an appropriate site for a forensic proceeding.[292] We can observe the forensic process in two ways: by comparing John 10:22–39 with the Judean trial found in the synoptic Passion narratives and by formal study of the choreography of the Johannine narrative in light of the typical elements of trials.[293]

Many observe that events clustered together in the synoptics are dispersed by the Johannine author.[294] We find here striking parallels between the questioning of Jesus by the high priest (Matt 26:62–64) and those who "surround" Jesus and demand that he answer them. In both cases, the questions asked are by no means a search for knowledge but a challenge, which is the rhetorical function of most questions.

Mark 14:61; Matthew 26:63; Luke 22:67	*John 10:22–39*
1. dramatis personae: high priests and Sanhedrin	1. dramatis personae: assembled elite
2. demand for testimony: "I adjure you by the living God, tell us if you are . . ."	2. demand for testimony: "How long will you keep us in suspense? If you are the Messiah, tell us plainly."
3. critical title: "Are you the Messiah?"	3. critical title: "If you are the Messiah, tell us."
4. charge against the questioners: "If I tell you, you will not believe; and if I question you, you will not answer" (Luke 22:67–68)	4. charge against the questioners: "I told you and you do not believe."
5. judgment: blasphemy	5. judgment: blasphemy (10:33)

---

[291] This feast commemorates the rededication of the Temple after its liberation from Greek rule (1 Macc 4:36–59; Josephus, *Ant.* 2.325). Whereas Jesus formally replaces other feasts, nothing of this sort occurs here.

[292] Solomon's "portico" or "stoa" was a colonnade along the east side of the temple platform (Josephus, *Ant.* 20.220–21). In general, it served as a meeting place for groups to study, discourse, and debate (Acts 3:11; 5:12).

[293] On the forensic shape and argument of John 10:22–39, see Jerome H. Neyrey, "'I Said: You are Gods,' Psalm 82:6 and John 10," *JBL* 108 (1989) 650–55.

[294] For example, the temple cleansing (John 2) occurs in the synoptics after Jesus' entry into Jerusalem; the cry of Jesus (John 12:27–28) resembles the prayer of Jesus in the garden. See R. E. Brown, *Gospel According to John* (1966), 1.405–6.

The parallels just noted cover only the beginning of John's scene. We need to bring to bear on the whole episode the formal elements of a trial to appreciate its forensic character.

Testimony Demanded (10:24). On the basis of what Jesus has previously said or done, the court demands that Jesus speak. Inasmuch as the "shepherd" has been the topic of the allegories spoken in 10:1–18, and because this title and role have traditionally belonged to Israel's king, it is logical that a court hostile to this would demand Jesus' clarification.

Testimony (10:25–27). In addition to those who testify boldly on Jesus' behalf, there is more cogent testimony on his behalf: "The works that I do in my Father's name testify to me" (10:25). Jesus, however, testifies against the court, accusing them of refusing to believe him and "not hearing his voice." In the logic of the Gospel, this is a very serious charge, for which one will die in one's sins (8:24). Returning to the sheep/shepherd materials in 10:1–16, Jesus reiterates the criteria for being "my sheep," which clearly excludes this court:

1. The sheep *hear* his *voice.* (10:3b)	1. My sheep *hear* my *voice.* (10:27a)
2. I *know my own* and my own know me. (10:14)	2. I *know them* (10:27b)
3. The sheep *follow him*; they know his voice. (10:4)	3. And they *follow me.* (10:27c)

The judges, however, are self-confessed nonsheep, who reject Jesus' basic claims to be God's agent and so are convicted of sin and unbelief (see John 3:18, 20; 5:40–45; 9:39–41; 12:46–48).

Testimony about Jesus (10:28–30). If the court took exception to Jesus' claims to be the "noble" shepherd, the new testimony by Jesus infuriates them. As he did in 5:21–29, Jesus claims to have God's eschatological power over life and death. He gives his sheep "eternal life" so that they never perish (10:28); this resembles the claim made in 8:51 that "whoever keeps my word will never see death." Nor will anyone "snatch them" from his hand (10:29), which we will shortly argue refers to death. Then Jesus testifies that in this matter he is equal to God.

When Jesus testifies about God, who is "greater than all," he affirms God's sovereignty and uniqueness (see 17:3). Yet having affirmed God as "greater," he then declares how he is "on a par" with God.[295]

---

[295] Many juxtapose 14:28 ("the Father is greater than I") with 10:29–30 ("My Father is greater than all.... I and the Father are one"). It seems best not to examine them as a coherent Christology but to assess the meaning of each in its context. In 10:29–30, Jesus claims parity with God in terms of the power given him. For a more theological analysis, see C. K. Barrett, "'The Father Is Greater Than I' (Jo 14, 28)," in Joachim Gnilka, ed., *Neues Testament und Kirche* (Freiburg: Herder, 1974), 150–52.

Jesus: "No one will snatch them out of my hand." (10:28)
Father: "No one can snatch it out of the Father's hand." (10:29)

The parity has to do with the bestowal of imperishable life, which Jesus claims was given him to give to others in 5:21–29. As we saw in the defense of the claim that Jesus has God's eschatological power, he is equal to God (5:18). Similarly, he claims the same power here and as a result states "I and the Father are one" (10:30). The Greek word *hen* commonly means the numeral "one," but in this context we translate it as "equal to" or "on a par with" (see 1 Cor 3:7).[296] It does not mean moral unity of purpose but rather equality of powers.[297]

Charge against Jesus (10:31–33). The court, which understands that "one" means "equal to," renders a verdict of blasphemy and prepares to execute a sentence of death by stoning. Jesus retorts by bringing back the argument earlier advanced by the man born blind in order to prove he is no sinner but in fact favored by God: "I have shown you many good works from the Father. For which of these are you going to stone me"? (10:32). They understand clearly what Jesus says but still judge him guilty: ". . . for blasphemy, because you, though only a human being, are making yourself God" (10:33). They charge him, then, with being an arrogant blasphemer, a deceiver, a consummate sinner.

JOHN 10:34–42 – WHO ELSE IS CALLED "GOD," AND WHY?

34 Jesus answered, "Is it not written in your law, 'I said, you are gods'?
35 If those to whom the word of God came were called 'gods' – and the scripture cannot be annulled –
36 can you say that the one whom the Father has sanctified and sent into the world is blaspheming because I said, 'I am God's Son'?
37 If I am not doing the works of my Father, then do not believe me.
38 But if I do them, even though you do not believe me, believe the works, so that you may know and understand that the Father is in me and I am in the Father."
39 Then they tried to arrest him again, but he escaped from their hands.
40 He went away again across the Jordan to the place where John had been baptizing earlier, and he remained there.
41 Many came to him, and they were saying, "John performed no sign, but everything that John said about this man was true."
42 And many believed in him there.

---

[296] J. H. Neyrey, "'I Said: You are Gods,'" *JBL* 108 (1989), 651–52.
[297] Patristic exegesis of this verse favored a trinitarian reading; see T. E. Pollard, "The Exegesis of John x.30 in the Early Trinitarian Controversies," *NTS* 3 (1957), 334–49.

Defense of Jesus. Jesus has already defended himself against charges such as these, denying that he "makes himself" anything, while affirming that his equality to God rests on God's gift of eschatological power (5:21–29). But here he shapes his defense as a holy person whom God has consecrated. Unlike other defenses in this Gospel, Jesus argues from Psalm 82:6, comparing the mortal persons in the psalm who are called "gods" with himself, the "Son of God," whom God consecrated and sent into the world (10:35–36).

A CLOSER LOOK – MIDRASH ON PSALM 82 IN JOHN 10:34

How is Psalm 82:6 understood, and how does it function? The following midrashim,[298] which draw parallels between Israel at Sinai with Adam in the Garden, argue that each was once judged "holy" and so "deathless," and thus validly called "god." The Gospel states "If those *to whom the word of God came* were called 'gods' . . .," whoever is called "god" is so named because "the word of God came" to them. This seems to be a reference to Israel at Sinai when God gave the Israelites the Torah.[299] One midrash emphasizes Israel's obedience at Sinai (that is, its holiness), for which it was called "god": "You stood at Mount Sinai and said, 'All that the Lord hath spoken will we do, and obey' (Exod 24:7), (whereupon) *'I SAID: YE ARE GODS'* (Ps 82:6); but when you said to the (golden) calf, 'This is thy god, O Israel' (Exod 32:4), I said to you, *NEVERTHELESS, YE SHALL DIE LIKE MEN* (Ps 82:7).[300] The basic lines of the midrash argue that receiving Torah meant obedience and so holiness, which resulted in deathlessness; hence Israel could be called "god" because it is "deathless." But Israel was disobedient and sinful and deserved the wages of sin; that is, death.

Similarly, Psalm 82:6 was used to interpret Adam's likeness to God, a point useful for understanding how the author uses this psalm in John 10. "The Holy one, blessed be He, said to them: 'I thought you would not sin and would live and endure for ever like Me; even as I live and endure for ever and to all eternity; *I SAID: YE ARE GODS, AND ALL OF YOU SONS OF THE MOST HIGH* (Ps 82:6). . . . Yet after all this greatness, you wanted to die! *INDEED, YE SHALL DIE LIKE MEN* (Ps 82:7) – Adam, i.e. like Adam whom I charged with one commandment which he was to perform and live and endure forever'; as it says, 'Behold the man was as one of us' (Gen 3:22). Similarly, 'And God created man in His own image' (Gen 1:27), that is to say, that he should live and endure like Himself. Yet [says God] he corrupted his

---

[298] On this topic, see J. A. Emerton, "Melchizedek and the Gods: Fresh Evidence for the Jewish Background of John X.34–36," *JTS* 17 (1966), 399–401; and James Ackerman, "The Rabbinic Interpretation of Psalm 82 and the Gospel of John," *HTR* 58 (1966), 186–91.

[299] Mekilta de-Rabbi Ishmael, Tractate *Bahodesh* 9, trans. Jacob Lauterbach (Philadelphia: Jewish Publication Society of America, 1933), 2.272.

[300] *Sifre: A Tannaitic Commentary on the Book of Deuteronomy.* Piska 320, trans. Reuven Hammer (New Haven, CT: YaleUniversity Press, 1986), 329.

deeds and nullified My decree. For he ate of the tree, and I said to him: 'For dust thou art' (Gen 3:19). So also in your case, *'I SAID YE ARE GODS'*; but you have ruined yourselves like Adam, and so *'INDEED, YE SHALL DIE'* like Adam."[301] This midrash parallels Israel at Sinai with Adam in the Garden, indicating that each was judged "holy" and so "deathless," and thus validly called "gods." But with sin, they died.[302]

Jesus' Defensive Use of the Midrash. The evangelist also understands Psalm 82 as referring to Israel at Sinai, for he contextualizes the psalm apropos of "those to whom the word of God came" (10:34–35). He does not explicitly link "gods" with holiness and "deathless," as the midrashim do. But indirectly he argues that some people were "equal to God" because they were deathless, as Psalm 82 indicates. In Jesus' case, he claims power over death; that is, "no snatching out of his hand." Moreover, if Israel became holy and was called *god*, then it is not blasphemy if Jesus, whom God consecrated and sent as his apostle into the world, is called *god* and *Son of God*. Holiness or sinlessness[303] again serves as the ground for calling someone, Israel or Jesus, "god."

Testimony on Jesus' Behalf. Is Jesus a sinner deserving of death, or a saint who enjoys deathlessness? The court judges negatively ("blasphemy," 10:33, 36) and so would stone him. But Jesus appeals to a witness whose testimony must be definitive in any court. God, who knows all secrets, has included Jesus in the inner circle of what is holy and trusts him as his unique agent.[304] The judges, then, contradict God's judgment, and by their wrong judgment they will be judged. But there is more testimony: Jesus' actions and powers serve as irrefutable testimony on his behalf, as we saw earlier in 9:31–33. God authorized his "works." But if Jesus does not do them, he disobeys God, becomes a sinner, and deserves death. But the "works," both miracles and powers, are authorized by God and prove God's favorable relationship with Jesus and that of Jesus with God. Yet the court rejects Jesus' testimony and so God's own judgment of him. In their eyes, he still blasphemes and so is guilty and deserves death.

Calling Jesus Names. We commonly find a series of titles ascribed to Jesus, often in an escalating or climactic manner. Curiously, except for the court's question

---

[301] *Numbers Rab.* 16.24.

[302] *Numbers Rab.* 16.24.

[303] The Gospel repeatedly notes the judgment that he was a sinner (9:16, 24) because of his healings on the Sabbath (5:1–17; 9:1–7). Enemies charge him with being thoroughly evil; that is, possessed of a demon (7:20; 8:48; 10:20). Here in 10:33 and 10:36 he is charged with a new sin, blasphemy, for claiming to be "equal to God."

[304] We have heard of God's evaluation of Jesus elsewhere: "The Father loves the Son" (3:35; 5:30). Sinners find no place in God's presence, yet Jesus was "face to face" with God (1:1–2) and in God's "heart" (1:18), to which Jesus will return at the completion of his mission (13:3; 17:5, 24). Jesus is sinless and worthy to stand in the divine presence.

about "Messiah," Jesus identifies himself with symbolic or titular names: "noble" shepherd; gate; "on a par" with God; and Son of God. The premier Christological testimony centers around "on a par with God," on which we focus. In 5:19–29, Jesus defended his "equality with God" by articulating that God gave him full creative and eschatological powers. John 10 articulates certain aspects of this eschatological power: First, Jesus has power to lay down his life and power to take it again (10:17–18), with emphasis clearly on the second part, the power to raise himself from the dead. God, who is immortal, has given Jesus the power to overcome death and be imperishable as well. Second, Jesus gives "eternal life" and there is "no snatching" from his hands (10:28). This parallels claims that "Just as the Father raises the dead and gives them life, so also the Son gives life to whomever he wishes" (5:21). Jesus did not say that his disciples would never "taste death" but that they would never "see death" (8:51–52). They may die, as do grains of wheat, but they do not remain dead, nor do they perish. Third, because saints are sinless, they are also deathless; hence those to whom the word of God comes may be called "god" – that is, deathless like God (10:34–36). These, then, are the people whom when Jesus raises the dead he will raise to the "resurrection of life" (5:29). One of the key themes that holds John 10 together is *death*, both the interpretation of Jesus' death as "noble" and the articulation of his eschatological power over death, both his own and that of others.

Geography of Safety. Since John 5, Jesus has been on trial by courts and crowds, which have sentenced him to death (5:18; 7:1, 32–36; 8:20, 37, 40, 59; 10:31, 39). All of this took place in "Jerusalem," not so much a specific location as a place of rejection and hostility. But when Jesus crosses the Jordan, he finds acceptance and safety. Moreover, he "remained" there, another indication of a place of close, friendly relationships.

JOHN 11:1–16 – AN ELEGANT OVERTURE

1 Now a certain man was ill, Lazarus of Bethany, the village of Mary and her sister Martha.

2 Mary was the one who anointed the Lord with perfume and wiped his feet with her hair; her brother Lazarus was ill.

3 So the sisters sent a message to Jesus, "Lord, he whom you love is ill."

4 But when Jesus heard it, he said, "This illness does not lead to death; rather it is for God's glory, so that the Son of God may be glorified through it."

5 Accordingly, though Jesus loved Martha and her sister and Lazarus,

6 after having heard that Lazarus was ill, he stayed two days longer in the place where he was.

7 Then after this he said to the disciples, "Let us go to Judea again."

8 The disciples said to him, "Rabbi, the Jews were just now trying to stone you, and are you going there again?"

9 Jesus answered, "Are there not twelve hours of daylight? Those who walk during the day do not stumble, because they see the light of this world.

10 But those who walk at night stumble, because the light is not in them."

11 After saying this, he told them, "Our friend Lazarus has fallen asleep, but I am going there to awaken him."

12 The disciples said to him, "Lord, if he has fallen asleep, he will be all right."

13 Jesus, however, had been speaking about his death, but they thought that he was referring merely to sleep.

14 Then Jesus told them plainly, "Lazarus is dead.

15 For your sake I am glad I was not there, so that you may believe. But let us go to him."

16 Thomas, who was called the Twin, said to his fellow disciples, "Let us also go, that we may die with him."

When? Where? Who?

When? We are between feasts, after Dedication (10:22) and before Passover (11:55); yet telling time in this Gospel is more complicated than mere calendar reckoning. On the one hand, it is a time of crisis, for a "beloved disciple" ("he whom you love") is near death; yet for all that, Jesus "stayed two days longer in the place where he was" (11:6), so that when Jesus arrived at Bethany, "Lazarus had already been in the tomb four days" (11:17). This telling of time serves to make the revivification of Lazarus all the more dramatic (see commentary on 5:5–6). Jesus speaks of "twelve hours in the day," daylight during which one must walk. In contrast, one stumbles in the darkness of nighttime. Jesus speaks not of clock time but discipleship time; those who believe in him act in the light, whereas pseudo-disciples like Nicodemus travel at night and traitors like Judas work evil at night. If Jesus himself is "light of the world," then disciples come to this light for revelation and grace. Thus, we know that "when?" is a time of crisis and time for appropriate action.[305]

Where? The three places identified are more than mere geographical loci. Jesus begins in safety, "across the Jordan . . . the place where John baptized" (10:40), suggesting a place where testimony to and revelation about Jesus proved successful: "Many believed in him there" (10:42). Bethany, home of these "beloved disciples," seems to be a safe place, where Jesus finds loyalty and belief. But "Judea," to which he returns, is known as a place of unbelief, trials, and death: "The Jews were just now trying to stone you, and are you going there again?" (11:8). Yet Jesus goes there, and his disciples declare readiness to go with Jesus, "that we

---

[305] Scholarship regularly indicates that a sign from the early stratum of John is now transformed because of a crisis in eschatological doctrine in the group; see James P. Martin, "History and Eschatology in the Lazarus Narrative: John 11.1–44," *SJTh* 17 (1964), 335–37.

may die with him" (11:16). Finally, Jesus' raising of Lazarus sets Jerusalem in an uproar, such that its elites plot Jesus' death (11:45–52). Space, as usual, is classified as friendly or hostile.

Who? We are told about two different networks of disciples: Jesus' inner circle, which includes a named disciple, Thomas; and three "beloved disciples" ("Jesus loved Martha and her sister and Lazarus," 11:5), all of whom are named. It is significant for the story that all three, especially Lazarus, be known as "beloved"[306] because the plot pivots around having a hard-core insider become ill and die, thus putting to the test Jesus' proclamation that believers have already passed from death to life. As regards Jesus himself, we have seen three times now that he is wont to refuse requests, even from family members. But now his intentional delay results in the death of a "beloved disciple" and raises the stakes; other beloved disciples, Martha (11:21) and Mary (11:32), reproach Jesus for the way he treated "beloved" Lazarus. Finally, Thomas,[307] the only named disciple, speaks only one line (11:16), which ironically boasts loyalty unto death with Jesus (11:16).

Gossip. The narrative begins with communication of information. First, Martha and Mary inform Jesus about Lazarus, presumably through a messenger (11:3); someone in Bethany tells Martha that Jesus has arrived (11:20), and Martha herself informs Mary of the same (11:28). Earlier, we observed that "gossip" networks naturally flourished in the ancient world as a typical way of conveying information. Already, we have seen in John how individuals brought messages to others (Andrew to Peter, Philip to Nathanael, 1:35–49; and the Samaritan woman to her village, 4:28–30; see also 20:17–18).

Request Refused Again. We observe the fourth instance of the pattern of "suggestion, negative response, positive action."[308] Twice already, Jesus' relatives have made requests of him and are put off: first the "woman" who is his mother (2:4); and then the men who are his "brothers" (7:3–4). We argued earlier that Jesus refuses them on very narrow but culturally significant grounds. Requests are positive honor challenges, which put Jesus on the spot and are perceived as forcing Jesus to act according to someone else's will.[309] His refusal, which is generally followed by positive action, indicates that Jesus has solved the honor challenge to his satisfaction and that all subsequent actions take place according to his timetable and purpose. Thus, the suggestion made by the sisters in 11:4 is refused; Jesus delays "two days longer" (11:6) and arrives after Lazarus is already

---

[306] The data include: "he whom you *love* is ill" (11:3); "now Jesus *loved* Lazarus" (11:5); "our *beloved* Lazarus has fallen asleep" (11:11); and "see how he *loved* him" (11:36).

[307] M. W. G. Stibbe, "A Tomb with a View: John 11:1–44 in Narrative-Critical Perspective," *NTS* 40 (1994), 45–48.

[308] C. H. Giblin, "Suggestion," *NTS* 26 (1980), 197–211.

[309] See the discussion of this at 2:3–7.

four days in the tomb (11:17). Were this just another sign, even the premiere sign, this delay would be disturbing.[310] Hence we are urged to attend to the special focus and emphasis Jesus has in mind, which is much more than the cure of a sick man.

Statement–Misunderstanding–Clarification. The entire Lazarus narrative functions as a catechetical experience of both "beloved" disciples (Martha and then Mary) and inner-circle disciples (Thomas and others). Jesus' first statement, "This illness does not lead to death; rather it is for God's glory, so that the Son of God may be glorified through it" (11:4), is typically misunderstood. After all, the disciples hear Jesus saying that this illness does not lead to death, so all will be well, which is not what Jesus meant but which he will clarify shortly (11:14). His second statement, "Let us go to Judea again" (11:7), sparks a practical but shallow understanding of this: "Rabbi, the Jews were just now trying to stone you, and are you going there again?" (11:8). Although they understand correctly based on past conflict, the full meaning will shortly come, for elite Judeans will shortly conspire to kill Jesus (11:45–52). Because the disciples miss what Jesus says, he clarifies by teaching them to tell time, namely the time to walk and act (11:9–10). Wise are they who walk in the twelve hours of the day and do not stumble; foolish, however, are those who ignore daylight, walk at night, and so stumble and fall. It would seem that "Let us go . . ." must be related to "walk in twelve hours of daylight." Thus, Jesus' "foolish" return to hostile territory is truly "wise" – but according to criteria different from those of the disciples.

Jesus' third statement escapes the disciples. They interpret "Our friend has fallen asleep, but I am going to awaken him" as health-restoring rest: "If he has fallen asleep, he will be all right" (11:12, 13). Jesus clarifies this for them: "Lazarus is dead" (11:15). What is not clarified here is the meaning of "I go to awaken him." Yet this exchange is in no way hostile, for Jesus treats it as an educational moment: "For your sake I am glad I was not there, so that you may believe" (11:15). Belief will mean understanding more fully Jesus' words and powers, but also adhering to him in loyalty. In anticipation of this, Thomas speaks words that are themselves glazed with irony: "Let us also go, that we may die with him" (11:16). This pattern, then, alerts us to an event, which is greater than a mere "sign" because it is revelatory[311] of Jesus' claim to God's power to raise the dead.

---

[310] See R. T. Fortna, *Gospel of Signs* (1970), 74–87; and W. Stegner, "Die Auferweckung des Lazarus (John 11, 1–45)," *TZ* 83 (1974), 17–19.

[311] Wilhelm Wuellner's "Putting Life Back into the Lazarus Story and Its Reading: The Narrative Rhetoric of John 11 as the Narration of Faith," *Semeia* 53 (1991), 113–32, argues that the raising of Lazarus is secondary to the enhancement of faith. Thus revelation of mysteries to Martha and her being led to a special insight is the center of the narrative.

JOHN 11:17–27 – REVELATION, NOT RESURRECTION

17 When Jesus arrived, he found that Lazarus had already been in the tomb four days.

18 Now Bethany was near Jerusalem, some two miles away,

19 and many of the Jews had come to Martha and Mary to console them about their brother.

20 When Martha heard that Jesus was coming, she went and met him, while Mary stayed at home.

21 Martha said to Jesus, "Lord, if you had been here, my brother would not have died.

22 But even now I know that God will give you whatever you ask of him."

23 Jesus said to her, "Your brother will rise again."

24 Martha said to him, "I know that he will rise again in the resurrection on the last day."

25 Jesus said to her, "I am the resurrection and the life. Those who believe in me, even though they die, will live,

26 and everyone who lives and believes in me will never die. Do you believe this?"

27 She said to him, "Yes, Lord, I believe that you are the Messiah, the Son of God, the one coming into the world."

Statement–Misunderstanding–Clarification. The exchange between Jesus and Martha repeats the pattern observed in 11:7–16. Martha begins "knowing" two things: If Jesus had been there, her brother would not have died; and if Jesus petitions God, presumably to raise Lazarus, God will respond. Although Martha "knows" much, she misunderstands much. Jesus makes a statement that moves the conversation to a new level: "Your brother will rise again" (11:23). Martha's misunderstanding indicates that she "knows" resurrection according to popular reckoning, but not the specific way Jesus intends: "I know that he will rise again in the resurrection on the last day" (11:24). Although her understanding is not perfect, Jesus reveals to this educatable, "beloved" disciple a remarkable thing: "I am the resurrection and the life" (11:25). Like other "I am . . ." statements, this one uniquely attaches a predicate to Jesus: He, and no one else, has power over death, a claim of uniqueness. Yet his clarification does not solve all problems, for it contains two conflicting statements:

those who believe in me,	even though they die, will live (11:25b)
everyone who lives and believes in me,	will never die (11:26).

We judged that 11:26 represents the traditional Johannine formula: belief = never die. But 11:25b seems to be a revision in light of the Lazarus event: belief = live, even if they die. But how does this clarify any of Martha's concerns?

Something is missing in her understanding. So, Martha hears Jesus but is still in the process of coming to full insight. Jesus' other remark ("believes in me . . . will never die") remains totally outside Martha's understanding because Lazarus, surely a believer, in fact died. Jesus then draws the catechesis to a climax: "Do you believe this?" In a Gospel where confessions are rare and reserved for elite people, Martha declares that she "knows" that Jesus is the Messiah, Son of God, and the one coming into the world. This pattern argues that "beloved" Martha now joins an elite inner circle who hear and understand Jesus' words (i.e., his sheep). Her speech is an expression of unique information reserved for elites in the group. Martha thus joins the circle of other special disciples who have immediate revelations of insider information given them by Jesus: Nathanael (1:47–50), the Samaritan woman (4:25–26), the man born blind (9:35–38), the "woman" and the beloved disciple (19:26–27), Mary Magdalene (20:16–18), the disciples (20:19–23), and finally Thomas (20:26–28).

Realized Eschatology. Here we find a theme that scholars call realized eschatology. A number of Jesus' remarks claim that by adherence to him true believers pass over from death to life. For example:

3:16   ". . . whoever believes in him should not perish, but have eternal life"
5:24   "Whoever hears my word and believes him who sent me has eternal life; he
             does not come into judgment, but has passed from death to life."
6:50   "This is the bread come down from heaven, that a man may eat it and not die."
6:51   "If anyone eats this bread he will live forever."
11:26b   "Whoever lives and believes in me shall never die."

What can "never die" mean, especially when a "beloved" disciple lies four days stinking in the tomb? Do disciples expect *not* to die?[312] Maybe ordinary or typical disciples die, but what of elites and those "beloved" of Jesus, such as Lazarus? Earlier, we observed people misunderstanding a remark by Jesus on death. He said, "If anyone keeps my word he will never see death" (8:51), which outsiders heard as "'If anyone keeps my word he will never taste death'" (8:52). But, in this Gospel, "seeing" is not "tasting." So, we expect an insider meaning to Jesus' words that true believers never "see" death, one that does not involve senses or body. The author, moreover, has prepared us earlier in 10:28–30 to understand 11:25–26, which led to the claim that in regard to dealing with death, Jesus is on a par with God: "I give them eternal life, and they will never perish. No one will snatch them out of my hand" (10:28). Three things are linked, in this precise order: (1) gift of "eternal life"; (2) they "never perish"; and (3) "no one will snatch them." While "eternal life" is already theirs, the sheep die but are not snatched.

---

[312] See John 21:22–23. On overly realized eschatology, see 2 Timothy 2:17–18; 1 Corinthians 4:8. See Richard Horsley, "'How Can Some of You Say that There Is No Resurrection of the Dead?' Spiritual Elitism in Corinth," *NovT* 29 (1978), 303–31; and A. C. Thistleton, "Realized Eschatology at Corinth," *NTS* 24 (1978), 510–26.

No wolf, enemy, or Angel of Death will dominate them. Jesus, then, shepherds his sheep through the end-time transformation into ultimate deathlessness and imperishability.

Martha, a Representative Figure.[313] We know that Martha is a "beloved" disciple along with her sister and brother.[314] Like the Samaritan woman, Jesus catechizes her, moving her from commonplace notions of afterlife to elite knowledge of Jesus as a unique source of imperishability: "I am the resurrection and the life." Because special knowledge and revelation mark characters as inner-circle elites, she should be evaluated as a singularly blessed person. Moreover, not many characters are presented as acknowledging Jesus with special titles; yet Martha acclaims Jesus as "Messiah, Son of God, the one coming into the world" (11:27). Thus, because of her revelations, she enjoys very high status.

But a Role? Does Martha, a high-status person, also play a role here?[315] Many interpreters confuse role and status, and so interpret Martha's next action as a *role*: "She called her sister Mary, and told her privately, 'The Teacher is here and is calling for you'" (11:28). We do not consider Martha commissioned to any role, much less that of "apostle," for the following reasons. (1) Jesus did *not* commission her to call Mary or to speak anything. (2) Martha and Mary have a "private," not a public, communication, which the mourners misinterpret (11:31); sister speaks to sister, whereas "apostles" speak publicly to non-related persons outside of their own households. (3) Martha's communication ("The Teacher is here and is calling for you") is information, not evangelization. (4) Martha, the recipient of Jesus' revelations, does not speak of these to Mary. All Mary knows is that the Teacher is here. (5) Having informed Mary, Martha's task is over; nothing more is expected of her. Roles simply do not evaporate in a matter of minutes but perdure over time. Thus, the narrative attributes to Martha very high status by virtue of Jesus' revelations, but not a formal role.

JOHN 11:28–33 – GATHERING ALL THE CAST

28 When she had said this, she went back and called her sister Mary, and told her privately, "The Teacher is here and is calling for you."

---

[313] See R. Collins, "Representative Figures in the Fourth Gospel," *Downside Review* 94 (1976), 26–32, 45, 124–26; S. van Tilborg, *Imaginative Love* (1993), 188–93; and C. M. Conway, *Men and Women in the Fourth Gospel* (1997), 139–43.

[314] To some, Martha is the central character in the narrative because of her extended communication with Jesus (11:5, 9, 20–27, 28).

[315] The Samaritan woman, although she enjoyed very high status, did not have an explicit role. See the commentary on 4:17–26; and J. H. Neyrey, "What's Wrong With This Picture?" *BTB* 24 (1994), 86–88.

29 And when she heard it, she got up quickly and went to him.

30 Now Jesus had not yet come to the village, but was still at the place where Martha had met him.

31 The Jews who were with her in the house, consoling her, saw Mary get up quickly and go out. They followed her because they thought that she was going to the tomb to weep there.

32 When Mary came where Jesus was and saw him, she knelt at his feet and said to him, "Lord, if you had been here, my brother would not have died."

33 When Jesus saw her weeping, and the Jews who came with her also weeping, he was greatly disturbed in spirit and deeply moved.

Representative Characters? Scholars often contrast Mary with Martha, either celebrating Mary's faith, illustrated by her "falling at his feet,"[316] or praising Martha's "ascending faith."[317] Unlike Martha, Mary is taught nothing by Jesus and receives no titles or insights. When Mary speaks to Jesus, she only repeats Martha's reproach: "Lord, if you had been here, my brother would not have died" (11:32 and 21). Hardly a confession, these words in fact challenge Jesus. We find no data in this story that set Mary apart or suggest she is representative of a Johannine virtue – yet (see 12:3–7).

Another set of characters appears: "Judeans who were with her in the house, consoling her." At this point, we cannot tell if they are sympathetic or hostile to Jesus. We do not know if friends of Jesus' friends are also Jesus' friends. Hence, we need to learn if they are insiders or outsiders. The divided reaction in 11:36–37 provides mixed information: some prove critical, others friendly. Yet all we know of them at this point is a misunderstanding. They read the scene literally and "suppose" that Mary departs for the tomb to weep. They know nothing about Jesus' presence because they are excluded from that news (11:28). A secret is successfully kept from them for the time being.

Disturbed in Spirit, Deeply Moved. Infrequently are Jesus' emotions and feelings narrated. Although we are told that he was "wearied" from travel (4:6) and "troubled" vis-à-vis his death (12:27; 13:21), the Johannine Jesus generally manifests power and control, which portray him as totally in charge and so not subject to passion or emotion.[318] Jesus' emotions in 11:33 are confusing for two reasons: They are said to be occasioned by Mary's weeping; and the Greek

---

[316] Francis J. Moloney, "The Faith of Martha and Mary: A Narrative Approach to John 11, 17–40," *Biblica* 75 (1994), 471–93.

[317] Thomas L. Brodie, *The Gospel According to John: A Literary and Theological Commentary* (Oxford: Oxford University Press, 1993), 394.

[318] Luke omits mention of Jesus' emotions; see Jerome H. Neyrey, "The Absence of Jesus' Emotions – The Lukan Redaction of Lk. 22, 36–46," *Biblica* 61 (1980), 153–57.

word translated as "disturbed" primarily means to "insist on something"[319] or
to be angry at. This suggests that Jesus shows an aggressive reaction to a grieving
woman. But Frederick Danker suggests another meaning, "to feel strongly about
something,"[320] which suggests that Jesus is depicted as feeling intensely about
death, in particular his own death.[321] In support of this, we notice that Jesus
is often "troubled": first, here with Mary and at the tomb (11:38); later, in the
Johannine version of the Gethsemane prayer (12:27), which is certainly about
his own death; and finally when he identifies his traitor (13:21). Yet some of the
crowd think he is "troubled" over Lazarus' death (11:36), whereas others think
that Jesus must be deceiving them (11:37). Thus there are three interpretations
of Jesus' emotions: that of the author, known only by clever insiders; that of the
crowd, who see it as testimony to his relationship with "beloved" Lazarus; and
that of cynical critics, who consider it a sham.[322] The literal or surface meaning
of words and events is never accurate in the Johannine world.

JOHN 11:34–44 – A TOMB WITH A VIEW

34 He said, "Where have you laid him?" They said to him, "Lord, come and see."
35 Jesus began to weep.
36 So the Jews said, "See how he loved him!"
37 But some of them said, "Could not he who opened the eyes of the blind man
have kept this man from dying?"
38 Then Jesus, again greatly disturbed, came to the tomb. It was a cave, and a stone
was lying against it.
39 Jesus said, "Take away the stone." Martha, the sister of the dead man, said to
him, "Lord, already there is a stench because he has been dead four days."
40 Jesus said to her, "Did I not tell you that if you believed, you would see the glory
of God?"
41 So they took away the stone. And Jesus looked upward and said, "Father, I thank
you for having heard me.

---

[319] *BDAG* 322. Other instances in the synoptic Gospels suggest a rebuke or anger; see Wendy
E. Sproston North, *The Lazarus Story within the Johannine Tradition* (Sheffield: Sheffield
Academic Press, 2001), 147–54.

[320] *BDAG* 322. See C. Bonner, "Traces of Thaumaturgic Technique in the Miracles," *HTR*
20 (1927), 171–81; and E. Bevan, "Note on Mark I 41 and John XI 33, 38," *JTS* 33 (1932),
186–88.

[321] W. E. S. North, *Lazarus Story* (2001), 153.

[322] Scholars generally classify the "Jews" in John as hostile outsiders; see S. Freyne, "Vilifying
the Other and Defining the Self: Matthew's and John's Anti-Jewish Polemic in Focus," in
Jacob Neusner and E. S. Frerichs, eds., *"To See Ourselves As Others See Us": Christians,
Jews, and "Others" in Late Antiquity* (Chico, CA: Scholars Press, 1985), 117–43. For a more
balanced view, see W. E. S. North, *Lazarus Story* (2001), 124–27.

42 I know that you always hear me, but I have said this for the sake of the crowd standing here, so that they may believe that you sent me."
43 When he had said this, he cried with a loud voice, "Lazarus, come out!"
44 The dead man came out, his hands and feet bound with strips of cloth, and his face wrapped in a cloth. Jesus said to them, "Unbind him, and let him go."

Private and Public. All events in the Lazarus story occur "outside": Both Martha and Mary encounter Jesus "outside" the family house, and the "tomb" also is "outside" the village. Yet "private" is the more significant classification of space here; "in private," Jesus enjoys intimacy with inner-circle disciples (11:6–16) and then in face-to-face meetings with two "beloved" friends (11:20–33). Only the gathering at the tomb is "public,"[323] which is intentional.[324] Everyone must witness the raising of Lazarus, either to believe Jesus (11:45) or to bring news of it to Jerusalem (11:46).

Miracle Form. The raising of Lazarus appears to be the last and climactic sign of a collection of miracle stories. Thus we can profitably analyze it in terms of typical miracle stories in antiquity (see the commentary on John 5:1–10). In the Greco-Roman and Israelite worlds, typical healings tend to have six elements, most of which are found here.

1. *Setting.* The author tells us who, what, where, and when (11:1–4).
2. *Confrontation.* The confrontation comes not from an aggressive spirit but from the two sisters who challenge Jesus, "Lord, if you had been here, my brother would not have died" (11:21, 38).
3. *Severity.* Lazarus could hardly be worse off: dead, in the tomb four days, already stinking.
4. *Healing.* Although Jesus smeared mud on the eyes of the blind man, here he cures by simple command, "Lazarus, come out."
5. *Proof.* "The dead man came out." When his burial clothes were removed, he rejoined society (see 12:1–6).
6. *Public Reaction.* Jesus already declared that Lazarus' death was about glory, both God's and that of the Son of God (11:4). As we shall see, this also sparks a plot to kill Jesus, whereas others believe in him because of this. As his fame increased, so did envy of him.

Jesus' Prayer. Bruce J. Malina defines prayer as: "A socially meaningful symbolic act of communication, bearing directly upon persons perceived as somehow supporting, maintaining, and controlling the order of existence of the one

---

[323] The title of this section is taken from M. W. G. Stibbe, "A Tomb with a View," *NTS* 40 (1994), 38–52.
[324] On the distinction between "public" and "private," see J. H. Neyrey, "Teaching You in Public and from House to House," *JSNT* 26 (2003), 69–102; and his "Territoriality," *BTB* 32 (2002), 64–65.

praying, and performed with the purpose of getting results from or in the interaction of communication."[325] In terms of communication theory, senders (mortals) send messages (petition and praise) to receivers for distinct purposes. Whatever its form, prayer is always addressed to God and aims to have an effect on, or to further interaction with, God. But what kinds of prayers do mortals pray? Because of the confusion over the classification of Jesus' prayer in 11:41–42,[326] we need a typology to distinguish prayers. Malina classifies prayers in terms of their purposes, identifying seven results or aims the one praying desires, only three of which are relevant here.[327] The types of prayer that concern us here are interactional, petitionary, and confessional. Interactional prayer presumes a relationship with God and seeks to enliven or quicken it. Petitionary prayer makes requests of the deity. Confessional prayer proclaims the glory of God and renders praise for benefaction. In John 11, Jesus makes no petition, despite Martha's insistence: "God will give you whatever you ask of him" (11:22). Jesus' address to God, "I thank you that you have heard me" (11:41), is confession praise for God's faithfulness. Jesus' "interactional prayer" celebrates emotional ties with God and confirms that relationship: "I give you thanks because you hear me" (11:41) and "I know that you always hear me" (11:42). In Jesus' prayer, only his relationship with God is in view. Lazarus, who is but meters away in the tomb, is omitted from this prayer.[328]

Lazarus, Another Representative Character? Scholars disagree over how to classify Lazarus, as a "symbolic" character,[329] an "ideal" character, or a "proto-typical" character.[330] All of these urge us to see Lazarus in terms of his status as a consummate insider. He is the unique recipient and proof of Jesus' power to raise the dead. What makes him particularly representative is the four-times-repeated note that Jesus loved him,[331] as well as his two sisters. No one before

---

[325] Bruce J. Malina, "What Is Prayer?" *Bible Today* 18 (1980), 215.

[326] See W. E. S. North, *Lazarus Story* (2001), 102–3.

[327] A full discussion of the types of prayer will be provided in the analysis of Jesus' prayer in John 17; see also Jerome H. Neyrey, "Prayer, in Other Words: A Social-Science Model for Interpreting Prayers," in John J. Pilch, ed., *Social Scientific Models for Interpreting the Bible: Essays by The Context Group in Honor of Bruce J. Malina* (Leiden: Brill, 2001), 351–77.

[328] W. E. S. North, in *The Lazarus Story within the Johannine Tradition* (2001), 102–4, lists three explanations of Jesus' prayer: Loisy's "prière pour la galerie" ("prayer for the crowd"), "pretense prayer," and prayer as "a demonstration of the Son's perfect unity with the Father."

[329] See, for example, C. R. Koester, *Symbolism in the Fourth Gospel* (1995), 32–39, 63–67, and 105–10.

[330] Philip F. Esler and Ronald A. Piper, "Lazarus, Mary and Martha as Group Prototypes: Social Identity, Collective Memory and John 11–12," forthcoming.

[331] "Love" means close social relationships; see Bruce J. Malina, "Love," in John J. Pilch and Bruce J. Malina, eds., *Handbook of Biblical Social Values*, rev. ed. (Peabody, MA: Hendrickson, 1998), 127–30. With regard to "insiders," God loves the world (3:16), the Son (3:35), and Jesus (10:17), Jesus loves the family at Bethany (11:5), but "outsiders" love darkness (3:19) or fail to love God (5:42) and so do not love Jesus (8:42).

this in the narrative is said to have such a relationship with Jesus. It now sets him apart as unique and favored. But the very relationship of being "beloved" creates the dramatic crisis. Surely those "beloved" by Jesus should not face illness and death? Surely, if Jesus truly loved him, he could have done something, at least come to attend his funeral (11:21, 32, 37). His death is all the more bitter because Jesus delays two days and arrives only after Lazarus is four days in the tomb. Thus Jesus' "love" is on trial, as well as his power to save this "beloved" Lazarus. If Jesus will not or cannot aid one whom he "loves," where does this leave the rest of the disciples? Of what value is Jesus' "love"?[332] All of this characterizes Lazarus as a consummate insider, whose illness and death severely test Jesus' loyalty and power.

But Who Is Lazarus? Only two males in this Gospel are "beloved" by Jesus, Lazarus and "the disciple whom Jesus loved." Some scholars[333] are thus drawn to equate the two figures for these reasons: (1) apart from Chapter 11, the "beloved disciple" does not appear until *after* the Lazarus story (13:23); (2) both are linked to Jerusalem and environs, Lazarus with Bethany and the Beloved Disciple with Jerusalem (18:15–17); (3) the question in 21:20–23 over whether the Beloved Disciple would not die (again) makes excellent sense if he is Lazarus, who has already died; and (4) the later figure is unnamed, except for the unique tag "Beloved."

So Much to Learn. Appreciating the significance of Lazarus' raising requires several catechetical sessions, first with the disciples (11:6–16) and then twice with Martha (11:20–27 and 39–40). These move in two directions: First, as Charles Giblin observed, disciples must learn that Jesus refuses to be manipulated and so "remains" to ensure that his interests are centrally honored; and second, knowing the value of the forthcoming sign will come after multiple proclamations that the events are for God's glory and that of Jesus (11:4 and 40) or with acknowledgment of Jesus' role and status as "Resurrection and Life" and "Messiah, Son of God." Within this setting, Martha and Mary learn that "beloved" associates do not lack Jesus' power or concern. But what they and the disciples learn is the apex of Jesus' eschatological power.

---

[332] P. F. Esler and R. A. Piper in "Lazarus, Mary and Martha as Group Prototypes," remind us that "love" language explodes with the Passion Narrative: The theme is stated that "Jesus loved his own unto the end" (13:1); the disciples are transformed into the high status of "friends" – that is, those whom Jesus loves (15:12–17); "friends" have a new commandment, to "love one another" (13:34–35; 15:12); and a new, unnamed figure appears, known as the Beloved Disciple (13:23; 18:15–18; 19:26; 20:2–9; 21:7, 20). Thus, Esler and Piper argue, "'Love' is a key identity-descriptor for believers in the Fourth Gospel."

[333] See Mark W. G. Stibbe, *John as Storyteller: Narrative Criticism and the Fourth Gospel* (Cambridge: Cambridge University Press, 1992), 77–81; and James H. Charlesworth, *The Beloved Disciple: Whose Witness Validates the Gospel of John?* (Valley Forge, PA: Trinity Press International, 1995), 185–92, 288–91.

A CLOSER LOOK – DEMONSTRATION OF ESCHATOLOGICAL POWER

We argued at the end of 5:29 that the eschatological power enunciated there serves as a topic statement developed in subsequent chapters.[334] Now is the time to assess how well the author has succeeded in this. It is one thing to claim power but another to demonstrate it. The following chart particularly focuses on power over death, either Jesus with life in himself or Jesus' ability to call disciples from death.

Eschatological Power in John 5:21–29	*Eschatological Power in John 10*	*Eschatological Power in John 11*
Give life: For just as the Father has life in himself, so he has granted the Son also to have life in himself. (5:26)	I have power to lay it down, and I have power to take it up again. (10:17–18)	I am the Resurrection and the Life. (11:25)
The dead hear and live: The dead will hear the voice of the Son of God, and those who hear will live (5:25); all in their graves will hear his voice and will come out. (5:28–29)	The sheep hear his voice. He calls his own sheep by name and leads them out. (10:3)	"Lazarus, come out!" The dead man came out. (11:43–44)
Honor and glory: All shall honor the Son just as they honor the Father. (5:23)	Honor denied: . . . blasphemy, because you, though only a human being, are making yourself God (10:33)	This illness is for the glory of God, so that the Son of God may be glorified by it (11:4). . . . Did I not say that if you believed you would see the glory of God? (11:40)

So we see that the eschatological power anticipated in Chapter 5 and claimed in Chapter 10 is manifested in John 11. All that remains to be demonstrated is that Jesus has life in himself and power to lay down his life and take it up again.

JOHN 11:45–52 – COUNCIL OF IRONY: CAUSING WHAT YOU DON'T WANT TO HAPPEN

45 Many of the Jews therefore, who had come with Mary and had seen what Jesus did, believed in him.
46 But some of them went to the Pharisees and told them what he had done.

---

[334] Commentators often link John 5 with John 11, but not in any systematic way. See R. Schnackenburg, *Gospel According to St. John* (1982), 2.322, 330; and C. H. Dodd, *Interpretation of the Fourth Gospel* (1968), 257.

47 So the chief priests and the Pharisees called a meeting of the council, and said, "What are we to do? This man is performing many signs.

48 If we let him go on like this, everyone will believe in him, and the Romans will come and destroy both our holy place and our nation."

49 But one of them, Caiaphas, who was high priest that year, said to them, "You know nothing at all!

50 You do not understand that it is better for you to have one man die for the people than to have the whole nation destroyed."

51 He did not say this on his own, but being high priest that year he prophesied that Jesus was about to die for the nation,

52 and not for the nation only, but to gather into one the dispersed children of God.

Irony. This episode contains numerous ironic elements.[335] (1) Jesus' gift of life now causes his death. (2) The sign that manifests his glory to many excites only envy in others. (3) If not challenged, "everyone will believe in him," a consequence terrible in envious eyes but wonderful in the mouth of the author. (4) Killing him, moreover, will have precisely this unintended effect (see 12:32). (5) Failure to act, they argue, will cause the Romans to come and "destroy both our holy place and our nation" (11:48); but the Romans will do that anyway.[336] (6) Caiaphas mocks his audience, "You know nothing at all" (11:49), but neither does he. True, he "prophesied" when he spoke.[337] But when prophets received or spoke oracles, it fell to another figure to interpret and communicate them.[338]

"Irony," of course, is no mere ornamentation. Because irony entails knowing (by insiders), whereas outsiders do *not* know, it serves as a sure marker of insiders and outsiders, respectively. Jesus often charges the crowds with *not* being in the know:

"You do not know": 3:10; 7:28; 8:14, 19, 43, and 55
"You do not hear/listen to my voice": 8:37, 47; 10:27; 18:37
"You do not believe": 8:45; 10:25
"You do not belong": 10:26

---

[335] For a detailed study of irony, see P. Duke, *Irony in the Fourth Gospel* (1985).

[336] For ancient Judean interpretations of the Temple's destruction, see Jacob Neusner, "Judaism in a Time of Crisis: Four Responses to the Destruction of the Temple," *Judaism: The Evidence of the Mishnah* (Chicago: University of Chicago Press, 1981), 313–27; Anthony J. Saldarini, "Varieties of Rabbinic Response to the Destruction of the Temple," *SBLSP* (1982), 437–58; and A. R. Kerr, *Temple of Jesus' Body* (2002), 34–66.

[337] On the tradition that Israelite priests were also prophets, see C. H. Dodd, "The Prophecy of Caiaphas," in his *More New Testament Essays* (Manchester: Manchester University Press, 1968), 64–66.

[338] See David E. Aune, *Prophecy in Early Christianity and the Ancient Mediterranean World* (Grand Rapids, MI: Eerdmans, 1983), 23–48.

Even when people claim to know, Jesus challenges that: "You *know* me, and you *know* where I am from? I have not come on my own. But the one who sent me . . . you *do not know*" (7:28). Some ask questions of Jesus, which he does not answer but continues to speak in the Johannine idiom of secrecy.[339]

According to the sociology of secrecy,[340] this elite group in Jerusalem receives spies' reports on Jesus' actions in Bethany (11:45–46). This "knowledge" enrages them to act in self-interest. One result of this meeting will be the recruitment of another spy to inform them how to capture and destroy Jesus (i.e., Judas). As we saw earlier, however, they truly do not know how their plot to kill Jesus will benefit the world. On one level, they practice secrecy, but ironically the real secrets are kept from them.

A CLOSER LOOK – THE REVEALER KEEPS SECRETS

Secrecy Defined. Secrecy is "the mandatory or voluntary, but calculated, concealment of information, activities, or relationships."[341] Secrets are "a social resource (or adaptive strategy) used by individuals, groups, and organizations to attain certain ends."[342] As a strategy, secrecy may be employed aggressively against rivals or defensively against attackers.[343] Secrecy enables certain types of associations to avoid political persecution or destruction, and it allows other groups to maintain an exclusive monopoly on esoteric knowledge. As an adaptive device, it contains five interrelated processes: security (control of information), entrusted disclosure, espionage, evaluation of spying, and post-hoc security measures.

Secrecy Process in the Fourth Gospel. It is a fact that many *secrets* are kept in the Fourth Gospel: lying, deception, and evasion; hiding either oneself or information; secret and public transmission of information; misunderstandings, ambiguity, and double-meaning words; people "in the know/ not in the know," and reasons why people know/do not know what they know; irony; and Jesus' perfect knowledge, his knowledge of his Father and knowledge of human hearts, all of which are secrets to all other people. Yet special persons are *entrusted with disclosure*: John the Baptizer (1:33–35), Nathanael (1:46–50), the Samaritan woman (4:25–26), the man born blind (9:35–38), Martha (11:21–27), all the disciples (13:1–17:26), Mary (20:15–18), and Thomas (20:24–28). *Spies*, such as the Pharisees in 4:1 and 11:46–47, conduct *espionage* to learn Jesus' secrets. They ask questions such as "Who are you?" (8:25, 53; 9:36), "What do you mean?" (7:36; 16:17–18), "Why . . .?"

---

[339] Examples of unanswered questions include 3:4, 9; 7:35–36; 8:19, 22, 25, 53; and 10:23.

[340] J. H. Neyrey, "Secrecy," in *What Is John?* (1998), 96–102.

[341] Stanton K. Tefft, "Secrecy as a Social and Political Process," in his *Secrecy: A Cross-Cultural Perspective* (New York: Human Sciences Press, 1980), 320.

[342] S. K. Tefft, "Secrecy as a Social and Political Process," in *Secrecy* (1980), 35.

[343] S. K. Tefft, "Secrecy As a Social and Political Process," in *Secrecy* (1980), 36.

(1:25; 9:27; 14:22), and "How can it be?" (3:4, 9; 6:42, 52, 8:33; 12:34). Those who spy and ask questions must then *evaluate what they learned*, a process unavailable to the Gospel's audience, except perhaps for 11:46–52. Judas the traitor is exposed; the subsequent security measures may be an intensification of anti-language, a code known only to insiders.

Limited Good and Envy. Earlier we interpreted the exchange between John and his disciples (3:25–30) in terms of limited good and envy.[344] Because all goods of creation exist in finite supply (i.e., "zero sum"), if someone increases, others necessarily decrease. The raising of Lazarus causes Jesus' fame to skyrocket, which the council correctly interprets: "This man performs many signs . . . everyone will believe in him" (11:47–48). As Jesus increases in fame and respect, they proportionately decrease. Moreover, people who think themselves thus injured by another's success are likely to engage in envy.[345] Their actions plotted in 11:45–52 are calculated to cause Jesus shame, cause the scattering of his followers, and cause the restoration of their honor. But, ironically, they will only increase Jesus' fame and benefit even more peoples.

Noble Death. We argued in regard to 10:11–18 that Jesus should be called a "noble" shepherd because he dies a "noble death." "Noble deaths," as we just saw, contain five elements: benefit to the polis; demonstration of virtue (courage and justice); voluntarily chosen; unvanquished in death; and posthumous honors. The topos on "noble death" influences our reading of 11:45–52, but not in the same fulsome way as in the case of 10:11–18. Here we ironically learn of the "benefit" of Jesus' death. Caiaphas states that it is profitable for Jesus to be destroyed "instead of" Israel, but the author clarifies that this means Jesus' death "for the benefit of" others.[346] Thus, insiders understand how "noble" Jesus' death will be because this one man will ironically "die for the people" but "gather into one the dispersed children of God" (11:52). The "justice" of Jesus is recognized only through the glasses of irony. Whereas this council considers him a sinner and denies him all virtue, insiders know that Jesus' death will be in obedience to God and in service of many. Jesus' death is also voluntary in that, despite the attempts to arrest and kill him, he enters Bethany (12:1–2, 9) and also Jerusalem (12:12–19) on his own. He lays down his life, but only when his hour has come, and so it is a thoroughly voluntary action.

A Final Trial. When "the chief priests and the Pharisees gathered the council" (11:47), the trial of Jesus draws to a close. The assembled judges sentence Jesus in

---

[344] Readers are referred back to the discussion of 3:22–30 and in particular to the article of Jerome H. Neyrey and Richard L. Rohrbaugh, "'He Must Increase, I Must Decrease' (John 3:30): Cultural and Social Interpretation," *CBQ* 63 (2001), 464–83.

[345] Envy of Jesus regularly turned into aggression; see J. H. Neyrey and A. C. Hagedorn, "It Was Out of Envy that They Handed Jesus Over," *JSNT* 69 (1998), 39–47.

[346] P. Duke, *Irony in the Fourth Gospel* (1985), 87–89.

absentia, a repeat of the phenomenon earlier declared illegal (7:51). Testimony is wasted on this court. Even irrefutable proof such as the signs worked on the man born blind (9:31–33) and the dead Lazarus fails to convince these judges. The Johannine audience, however, knows how to interpret these proceedings. They know that the judges sentence Jesus out of envy, and so they judge unjustly. As they always have, these judges judge according to appearances (7:24) and so deny the probative power of Jesus' giving sight to the blind (9:31–33) and life to the dead (11:43). The correct judgment is "if this man were not from God, he could do nothing" (9:33), but the judges come to the opposite conclusion.

JOHN 11:53–57 – PLAYING CAT AND MOUSE

53 So from that day on they planned to put him to death.
54 Jesus therefore no longer walked about openly among the Jews, but went from there to a town called Ephraim in the region near the wilderness; and he remained there with the disciples.
55 Now the Passover of the Jews was near, and many went up from the country to Jerusalem before the Passover to purify themselves.
56 They were looking for Jesus and were asking one another as they stood in the temple, "What do you think? Surely he will not come to the festival, will he?"
57 Now the chief priests and the Pharisees had given orders that anyone who knew where Jesus was should let them know, so that they might arrest him.

Bridge to the Future. This transition passage contains the seeds of the events that immediately unfold. First, we learn that the council seeks Jesus' death and that he no longer walks openly in the environs of Jerusalem. Nevertheless, the author does not imply that Jesus fears his adversaries and hides to save his life. Rather, Jesus has always worked on his own timetable, and the "hour," although close, is not yet. When all suits the honorable Jesus, he will come to Bethany (12:1–2) and then Jerusalem (12:12–19). Second, Jesus "remained" in Ephraim with his disciples, not so much a calendar reckoning of time here as an indication of acceptance and respect. Finally, the question of some, "Will he come to the feast?" and the spying of the council to learn Jesus' whereabouts, indicate that they are "not in the know." The secrets all belong to Jesus; insiders know, but the rest are in the dark.

JOHN 12:1–11 – THE BELOVED DISCIPLES ONCE MORE

1 Six days before the Passover Jesus came to Bethany, the home of Lazarus, whom he had raised from the dead.
2 There they gave a dinner for him. Martha served, and Lazarus was one of those at the table with him.

3 Mary took a pound of costly perfume made of pure nard, anointed Jesus' feet, and wiped them with her hair. The house was filled with the fragrance of the perfume.

4 But Judas Iscariot, one of his disciples (the one who was about to betray him), said,

5 "Why was this perfume not sold for three hundred denarii and the money given to the poor?"

6 (He said this not because he cared about the poor, but because he was a thief; he kept the common purse and used to steal what was put into it.)

7 Jesus said, "Leave her alone. She bought it so that she might keep it for the day of my burial.

8 You always have the poor with you, but you do not always have me."

9 When the great crowd of the Jews learned that he was there, they came not only because of Jesus but also to see Lazarus, whom he had raised from the dead.

10 So the chief priests planned to put Lazarus to death as well,

11 since it was on account of him that many of the Jews were deserting and were believing in Jesus.

The Story Continued. The narrative about the "beloved" Martha, Mary, and Lazarus turns from one tomb to another. We last saw Jesus and the sisters at Lazarus' tomb, and now, with all reassembled, Mary anoints Jesus to prepare him for his tomb (12:1–8). In acknowledgment of the benefaction Jesus gave Lazarus, they host him at a meal. We learn then that Jesus' enemies now target Lazarus for another death because the fame of his revivification has caused Jesus to grow in honor and fame – at their expense (12:9–11; see also 11:45–51). Lazarus' death and tomb, then, are linked with Jesus' death and tomb, indicators of elite status. Of no other person in this Gospel are so many stories told, especially those that touch on elite behavior.

Johannine Version of a Familiar Story. Although modern readers of the Gospels immediately link John's story of the anointing of Jesus' feet with two other ones, Mark 14:3–9 and Luke 7:36–38, we are uncertain about the relationship of these seemingly parallel accounts. Some argue that all of these reflect a single anointing story,[347] and others see different stories in the background.[348] The following synopsis aims to sharpen our perception of the likenesses and differences between the two accounts of the same event.

---

[347] For example, C. H. Dodd, *The Historical Tradition in the Fourth Gospel* (Cambridge: Cambridge University Press, 1963), 162–73; and Joseph A. Fitzmyer, *The Gospel According to Luke I–X* (Garden City, NY: Doubleday, 1981), 686–87.

[348] A. Legault, "An Application of the Form-Critique Method to the Anointings in Galilee and Bethany," *CBQ* 16 (1954), 131–41; and R. E. Brown, *Gospel According to John* (1966), 1.449–52.

A CLOSER LOOK – ANOINTINGS COMPARED: MARK 14:3–9 AND
JOHN 12:1–8

Mark 14:3–9	*John 12:1–8*
1. *Date*: "It was two days before the Passover and the festival of Unleavened Bread." (14:1)	1. *Date*: "Six days before the Passover . . ." (12:1)
2. *Plot*: The chief priests and the scribes were looking for a way to arrest Jesus by stealth and kill him; for they said, "Not during the festival, or there may be a riot among the people." (14:1–2)	2. *Plot*: The chief priests and the Pharisees called a meeting of the council, and said, "If we let him go on like this, everyone will believe in him, and the Romans will come and destroy both our holy place and our nation." Caiaphas said to them, "It is better for you to have one man die for the people than to have the whole nation destroyed." (11:47–51)
3. *A home in Bethany*: "While he was at Bethany in the house of Simon the leper, as he sat at the table . . ." (14:3)	3. *A home in Bethany*: "The home of Lazarus . . . There they gave a dinner for him. Martha served; one of those at the table with him was Lazarus." (12:1–2)
4. *An (anonymous) female*: "a woman came . . ." (14:3)	4. *A named and known female*: "Mary took a pound of costly perfume." (12:3)
5. *Ointment*: ". . . with an alabaster jar of very costly ointment of nard, and she broke open the jar and poured the ointment on his head" (14:3)	5. *Ointment*: ". . . a poured of costly perfume made of pure nard, anointed Jesus' feet, and wiped them with her hair. The house was filled with the fragrence of the perfume." (12:3)
6. *Objectors*: "But some were there who said to one another in anger, 'Why was the ointment wasted in this way? For this ointment could have been sold for more than three hundred denarii, and the money given to the poor.' And they scolded her." (14:4–5)	6. *Objectors*: "But Judas Iscariot, one of his disciples, said, 'Why was this perfume not sold for three hundred denarii and the money given to the poor?' (He said this not because he cared about the poor, but because he was a thief; he kept the common purse and used to steal what was put into it.)" (12:4–6)
7. *Jesus' defense of the woman*: "Let her alone; why do you trouble her? She has performed a good service for me. . . . She has done what she could; she has anointed my body beforehand for its burial."(14:6, 8)	7. *Jesus' defense of Mary*: "Leave her alone. She bought it so that she might keep it for the day of my burial." (12:7)
8. *Jesus' justification for the expense*: "For you always have the poor with you, and you can show kindness to them whenever you wish; but you will not always have me." (14:7)	8. *Jesus' justification for the expense*: "You always have the poor with you, but you do not always have me." (12:8)

Examining the Johannine version of this story, we note the following.

Where. It is located in the house of the "beloved" disciples – Martha, Mary, and Lazarus. Mary's anointing and Martha's serving stand out as marks of affection and respect (cf. Luke 10:38–42). Thus all of the actions and gestures express intimacy and elite status.

Who. Whereas in Mark and Luke an unknown woman approaches Jesus, here it is Mary, herself a "beloved disciple."

Body Part Anointed. Mark says that the perfume is poured on Jesus' head, whereas John states that Mary anoints his feet. Although the head, which is the most honorable body part, is anointed for major political roles such as king, prophet, or priest, nevertheless Jesus' feet are anointed in John.

Elite Status. We do not know the social status of Mark's unidentified female but only that the perfume is very expensive, so costly that it is unthinkable for a peasant woman or a beggar. Mary, on the other hand, seems to belong to a well-to-do household. "Many of the Jews," presumably Jerusalem elites, came to the house to mourn (11:18–19), and many who came were on such close terms with "the Pharisees" in Jerusalem that they had immediate access to them to relate the news about Lazarus' restoration (11:46).

Critics. Unknown figures, presumably disciples, criticize Mark's female, whereas in John the critic has a face and name, Judas, keeper of the purse (see 13:27–29). Mark's characters argue that use of the ointment is excessive; the poor should have been cared for by its sale. So, too, Judas, except that we are told the secret that Judas as a thief sought to fatten the common purse, from which he helped himself. His criticism that the poor should have been fed the ointment's sale is a lie because he intends to take such moneys for his own use. Thus, he is both liar and thief, and will soon aid in murder.

Hidden Meaning. Both Mark and John see a hidden meaning in the anointing that only insiders comprehend, namely anticipation of Jesus' burial. The preparation of a body for burial, a female act of piety, typically consisted of washing the corpse, clothing it in funeral cloths, and anointing it with oils and spices. Jesus honors the woman's gesture, calling it "a noble work." Moreover, very few people ever have such intimate access to Jesus' body, this access itself a mark of high status.

Linked in a Second Death. The plot against Lazarus in 12:9–11 ironically repeats the events subsequent to Jesus' calling him from the tomb (11:45–53). Then, informers brought back the news of Lazarus' revivification to the Pharisees, who called a council at which they lamented that Jesus' sign gained him many disciples, diminishing the Pharisees' respect. They decided to kill him. Here, crowds come to this same Lazarus because he is the icon of Jesus' power. This increase in honor causes the same council to plot Lazarus' death, too. In both instances, envy poisons the hearts of Jesus' rivals against him and Lazarus; the elite interpret the gain in fame and respect of Jesus and Lazarus as their own loss (see the discussion of "limited good" at 3:21–30; see also Mark 15:10). Lazarus' death would seem to be noble in the eyes of the Johannine group because he will die precisely because of his association with Jesus.

Classifying the Characters. The dramatis personae in John are often representative of some virtue or vice or are characterized in terms of high or low status within the group. On the one hand, "the beloved ones" host Jesus, a gesture of intimacy that no one else in the narrative performs. Lazarus, the object of Jesus' greatest sign, is targeted in 12:10–11 to share Jesus' own fate. Both are marks of very high status. Martha, who once received the great revelation that Jesus is "the resurrection and the life" (11:25), now serves Jesus. Mary, a lesser figure at Lazarus' death, performs the intimate gesture of touching Jesus' body and anointing his feet. By virtue of what these characters know and have experienced at Jesus' hand, and their physical closeness to Jesus, they are all elites and genuinely "beloved ones." In contrast stands Judas. Invited to a supper only because of Jesus, he proves to be the consummate antagonist. He disrupts the meal with criticism of his hosts and in the process shames Jesus by protesting the gesture done him by Mary. Judas, moreover, will later disrupt the farewell meal (13:21–30). Worse, we learn that he is a liar and a thief and that his indignation is a sham; he wants the perfume's worth for himself. Thus elite disciples are contrasted with a person who is a disciple only in name, their physical service of Jesus contrasts with Judas' hostility, and their patent honoring of Jesus is juxtaposed with Judas' deception and lying.

JOHN 12:12–19 – YOUR KING COMES, RIDING ON A DONKEY

12 The next day the great crowd that had come to the festival heard that Jesus was coming to Jerusalem.

13 So they took branches of palm trees and went out to meet him, shouting, "Hosanna! Blessed is the one who comes in the name of the Lord – the King of Israel!"

14 Jesus found a young donkey and sat on it; as it is written:

15 "Do not be afraid, daughter of Zion. Look, your king is coming, sitting on a donkey's colt!"

16 His disciples did not understand these things at first; but when Jesus was glorified, then they remembered that these things had been written of him and had been done to him.

17 So the crowd that had been with him when he called Lazarus out of the tomb and raised him from the dead continued to testify.
18 It was also because they heard that he had performed this sign that the crowd went to meet him.
19 The Pharisees then said to one another, "You see, you can do nothing. Look, the world has gone after him!"

Johannine Redaction of a Common Source. All four Gospels tell of Jesus' entry into Jerusalem, but John's version appears to be the most idiosyncratic. A comparison with the synoptic accounts helps us identify the Johannine interpretation of it.

Brackets. Significant Johannine editorial changes occur in the bracketing of the event with mention of Lazarus' being raised from death (12:9–11, 17–19), indicating how significant a sign this was and how ironic it is that raising the dead would cause the death of the one who performed it.

King. The citations from Zechariah and Psalm 118 are shaved to emphasize the acclamation of Jesus as "King" (12:13, 15) – "Blessed is the king of Israel" and "See, your king comes to you." This title figures dramatically in Jesus' trial before Pilate (18:33–37) and is the title over Jesus' cross (19:19–22).

Posthumous Understanding. As with the earlier citation, "Destroy this temple ..." (2:19), which was misunderstood until Jesus was raised from the dead (2:21–22), the disciples misunderstand this episode. Only "when Jesus was glorified, then they remembered that these things had been written of him and had been done to him" (12:16).

Public Confession. According to 9:22 and 12:42, those who publicly acclaimed Jesus were censured by expulsion from the synagogue. How remarkable it is, then, to see crowds from Jerusalem publicly hailing Jesus in the praiseworthy tones of Psalm 118 (12:13). Public, bold speech such as this is highly valued in the Johannine group.

Signs and Faith. In the Johannine version, the testimony of the crowd is a response to Jesus' sign. As 20:30–31 will state, "these signs were written that you may believe that Jesus is the Christ, the Son of God." This sign, at least, achieved what it was supposed to. But not all who tell of Jesus' signs do so for his honor and glory (11:46).

Irony. The Pharisees' envy over Jesus' success contains ironic sweetness: "Look, the world has gone after him!" (12:19).

JOHN 12:20–26 – GREEKS AND GRAINS

20 Now among those who went up to worship at the festival were some Greeks.

21 They came to Philip, who was from Bethsaida in Galilee, and said to him, "Sir, we wish to see Jesus."

22 Philip went and told Andrew; then Andrew and Philip went and told Jesus.

23 Jesus answered them, "The hour has come for the Son of Man to be glorified.

24 Very truly, I tell you, unless a grain of wheat falls into the earth and dies, it remains just a single grain; but if it dies, it bears much fruit.

25 Those who love their life lose it, and those who hate their life in this world will keep it for eternal life.

26 Whoever serves me must follow me, and where I am, there will my servant be also. Whoever serves me, the Father will honor.

Gross Anatomy. This brief story contains two scenes: disciples networking to provide access to Jesus; and the sayings of Jesus to those brought to him. The first scene tells of Greeks coming to Philip, who approaches Andrew so that both Philip and Andrew go to Jesus. This would seem clumsy except for the fact that this pattern of disciples bringing new persons to Jesus is a dynamic observed in the Gospel's opening, where Andrew brought Simon to Jesus and Philip brought Nathanael.[349] Similarly, the Samaritan woman brought the men of her village to "come and see," just as Martha brought Mary to Jesus. What do we make of this pattern? First of all, Jesus never calls anyone to be a disciple; they are all brought to him by others, whose association he then confirms. It is argued that we are observing ancient "networking,"[350] the "way people interact on the basis of established pathways of social relationships." John the Baptizer was Andrew's mentor; Andrew is Simon's brother; Philip "was from Bethsaida, the city of Andrew and Peter" (1:44; 12:21); Martha is Mary's sister. We surmise, then, that the "Greeks" sought out Philip because he is identified as "from Bethsaida in Galilee": perhaps they knew him or about him , were in the same trade, or there was some such network link.

Yet there is more than meets the eye, for unlike the networking process, the Greeks "volunteer" or approach Philip to mediate access to Jesus. Do we ever find volunteers in the Gospels who are accepted for discipleship? In Matthew 8:19–22 and Luke 9:57–62, volunteers initiate contact with Jesus and declare that they will "follow you." But to each Jesus says a discouraging word; and although the text does not literally say that they were dismissed, that would be the correct cultural reading. As we say in the case of "positive challenges" in our discussion

---

[349] For a full discussion of this pattern, see the commentary on 1:35–51.

[350] B. J. Malina and R. L. Rohrbaugh, *Commentary on John* (1998), 57–59.

of 2:4–6, volunteering puts on the spot the person to whom the volunteers offer their allegiance. Just as Jesus refused requests for aid until it was clear that he was in control of the situation, there is no reason to think otherwise with these volunteers. Maybe he will accept them, but not until they know how they must conform to his pattern of rejection and dying. Do any other people volunteer? Nicodemus? How was he treated, and is that different from the way the Greeks are treated?

In the second scene, Jesus' address to these "Greeks" is cast in a distinctive chiastic structure, which aids us in appreciating its major themes:

A. The hour has come for the Son of Man to be *glorified*.
B. Unless a grain of wheat *falls* into the earth and *dies*, it remains just a single grain; but if it *dies*, it *bears much fruit*.
B′. Those who *love* their life. *lose* it, and those who hate their life in this world will *keep* it for eternal life. Whoever *serves* me must *follow me*, and where I am, there will my servant be also.
A′. Whoever serves me, the Father will *honor*.

Assuming that "glory" and "honor" refer to the same value in antiquity, the two brackets (A and A′) speak of divine honor shown, first to Jesus ("glorified") and then to his servants ("honor"). Why? – for walking the way described in B and B′. The talk there is of dying and bearing fruit, hating and keeping, or becoming a servant and being honored. All recognize this as the type of radical discipleship demanded by Jesus (see Mark 8:34–38).

Deciphering Discipleship. Given the fact that the Jerusalem elite have already plotted to kill first Jesus and then Lazarus, the references to "fall into the earth and die" and "lose one's life" resonate with intensity. Jesus, in effect, is demanding that they "follow me" even unto death; that is, "lay down their lives" for him (see 10:4, 27; 13:37). The demand for discipleship begins with "*Unless . . . ,*" which we have seen prefacing many rites of transformation.

3:3	"*Unless* you are born from above, you cannot see the kingdom of God."
8:24	"*Unless* you believe that I AM, you will die in your sins."
12:24	"*Unless* a grain of wheat dies and falls into the ground . . ."
13:8	"*Unless* I wash you, you have no share with me."

This demand, too, is not an entrance ritual (3:3) but one whereby an insider is transformed into an elite by virtue of radical imitation of Jesus. If those afraid to speak publicly on Jesus' behalf stand on the periphery of the group (9:22; 12:42), these disciples would be highly honored according to criteria for elite status in the group, such as rejection from the synagogue (9:34) and even death for Jesus (16:1–2).

Finally, the exhortation by Jesus argues according to "advantage,"[351] the aim of deliberative rhetoric. Why do this? Because it leads to great benefits: One "bears much fruit" and "keeps it for eternal life." Moreover, just as God "glorifies" the Son of Man in his death, so, too, God will "honor" the disciple who follows Jesus. Honor is lost before the people, but divine honor is awarded later by God.

JOHN 12:27–36 – JESUS' PUBLIC PRAYERS

27 "Now my soul is troubled. And what should I say – 'Father, save me from this hour'? No, it is for this reason that I have come to this hour.
28 Father, glorify your name." Then a voice came from heaven, "I have glorified it, and I will glorify it again."
29 The crowd standing there heard it and said that it was thunder. Others said, "An angel has spoken to him."
30 Jesus answered, "This voice has come for your sake, not for mine.
31 Now is the judgment of this world; now the ruler of this world will be driven out.
32 And I, when I am lifted up from the earth, will draw all people to myself."
33 He said this to indicate the kind of death he was to die.
34 The crowd answered him, "We have heard from the law that the Messiah remains forever. How can you say that the Son of Man must be lifted up? Who is this Son of Man?"
35 Jesus said to them, "The light is with you for a little longer. Walk while you have the light, so that the darkness may not overtake you. If you walk in the darkness, you do not know where you are going.
36 While you have the light, believe in the light, so that you may become children of light." After Jesus had said this, he departed and hid from them.

The Unshakeable One Is Shaken. Our narrator occasionally states that Jesus is "deeply moved" (11:33–35) or "troubled" (12:27; 13:21). At his farewell, he exhorts his disciples, "Do not let your hearts be troubled" (14:1). Although Jesus is generally portrayed as being in endless conflict, he is always in control of the situation and superior to his enemies. He is never at a loss for a clever word, and throughout the Passion story, Jesus will be unshakeable. All of this is probably an extension of the idea of the "noble death" that Jesus dies: voluntary, unconquered, and honorable. Then why should he be "deeply troubled" when he

---

[351] Aristotle describes deliberative rhetoric: "For the deliberative speaker [the end] is the advantageous and the harmful (for someone urging something advises it as the better course and one dissuading dissuades that it is worse)." See Aristotle, *Rhetoric* 1.3.3, trans. George Kennedy, *Aristotle, On Rhetoric* (Oxford: Oxford University Press, 1991), 49.

stands before Lazarus' tomb and troubled when he reveals that his betrayer is at table? In a Greek setting, such overpowering emotions might be considered vices that cloud reason and deter one from what is right.[352] The simple explanation lies in considering this episode as John's version of the synoptic garden story, which began with Jesus praying psalms of distress ("My soul is sorrowful even unto death," Mark 14:34 and Ps 42:5) and then petitioning to escape the cup, only to declare his obedience. Perhaps Jesus models the triumph of obedience over fear by displaying emotions others experience but trumping them with total loyalty to God.

Jesus' Prayers. Two types of prayer are evident here: *petitionary* prayer ("Father, save me from this hour") and *informational* prayer ("Father, glorify your name"). Readers are asked to consult the full discussion of Jesus' prayer in John 17. Only some summary remarks about prayer can be made. Jesus here does *not* petition God to rescue him from death but only mentions it as a possibility; rather, he says "No! It is for this reason that I have come to this hour." This contrasts with the synoptic account of the garden, where Jesus explicitly petitioned God that the "cup be taken away," after which he confessed his obedience to God: "Thy will be done" (Mark 14:36). *Informational* prayer gives praise and respect to God, such as we see in the first half of the sanctioned Christian prayer, the Our Father. Present here are three elements from that prayer: the address of God as "Father," the equivalent of "Your will be done," and "hallowed be your name" = "Father, glorify your name." This prayer wins a dramatic response, as God says: "I have glorified it and will glorify it again." Jesus, then, makes no petition but manifests loyalty to God.

A CLOSER LOOK – GIVE GOD THE GLORY

"Glory"[353] is synonymous with reputation, respect, and honor.[354] When one gives glory, one *acknowledges* the status or prowess of another, according to the following indices.

Role and status. "Glory" relates to *role and/or status.* For example, some Israelites "have seen his glory, the glory as of a father's only son, full of grace and truth" (1:14), thus acknowledging the elite role and status of "the

---

[352] On the "absence of emotions" in Luke's Passion narrative, see J. H. Neyrey, *Passion According to St. Luke* (1985), 49–54.

[353] See B. J. Malina, *New Testament World* (2001), 27–57; and J. H. Neyrey, *Honor and Shame* (1998), 14–90.

[354] G. B. Caird, in his "The Glory of God in the Fourth Gospel: An Exercise in Biblical Semantics," *NTS* 15 (1969), 266–72, often translated "glory" as "honor," but his attention focused on the Septuagint to interpret it. See Ronald Piper, "Glory, Honor and Patronage in the Fourth Gospel: Understanding ΔOXA Given to the Disciples in John 17," in John J. Pilch, ed., *Social Scientific Models for Interpreting the Bible: Essays by The Context Group in Honor of Bruce J. Malina* (Leiden: Brill, 2001), 239–59.

Father's only son." Similarly, Jesus' signs occasion acknowledgment of his relationship to God: "Jesus did this, the first of his signs . . . and revealed his glory; and his disciples believed in him" (2:11; see also 6:14–15; 7:31; 10:21; 11:47).

Whose approval? Jesus criticizes those who prefer glory and praise from one another rather than from God. For his part, Jesus says, "I do not accept glory from human beings" (5:41), although others do: "[they] loved human glory more than the glory that comes from God" (12:43). Glory's synonym, "honor," appears in terms of the respect and recognition given or denied Jesus (4:44; 5:23; 8:49; see also 12:26). Of those who refused to acknowledge him, Jesus says: "How can you believe when you accept glory from one another and do not seek the glory that comes from the one who alone is God"? (5:44).

Sources of glory and honor. Glory may be bestowed or earned. It is bestowed upon sons born of noble fathers, who enjoy great honor simply because of their birth into a noble line (1:14; 8:33). God the Father ceaselessly bestows glory and honor on Jesus (8:50, 54; 16:14; 17:1, 5, 22). Earned glory, however, depends on prowess (military, athletic, and aesthetic), virtue, or benefaction. Jesus, however, does not compete with others to earn honor and respect. How false are the accusations that he "makes himself anything" (5:18; 8:53; 10:33; 19:7, 12). In fact, Jesus' refusal to seek his own glory becomes a criterion of his authenticity: "Those who speak on their own seek their own glory; but the one who seeks the glory of him who sent him is true, and there is nothing false in him" (7:18; 8:50).

Give God the glory. The psalmist got it right: "Not to us, O LORD, not to us, but to your name give glory" (Ps 115:1). But what does it mean to give glory to God? First, mortals do not "give" God anything, including glory. Mortals only acknowledge God's power, sovereignty, and benefaction. When God manifests his glory, mortals then have a duty to acknowledge it. When they "give honor" to God, they are in effect doing what all children are commanded in the Law: They "honor their Father" by being loyal children of their Father. Lazarus' illness was for the "glory of God" (11:4), the means whereby the disciples "see the glory of God" (11:40). Jesus models this acknowledgment of God's honor: "I glorified you on earth, having accomplished the work which you gave me to do" (17:5).

Glory is shame and shame is glory.[355] Although the crucifixion was "shame" (Heb 12:2), in the logic of Jesus' circle it was "glory" (12:23; 13:31–32). Even Peter's death, while not itself "glory," nevertheless is for the "glory of God" (21:19). Similarly, statements about "lifting" up are ironic remarks about the honor of the cross, not its shame.

---

[355] J. H. Neyrey, "Despising the Shame," *Semeia* 68 (1994), 113–37.

Equal glory, equal honor. God, of course, is glory personified. Only to God belongs the glory. Nevertheless, this Gospel states that God wants Jesus to share equally in that glory. In defining his eschatological power in 5:21–29, Jesus states: "All may honor the Son just as they honor the Father. Anyone who does not honor the Son does not honor the Father who sent him" (5:23). This honor, moreover, is no new status for Jesus, for he later prays for its restoration: "Father, glorify me in your own presence with the glory that I had in your presence before the world existed" (17:5).

In regard to "glory" in 12:28–29, Jesus has not asked for glory; rather, he glorifies God: "Father, glorify your name." Although mortals "give" glory to God (i.e., acknowledge God's sovereignty), only God can glorify Himself. Ancient philosophical thinking had begun to argue that God is unchanging,[356] and so God cannot either grow or diminish in glory. But God can manifest power and majesty that create awe in mortals, whose duty it is to acknowledge God's glory, which means honoring God and showing respect and reverence (see Rom 1:19–23).

But in 12:23, 12:29, and 13:31–32, Jesus links his glory with that of God and in a distinctively Johannine way: "Now the Son of Man has been glorified, and God has been glorified in him. If God has been glorified in him, God will also glorify him in himself and will glorify him at once" (13:31–32). The parallels between materials in 12:23 and 12:29 and in 13:31–32 deserve attention. First, both begin with the declaration that "Now the Son of man is glorified" (12:23; 13:31); "glory" means God's honoring of Jesus in and because of his death. "Glory," then, entails the paradoxical reversal of honor and shame as the world knows them. Second, Jesus' obedience and faithfulness unto death "glorify" God because these actions acknowledge that God has the right to command (and have others obey) – the sign of an honorable Father. Third, God's "glory" is acknowledged by Jesus' loyalty unto death, and in return God will reward Jesus for this obedience: "God will also glorify him in himself and will glorify him at once." Parallel to this is God's voice to Jesus in 12:29: "I have glorified it, and I will glorify it again." Because 12:27–29 speaks in a veiled way of Jesus' death, the heavenly remark in 12:29 would safely be paraphrased as "I am manifesting my power and sovereignty now and in your death vindication I will manifest it again."

Statement–Misunderstanding–Clarification–Twice! The pattern with which we are now familiar occurs twice in this story:

---

[356] See H. A. Wolfson, "Albinus and Plotinus on Divine Attributes," *HTR* 45 (1952), 115–30; and "Negative Attributes in the Church Fathers and the Gnostic Basilides," *HTR* 50 (1957), 145–56; William R. Schoedel, "Enclosing, Not Enclosed: The Early Christian Doctrine of God," in William R. Schoedel and Robert L. Wilken, eds., *Early Church Literature and the Classical Intellectual Tradition* (Paris: Éditions Beauchesne, 1979), 75–86.

Pattern	Cycle One 12:27–32	Cycle Two 12:32–36
Statement	"I have glorified it, and I will glorify it again." (12:28)	"And I, when I am lifted up from the earth, will draw all people to myself." He said this to indicate the kind of death he was to die. (12:32–33)
Misunderstanding	The crowd standing there heard it and said that it was thunder. Others said, "An angel has spoken to him." (12:29)	The crowd answered, "We have heard from the law that the Messiah remains forever. How can you say that the Son of Man must be lifted up?" (12:34)
Clarification	"This voice has come for your sake, not for mine. Now is the judgment of this world; now the ruler of this world will be driven out." (12:30)	"The light is with you for a little longer. Walk while you have the light, so that the darkness may not overtake you. . . . While you have the light, believe in the light, so that you may become children of light." (12:35–36)

How do we interpret these misunderstandings? In 12:29, although only Jesus understood what God said, we find a characteristic division of opinion. Some equate the voice of God with thunder, whereas others closer to the truth claim that an "angel" spoke; that is, a messenger from God. The pattern, then, clues us in to the spectrum of how people hear: Elite disciples hear well, others less well, and so on until we find those who are not Jesus' sheep and so do not hear at all.

Double-Meaning Words. In 12:32–33, we find Jesus again speaking double-meaning words.[357] "Lifted up" can mean either exalted and glorified (by God) or crucified.[358] These bystanders resemble others who did not understand Jesus' cryptic reference to death (see 7:33–36; 8:21–22). The remark about the Messiah is true enough (see 3:2),[359] except that they do not acknowledge Jesus as "Messiah." Although they refer to the "Son of Man," they acknowledge ignorance of the title and person to whom it applies (12:34). Hence, although the words are on their lips, they make no confession because they just do not get it. Thus we conclude that the crowd has not been part of Jesus' group because they do not know his voice. They claim knowledge ("we know that the Messiah

---

357 Readers should consult the introduction to this motif in the commentary on 2:20; the bibliography cited there is of importance here.

358 B. J. Malina and R. L. Rohrbaugh's *Commentary on John* (1998), 212–13, cites from Artemidorus several dreams in which "lifting up" was a positive omen for a poor man ("the crucified is exalted") but an ironic death sentence to enemies (Alexander condemns certain assassins, "Make them exalted above all men").

359 Marinus de Jonge, "Jewish Expectations about the 'Messiah' According to the Fourth Gospel," in *Jesus: Stranger* (1977), 94–96.

remains") but are ultimately reduced to questions ("Who is this Son of Man"?). They are not "in the know."

Revelation and Hiding. Jesus next exhorts the audience to act while there is time, contrasting walking in the light with stumbling in the dark. But this proverb is spiced with extra Johannine meanings. Jesus, the light, with them only a little longer, has been saying this repeatedly throughout the narrative: "I am the light of the world" (8:12); and "We must work the works of him who sent me while it is day; night is coming when no one can work. As long as I am in the world, I am the light of the world" (9:4–5; see also 11:9–11). As if to dramatize how little light is left, Jesus then "departed and hid from them." The light is quickly going out.

JOHN 12:37–43 – SOME GET IT, MOST DON'T

37 Although he had performed so many signs in their presence, they did not believe in him.
38 This was to fulfill the word spoken by the prophet Isaiah: "Lord, who has believed our message, and to whom has the arm of the Lord been revealed?"
39 And so they could not believe, because Isaiah also said,
40 "He has blinded their eyes and hardened their heart, so that they might not look with their eyes, and understand with their heart and turn – and I would heal them."
41 Isaiah said this because he saw his glory and spoke about him.
42 Nevertheless many, even of the authorities, believed in him. But because of the Pharisees they did not confess it, for fear that they would be put out of the synagogue;
43 for they loved human glory more than the glory that comes from God.

Representative Characters. It seems that every type of representative character in the Gospel narrative is presented in John 12. They are listed in terms of status, from very high to very low.

1. *Beloved Disciples.* Elite, "beloved" disciples, who honor Jesus with meals, anointings or sharing in his death, enjoy exceptionally high status.
2. *Publicly Confessing.* Others greet Jesus, acclaiming him as "King" (12:12–16), an indicator of insider status because public confession is a special badge of honor.
3. *Cowards.* Many authorities believed in him, but "because of the Pharisees they did not confess it, for fear that they would be put out of the synagogue" (12:42). These are borderline disciples, at best.

4. *Greeks.* Would-be disciples are exhorted to die and lose themselves as Jesus does, which would identify them as genuine insiders (12:23–26).

5. *Those Who Cannot Understand Heavenly Speech.* Some hear Jesus' prayer and a heavenly noise in response, but cannot break the code on this (12:29–35). They are outsiders, for, although the light shines before them, they remain in darkness (12:36).

6. *Spies for the Opposition.* Some see what Jesus does and sing his praises, but not these for whom the news excites envy (12:17–19); they can hardly be insiders.

7. *Pharisees* are the certified enemies of Jesus, trying to arrest or suppress public loyalty to him (9:22; 12:42).

8. *Judas*, who appears to be an insider of some status (he held the purse), is revealed as liar, thief, and murderer (i.e., the agent of Jesus' arrest). He, then, is the ultimate outsider. Thus we can discern many of the criteria for elite discipleship: physical proximity to Jesus, imitation of Jesus in death, bold public confession of him, and knowing the secret meaning of his words and actions.

JOHN 12:44–50 – HAVING THE LAST WORD

44 Then Jesus cried aloud: "Whoever believes in me believes not in me but in him who sent me.

45 And whoever sees me sees him who sent me.

46 I have come as light into the world, so that everyone who believes in me should not remain in the darkness.

47 I do not judge anyone who hears my words and does not keep them, for I came not to judge the world, but to save the world.

48 The one who rejects me and does not receive my word has a judge; on the last day the word that I have spoken will serve as judge,

49 for I have not spoken on my own, but the Father who sent me has himself given me a commandment about what to say and what to speak.

50 And I know that his commandment is eternal life. What I speak, therefore, I speak just as the Father has told me."

A CLOSER LOOK – "CONCLUSION" TO THE BOOK OF SIGNS

Rhetoricians instruct on how to write a "conclusion" (epilogue, peroration) to speeches, which is of value to us as we conclude the "Book of Signs." An epilogue, says Aristotle, does four things: (1) disposes the hearer favorably to us and unfavorably to opponents; (2) amplifies and minimizes; (3) moves the hearer to an emotional reaction; and (4) reminds the audience of the main points (*Rhet.* 3.19.1). Quintilian compresses this into two kinds of peroration: facts and emotions (*Inst. Orat.* 6.1.1). He highlights the first, namely the repetition and enumeration of the facts. We suggest that John does both. He appeals to emotions by inviting the audience to praise or blame the characters in the narrative, and he enumerates many of the themes and motifs that characterize Chapters 1–12. If 1:1–18 is a genuine prologue, then John 12 is a potential conclusion.

Emotional Reaction. Having examined the "representative" characters in John 12, we focus now on the emotional reaction that the author wishes us to have toward them, either praise or blame. Because the conclusion ends with extensive material on judgment, praise is awarded for closeness to Jesus, bold public acknowledgment of him, and suffering and even dying like him, but shame or dishonor is given for hostility to Jesus, fear of publicly acknowledging him, and spying for the enemy. The highest praise is given to Martha, Mary, and Lazarus, who host Jesus, honoring him with special anointing and even potential sharing of his death. Lesser praise also goes to the crowd, who publicly acknowledges Jesus upon his entry to Jerusalem (12:12–17). Philip and Andrew (12:20–22) are neutrally presented. They only broker access for the Greeks to Jesus and do not themselves recruit or display bold behavior or special knowledge. They are only minor players here. In contrast, the author provides grounds to evaluate other characters as deserving of shame and dishonor. Shame is heaped on those who, despite the evidence of the signs, did not believe in him (12:37–41). Worse, however, is the judgment that "many, even of the authorities, believed in him. But because of the Pharisees they did not confess it, for fear that they would be put out of the synagogue" (12:42). The Pharisees (12:19) repeat their envious grounds for killing Jesus (11:47–48). Finally, Judas is exposed as a thief and disguised traitor (12:4–6). Emotional reactions to these characters provide both a recapitulation of the dramatis personae of the narrative, praising group virtues (courage, loyalty, belief, and "belovedness") and declaring certain vices shameful (fear, envy, and hate).

Recapitulation. As true conclusions do, John 12 can be shown to enumerate and recapitulate many of the topics, themes, and motifs seen earlier. For example, the prayer of Jesus in which he is "shaken" (12:27–28) reminds us of the same presentation of Jesus in 11:41–42. The glorification of God's name (12:28–29) is the latest extension of this motif, as the "Closer Look" on God's glory indicates. Just as outsider ideas of the Messiah exclude Jesus in 12:34–35, so did similar a priori notions about the Messiah exclude him in 7:40–43. The pun on "lifting" in 12:33 recalls the same double meaning of the verb in 3:14 and 8:28. Moreover, because "lifting" refers to Jesus' glorious return to

God, it repeats the descent/ascent pattern of the prologue (1:1–18), the Son of Man (3:13–14), and the omnipresent "whence" and "whither" debates. The infertile result of signs in 12:37 reminds the audience of previous refusals to accept the probative value of signs (2:23; 4:48; 6:1–15; 7:31; 9:24–34). Patterns of light and darkness in 12:35–36 and 12:46 begin in 1:4–5 and are repeated in the contrast between "night" (Nicodemus) and "noon" (Samaritan woman) and in numerous other parallels (3:19–21; 8:12; 9:4–5; 11:9–10). That Isaiah "saw his day" (12:41) picks up the claim that Abraham "saw my day" (8:56) and possibly the claim in 1:18. The most significant recapitulation finalizes the judgment begun in John 3, as the following commentary will illustrate.

The End of the End. Raymond Brown[360] divided the Fourth Gospel into two unequal parts: the Book of Signs (1:1–12:50) and the Book of Glory (13:1–21:25). Here, at the end of the Book of Signs, Jesus summarizes his case in judicial language and effectively judges all characters in the narrative. Earlier, when people were able to see and hear Jesus, he warned them, "Do not judge by appearances, but judge with right judgment" (7:24). So in 12:44–50, although no specific audience is identified, Jesus gives a plenary judgment that applies to the whole of the Book of Signs. This "last" judgment contains typical Johannine features, arranged in a chiastic form:

A = Jesus' legitimacy as agent (12:44–45)
B = the Judge, which is the word of God, spoken by the Word (12:46–48)
A′ = Repetition of Jesus' legitimacy (12:49–50)

The Last Judgment. The language here appeared much earlier, in the discourse with Nicodemus. The following tables indicate the close repetition of the statement on judgment there and now at the end of the Book of Signs.

3:19–21	*12:31–36*
1. This is the *judgment*. (3:19)	1. Now is the *judgment*. (12:31)
2. The *light* has come into the world. (3:19b)	2. The *light* is with you for a little longer. (12:35a)
3. But those who *do what is true* come to the light, so that it may be clearly seen that their *deeds* have been *done* in God. (3:21)	3. *Walk* while you have the *light*, so that the darkness may not overtake you. (12:35b)
4. For all who *do* evil hate the light and *do not come to the light*, so that their deeds may not be exposed. (3:20)	4. If you *walk* in the darkness, you *do not know* where you are going. (12:35c)

[360] R. E. Brown, *Gospel According to John* (1996), 1.cxxxviii–cxliv and 2.541–42.

This comparison proclaims that Jesus himself occasions the judgment, even a schism of contrasting judgments, about him (7:40–43; 9:16; 10:19–21; 11:36; and 12:29). Some accept him, his agency, and his word, whereas others do not. For the former there is praise, for the latter, dishonor. A subsequent passage, 12:45–50, repeats much of the judgmental material seen earlier in John 3 but highlights different aspects of judgment.

3:17–19, 34–36	*12:45–50*
1. *God sent the Son* into the world. (3:17)	1. Whoever believes in me believes not in me but *in him who sent me.* And whoever sees me sees *him who sent me.* (12:44–45)
2. And this is the judgment, that the *light has come into the world,* and people loved *darkness* rather than light. (3:19)	2. I have come as *light into the world,* so that everyone who believes in me should not remain in the *darkness.* (12:46)
3. God did *not* send the Son into the world *to condemn* the world, but in order that the *world might be saved through him.* (3:17)	3. *I do not judge anyone* who hears my words and does not keep them, for I came *not to judge the world,* but *to save the world.* (12:47)
4. *He whom God has sent speaks the words of God,* for he gives the Spirit without measure. (3:34)	4. I have *not spoken on my own;* the *Father who sent me* has himself given me a commandment *about what to say and what to speak.* (12:49)
5. Whoever believes in the Son has *eternal life;* whoever disobeys the Son will *not see life,* but must endure God's wrath. (3:36)	5. And I know that his commandment is *eternal life.* What I speak, therefore, I speak just as the Father has told me. (12:50)

Both 12:35–36 and 12:45–50 repeat materials characteristic of an early pattern in the Gospel, that those who hear and see Jesus are judges trying to evaluate him. When they declare him saint or sinner, they make a momentous judgment, for, when judges judge, they are themselves subject to judgment depending on whether they judge justly and not according to appearances: "With the judgment you make you will be judged, and the measure you give will be the measure you get" (Matt 7:2). This entire chapter contains a vast range of judgments about Jesus, as we have seen in the comments on "representative characters." Judgment, moreover, is an apt conclusion to John 1–12 because it summarizes the role and status of Jesus as "light of the world," concludes the trial of the Word that has been formally conducted since John 5, and articulates the criteria for praise and blame.

JOHN 13:1–3 – A SECOND PROLOGUE

1 Now before the festival of the Passover, Jesus knew that his hour had come to depart from this world and go to the Father. Having loved his own who were in the world, he loved them to the end.
2 The devil had already put it into the heart of Judas son of Simon Iscariot to betray him. And during supper.
3 Jesus, knowing that the Father had given all things into his hands, and that he had come from God and was going to God.

Prologue to the Gospel's Second Half. Because many scholars describe John 1–12 as the "Book of Signs," they identify John 12 as the conclusion of Jesus' signs and his forensic engagement with the Jerusalem elite. Correspondingly, they consider John 13 as beginning a new section of the story, namely the farewell, death, and resurrection of Jesus, which they call the "Book of Glory."[361] Just as the Book of Signs began with a prologue (1:1–18), so, too, does the Book of Glory.[362] Although the two prologues are similar in many aspects, they sharply contrast in other ways, as the following table demonstrates.

First Prologue (1:1–18)	*Second Prologue (13:1–3)*
1. Jesus, a *descending* figure: "The true light, which enlightens everyone, was coming into the world."	1. Jesus, an *ascending* figure: "Jesus knew that his hour had come to depart from this world and go to the Father. . . . Jesus, knowing that he had come from God and was going to God . . . "
2. Intended audience: "He came to what was *his own.*"	2. Intended audience: "Having loved *his own* who were in the world, he loved them to the end."
3. Hostility: "And his own people did *not accept him.*"	3. Hostility increased: "The devil already *put it into the heart* of Judas son of Simon Iscariot *to betray him.*"
4. *Creative* power showcased	4. *Eschatological* power on display

If Jesus enters the world in 1:1–18, he prepares to leave it in 13:1–3. His first audience, "his own," consisted of ethnic Israelites, but the people he leaves are not blood relatives but disciples he has selected out of the world. The rejection foretold in 1:11 is realized now as Jesus is attacked by the devil, betrayed by a deceiving disciple, and sought by enemies seeking to kill him.

---

[361] For example, R. E. Brown, *Gospel According to John* (1966), 1.541–42.
[362] See E. Harris, *Prologue and Gospel* (1994), 165, 158; and W. K. Grossouw, "A Note on John XIII 1–3," *NovT* 8 (1966), 124–31.

Finally, the first prologue stressed Jesus' creative power (1:1–3), whereas the power exclusively in view in the Book of Glory is his eschatological power, the power of Jesus over death – power to lay down his life and take it back (10:17–18). As Jesus was named "God" (*Theos*) in regard to his creative power (1:1–2), he will be named "Lord" (*Kyrios*) after demonstrating eschatological power (20:28).

Characters in the Second Act. Five characters pivotal to the Passion narrative are identified in this prologue: Jesus, "his own," Judas, and the Father. *Jesus* is characterized by key verbs used to describe him. He *knows* the most important knowledge, namely that the hour had come to return to the Father and that as he came from God, he was returning there. Thus he knows the secret of secrets, which escapes all others; that is, whence he comes and whither he goes. He also knows that God has put all things into his hands, especially power to lay down his life and take it back. He *loved* his own who were in the world, even to the end. Included here are his sheep, whom as shepherd he guards from the wolf, as well as the "beloved" Lazarus, Martha, and Mary, and now his disciples. "Love," we have come to know, means loyalty, faithfulness, and commitment. *The devil*, Jesus' antagonist, appears on stage, corrupting one of the inner circle and seducing him to betray Jesus. This refusal of loyalty means hatred. "*His own*" refers to his disciples, not his blood relatives (see Mark 3:31–35). *Judas*, of course, is a pseudodisciple, even a traitor, whose degree of wickedness is expressed by labeling him as a pawn of the devil. *The Father* is the figure from whom Jesus descended and to whose heart he reascends. "His own" will be described as "one" with Jesus, who is "one" with the Father (14:20). Thus their group association includes Jesus and God.

Loved Them to the End. Does Jesus love them "perfectly" or "to his last breath"? To determine the meaning of the Greek words *telos* and *teleō*, let us compare 13:1 with places where these words are used.

4:34	"... do the will of the one who sent me.... I will *finish* his work."
5:36	"... the works which the Father gave me for the purpose that I *finish* them."
13:1	"He loved them to the *end/finish*."
17:4	"I have glorified you on earth, *finishing* the work you gave me to do."
19:28	"Jesus knew that already all was *finished*."
19:30	"He said, 'It is *finished*.'"

Several meanings are possible. Overwhelmingly, these words refer to Jesus' complete loyalty and obedience to God (4:34, 5:36; 17:4, 19:28, 30), whereas in 13:1, it is directed to the disciples, not God. Yet it, too, expresses maximum loyalty to them, not merely the chronological termination of a task. The quality of Jesus' loyalty will be explained shortly in 15:12–17 and 17:11–12, 15.

JOHN 13:4–20 – FOOTWASHING AND ITS INTERPRETATIONS

4 Jesus got up from the table, took off his outer robe, and tied a towel around himself.

5 Then he poured water into a basin and began to wash the disciples' feet and to wipe them with the towel that was tied around him.

6 He came to Simon Peter, who said to him, "Lord, are you going to wash my feet?"

7 Jesus answered, "You do not know now what I am doing, but later you will understand."

8 Peter said to him, "You will never wash my feet." Jesus answered, "Unless I wash you, you have no share with me."

9 Simon Peter said to him, "Lord, not my feet only but also my hands and my head!"

10 Jesus said to him, "One who has bathed does not need to wash, except for the feet, but is entirely clean. And you are clean, though not all of you."

11 For he knew who was to betray him; for this reason he said, "Not all of you are clean."

12 After he had washed their feet, had put on his robe, and had returned to the table, he said to them, "Do you know what I have done to you?

13 You call me Teacher and Lord – and you are right, for that is what I am.

14 So if I, your Lord and Teacher, have washed your feet, you also ought to wash one another's feet.

15 For I have set you an example, that you also should do as I have done to you.

16 Very truly, I tell you, servants are not greater than their master, nor are messengers greater than the one who sent them.

17 If you know these things, you are blessed if you do them.

18 I am not speaking of all of you; I know whom I have chosen. But it is to fulfill the scripture, 'The one who ate my bread has lifted his heel against me.'

19 I tell you this now, before it occurs, so that when it does occur, you may believe that I am he.

20 Very truly, I tell you, whoever receives one whom I send receives me; and whoever receives me receives him who sent me."

Two Different Scenes. Footwashing, a ritual event, first takes place in 13:4–11 and is subsequently interpreted in 13:12–20. But careful readers will note that the two scenes are mismatched and do not describe the same phenomenon.[363] We can observe six items in them, which are more contrasting than similar.

---

[363] Scholarship regularly notes that 13:4–11 differ from 13:12–20; see R. E. Brown, *Gospel According to John* (1966), 2.559–62; and Arland Hultgren, "The Johannine Footwashing (13:1–11) as Symbol of Eschatological Hospitality," *NTS* 28 (1982), 540–44.

Audience. Jesus has a sharp exchange only with Peter (13:6–11), but later delivers an irenic discourse to all the disciples (13:12–20).

Knowledge. Peter is told "You do *not* know" (v. 7) but will understand later, whereas all of them are clearly "in the know" during Jesus' general explanation: "You know what I have done" (v. 12) and "If you know these things, honored are you if you do them" (v. 17).

Necessity/Obligation. Jesus tells Peter, "Unless I wash you . . . " (v. 8), whereas all "ought" to wash others' feet (v. 14) – different notions of necessity and obligation.

Effect. Whereas Jesus' action will make Simon and others "pure," their washing of the feet of others will make them "honored."

Judas. The remark in 13:10 identifies someone who is not pure, "You are clean, but not every one of you." The evangelist says that this refers to Jesus' betrayer: "He knew who was to betray him; that was why he said, 'You are not all clean'" (13:11). In contrast, when Jesus mandates the washing of feet, he alludes to a traitor, "I am not speaking of you all; I know whom I have chosen" (v. 18); he quotes Psalm 41:9 about a treacherous table companion. "Clean" and "chosen" refer to quite different things.

Time. The "now/later" distinction functions differently in each part. Peter does not understand now but will later (13:7), whereas all of them know "now," so that "later," when the prophecy comes true, they will remain faithful (13:19). Surely there is a link between the foot washing in 13:4–11 and the one interpreted in 13:12–20, but each refers to a different kind of ritual action, as we shall shortly see.[364]

Footwashing as Transformation and Footwashing as Confirmation. The differences between 13:4–11 and 13:12–20 can be sharpened by reference to two different ritual actions. All know that birth, marriage, and death transform us, either elevating us in status and role or demoting us. But meals, feasts, and anniversaries ("Rededication," 10:22; "Passover," 13:1) confirm membership in a group. In 13:4–11, Jesus requires Peter to undergo a *status-transformation ritual* to become "wholly clean" in order to merit a new, elite inheritance or status with Jesus. But in 13:12–20, the disciples are told to practice a *ceremony* in which their role and status are confirmed by acts of hospitality toward group members. Peter's footwashing *ritual* has to do with his transformation into the role of an elite, public witness to Jesus with accompanying risk of death – a one-time event. Conversely, the *ceremony* the disciples will perform confirms their role and status as leaders of the group – an action to be repeated regularly.

Transformation Rituals versus Confirmatory Ceremonies. Victor Turner described the difference between transformation rituals and confirmation

---

[364] J. H. Neyrey, "Footwashing," in *Social World of the First Christians* (1995), 198–99.

ceremonies in this way: "I consider the term 'ritual' to be more fittingly applied to forms of religious behavior associated with social *transitions,* while the term 'ceremony' has a closer bearing on religious behavior associated with religious *states.* . . . Ritual is transformative, ceremony confirmatory."[365] Structurally, then, the differences look like this:

Status Transformation (transition)	Ceremony (confirmation)
1. calendar: unpredictable, when needed	1. calendar: predictable and planned for
2. time focus: present to future	2. time focus: past to present
3. presided over by professional	3. presided over by official of the institution
4. purpose: status transformation	4. purpose: confirmation of roles or status within an institution[366]

(1) *Calendar.* Footwashing occurs just once in the Gospel, as an irregular pause in the Passover meal. Although occurring in this meal, it is not a planned or fixed element of the meal but an irregular, unpredictable pause that suddenly arises. (2) *Time focus.* The present footwashing looks to the future, *"Unless* I wash you, you have no part in me" (13:8), and hence a new, future relationship with Jesus depends on what is presently happening. (3) *Presiding.* Jesus presides over this transformation ritual. Were this an act of etiquette that welcomes guests to a ceremonial meal, Jesus would be an official of the kinship institution that celebrated its commitment through commensality. But the washing of Peter's feet has nothing to do with welcome etiquette or meal participation. Jesus seeks to change Peter – that is, to make him "wholly clean" – a status that he does not now and will not enjoy unless Jesus performs this ritual. (4) *Purpose.* Whatever role and status Peter enjoyed prior to 13:6, Jesus requires that he undergo this ritual for two reasons. First, unless he accepts this, "You will have no part in me." Second, when completed, Peter will be "wholly clean." As regards the former purpose, this footwashing resembles other status-transformation rituals in the Fourth Gospel, many of which are presented under the rubric of "unless," just like Jesus' demand to Peter:

3:3	*"Unless* one is born anew, one cannot see the kingdom of God."
6:53	*"Unless* you eat the flesh of the Son of Man and drink his blood, you have no life in you."
12:24	*"Unless* a grain of wheat falls into the earth and dies, it remains just a single grain; but if it dies, it bears much fruit."

In view are an entrance ritual (3:3–5) and transformations to a new status (6:53; 12:24). Similarly, in 13:8 Jesus tells Peter, already a member of the circle,

---

[365] Victor Turner, *The Forest of Symbols: Aspects of Ndembu Ritual* (Ithaca, NY: Cornell University Press, 1967), 95 (italics added); see also Raymond Firth and John Skorupski, *Symbol and Theory: A Philosophical Study of Theories of Religion in Social Anthropology* (Cambridge: Cambridge University Press, 1976), 164.

[366] B. J. Malina, *Christian Origins and Cultural Anthropology* (1986), 139–43.

that still more is needed, that his current status is inadequate. Another transformation must occur. Thus, the "unless" statements just examined all describe
transformations. Some represent the radical change of status from outsider to
insider (3:3, 5), whereas others indicate a change of insider status from less complete to more complete or from imperfect to perfect follower. Thus disciple
Peter has passed one loyalty test (6:67–69) and so enjoys basic membership. The
"part" Jesus offers in 13:8 would seem to be a new elite status.

A CLOSER LOOK — SYMBOLIC MEANING OF FOOTWASHING

Granted that 13:4–11 describes a status transformation, but why washing,
and why foot washing? This is unlike all other purifications found in Israel,
such as the washing of hands and vessels (Mark 7:1–7), which are perpetu-
ally repeated; they do not make the person washing "wholly clean." Unlike
those purifications, this one cannot be repeated. It certainly is not a gesture
of hospitality or hygiene.[367] Peter and the others are already disciples who
have seen and heard Jesus with sympathy, if not always with understanding.
Yet something more is needed, which will make them "wholly clean." This
washing, then, functions primarily as a preparation for a new phase of being
an elite disciple.

Explanatory parallels describe how priests wash before offering sacrifice
(Exod 30:17–21 and 40:30–32), but Jesus is not consecrating the disciples as
priests.[368] Warriors in a Holy War washed their feet to symbolize that they
were assuming duties requiring ritual purity.[369] The closest parallel might
be Jesus' question to James and John: "Are you able to be baptized with
the baptism that I am to be baptized with?" (Mark 10:38). The Johannine
washing thus transforms them into disciples who "wholly" share in Jesus'
own "baptism." We take the term "'part' of me" (*meros*) to imply sharing
Jesus' lot, which as the Passion narrative progresses, means "like a grain of
wheat dying" or "like a branch purified by the vine dresser."[370]

---

[367] John C. Thomas identifies three different functions for footwashing in the ancient
world: cultic settings, domestic hygiene or comfort, and hospitality. See his *Footwashing in John 13 and the Johannine Community* (Sheffield: Sheffield Academic Press,
1991), 27.

[368] "I bless You that I may share, among the number (*meros*, as in "share the lot") of the
martyrs, in the cup of thy Christ.... And may I be received among them before Thee, as a
rich and acceptable sacrifice.... I glorify Thee through the everlasting and heavenly high
priest" (*Martyrdom of Polycarp* 14.2–3).

[369] See James Swetnam's review of Richter's *Die Fusswaschung* in *Biblica* 49 (1968), 441–43.
Although no evidence of Holy War is found in John 13, the suggestion of ritual purification
before confronting mortal danger has much to recommend it.

[370] "Part" (*meros*) is often interpreted in reference to Jesus' glorious post-resurrection future;
see R. E. Brown, *Gospel According to John* (1966), 2.565–66. Some see this as echoing the
synoptic command that disciples "take up their cross and follow me" (Mark 8:34). See
Herold Weiss, "Footwashing in the Johannine Community," *NovT* 21 (1971), 315–17.

Footwashing as Ceremony. Scholarship rightly understands Jesus' remarks in 13:12–20 as a ceremony that seemingly has become a regular part of the Johannine group's worship. Let us examine this ceremony in terms of the four characteristics noted earlier. Jesus mandates that the disciples wash the feet of group members as a regular part of their gatherings. How often? If, as an act of etiquette, footwashing welcomes people to a ceremonial meal (see Luke 7:44–46; 1 Tim 5:10), then presumably it would be repeated whenever the group gathered. (1) *Calendar.* This footwashing, if similar to other ceremonial foot-washing in the New Testament, would occur regularly at the *beginning* of the ceremony. Hence it is not the emergency ritual that interrupted the meal in progress when Jesus demanded to wash Peter's feet, something never repeated. (2) *Time focus.* It harkens back to the past; that is, some example of Jesus that is imitated in present time by the group's leaders. Jesus' past action, then, serves as warrant for the present action: "Do you know what I have done to you?" (13:12, 14). (3) *Presiding.* If footwashing belongs in the orbit of etiquette associated with commensality, then the group's leaders, the officials who preside over that ceremony, perform the washing. (4) *Purpose.* The purpose of the footwashing in 13:12–16 is manifold. Jesus confirms his own role and status by this act: "You call me 'Teacher' and 'Lord'; and you are right, for so I am" (13:13); he is also "Master" (13:16). Yet the appropriate act of this Teacher-Lord-Master is to wash the feet of disciples and servants, thus offering them welcome. By presiding at this ceremonial washing, Jesus confirms his unique role as Teacher-Lord-Master, even if the action done is "humble" in our eyes. Only the person in this exalted role may perform this action.

JOHN 13:21–30 – WHO KNOWS WHAT?

21 After saying this Jesus was troubled in spirit, and declared, "Very truly, I tell you, one of you will betray me."

22 The disciples looked at one another, uncertain of whom he was speaking.

23 One of his disciples – the one whom Jesus loved – was reclining next to him;

24 Simon Peter therefore motioned to him to ask Jesus of whom he was speaking.

25 So while reclining next to Jesus, he asked him, "Lord, who is it?"

26 Jesus answered, "It is the one to whom I give this piece of bread when I have dipped it in the dish." So when he had dipped the piece of bread, he gave it to Judas son of Simon Iscariot.

27 After he received the piece of bread, Satan entered into him. Jesus said to him, "Do quickly what you are going to do."

28 Now no one at the table knew why he said this to him.

29 Some thought that, because Judas had the common purse, Jesus was telling him, "Buy what we need for the festival"; or, that he should give something to the poor.

30 So, after receiving the piece of bread, he immediately went out. And it was night.

Who Knows What? Jesus, of course, knows all things, but the disciples either don't know or will soon know. If "knowledge" is currency in this Gospel, then tracking who knows what serves to classify the characters. The following list covers all instances just in John 13, indicating how prevalent and significant this theme is here.

13:1	"Jesus *knew* that his hour had come to depart."
13:3	"Jesus, *knowing* that the Father had given all things into his hand."
13:7	"What I am doing you do not *know* now, but afterwards you will understand."
13:11	"For he *knew* who was to betray him; that is why he said 'You are not all clean.'"
13:12	"You *know* what I have done to you."
13:17	"If you *know* these things, honorable are you."
13:18	"I *know* whom I have chosen."
13:19	"I tell you this now [i.e., "you know it"] so that when it happens you will believe."
13:21	"[I know that] One of you will betray me."
13:22	"Disciples lack knowledge of whom he spoke."
13:24–26	"[Seeking to know] Simon asks the Beloved Disciple who asks Jesus."
13:28	"No one *knew* why he [Jesus] said this to him [Judas]."
13:29	"Some thought that Jesus was telling him 'Buy what we need for the feast'; or that he should give something to the poor." (mistaken knowledge)
13:35	"By this all will *know* that you are my disciples."
13:36–38	Jesus' prediction [knowledge given]

Jesus knows the most important knowledge, whence he comes and whither he goes (13:1–3). He knows, moreover, of God's extraordinary benefaction of "putting all things in his hands." His knowledge, then, binds him most closely to God.[371] He also knows like a prophet, for he can penetrate disguises and read hearts; hence he knows his betrayer. The disciples, however, do and do not know. They *know* what Jesus' exemplary footwashing means. They *don't know* what Jesus is doing, who the traitor is, or why Judas does what he does. Although all will become clear to them later, they are still in transition and still lost in a fog of unknowing.

---

[371] On "knowledge" in John 13, see Alan Culpepper, "The Johannine *Hypodeigma:* A Reading of John 13," *Semeia* 53 (1991), 133–45.

Form of the Episode. Here again we find the familiar form statement, misunderstanding, and clarification. It occurs twice in 13:21–30:

	13:21–27a	*13:27b–30*
Statement	"One of you will betray me."	"Do quickly what you are going to do."
Misunderstanding or nonunderstanding	"The disciples looked at one another, uncertain of whom he was speaking."	"No one at the table knew why he said this to him. Some thought that, because Judas had the common purse, Jesus was telling him, 'Buy what we need for the festival'; or, that he should give something to the poor."
Clarification	"So while reclining next to Jesus, he asked him, 'Lord, who is it?' Jesus answered, 'It is the one to whom I give this piece of bread when I have dipped it in the dish.'"	"Now the Son of Man has been glorified, and God has been glorified in him."

In both instances, Jesus' *statement* concerns Judas, one of the disciples, and it serves as notice of the dirty business that is under way. In the first case, no one knows who the betrayer is. Peter seeks to know by asking the Beloved Disciple to learn the betrayer's identity. In the second instance, the disciples completely *misunderstand* Jesus, ironically crediting a positive motive to the worst of sinners. As regards *clarification,* Jesus identifies the traitor to the Beloved Disciple, whereas in the second cycle, he declares that Judas' actions will be for his glory, even if the disciples do not grasp this.

Commensality Poisoned. Meals are ceremonies[372] because they confirm various roles and statuses in a given institution. Those sharing this meal with Jesus are the inner circle of his group, not just anyone; Jesus is "Lord and Teacher...Master" (13:14, 16), a role confirmed by his commanding actions and words. The meal, moreover, is no ordinary consumption of food but a farewell meal that climaxes Jesus' association with his disciples. Whereas the rule is "Likes eat with likes," in this case an enemy eats at the table and so poisons the commensality while present. The author twice notes the presence of Judas at this meal, each time indicating that he is out of place here, as he was at

---

[372] See J. H. Neyrey, "Ceremonies in Luke-Acts," in *Social World of Luke-Acts* (1991), 361–74; and his "Meals, Food, and Table Fellowship," in Richard L. Rohrbaugh, ed., *The Social Sciences and New Testament Interpretation* (Peabody, MA: Hendrickson, 1996), 159–82.

the meal with Mary, Martha, and Lazarus (12:4–6). First, Jesus declares that the commensality is fouled by the table fellowship of a betrayer, as was predicted in Psalm 41:9: "'The one who ate my bread has lifted his heel against me'" (13:18). Second, in an ironic gesture, the victim of betrayal knowingly gives food to his betrayer, generally understood as a mark of respect and honor (13:26). This betrayer will later mark Jesus for the soldiers by kissing him, another mark of respect.

An Unknown Disciple. Peter turns to a disciple who must enjoy very high status in the group because of his physical closeness to Jesus. Relying on this elevated status, he turns to Jesus and asks to know a secret, the identity of the traitor. Thus, besides having the status associated with physical closeness, he learns highly restricted knowledge.[373] Moreover, he is called "the one whom Jesus loved," a remark that thus far applies only to Lazarus and his sisters. Hence, it is a restricted label, signaling very high status because of his close relationship to Jesus. He also immediately assumes the role of broker or middleman, a role he will exercise for the rest of the narrative. Here he brokers Peter's question, soon he will mediate Peter's entrance into Annas' palace (18:15–18), later he receives Jesus' mother into his house, a mark of incalculably high status, and finally, on the lake with Peter and others, he alone knows what they do not know: "It is the Lord" (21:7).

JOHN 13:31–35 – NOW GLORY

31 When he had gone out, Jesus said, "Now the Son of Man has been glorified, and God has been glorified in him.

32 If God has been glorified in him, God will also glorify him in himself and will glorify him at once.

33 Little children, I am with you only a little longer. You will look for me; and as I said to the Jews so now I say to you, 'Where I am going, you cannot come.'

34 I give you a new commandment, that you love one another. Just as I have loved you, you also should love one another.

35 By this everyone will know that you are my disciples, if you have love for one another."

---

[373] In terms of representative characters, the Beloved Disciple seems to be all that Peter is not; that is, ideal behavior is presented in contrast to Peter's weakness. See William S. Kurz, "The Beloved Disciple and Implied Readers," *BTB* 19 (1989), 100–7; and Brendan J. Byrne, "The Faith of the Beloved Disciple and the Community in John 20," *JSNT* 23 (1985), 83–97.

Glory All Around. Jesus' remark on "glory"[374] is chiastic in shape:

A.   The *Son of Man* has been glorified.
B.   and *God* has been glorified in him.
B'.   If *God* has been glorified in him.
A'.   God will also glorify *him in himself* and will glorify *him* at once.

In the "A" parts, God acts to glorify the Son of Man, whereas in the "B" parts, God in turn is honored by the obedient Son. "Glory" belongs to the world of honor; that is, the respect or worth a person has in the eyes of others. But the only honor that matters is what God thinks, not what one's peers or neighbors value. For example, many prefer the glory from their peers to glory from God, and so refuse to honor Jesus: "Many, even of the authorities, believed in him, but they did not confess it, for fear that they would be put out of the synagogue; for they loved human glory more than the glory that comes from God" (12:42–43). Jesus refused to play this game, stating "I do not accept glory from human beings" (5:41) but only from God.[375]

Their Shame but God's Honor. Two different times are indicated in 13:31–32: the "Son of man *has been* glorified" indicating God's honoring of Jesus in the past when others dishonored him; and "God *will* glorify him . . . at once," which refers to his passage through death and so his return back to the "heart" of the Father. Honor, then, is couched in terms of shame: Jesus finds honor in God's eyes but rejection in the eyes of the crowds. The glory of Jesus is his shame; that is, his death. Yet his death and shame are glory in God's eyes.

Coming and Going. Jesus has always known *whence* he comes and *whither* he goes. But outsiders and enemies never have this knowledge. Are the disciples among the ignorant? After all, Jesus said: "I am with you only a little longer. You will look for me; and as I said to the Jews so now I say to you, 'Where I am going, you cannot come'" (13:33). Yet immediately in 14:1–7 and 17:1–5, Jesus will give them privileged discourse on this matter; and Mary Magdalene will carry to them a revelation from Jesus on the same topic (20:17–18). There is a lot of learning left to do, and of the highest order.

New Commandment: Love One Another.[376] Except for 12:24–26, Jesus issued virtually no commands relative to discipleship in the Book of Signs. But starting

---

[374] For a description of honor/glory suitable to the New Testament, see J. H. Neyrey, *Honor and Shame* (1998), 14–17.

[375] See the remarks on "glory" in the discussion of 12:28; see also G. B. Caird, "The Glory of God in the Fourth Gospel," *NTS* 15 (1969), 265–77.

[376] Raymond F. Collins, "'A New Commandment I Give You . . .' (Jn 13:34)," *LTP* 35 (1979), 235–61.

with Chapter 13, the narrative records over a dozen. This one is labeled "new," probably because of its timeliness in light of Jesus' death. It may be "new," but it will be repeated shortly in John 15.

13:34–35, 37	*15:12–13*
Jesus to disciples:	Jesus to disciples:
I give you a new commandment, that you love one another. Just as I have loved you, you also should love one another.	This is my commandment, that you love one another as I have loved you.
By this everyone will know that you are my disciples, if you have love for one another.	
Peter to Jesus:	Jesus to disciples:
I will lay down my life for you.	No one has greater love than this, to lay down one's life for one's friends.

This comparison yields several points: Jesus' "love" for the disciples is the model for and measure of group love; group love distinguishes the disciples from all other peoples, an identity marker; and an elitist note is sounded – "Greater" love is expressed by "laying down one's life for one's friends." We have, then, another status marker associated with how one "loves."

But what does "love" mean? Most frequently it is linked to "laying down one's life" for another (10:11, 15, 17–18; 15:13), which is what Peter claims that he will be willing to do (13:37–38). Bruce Malina proposes a cultural meaning of "love": "This [love] is the value of group attachment and group bonding. It may or may not be coupled with feelings of affection. Such group attachment and group bonding are one type of social glue that keeps groups together." "Laying down one's life" contains strong elements of faithfulness and loyalty, hallmarks of a "noble" death. The opposite here is cowardice,[377] disloyalty, and unfaithfulness, first in the case of Judas and then in Peter's denial. Love, then, means that disciples must be loyal and faithful to the group; they do this by remaining attached to Jesus. Jesus' disciples are to love (i.e., be attached to) him (John 14:15, 21, 23, 24; 21:15–17).

JOHN 13:36–38 – PETER: "HAVE PART WITH ME" OR DENY ME?

36 Simon Peter said to him, "Lord, where are you going?" Jesus answered, "Where I am going, you cannot follow me now; but you will follow afterward."

---

[377] Recall how the threat of excommunication silenced some people (9:22; 12:42); others come to Jesus at night, presumably to avoid notice (3:2).

37 Peter said to him, "Lord, why can I not follow you now? I will lay down my life for you."
38 Jesus answered, "Will you lay down your life for me? Very truly, I tell you, before the cock crows, you will have denied me three times."

Challenge/Riposte? Peter's question "Where are you going?" is, as most questions are, challenging to Jesus because Jesus just told all the disciples, "Where I am going you cannot come."[378] To pry secrets from Jesus is aggressive behavior. Although Jesus halts Peter, he promises that "afterward" he will follow Jesus. Peter then makes a rash or vainglorious claim, that he will "follow" Jesus now and even lay down his life. Jesus challenges this claim, mocking Peter not only by repeating his words but adding the prediction of Peter's shameful failure, for he will "deny me three times." Boasting and bragging are forms of honor claims inappropriate with Jesus.

A CLOSER LOOK — PETER'S PERPETUAL MISUNDERSTANDINGS

The exchange between Jesus and Peter in 13:36–38 strongly parallels that in 13:7–9. Twice in this chapter, Jesus and Peter speak to each other, both times in the familiar form of statement–misunderstanding–clarification.

13:7–9	*13:36–38*
1. *Statement of Jesus:* "What I am doing you *do not know* now; afterwards you will understand (v. 7)."	1. *Statement of Jesus:* "Where I am going your *cannot come* now, but afterwards you will follow (v. 36)."
2. *Misunderstanding by Peter:* "You shall not wash my feet forever (v. 8a)."	2. *Misunderstanding by Peter:* "Why can I not follow you now? I will lay down my life for you (v. 37)."
3. *Clarification by Jesus:* "If I do not wash you, you will have no part in me (v. 9)."	3. *Clarification by Jesus:* "The cock shall not have crowed till you have denied me three times (v. 38)."

Failure in Peter's Transformation Ritual. We interpreted the footwashing in 13:4–11 as a status-transformation ritual. If all goes well, the candidates will be changed by becoming "wholly clean" and by having "a share with me." Thus, they will be prepared for the death of Jesus, either by physically sharing in it or

---

[378] J. H. Neyrey, "Questions," *CBQ* 60 (1998), 658–67; see the discussion of questions in the commentary on 3:3–5.

by being participants in Jesus' own arrest, trial, and death. Who undergoes this ritual and how do they fare?[379]

Peter: footwashing transformation ritual: *still a candidate;* failed
              loyalty to Jesus = failed transformation
Judas: footwashing transformation ritual: *never a candidate;* hostility
              to Jesus = no possible status transformation ("One is *not*
              clean")
BD: footwashing transformation ritual: *successful candidate;*
              courage to enter Annas' place and stand at the cross =
              successful transformation

Moreover, is there a *role* transformation beyond a *status* change? When Peter boasts "I will lay down my life for you" (13:37), he makes the same claim that the Noble Shepherd repeatedly made in 10:11–15, namely that "The noble shepherd lays down his life for his sheep." A role is in view here: "shepherd" of the flock. Jesus challenges Peter's claim, effectively declaring that Peter has failed the test for being a "shepherd" as of this time; rather, he resembles the "hireling" instead. Moreover, there are several episodes coming in which Peter acts as a sheep, not shepherd (18:15–18). Only later does Jesus declare him qualified for the transformation to the role of shepherd (21:15–19).

JOHN 14:1–6 – GOING AWAY AND COMING BACK

1 "Do not let your hearts be troubled. Believe in God, believe also in me.
2 In my Father's house there are many dwelling places. If it were not so, would I have told you that I go to prepare a place for you?
3 And if I go and prepare a place for you, I will come again and will take you to myself, so that where I am, there you may be also.
4 And you know the way to the place where I am going."
5 Thomas said to him, "Lord, we do not know where you are going. How can we know the way?"
6 Jesus said to him, "I am the way, and the truth, and the life. No one comes to the Father except through me."

Farewell Address: Gross Anatomy. Readers of John 13–17 quickly learn that this seemingly disorganized assemblage of materials makes excellent sense when viewed as a farewell address. The ancient world contains numerous examples

---

[379] J. H. Neyrey, "Footwashing," in *Social World of First Christians* (1995), 206–8.

of a dying leader or patriarch delivering a last will and testament. For example, Moses delivers his farewell address in Deuteronomy 32 and Jacob his in Genesis 49; see also *Testaments of the Twelve Patriarchs*.[380] The most celebrated Greek example is Plato's *Phaedo*, which contains Socrates' farewell.[381] Luke creates a farewell address both for Jesus (Luke 22:14–36) and for Paul (Acts 20:18–35).[382] Farewell addresses have a range of purposes, from honoring the dying patriarch to encouraging his followers and designating a successor.

Typical farewell addresses contain the following elements: (1) announcement of death or departure (hence "farewell" address); (2) review of the patriarch's life, setting the record straight; (3) relationships to be maintained; (4) revelations of beneficial things to come; (5) predictions of future hard times; (6) exhortation to practice a group-specific virtue and to avoid a group-specific vice; (7) successor named; (8) legacy bestowed; and (9) occasionally a final prayer or blessing. Adjusting the typical form for the specific Johannine Farewell Address, we offer the following chart to help readers identify and interpret the elements in John 14–17.[383]

1. Announcement: Death or departure	"Yet a little while I am with you" (13:33); "I go away" (14:2–3, 28). Reaction: "Do not be troubled" (14:1, 27; 16:4b–6).
2. Review of patriarch's life	"I do as the Father has commanded me, so that the world may know that I love the Father" (14:31); "I have glorified you on earth (17:4); "I have manifested your name" (17:6, 26); "I have given them the words which you have given me" (17:8, 14); "I have kept them in your name" (17:12); "I have sent them into the world" (17:18).

---

[380] See Fernando F. Segovia, *The Farewell Address of the Word* (Minneapolis, MN: Fortress Press, 1991); Bruce Woll, *Johannine Christianity in Conflict: Authority, Rank, and Succession in the First Farewell Discourse* (Chico, CA: Scholars Press, 1981); and John Painter, "The Farewell Discourses and the History of Johannine Christianity," *NTS* 27 (1981), 525–43.

[381] William S. Kurz, "Luke 22:14–38 and Greco-Roman and Biblical Farewell Addresses," *JBL* 104 (1985), 253–55.

[382] J. H. Neyrey, *Passion Narrative in St. Luke* (1985), 5–48.

[383] This should be supplemented with the reading scenario "Final Address" by Bruce J. Malina and Richard L. Rohrbaugh in their *Social-Science Commentary on the Synoptic Gospels*, 2nd ed. (Minneapolis, MN: Fortress Press, 2003), 361–63; and "Final Words" in their *Social-Science Commentary on the Gospel of John* (Minneapolis, MN: Fortress Press, 1998), 221–23.

3. Relationships maintained	Jesus and God: 14:8–11, 20; Jesus and the disciples: 14:3, 21; 15:1–11, 12–17; Jesus, God, and the disciples: 14:6–7, 13, 23.
4. Knowledge and revelations given	Knowledge of the way: 14:4–7; seeing the Father: 14:8–11; knowledge about Jesus in the Father: 14:20–24; revelation by the spirit: 14:25–26; 15:25–26.
5. Predictions of the future	Future crises: 14:29; 15:18–25; 16:1–4, 29–33; future blessings: 14:2–3, 12–14, 18; 16:20–24, 25.
6. Exhortation to virtue; avoidance of vice	Believe: 14:10–11, 29; love: 14:15, 21, 23–24, 28; 15:12–17; 16:27; abide: 15:1–11; hate: 15:18–25.
7. Successor named	"Another Advocate": 14:25–26; 15:25–26; 16:7–15.
8. Legacy	Greater works: 14:12–14; revelation of "your name": 17:6, 11–12, 26; knowledge: see #4, knowledge and revelations.
9. Farewell prayer	Worship 17:1–26.

How Many Farewells? John's Farewell Address begins in 13:31 with Jesus' announcement of his imminent departure. Although it officially ends in 18:1, we find an earlier terminus marker in 14:31, where Jesus says "Arise, let us go hence," signaling an end to the address, at least in the supper room.[384] Many take this as evidence that the Farewell Address underwent a second edition with significant new additions.

In My Father's House There Are Many Dwelling Places. Two phrases in 14:2 require attention: "In my Father's house there are many rooms (*monai pollai*)"; and "I am going to prepare a place (*topon*) for you." "My Father's house" has been variously explained as heaven, the heavenly temple, the messianic kingdom, or even the universe.[385] Because in John there is no longer any fixed sacred space[386] or earthly temple made sacred by God's dwelling (4:21), we look to God's "realm" as the place for worshiping God – wherever that may be. McCaffrey offers an important contribution, namely, that "house" suggests relationships such as Father–Son or intimate kinship relationships.[387] In this household, then, there are many relations – Father, Son, and current disciples, and perhaps other Christians yet to be brought in.[388] And when Jesus states that "I go to prepare a place for you," he goes not as an architect to build something but as a broker of

---

384 Bruce Woll, "The Departure of 'the Way': The First Farewell Discourse in the Gospel of John." *JBL* 99 (1980), 225–39; and F. F. Segovia, *Farewell of the Word* (1991), 61–121.

385 James McCaffrey, *The House with Many Rooms: The Temple Theme of Jn. 14, 2–3* (Rome: Pontifical Biblical Institute, 1988), 29–35.

386 J. H. Neyrey, "Territoriality," *BTB* 32 (2002), 665–66, 668–69.

387 J. McCaffrey, *The House with Many Rooms* (1988), 49–64. See also S. van Tilborg, *Imaginative Love* (1993).

388 See John 17:20–22; and also Tod D. Swanson, "To Prepare a Place: Johannine Christianity and the Collapse of Ethnic Territory," *JAAR* 62 (1994), 244–45, 248–51, 257–60.

relationships that will secure access to God through himself. Thus we are inclined to read 14:2 in terms of personal relationships and not in terms of buildings or space.

A CLOSER LOOK – JOHANNINE GEOGRAPHY: SPACE = RELATIONSHIPS

Category	*Data*
1. No fixed sacred space	"Neither on this mountain, nor in Jerusalem will you worship" (4:21). "He spoke of the temple of his body" (2:21).
2. Whence and whither	The Messiah is not from Nazareth or Galilee (1:46; 7:41–42, 52). Whence: from heaven (3:13; 6:38, 41–42) and from God (17:5). Whither: to God (1:18; 14:2–4; 16:5; 20:18)
3. "Remain" and "dwell in"	In: "I am in the Father and the Father is in me" (14:10, 11); "I am in my Father and you in me and I in you" (14:20). Remain: "The Father dwells in me" (14:10b); "The branch cannot bear fruit unless it 'dwells' in the vine" (15:4, 5b); "If you 'dwell' in me and my words 'dwell' in you" (15:7).
4. Rooms, place, home	"In my Father's house there are many rooms. . . . I go to prepare a place for you" (14:2); "We will come to him and make our home with him" (14:23).

With the advent of the Farewell Address, the language of space and place becomes frequent because of the immediate question of Jesus' spatial departure. Hence, in light of Jesus' absence, the document must focus on the antidote proposed in terms of references to Jesus' return and the benefit to his disciples through his departure. Moreover, in light of this absence, the data argue that "relationships"[389] substitute for absence. One worships "in" Jesus and "remains" loyal and faithful to him, and he "remains" in the disciple. God's "house" is a household, not a building, which allows for endless relationships between God and his disciples.

Jesus the Broker. Jesus "goes away and comes back" – he goes "to prepare a place for you" and then "comes back and will take you" to himself. His purpose is that "where I am you also may be." Having solidified his relationship with the Patron-Father, he returns to solidify his relationship with God's clients. He does

---

[389] See J. H. Neyrey, "Territoriality," *BTB* 32 (2002), 60–74; and W. H. Oliver and A. G. Van Aarde, "The Community of Faith as the Dwelling Place of the Father: *Basileia ton theou* as 'Household of God' in the Johannine Farewell Address," *Neotestamentica* 25 (1991), 379–400.

not say that he will take the disciples to the "Father's house" but rather broker and maintain a favored relationship between the heavenly Patron and his clients on earth. Thus, Jesus is in two "places" at once: in heaven (in relationship with God, wherever God is) and on earth (in relationship with disciples, whenever they gather). Balancing his remark that he has access to God's presence, he also "takes the disciples to myself." Thus they, too, have access to God's house, but only in relation to Jesus. Poor Thomas does not know the way to the Father's house! Jesus tells him "I am the way . . ." (14:6); that is, he enjoys an exclusive relationship with God: "No one comes to the Father, but by me." Jesus, then, is both relationship and access, but he is not "place."

Way, Truth, and Life. These three words are but the latest examples of the Johannine pattern whereby Jesus claims to be something unique:[390] "I am + predicate"; for example, "I am the bread of life" or "I am the light of the world." These claim that Jesus under this or that rubric is the unique, only, and genuine item; all others are defective, unreliable, or false. The claim here is particularly dense (three claims: way, truth, and life) and expressed in the context of crisis (his departure and the disciples' persecution). Hence, we look for Johannine meanings to the three predicates that match the context. "Way" refers to exclusive access to God: "No one comes to the Father except through me" (14:6; see also 1:18). Jesus acts as the unique broker between God and the disciples. "Truth" can be read in two ways, either as knowledge and revelation or as faithfulness. Certainly Jesus mediates heavenly secrets in abundance, especially at this farewell time, but he also exhorts and exemplifies "remaining" in God and himself. "Life" should be seen in the context of death. Jesus has demonstrated that he can call the dead from their tombs (5:25; 11:43) and will soon demonstrate that in virtue of God's benefaction "to have life in himself" (5:26), he has power to lay down his life and power to take it back (10:17–18). Thus he can mediate to enable loyal disciples to survive death.

JOHN 14:7–12 – KNOWING, SHOWING, AND SEEING

7 If you know me, you will know my Father also. From now on you do know him and have seen him."
8 Philip said to him, "Lord, show us the Father, and we will be satisfied."
9 Jesus said to him, "Have I been with you all this time, Philip, and you still do not know me? Whoever has seen me has seen the Father. How can you say, 'Show us the Father'?

---

[390] On the rhetoric of "uniqueness," see J. H. Neyrey, "Uniqueness," *Biblica* 86 (2005), 59–87; readers are referred to the discussion of this material in the commentary on 3:13.

10 Do you not believe that I am in the Father and the Father is in me? The words that I say to you I do not speak on my own; but the Father who dwells in me does his works.

11 Believe me that I am in the Father and the Father is in me; but if you do not, then believe me because of the works themselves.

12 Very truly, I tell you, the one who believes in me will also do the works that I do and, in fact, will do greater works than these, because I am going to the Father.

Statement – Misunderstanding – Clarification. When people in John 13 misunderstand Jesus' words, not much is made of it; here, the full catechetical thrust of this pattern is operative, presumably because this part of the Farewell Address deals with revelations, knowledge, and secrets.[391] It matters greatly that disciples understand Jesus' last words. The following chart illustrates this pattern in John 14.

1. Statement	14:1–4	14:7	14:21
2. Misunderstanding	14:5	14:8	14:22
3. Clarification	14:6	14:9–12	14:23ff.

Jesus addresses named disciples: Thomas (14:5), Philip (14:8), and Judas, not Iscariot (14:22). Thus, we do not take their challenges and questions to Jesus as seriously as in other contexts, for here each disciple receives a rich, full response, not a riposte or insult. Moreover, they receive unique, esoteric insider information, not fit for outsiders to hear.

"Being in" and "Dwelling in." Jesus' remarks in John 14–15 describe his relationship with either the Father or the disciples, which is expressed in spatial terms ("in" and "dwell in"). For example, "I am in the Father and the Father is in me" (14:10, 11, 20), and "the Father dwells in me" (14:10b). Similarly, Jesus' relationship with the disciples parallels that between him and God: "I am in my Father and you in me and I in you" (14:20). But the perspective is hardly a spatial one, for the disciples do not travel to another place; nor does "being in" necessarily imply spatial location. Likewise with "dwell in." In terms of Jesus' relationship with God, we are told that "the Father dwells in me" (14:10b). The same verb is used ten times in 15:4–10 to express Jesus' relationship with the disciples. On the one hand, the disciple must "dwell" in, remain in, or sustain loyalty to Jesus: "The branch cannot bear fruit unless it *dwells* in the vine" (15:4). Conversely, if a branch "dwells" in the vine, the vine curiously will "Dwell" in the branch: "Dwell in me and I in you" (15:4, 5b). An alternate way of expressing this in 15:7 indicates a basis for this type of dwelling: "If you 'dwell' in me and my words 'dwell' in you ... " So, "knowledge" or "words" can dwell in the disciples. Finally, the Spirit will "dwell" in you and "be" in you (14:17). Recall that we best understand "in" and "dwell" in terms of relationships.

---

[391] On farewell addresses as occasions for revelations, see B. J. Malina and R. L. Rohrbaugh, *Commentary on the Synoptic Gospels* (2003), 361–63.

JOHN 14:13–24 – PATRON-GOD, BROKER-JESUS, AND CLIENTS-DISCIPLES

13 I will do whatever you ask in my name, so that the Father may be glorified in the Son.

14 If in my name you ask me for anything, I will do it.

15 "If you love me, you will keep my commandments.

16 And I will ask the Father, and he will give you another Advocate, to be with you forever.

17 This is the Spirit of truth, whom the world cannot receive, because it neither sees him nor knows him. You know him, because he abides with you, and he will be in you.

18 "I will not leave you orphaned; I am coming to you.

19 In a little while the world will no longer see me, but you will see me; because I live, you also will live.

20 On that day you will know that I am in my Father, and you in me, and I in you.

21 They who have my commandments and keep them are those who love me; and those who love me will be loved by my Father, and I will love them and reveal myself to them."

22 Judas (not Iscariot) said to him, "Lord, how is it that you will reveal yourself to us, and not to the world?"

23 Jesus answered him, "Those who love me will keep my word, and my Father will love them, and we will come to them and make our home with them.

24 Whoever does not love me does not keep my words; and the word that you hear is not mine, but is from the Father who sent me.

Broker. To interpret this passage, we need to know the ancient model of patron–broker–client relationships. God, the Patron of Patrons, bestows benefaction and favors on his clients. At no time and in no way does Jesus present himself as a patron, but only as the Patron's mediator and broker. He bridges and joins clients and Patron; he is the go-between, or the exclusive "way" to the Father. Let us use this model to observe how the dramatis personae of the patron–broker–client relationship are described here. First, the broker cements his relationship with the patron, the source of all benefaction; in many ways he declares it to be strong and solid: "Do you not believe that I am in the Father and the Father is in me? . . . The Father who dwells in me does his works. Believe me that I am in the Father and the Father is in me" (14:10–11). The broker–patron relationship is utterly reliable. Jesus, moreover, brokers the Patron's works (14:1) and words (14:24). Similarly, the Broker facilitates the clients' access to the Patron: They may ask in his name (14:13–14). He, in fact, will broker the Paraclete for them

(14:16–17, 26). The Broker, moreover, is solicitous for his clients: He warns them of coming crises, exhorting them not to be disturbed (14:1, 28); he tells them prophecies of future hard times for the express purpose of alerting them how to weather those storms successfully (14:29; see also 13:19); and finally, he gives them otherworldly peace (14:27). Although he leaves them, he declares that he will not leave them orphans (14:18). The clients know that they are truly connected to their patron if they keep his commands (14:15) and feed on his words (14:23). Finally, we glimpse the complete relationship of patron, broker, and clients: "On that day you will know that I am in my Father, and you in me, and I in you" (14:20). This completeness is reflected also in Jesus' remarks "and you in me, and I in you" (14:20)[392] and "Those who love me will keep my word, and my Father will love them, and we will come to them and make our home with them" (14:23).

What kind of broker is he? Clients may petition the Patron through Jesus: "If in my name you ask for anything, I will do it" (14:14). The Broker himself petitions the Patron on their behalf: "I will ask the Father, and he will give you another Advocate" (14:16). Jesus, moreover, is a reliable broker: "I will not leave you orphaned; I am coming to you. In a little while . . . you will see me" (14:18–19). He typically manifests favoritism to certain clients: "How is it that you will reveal yourself to us, and not to the world?" (14:22). As a proactive broker, he anticipates the clients' needs (14:16) and urges them to petition in his name, even affirming that "I will do it" (14:13–14).

A CLOSER LOOK — JESUS, THE BROKER

Jesus is frequently labeled a broker in the New Testament, usually with synonyms such as "mediator" (1 Tim 2:5), "priest" (Heb 3:1; 5:6; 7:1–25), or "apostle" (Heb 3:1).[393] Moreover, practically all commerce with the heavenly world takes place "through" Jesus, another way of describing his role as mediator,[394] including prayer made "in my name" (John 14:13, 14, 26). Such a role was well known in ancient Israel, for both Abraham (Gen 18:23–33) and Moses (Exod 32:11–14) brokered God's mercy (see John 5:45–46). Throughout this commentary, we have chosen to describe such a relationship in

---

[392] For another reading of this material from the sociology of space, see J. H. Neyrey, "Territoriality," *BTB* 32 (2002), 69.

[393] See P. Borgen, "God's Agent," in *Religions in Antiquity* (1968), 137–48; G. W. Buchanan, "Apostolic Christianity," *SBLSP* (1986), 172–82; and A. E. Harvey, "Christ as Agent," in *Glory of Christ in the New Testament* (1987), 239–50.

[394] For example, 1 Corinthians 8:6; 15:57; Romans 1:8; 5:1–2; 11:36; Hebrews 2:10; Acts 2:22; Galatians 6:14; Philippians 3:8; Colossians 1:16–17, 3:17; see Gregory E. Sterling, "Prepositional Metaphysics in Jewish Wisdom Speculation and Early Christian Liturgical Texts," *Studia Philonica* 9 (1997), 219–38.

terms of the well-known social model of patron–client relations, with Jesus in situations such as these taking the role of broker or mediator.[395]

When the Gospel states that Jesus is "sent," he acts as an intermediary between the Patron and those clients to whom God's benefaction is intended. Jesus makes clear that the Patron (God, Father) has given him complete resources to distribute as he wills: "The Father loves the Son and has placed all things in his hands" (3:35). Specifically, Jesus mediates God's power (9:31–33), as well as God's word (14:24; 17:14) and God's worlds (3:34; 8:47; 14:10; 17:8). Successful brokers belong in two worlds, those of the Patron and the clients. Illustrative of this is the insistence that Jesus comes from the Patron, as well as the reminder that Jesus will return to Him (7:33, 13:1, 14:12, 28; 16:5, 10, 17, 28; 20:18), suggesting that the Broker has ready access to the Patron, who sent him. Jesus, of course, belongs to this world, where he became flesh and pitched his tent (1:14). Eventually Jesus will turn over the broker role to the Paraclete and to his own favored clients (disciples), who will take up their role on behalf of Jesus: "As you have sent me into the world, so I have sent them into the world" (17:18).[396]

All brokers deserve recompense for services and goods provided; God's clients have a duty to acknowledge Jesus as broker, which can only be paid by keeping his "words" and "commandments." Jesus claims here that disciples have a dual duty. They owe God, their patron, acknowledgment and honor: "Believe in God" (14:1). Jesus, too, honors God: "I do as the Father commanded me" (14:31). But the disciples' duty is owed to Jesus in terms of acknowledging his relationship to God; that is, as their broker (14:10–11, 13–14, 15, 21, 26).

Love and Duty.[397] Twice the author defines "love" in terms of "keeping my commandments" (14:15, 21).[398] "Love," moreover, bespeaks adhesion, loyalty, and faithfulness. An index of adhesion to Jesus is paying him his due by honoring his commandments. He is, then, an honorable teacher, a respected Master and Lord. Later, Jesus presents a contrast between those who do not love and those who do (14:23–24). On the positive side, those who love Jesus keep his word, with the wonderful result that "my Father will love them." Moreover, "we will

---

[395] See Bruce J. Malina, *The Social World of Jesus and the Gospels* (London: Routledge, 1996), 143–57. On the use of this model to describe the role of the Spirit, see Tricia Gates Brown, *Spirit in the Writings of John* (New York: T and T Clark, 2003), 23–61.

[396] This material on Jesus as broker is a paraphrase of B. J. Malina and R. L. Rohrbaugh, *Commentary on John* (1998), 118.

[397] See Fernando F. Segovia, "The Love and Hatred of Jesus in Johannine Sectarianism," *CBQ* 43 (1981), 260–66.

[398] Readers are referred back to the discussion of this material at 13:31–35.

come to them and make our home with them," which repeats what he previously said.

<table>
<tr><td>

1. "They who have my commandments and keep them are those who love me;

2. and those who love me will be loved by my Father,

3. and I will love them and reveal myself to them" (14:21).

</td><td>

1. "Those who love me will keep my word,

2. and my Father will love them,

3. and we will come to them and make our home with them" (14:23).

</td></tr>
</table>

Adhesion begets adhesion, which results in "housing" Jesus and God with the disciples or in receiving his manifestation. Yet, those who do not love Jesus and so do not keep his words forfeit these benefits. All hinges on a disciple's duty to "keep the word" of his teacher.

A CLOSER LOOK — JUSTICE, DUTY, AND LOVE

Why do disciples have duties in the first place? Why take up this topic when discussing "love"? Are they related? Typical descriptions of the virtue of "justice" speak of duties, love, and loyalty; Pseudo-Aristotle was hardly alone in arguing that:

To righteousness [i.e., justice] it belongs to be ready to distribute according to desert, and to preserve ancestral customs and institutions and the established laws, and to tell the truth when interest is at stake, and to keep agreements. First among the claims of righteousness are our duties to the gods, then our duties to the spirits, then those to country and parents, then those to the departed. Righteousness is also accompanied by holiness and truth and faithfulness (*pistis*) and hatred of wickedness. (*Virtues and Vices*, 5.2–3)

When we use this to interpret "love" in 14:13–24, we find the following sets of duties:

1. Disciples are indebted to Jesus: "If you love me . . . keep my commandments" (14:15, 21, 23).
2. Jesus has duties to his disciples, which he fulfills in the following way:

   "I will ask the Father . . . another advocate, to be with you forever" (14:16)
   "You know him, because he abides with you and will be in you." (14:17)
   "I will not leave you orphaned. . . ." (14:18)
   "You will see me. . . ." (14:19)
   "You will know that I am in the Father, and you in me and I in you." (14:20)

3. The Father's duties to Jesus' disciples: "My Father will love them and we will come to them and make our home in them." (14:23)

But in another description of justice, we find a remarkable statement on "justice" and "love" that has bearing on how we read 14:13–25:

The parts of justice are piety, fair dealing and reverence: piety toward the gods, fair dealing towards men, reverence toward the departed. Piety to the gods consists of two elements: being god-loved and god-loving. The former means being loved by the gods and receiving many blessings from them, the latter consists of loving the gods and having a relationship of friendship with them. (*Menander Rhetor* 1.361.17–25)

In this vein, we have ample data that both the world (3:16) and Jesus are "god-loved" (3:35; 5:20; 10:17; 15:9; 17:23, 26). On occasion, we hear that God loves Jesus' disciples (16:27; 17:23, 26). This should help us understand 14:23, where we are told that those who pay their duties to Jesus "my Father will love, and we will come and make our home with them." Thus "obey my commandments" and "keep my word" are the grounds for the special status of being "God-loved."

Word and Commandments. Yet what are this "word" and these "commandments"? What does it mean to "keep" them? All this belongs in the category of knowledge, revelation, and esoteric wisdom that Jesus teaches. This includes commandments to be obeyed (13:34; 14:15), which focus on love or loyalty; accepting the authorization of Jesus' discourse as coming from God (14:10, 24b); revelations such as "I am the way, the truth, and the life" (14:5); a description of God's house and its dwelling (14:2–3, 23); time and travel plans (14:3, 18–19, 28); and manifestations (14:21). Thus we learn that Jesus the broker primarily mediates information to God's clients. We will return to this passage shortly, but the "other Advocate" functions in this vein also. He "will teach you everything, and remind you of all that I have said to you" (14:26). Thus he will broker Jesus' information, word, and commandments to the disciples; even brokers have brokers.

JOHN 14:25–31 – PEACE, CRISIS, AND DEPARTURE

25 "I have said these things to you while I am still with you.

26 But the Advocate, the Holy Spirit, whom the Father will send in my name, will teach you everything, and remind you of all that I have said to you.

27 Peace I leave with you; my peace I give to you. I do not give to you as the world gives. Do not let your hearts be troubled, and do not let them be afraid.

28 You heard me say to you, 'I am going away, and I am coming to you.' If you loved me, you would rejoice that I am going to the Father, because the Father is greater than I.

29 And now I have told you this before it occurs, so that when it does occur, you may believe.

30 I will no longer talk much with you, for the ruler of this world is coming. He has no power over me;

31 but I do as the Father has commanded me, so that the world may know that I love the Father. Rise, let us be on our way.

Advocate and Spirit. Our author twice remarks about the Advocate, first in 14:16–17 and then in 14:25–26. We best interpret them by working our way slowly through them.

Paraclete or Advocate? In times past, we simply used to borrow the Greek word "Paraclete" without addressing its meaning. Several recent studies have surveyed the instances of "paraclete" and offer the following interpretations: "Prior to the Gospel of John the term usually carries a connotation of 'mediator' or 'broker'"[399], or, it should be translated as "patron" or "supporter."[400] These scholars find little support for interpreting the Advocate in forensic terms as a spokesman or defense lawyer.

Jesus and Advocate. Although in some places Jesus himself gives the Spirit to his disciples (John 20:22–23; 3:34), the Spirit in no way replaces Jesus but rather continues Jesus' benefaction to the disciples. But in 14:15–16 and 14:25–26, the Father alone sends the Advocate, albeit at Jesus' request, and here the Advocate/Spirit would appear to be Jesus' successor.

Knowledge and Spirit. We have noted how Jesus' knowledge, revelations, and words constitute the chief elements of his legacy. So the Advocate serves to ensure access to this legacy now that Jesus has gone away. Tricia Brown argues this cogently: "The Paraclete makes possible continued access to Jesus after Jesus has departed.... In the Discourses Jesus' exclusive ability to provide a way to the Father is strongly reasserted, and the Paraclete is depicted as providing the believers with continual access to Jesus."[401] At least here, the sole function of the Advocate is to keep Jesus current to the disciples: "the Advocate, the Holy Spirit, will teach you everything, and remind you of all that I have said to you."

Advocate Remaining. Just as God's Spirit "remained" on Jesus (1:33), similarly the Advocate/Spirit will "remain in" you. Jesus may depart, but the Advocate remains and dwells in the group.

[399] T. G. Brown, *Spirit in the Writings of John* (2003), 170–86.
[400] Kenneth Grayston, "The Meaning of PARAKLETOS," *JSNT* 13 (1981), 67–82.
[401] T. G. Brown, *Spirit in the Writings of John* (2003), 22.

Spirit of Truth. The Advocate is the Spirit of "truth" in two senses. First, as mediator of Jesus' words, he does so honestly and accurately, hence truthfully. And because "truth" has to do with loyalty and faithfulness, the Spirit is therefore reliable and steadfast.

Spirit Looks to Past and Future. Is there a difference in the two functions of the Spirit in 14:26, "He will teach you everything, and remind you of all that I have said to you"? "Remind you of all that I have said" looks to the past and brings it into the present (e.g., 2:17, 21–22; 12:15–16). Spirit in this sense could be normed by or tested with the memory of those who heard it; let us call this a "conservative" function. But "teach you everything"seems to look from the present to the future: At some time in the future, the Spirit will teach new things, which might be different from the words of Jesus or the evaluation of his actions (e.g., 1 John 4:2–3; 1 Cor 12:3). Such future words cannot be tested or normed, although later we hear of cries for "discernment of the spirits" (1 John 4:1; 1 Cor 12:10).[402] Let us call this a "progressive" function.

A CLOSER LOOK – TYPES OF SPIRITS IN JOHN

Raymond Firth proposed an anthropological model for interpreting spirit possession,[403] which was expanded by Mary Douglas.[404] The central insight indicates that attitudes toward spirit run along a spectrum from welcome to dangerous. Hence there will tend to be little or no control of the spirit when welcomed, but strong control will be exercised if the spirit is considered dangerous or ambiguous, as the following scheme indicates:

CONTROL			CONTROL
weak			**strong**
positive	spirit	shamanism	spirit
possession	mediumship		possession
welcome	useful	domesticated	dangerous
ATTITUDE			ATTITUDE

This can be expanded by considering how spirit functions in the two extreme positions: weak control and welcome; and strong control because it is dangerous.

---

402 Raymond E. Brown, *The Epistles of John* (Garden City, NY: Doubleday, 1982), 485–89.
403 Raymond Firth, *Essays on Social Organization and Values* (London: Athlone Press, 1964), 247–56.
404 Mary T. Douglas, *Natural Symbols* (New York: Pantheon, 1982), 65–81.

Spirit: Weak Control, Welcome	Spirit: Strong Control, Dangerous
1. *Definition of spirit* by: *nature*: approved, welcome *time orientation*: in service of the future *normed*: emphatically unnormed *freedom*: freedom from former systems, new individualized choices *persons*: available to all individuals	1. *Description of spirit* by: *nature*: dangerous *time orientation*: in service of past *normed*: restrained, institutionalized *freedom*: spirit frees individuals to promote common good *persons*: limited to group of experts
2. *Spirit in matter*: against matter, superior to it, completely unnormed; is found in unmediated experience of God prophecy, which is fulfilled in future revolt against tradition and social structures	2. *Spirit in matter*: must be in or with matter; found in rituals and ceremonies, fixed sacred space in service of ascribed, traditional leadership in service of interpreting history and tradition and normed by them
3. *Social strategy*: Because of strong individualism and its challenge to former structures, spirit is positively valued, sought after, and manipulated.	3. *Social strategy*: Because of the strength of the system, an uncontrolled spirit is not allowed but is either controlled or limited to a group of experts.
4. *Function*: Spirit against matter supports the liberties of individuals and points to a program for freeing them from social constraints.	4. *Function*: Spirit in matter implies that individuals are by nature subordinate to society and find their freedom in its forms

When signs manifested benefaction and power and when rituals such as baptism, Eucharist, and declaring sins forgiven (20:22–23) were valued in the community, spirit was comfortably in matter, normed by Jesus traditions, and associated with but a few figures, such as John the Baptizer and Jesus. The community looked to the past, to what Jesus said and did, as directives for present discipleship. In short, it "remembered" a lot. But there is evidence of a change in perspective such that no value is given to this world and material things (6:63; 8:23). A gnostic elitism develops that elevates those with spirit over traditional leaders, such as Peter; these elites are supremely "in the know." But their knowledge is not so much "remembering" the past but knowing double meanings and secrets and revelations, and even knowing the future. In this context, "the Spirit will teach you all things" (14:26). Examples of such a spirit may be found in 1 John 4:2–3 and 5:6–8.[405]

---

[405] On this typology of "spirit" and the Fourth Gospel, see J. H. Neyrey, *Ideology of Revolt* (1988), 151–206.

Advocate As Broker. Throughout this study, we have considered Jesus as God's broker to God's earthly clients. Tricia Brown's thesis argues that we also consider the Advocate/Paraclete as a broker. But whose? He is Jesus' sub-broker because Jesus himself "prays the Father" to send the Advocate (14:16) and because the Advocate is "sent in my name" (14:26). Moreover, the Advocate basically reminds the disciples of Jesus' words and so can be said to keep Jesus' own brokerage operative.

Peace. In classical Greek, "peace" refers to the cessation of hostilities, but in Israelite writings it means much more because it translates as "shalom," which means plentitude of blessings or completeness of benefaction. The exhortation "let not your hearts be troubled" both begins this part of the Farewell Address (14:1) and concludes it (14:27). But in the conclusion it is joined with Jesus' benefaction of "peace." The context of these sayings, then, influences how we should read them. Faced with the emptiness of Jesus' departure (14:28–29), the disciples are given fullness; that is, shalom, or peace. And faced with "trouble," Jesus bequeaths them security and peace. Similarly, Jesus calms the terror of his disciples in the upper room when he announces, "Peace be with you" (John 20:19, 21). Inasmuch as the meaning of "peace" comes from its context, here it would be the successful endurance of crises and trials.

Ruler of This World. We are told three more or less parallel remarks about this "ruler of the world":

> "Now is the judgment of this world. . . . The ruler of this world will be cast out." (12:31)
> "The ruler of the world is coming. He has no power over me." (14:30)
> " . . . judgment: for the ruler of this world is judged" (16:11)

Most agree that this "ruler" is the devil, who functioned as the father/patron of the pseudo-disciples whose testimony Jesus examined. They are sons of the devil because like him they lie and murder (8:44).[406] If we stress "ruler *of this world*," the emphasis falls on the world of hostility in which Jesus the alien resides and yearns to leave. He is not of this world, but his enemies are; he is from above, but they are from below (8:24). "Judgment" seems to refer to a trial of the devil and all his sons who judge Jesus unjustly and seek his death. When they are judged, Jesus will be vindicated and glorified even as the devil and his clients are shamed and brought low. The devil is dethroned, but Jesus is enthroned.

---

[406] Ronald A. Piper's "Satan, Demons and the Absence of Exorcisms in the Fourth Gospel," in Richard G. Catchpole and David R. Horrell, eds., *Christology, Controversy, and Community* (Leiden: Brill, 2000), 225, cites all the data on the devil and devils in John. More importantly, he argues at 264–65 that "the language of demon possession is not . . . related to matters of magical healing, but to rivalry. It is reserved for demonizing one's opponents."

JOHN 15:1–8 – ABIDING IN THE VINE

1 "I am the true vine, and my Father is the vinegrower.
2 He removes every branch in me that bears no fruit. Every branch that bears fruit he prunes to make it bear more fruit.
3 You have already been cleansed by the word that I have spoken to you.
4 Abide in me as I abide in you. Just as the branch cannot bear fruit by itself unless it abides in the vine, neither can you unless you abide in me.
5 I am the vine, you are the branches. Those who abide in me and I in them bear much fruit, because apart from me you can do nothing.
6 Whoever does not abide in me is thrown away like a branch and withers; such branches are gathered, thrown into the fire, and burned.
7 If you abide in me, and my words abide in you, ask for whatever you wish, and it will be done for you.
8 My Father is glorified by this, that you bear much fruit and become my disciples.

Farewell Address. Several of the typical elements of a farewell address appear here.

Predictions of Hard Times. The chief elements here of a typical farewell address are both predictions of hard times and exhortations to group-specific virtues. Hard times include the "cleansing" of the branches by the vine dresser (15:2), whose distress is transcended by the metaphor of "pruning," which leads to richer growth. Similarly, the predictions of "hatred" from the world are likewise tempered by the note that Jesus himself has been subject to the same (15:18–25).

Exhortations. Here they focus on two virtues: "remaining" during crisis (15:1–8) and "love," understood as loyalty to the group, especially during this difficult time (15:9–17).

Legacy? The following items seem to be Jesus' departing legacy: "joy" (15:11), "much fruit" (15:4–5, 8, 16), and "asking for anything" (15:7, 16).

Successor. The Advocate seems to be Jesus' replacement and so his successor (15:26).

Vine, Branches, and Vine Dresser.[407] The author provides in 15:1–2 a characteristic topic statement of six elements, which he will subsequently develop in detail. They are not discussed sequentially, but each is explained at length: I am the *true vine*; *My Father* is the vine grower; He *removes* every branch; *In me*; Every branch that *bears fruit*; He *purifies* to make it bear more fruit.

---

[407] On the structure and composition of John 15, see Fernando F. Segovia, "The Theology and Provenance of John 15:1–17," *JBL* 101 (1982), 118–28.

The True Vine. This vine stands in contrast to other vines, for it is "true"; that is, genuine and enduring.[408] It is "true" also in the sense that it alone is the unique source of fruitfulness: "Those who abide in me and I in them bear much fruit, because apart from me you can do nothing" (15:5). It makes horticultural sense to state that branches are "in" the vine and the vine "in" the branches, but Jesus' remark is not spatial but relational. Even if the future of disciples includes being expelled from some places (16:1–2), their benefaction lies in being securely in another "place," namely the vine. And the vine is a secure and reliable broker of the ministrations of the vine dresser.

My Father. Although Jesus' Father first appears as a vine dresser, doing what vine dressers do, he later appears twice in 15:7–8 in a different role. First, Jesus describes a situation of petitionary prayer, in which disciples make a request through Jesus to the "Father." The success of this prayer is assured, for "it will be done for you" surely by the Father, who answers prayers. Second, Jesus' Father is honored by the loyalty and faithfulness of the branches and their willingness to accept the Father's will. Hence, all of the seemingly shameful, dishonorable things the disciples will endure are truly honorable in God's eyes and likewise honor the Father as only obedient sons can. "My Father is glorified by this, that you bear much fruit and become my disciples."

Removes/Throws Away. Jesus pronounces severe sanctions for failing to be a branch of this vine: Those who do not abide in Jesus are "thrown away like a branch and wither.... They are gathered, thrown into the fire, and burned" (15:6). Obviously the branches who are "thrown away" stand in contrast with those who are "pruned." The first suffer great and permanent loss, whereas the second endure purification so as to be fruitful. The sanction described here resembles the fate of weeds and chaff, which are separated from the wheat and burned (Matt 3:12; 13:30).

In Me. "Abide in me as I abide in you" (15:4). "Abide" refers not to geograph- ical space but to social relationships and group adhesion. Jesus already spoke about this when he described how he is "in my Father, and you in me and I in you" (14:20); and Jesus and the Father will "come to him and make our home with him" (14:23). "Abiding, . . . in Jesus," then, is an absolute qualification for "bearing fruit": "Apart from me you can do nothing" (15:5).

Bear Fruit. No branch can bear fruit apart from the vine (15:4). Bearing fruit can refer to one's deeds (Matt 7:16) or the success of one's labors (John 4:36). But we have an immediate echo in the metaphor of grains of wheat, which die,

---

[408] On the significance of "vine" in Israelite literature, see R. E. Brown, *Gospel According to John* (1970), 2.669–72.

fall into the ground, and "bear fruit" (12:25; see also 1 Cor 15:37–38), suggesting that death produces life. Thus, we are inclined to consider it as the good result of being "pruned" or "laying down one's life." Either new members will be added when disciples endure hostility or the life that the group enjoys will be exponentially increased.

He Purifies. "You have already been 'purified' by the word that I have spoken to you" (15:3). The verb "purify" in 15:2–3 is the same word Jesus used to describe his footwashing in 13:7–9, which would make Peter "wholly pure." One is tempted to link the preparation for martyrdom symbolized by footwashing with the pruning of the branches. God brings life from crisis and death, just as gold is purified in fire.

From this analogy, genuine disciples learn the following. There is only one place to be; that is, attached in loyalty to Jesus ("abide"; 15:4–10). There are two types of branches: unfaithful, disloyal branches, which bear no fruit, and loyal branches, which abide and bear much fruit. The two types of branches have two contrasting fates: true branches, because of trials and suffering, bear much fruit, but false branches bear no fruit and are taken away, gathered, and burned. The disciples also learn that success is assured and that the elite members of the Jesus group are the true branches; their future, although fearful, will produce great rewards. They are the tested and "proven" disciples (15:8).

JOHN 15:9–17 – LOVE AND FRIENDS

9 As the Father has loved me, so I have loved you; abide in my love.

10 If you keep my commandments, you will abide in my love, just as I have kept my Father's commandments and abide in his love.

11 I have said these things to you so that my joy may be in you, and that your joy may be complete.

12 "This is my commandment, that you love one another as I have loved you.

13 No one has greater love than this, to lay down one's life for one's friends.

14 You are my friends if you do what I command you.

15 I do not call you servants any longer, because the servant does not know what the master is doing; but I have called you friends, because I have made known to you everything that I have heard from my Father.

16 You did not choose me but I chose you. And I appointed you to go and bear fruit, fruit that will last, so that the Father will give you whatever you ask him in my name.

17 I am giving you these commands so that you may love one another.

A CLOSER LOOK – DELIBERATIVE RHETORIC: "ABIDE" (15:1–8) AND "LOVE" (15:9–17)

Classical rhetoric distinguished three species of rhetoric: judicial, deliberative, and epideictic: Judicial rhetoric is either accusative or defensive, looking to the past (what was done) and evaluating what is just or unjust; deliberative rhetoric is either exhortation or dissuasion, looking to the future (what should be done) and arguing that something is either advantageous or harmful; and epideictic rhetoric is either praise or blame and looks to the present (what is current) and tries to show what is honorable or shameful (Aristotle, *Rhet.* 1.3).

One may profitably examine the trials of Jesus and the man born blind in terms of judicial rhetoric (Chapters 5, 7–8, 9, 10, 18–19). Epideictic rhetoric occurs in the debates over the nobility of Jesus' origins and his parents, typical topics of this sort of rhetoric. Also, according to the logic of the Gospel, shame in some eyes is honor in others; hence Jesus' Passion may be considered a study in ironic honor.[409]

Deliberative rhetoric is rare in the Fourth Gospel because Jesus reveals wisdom and secrets but rarely exhorts.[410] But in 15:1–8 and 15:9–17 we find two exhortations, to "abide" and to "love." Although one may classify them according to the elements of a farewell address, namely exhortations to group-oriented virtue, they are also worth considering in terms of deliberative rhetoric. Argument in deliberative rhetoric is generally based on "advantage" and so makes appeals for future action on the basis of future benefits. An action benefits and so should be adopted; another harms and should be avoided. As regards John 15, "remaining" brings great advantage, just as "not remaining" leads to severe sanctions. A branch that remains and is cleansed by the vine dresser "bears much fruit" (v. 2), a verse that is repeated three times (vv. 4, 5, 8) to underscore the advantage that comes from "remaining." Similarly, branches that "remain" may petition God for "whatever you will" and expect God's positive response (v. 7) – advantage indeed! In contrast, we are told of the sanctions imposed on those who do "not remain." They are taken away (v. 1), and worse, "cast forth . . . wither . . . thrown into the fire and burned" (v. 6). What must be decided, then, is whether to be associated with Jesus in loyalty and faithfulness.

Balancing this exhortation, another begins with a command, "remain in my love" (15:9), and concludes with "love one another" (15:17). Although

---

[409] See J. H. Neyrey, "Despising the Shame," *Semeia* 68 (1994), 113–38.
[410] Scholarship on the ancient homily has ignored John 15. For a recent investigation of "homily" or "sermon," see Lawrence Wills, "The Form of the Sermon in Hellenistic Judaism and Early Christianity," *HTR* 77 (1984), 277–99; and C. Clifton Black, "The Rhetorical Form of the Hellenistic Jewish and Early Christian Sermon: A Response to Lawrence Wills," *HTR* 81 (1988), 1–18.

the exhortation is focused on "love," verses 9–17 are linked with verses 1–8 by four more references to "remain" (vv. 9–10, 16). Thus 15:1–8 and 15:9–17 should be seen as parallel and linked exhortations. Arguing from advantage, the author first tells the disciples that "remaining" and "loving" elevate their status from that of "servants" to "friends." The benefit of "remaining" and "loving," then, effects a status elevation of the disciple. Jesus' final argument exhorts the disciples to honor their debt of justice to him: "You did not choose me, but I chose you and appointed you that you should go and bear fruit and that your fruit should remain" (15:16).

Literary Analysis. Once again, Jesus speaks a topic statement consisting of three elements, each developed in detail in the discourse that follows.

1. As the Father has *loved* me, so I have *loved* you;
2. *abide* in my love.
3. If you keep *my commandments*, you will abide in my love, just as I have kept my Father's *commandments* and abide in his love (15:9).

Love/Greater Love. One senses a certain elitism in the statement that there is no "greater love" than to lay down one's life for one's friends (15:13).[411] Frequently in this Gospel, persons, things, and behaviors are compared to determine who or what is "greater." As regards things, "greater works" remain to be done, either by Jesus (5:20) or by the disciples (14:12). As regards persons, Jesus has always been superior to the disciples (see 15:13). As regards behavior, "laying down one's life for one's friends" expresses the greatest love.[412]

A CLOSER LOOK – COMPARISONS: "GREATER THAN" AND "TRUE"

Students in the second level of education in antiquity learned to compose various traditional forms that would be serviceable in writing public speeches when they matured into men with public voice. Among these exercises are comparison (σύγκρισις), encomium, chreia, and proposing a law. Comparisons basically function to honor one thing above another. What is compared? Aelius Theon writes:

There are comparisons of characters and subjects: of characters: for example, Ajax, Odysseus; of subjects: for example, wisdom and courage. . . . First, let it be established that comparisons are made not with matters that differ greatly from one another (for the person who does not know whether Achilles or Thersites was more courageous is ridiculous), but with matters that are similar and concerning which we disagree about which of the two we must prefer because we see no superiority of one over the

---

[411] See S. van Tilborg, *Imaginative Love* (1997), 149–54.

[412] This love first characterized the Noble Shepherd (10:11, 15) but is rashly claimed by Peter (13:37–38).

other. After these items, we will compare their actions by choosing those which are more noble and reasons for the numerous and greater blessings, those actions that are more reliable, those that are more enduring, those that were done at the proper time, those from which great harm results, when they have not been done, those that were done with a motive rather than those done because of compulsion or chance, those which few have done rather than those that many have done (for the common and hackneyed are not at all praiseworthy), those we have done with effort rather than easily, and those we have performed that were beyond our age and ability rather than those which we performed when it was possible.[413]

The Fourth Gospel compares both persons and things, using either the comparative adverb "greater" or the adjective "true." Jesus is "greater than": "greater than our father Jacob" (4:12) and "greater than our father Abraham" (8:53). Although "greater than" does not appear in 1:17 and 5:38, Jesus is surely compared with Moses. Alternatively, "the Father is greater than I" (14:28; see 10:29), and "servants" are never greater than their masters, nor students their teachers (13:16; 15:20). "Greater" objects and behaviors are compared: "greater than this" (1:51); "greater deeds he will do" (14:12); and "greater love no one has" (15:13). Comparisons using "true" include: "the true light" (1:8); "true worshipers" (4:23); "the true bread which comes down from heaven" (6:32); and "the true vine" (15:1). Comparisons also use replacement. When Jesus replaces various cultic objects and feasts, he is effectively claiming that his are "better," such as entrance rites (3:3–5); festival benefits (6:32; 7:37; 8:12); and feasts (6:1–14; 7:1–8:20).

What does this "love" look like?[414] From the beginning, we have been repeatedly told that people "loved darkness" rather than the light (3:19), or they have loved the praise of mortals more than the praise of God (12:42–43). If they were from God, they would love Jesus (8:42). "Love" functions in a series of binary opposites that reflect the social turmoil in which the community finds itself: love versus hate, light versus darkness, belief versus unbelief, praise of God versus praise of men, and community versus synagogue. Hence, "love" means allegiance to Jesus and loyalty to the group, and also being opposed by outsiders. We shall shortly see this expressed in the discourse on "hate," which balances this one on "love."[415]

---

413 J. Butts, *"Progymnasmata" of Theon* (1987), 495–505. Other texts include: Quintilian, *Inst. Orat.* 2.4.24–25; Aphthonius, in Patricia Matsen and P. Rollinson, eds., *Readings from Classical Rhetoric* (Carbondale: Southern Illinois University Press, 1990), 279–80; and David H. J. Lamour, "Making Parallels: *Synkrisis* and Plutarch's 'Themistocles and Camillus,'" *ANRW* 2.33.6 (1991), 4154–204.

414 Readers are referred to the commentary on "love" in 14:13–24. Wayne Meeks's essay on the absence of Johannine ethics, "The Ethics of the Fourth Gospel," in R. Alan Culpepper and C. Clifton Black, eds., *Exploring the Gospel of John* (Louisville, KY: Westminster John Knox, 1996) 317–26, cautions against attempting to build an ethics on the basis of "love."

415 See Jan G. Van der Watt, *Family of the King: Dynamics of Metaphor in the Gospel According to John* (Leiden: Brill, 2000), 304–23.

An important clue for understanding "love" is found in 15:9–10 about the way it is intertwined with "abide": "Abide in my love" (15:9); "You will abide in my love" (15:10); and "I abide in his love" (15:10b). Thus "abide" means steadfastness in crisis and loyalty in peril. But this is also what "love" means, especially when it is explained as "lay down one's life for one's friends." If "love" means "abide," then "hate" suggests hostility and apostasy.

Abide. We know that "abide" implies not spatial but personal relationships. For example, "abide" describes how God and Jesus relate ("the Father abides in me," 14:10b) and how disciples must abide in Jesus (15:4–7, 9–10). In fact, "abide" is used ten times in the vine branch discourse to express the ideal relationship of Jesus with his disciples. On the one hand, the disciple must "dwell" in, remain in, or sustain loyalty to Jesus: "The branch cannot bear fruit unless it *abides* in the vine" (15:4). But if a branch "abides" in the vine, the vine curiously will "abide" in the branch: "Abide in me and I in you" (15:4, 5b). Thus we equate "abide" with faithfulness and loyalty. It expresses the same kind of group adhesion that love does. Finally, because this Gospel talks about people failing to act because of fear of expulsion from the synagogue (9:22; 12:42; see also 16:1–2), "abide" may be the exhortation juxtaposed with "fall away."

My Commandment. Jesus commands in 15:12 that the disciples love one another, which seems to be repeated in 15:14, where the disciples are then called "loved ones" if they do what Jesus commands. It might strike the reader as odd that the "command" is "love." How does one command love? Although we will examine "love" shortly, let us now consider what "commandment" means in the Farewell Address.

Jesus' "commandments" are unrelated to the Ten Commandments and even exhortations such as the Sermon on the Mount. Jesus earlier identified "commands" given him by God: "to lay down his life and take it again" (10:18) and "what to say and what to speak" (12:49–50). Now he issues commands. It is truly surprising how numerous are the references to "command" in this farewell address, either the use of the imperative mood or actual mandate to do this or that:

13:4–15	Command: footwashing
13:27	(to Judas) "Whatever you are going to do, do quickly."
13:34	A new command: love one another
14:1a	"Let not your hearts be troubled."
14:1b	"Believe in God and keep on believing in me."
14:11	"Believe me: that I am in the Father and the Father is in me."
14:15	"If you love me, you will keep my commandments."
14:21	"He who has my commandments and keeps them is the one who loves me."
14:27	"Do not let your heart be troubled, nor let it be afraid."
14:31	"Arise, let us go hence"!
15:4	"Abide in me"!

15:9	"Abide in my love"!
15:12	"This is my commandment: that you love one another as I have loved you."
15:14	"You are my friends, if you do what I command."
15:17	"This is my command: love one another."

In this list, we find three commands: believe, love, and abide. The relationship of "abide" and "love" implies that these two commands greatly overlap. These three commands differ greatly from the material care of others, as is found in 1 John 3:16–17, for "believe," "love," and "abide" look to group cohesion, not welfare.

Friends Equals Clients. The labeling of the disciples in 15:14 as "friends" is explained by subsequent affirmation that they are no longer "servants." Servants are "not in the know" about the master's business, but Jesus has told these "friends" "all that I have heard from my Father" and so they are no longer "servants" but "friends" (15:15). Should we immediately equate "love" and "friend"? No, for God indeed has "friends," such as "Abraham, my friend" (Isa 41:8), Moses, with whom God spoke face to face "as a man speaks to a friend" (Exod 33:11), and holy and wise men.[416] Rather, let us consider "friend" in terms of the patron–client model of relationships.[417] First of all, the author clearly knows that "friend" equals "client" when he describes the crowd threatening Pilate with loss of imperial patronage: "If you release this man, you are no *friend* of the emperor" (19:12). Pilate's role as procurator rests entirely on the favor of his patron (i.e., Caesar). Thus "friend" here means "client."[418] Second, Jesus elevates the status of the disciples from "servant" to "friend"; that is, they share the most precious benefaction of Jesus' patron, in this case "*everything that I have heard from my Father*" (15:15). With his departure, he acknowledges them as his preferred clients. Ideally, this kind of discourse will confirm them in their relationship to him and thus to God. "Abiding" in him will ensure their privileged status as "friends" and clients.

Patron–Broker–Clients. God's relationship with Jesus is, of course, that of patron and broker. The Father-Patron "loves Jesus" (15:9), and Jesus responds appropriately by keeping his Father's commands and so abiding in the Patron's love (15:10). Jesus relates to the disciples as broker to clients. He mediates to them many benefactions: commandments (15:10, 12), love or faithfulness (15:9), joy (15:11), election or choice (15:16), secret knowledge (15:15), and ability to bear

---

416 C. H. Talbert, *Reading John* (1992), 214; and van der Watt, *Family of the King* (2000), 358–66.

417 On "friendship," see C. S. Keener, *Gospel of John Commentary* (2003), 1004–16.

418 See S. van Tilborg, *Imaginative Love* (1993), 149; Alan C. Mitchell, "'Greet the Friends by Name': New Testament Evidence for the Greco-Roman *topos* on Friendship," in John T. Fitzgerald, ed., *Greco-Roman Perspectives on Friendship* (Atlanta: Scholars Press, 1997), 257–58. In Luke 7:6, 34; 14:10–12; and 16:9, "friend" means "client."

fruit (15:16b). Moreover, Jesus raises their status from "slaves" to "friends," a euphemism for "clients" in the ancient world (15:13–15). What do clients, even "friends," owe their brokers and patrons? Primarily loyalty, which is how we read "abide" and "love" in this part of the Farewell Address.

JOHN 15:18–27 – ENEMIES AND HATE

18 "If the world hates you, be aware that it hated me before it hated you.

19 If you belonged to the world, the world would love you as its own. Because you do not belong to the world, but I have chosen you out of the world – therefore the world hates you.

20 Remember the word that I said to you. 'Servants are not greater than their master.' If they persecuted me, they will persecute you; if they kept my word, they will keep yours also.

21 But they will do all these things to you on account of my name, because they do not know him who sent me.

22 If I had not come and spoken to them, they would not have sin; but now they have no excuse for their sin.

23 Whoever hates me hates my Father also.

24 If I had not done among them the works that no one else did, they would not have sin. But now they have seen and hated both me and my Father.

25 It was to fulfill the word that is written in their law, "They hated me without a cause."

26 "When the Advocate comes, whom I will send to you from the Father, the Spirit of truth who comes from the Father, he will testify on my behalf.

27 You also are to testify because you have been with me from the beginning.

Hate. "Hate" for the author is the opposite of "love."[419] All references to "hate" in 15:18–25 are predictions of future trials for the disciples, a common element of farewell addresses. R. E. Brown, moreover, highlights this aspect by attending to the parallels between John 15:18–16:4 and the missionary discourse in Matthew 10:17–25 and the predictions of future trials in Matthew 24:9–10.[420] "Hate," then, suggests an attack on group adherence and loyalty. Third, we should contextualize "hate" in terms of the ancient system of honor and shame.[421] In this Gospel, refusing to honor Jesus means rejection of him and hence hating

---

[419] See F. F. Segovia, "Love and Hatred of Jesus and Johannine Sectarianism," *CBQ* 43 (1981), 258–72.

[420] R. E. Brown. *Gospel According to John* (1970), 2.692–95.

[421] Frederick Danker warns: "The English term 'hate' generally suggests affective connotations that do not always do justice to some Semitic shame-honor oriented uses of the

him. For example, when Jesus says that no prophet is without honor except in his home place (4:44), he speaks of his rejection and death. Later, he states, "I honor my Father, and you dishonor me" (8:49); the dishonor in John 7 consisting in trying to arrest and kill Jesus. If "love" means "abide," then "hate" suggests expulsion, disvaluing, and persecuting.

Servants. Three times in the Farewell Address, the disciples are referred to as "servants," twice reminding the disciples that their status is inferior to that of Jesus and once transforming them to a higher status but not equal to that of Jesus.

13:16	"I tell you, *servants are not greater than their master,* nor are messengers greater than the one who sent them."
15:15	"I do not call you *servants any longer* . . . but I have called you *friends,* because I have made known to you everything that I have heard from my Father."
15:20	"Remember that I said to you, '*Servants are not greater than their master.*' If they persecuted me, they will persecute you; if they kept my word, they will keep yours also."

In 15:15, Jesus tells the disciples that they are no longer servants because of a benefit received; that is, a status transformation from "servant" to "friend." But in 13:16 and 15:20 they are still servants in the sense that they are not greater than their master but must imitate him in some way. In fact, their sharing in the master's fate confirms them as servants. Even though their status is changed from "servant" to "friend," these disciples are still identified as Jesus' clients.

World. At one time, the "world" (i.e., the people in the world) was highly favored by God and Jesus. God so loved this world that He sent Jesus to be its savior (3:16–17; 10:36), not its judge (12:47). And Jesus, "the one coming into the world" (1:9; 6:14; 11:27), came as broker to it of God's benefaction. As regards the peoples of this world, he was their savior (4:42), life (6:33), and light (8:12; 9:5); he spoke God's words to them (8:26). But at some point the world became the enemy of Jesus, for it rejected him (1:10), hating both him (7:7; 15:18–19) and his disciples (15:18–20). "World," moreover, functions as a social marker, in opposition to which Jesus and his disciples are the elite few.[422] For example, Jesus does not belong to this world (8:23) but to God's realm, and he cannot leave "the world" quickly enough (13:1). The hostility between Jesus and the world ripens with remarks about judging it (9:39; 12:31), convicting it of sin (16:8), and battling with its ruler (14:30; 16:11). Alas, the disciples cannot escape this hostile

---

word (e.g., Deut 21:15, 16) in the sense of 'hold in disfavor, be disinclined to, have relatively little regard for' " (*BDAG*, 3rd ed., 652).

[422] B. J. Malina and R. L. Rohrbaugh, in their *Commentary on John* (1998), 245–46, interpret "world" in this way: "[It] refers to three entities: the physical world, Israel as God's chosen humanity, and Judeans as enemies of John's community. What 'world' never refers to in John is all human beings, the whole human race."

world but must face its hatred (17:11, 15). "World," then, is less a geographical term than a social one. When one thinks of "world" at this point of the group's history, one thinks of rejection, hostility, and murder.

Jesus' Riposte. Throughout the Gospel, Jesus has repeatedly made claims about his role and status, which are invariably challenged. On occasion, he gives a riposte to these challenges, of which 15:18–25 seems to be an example. The context is "hate," clearly hostility and dishonor. Although we considered these remarks earlier as predictions of future crises, Jesus nevertheless speaks in such a way as to provide an apology for them. First, we note that the evil of the world is long-standing and handed on from generation to generation: The world hated Jesus and then his disciples (15:18) and persecuted Jesus and then his disciples (15:20). Twice Jesus mounts a forensic argument about his enemies: If Jesus had not come, they would have no sin (15:22), and if he did not work his works in their midst, they would have no sin (15:24). But Jesus did come and did his works, which they reject. They hate not just Jesus but his Father as well (15:23). Worst of all, they hated without cause (15:25); that is, without provocation. They are radically evil people. Why talk this way? In addition to being predictions of future crises, these remarks serve to confirm the disciples in loyalty to Jesus; that is, he "loves" them and they should remain faithful to him and to the other disciples. If a man is known by his enemies, the status of the disciples is very high because they are the elite few who stand apart from the crowd and are hated by the world.

The Advocate's New Role. In the face of such evil, Jesus speaks further about the Advocate. The disciples need someone to aid them in responding to "hate" and "persecution." The Advocate's function in 15:26, however, differs from that in 14:26, where he brought to remembrance all that Jesus said. Here he "witnesses" on Jesus' behalf, which some have thought suggested a forensic or conflict situation (see Matt 10:19–20). Hence, the Advocate will function as the riposte to the challenges raining down on Jesus and the disciples.[423]

JOHN 16:1–15 – STILL ANOTHER ROLE FOR THE ADVOCATE

1 "I have said these things to you to keep you from stumbling.
2 They will put you out of the synagogues. Indeed, an hour is coming when those who kill you will think that by doing so they are offering worship to God.
3 And they will do this because they have not known the Father or me.

---

[423] The Spirit will also function as the sub-broker of Jesus, who secures for the group access to Jesus and benefaction from him; see T. G. Brown, *Spirit in John* (2003), 170–234.

4 But I have said these things to you so that when their hour comes you may remember that I told you about them. "I did not say these things to you from the beginning, because I was with you.

5 But now I am going to him who sent me; yet none of you asks me, 'Where are you going?'

6 But because I have said these things to you, sorrow has filled your hearts.

7 Nevertheless I tell you the truth: it is to your advantage that I go away, for if I do not go away, the Advocate will not come to you; but if I go, I will send him to you.

8 And when he comes, he will prove the world wrong about sin and righteousness and judgment:

9 about sin, because they do not believe in me;

10 about righteousness, because I am going to the Father and you will see me no longer;

11 about judgment, because the ruler of this world has been condemned.

12 "I still have many things to say to you, but you cannot bear them now.

13 When the Spirit of truth comes, he will guide you into all the truth; for he will not speak on his own, but will speak whatever he hears, and he will declare to you the things that are to come.

14 He will glorify me, because he will take what is mine and declare it to you.

15 All that the Father has is mine. For this reason I said that he will take what is mine and declare it to you.

Farewell Address. We find once more many elements of a farewell address in John 16: predictions of death or departure ("I am going to him . . . ," 16:5, 7; "a little while and you will not see me," 16:16); predictions of future bad times (16:31–32) and good times (16:33b) or both in tandem ("you will weep and lament . . . but your sorrow will turn to joy," 16:20–22); legacy of revelations and knowledge ("a little while and you will not see me and a little while you will see me again," 16:16–19; "I have said these things to you in figures of speech. The hour is coming when I will no longer speak to you in figures," 16:25–30); and a successor, the Advocate, who will continue Jesus' forensic engagement with the world (16:7–11) and broker Jesus' words to the disciples (16:12–15).

Gross Anatomy. Scholarly judgment on John 16 attaches 16:1–4 to the material on hate in 15:18–27.[424] But, we note two rhetorical qualifications to that. First, there appears to be an inclusion between 16:1–4 and 16:32–33, suggesting that 16:1–33 is a conscious unit, bracketed by repeated materials.

   A. *I have said these things to you* to *keep you from stumbling* (16:1).
   B. They will *put you out of the synagogues.* Indeed, an hour is coming when those who will kill you think that by doing so they are offering worship to God (16:2).

---

[424] R. E. Brown, *Gospel According to John* (1970), 2.692–95; Francis J. Moloney, *Glory Not Dishonor* (Minneapolis, MN: Fortress Press, 1998), 55–56, 70–73.

C. I have said these things to you so that *when their hour comes* you may remember that I told you about them (16:4).

C′. *The hour is coming*, indeed it has come (16:32).

B′. *You will be scattered*, each one to his home, and you will leave me alone (16:32b).

A′. *I have said this to you*, so that in me *you may have peace* (16:33).

Thus John 16 begins and ends with Jesus making predictions of future hard times, with the express purpose of keeping the disciples from panic and flight, which will occur (16:1, 4, and 33). Although the predictions are not identical, both describe expulsion (from the synagogue) or scattering (of the group). The future of the disciples is identified just as Jesus identified his own future crisis: "The hour is coming." The chiastic figure, moreover, calls attention to important material and highlights it.

A second noteworthy item is the density of predictions made here.

1–4	"They will put you out of the synagogues . . . those who kill you . . ."
5–6	"I go away . . . and sorrow fills your hearts."
7–11	"If I go, I will send him [Advocate] to you."
12–15	"The Spirit of Truth will guide you into all truth."
16	"A little while, you will see me no more and . . . you will see me again."
20–21	"You will weep and lament. . . . Your sorrow will be turned into joy."
22	"I will see you again and your hearts will rejoice."
25	"The hour is coming when I will no longer speak in figures, but tell you plainly of the Father."
32	"The hour is coming when you will be scattered. . . . You will leave me alone."

This material contains predictions about Jesus' future (going away, sending the Advocate, not speaking in figures), but especially about the future crises of the disciples (expulsion from the synagogue, sorrow, weeping and lamenting, being scattered). These predictions provide the realistic background for the exhortation about "abide," "love," and "hate." This material, then, constitutes the Passion predictions of the disciples. But more needs to be said about these prophecies. The author speaks a quartet of prophecies of future crises, which are given in advance to strengthen the courage and faithfulness of the disciples.

> I tell you this now, before it occurs,
> so that when it does occur,
> you may believe that I am he (13:19).

> And now I have told you this before it occurs,
> so that when it does occur,
> you may believe (14:29).

I have said these things to you
so that my joy may be in you,
and that your joy may be complete (15:11).

I have said these things to you
so that when their hour comes
you may remember that I told you about them (16:4).

Four times, then, Jesus not only predicts future hard times but explains why
the disciples need his revelations of them. The issue is not one of information
but exhortation ("joy," loyalty, and "remaining"), which Jesus explains as such:
"That you may *believe* . . . that you may *believe* . . . that you may *remember.*" Jesus
is no mere prophet but someone who, knowing and controlling events, cares
about the fate of his disciples.

Expulsion from the Synagogue.[425] Three issues need be considered in interpreting the prediction in 16:1–2: What is referred to? When might it have
occurred? What is the social impact of such an action? We have already been told
that people inclined to join Jesus were threatened with social sanctions (9:22;
12:42). In Matthew 5:1–12 and /Luke 6:22–24, some disciples truly experienced
sanctions from their families. Others experienced spontaneous mob actions
against them, such as Stephen (Acts 7:54–60) and Paul (Acts 13:50; 21:27–31). J.
Louis Martyn has argued that John 9:22; 12:42; and 16:1–2 reflect the disciplinary
practice in the synagogue known at a later time as the "curse on the heretics."[426]
His precise linking of curse and excommunication has been hotly contested.
Expulsion might have occurred at any time, as it seems to be a common practice
at Qumran (1QS 6.24–7.25) and in Corinth (1 Cor 5) and was the fate of Paul
throughout Acts. We consider expulsion as a social sanction intended to prevent
certain social behavior or to penalize it when it occurs. In group-oriented societies such as those existing in the ancient world,[427] people are acutely aware of
how others perceive them, either in terms of praise (for conformity to customs)
or blame (for nonconformity). One's "conscience" meant knowledge from the
group and held within the group (*con* = with, *scientia* = knowledge). To reject
this knowledge and to stand apart from group expectations was to risk censure,
shame, and rejection. Expulsion from the synagogue would affect not just an
individual but his family, parents, and other kin, all of whom would be tainted
with this shame. They, in turn, would put pressure on the individual to conform.
Hence, if the matter came to expulsion, we envision a severe social crisis in which
an individual would suffer an immediate and profound loss of standing in the

---

[425] See G. Forkman, *Limits of Religious Community* (1972).
[426] J. L. Martyn, *History and Theology* (1979), 37–63.
[427] B. J. Malina, *New Testament World* (2001), 58–80; B. J. Malina and J. H. Neyrey, *Portraits of Paul* (1996), 154–76.

eyes of family, kin, and neighbors. Given the importance of kinship, expulsion from the synagogue must have served as a very effective sanction. Christians also employed this form of coercion (2 Thess 3:14; Titus 3:10–11).

Killing a Sacrifice? Before we can assess the remark in 16:1–2, we need to be clear about the meaning of a sacrifice. Sacrifice may be defined as "a ritual in which a deity/deities is/are offered some form of inducement (i.e., goods, such as animals, wine, grain), rendered humanly irretrievable, with a view to some life-effect for the offerer(s)."[428] Its purpose may be either life maintenance, which celebrates life in festivity, or life restoration, which revitalizes after accidental deviance. In Israel, sacrifice could be offered in the kinship group or in the political shrine, namely the Temple. Life-maintenance sacrifices were consumed, whereas life-restoration ones were completely burned up. But how could anyone think that killing would be sacrifice?

Paul's thinking in 1 Corinthians 5 offers a valuable clue here. He labeled the sexual union of one member a "corruption," equating it with leaven. Something labeled as a contagious corruption provokes intolerance: It must be expelled or all will be ruined. Similarly, the label "gangrene," which is attached to the teaching of Hymenaeus and Philetus (2 Tim 2:17), provokes radical hostility. Because it is life-threatening, "gangrene" must be cut. Hence, the synagogue labeled Jesus a "deceiver" who led others astray (7:12, 47). If the Judeans do nothing, only disaster will follow: "If we let him go on like this, everyone will believe in him" (11:48). The appropriate strategy is to destroy him and so rid Israel of this corruption. "Killing," then, suggests an attempt to drive out the pollution from Israel; it would then be a life-restoring act, a sacrifice of purification. Purification, then, seems the most likely aim of sacrifice.

Advocate Again. The Spirit functions in this Gospel as "another Advocate" for the group, a broker who replaces Jesus and secures the disciples' access to Jesus. Recent studies challenge the conventional opinion that the Advocate belongs in a forensic context, either as defender or witness.[429] Although "advocates" appear in a court, they more readily appear in other venues, such as palaces, temples, and forums. Even in a court, an advocate does not function in a forensic role but rather as a partisan supporter. In Philo, an "advocate" may give advice about a difficult decision or provide support for someone making a claim or settling a dispute.[430] But Advocate/Paraclete "did not mean an advocate in the sense of a lawyer. It meant rather a man who would appear in court to lend the weight of

---

[428] Bruce J. Malina, "Mediterranean Sacrifice: Dimensions of Domestic and Political Religion," *BTB* 26 (1996), 37.

[429] Raymond E. Brown, "The Paraclete in the Fourth Gospel," *NTS* 13 (1967), 113–26; and Kenneth Grayston, "The Meaning of PARAKLETOS," *JSNT* 13 (1981), 67–82.

[430] K. Grayston, "The Meaning of PARAKLETOS," *JSNT* 13 (1981), 71–72; T. G., Brown, *Spirit in John* (2003), 170–80.

his influence and prestige to the case of his friend, to convince the judges of his probity, and to seek a favourable verdict."[431]

Does the Advocate Prove or Convince?[432] In 16:8–11, this Advocate "will prove the world wrong about sin and righteousness and judgment." But does he "prove" or "convict" the world? Which meaning is preferred? To whom will the Advocate prove whatever he proves? And does the Advocate perform an internal or external action? The Greek word *elencho* is generally translated either as "to prove someone wrong" or "to convince someone of guilt."[433] Moreover, the action of the Advocate is not in some civic or cosmic forum; rather he testifies to the Johannine insiders within the group itself. The group that is hated, expelled from the synagogue, and even killed requires this support to know for sure that they are right and their enemies are wrong. Thus, as broker, the Advocate labors to support the group steadfastly in its trials and in its loyalty to Jesus.

"Sin, Righteousness, and Judgment." Let us closely examine what each of these three items is about.

Sin. As always, the premier sin is "they do not believe in me" (3:19; 8:21, 24; 9:41; 15:22). This means that some never had any belief and were always hostile; others were liars who faked belief to escape censure (8:30) but were exposed as "liars and murderers." The sole criterion for life or death in the Gospels has always been belief or nonbelief.

(False) Righteousness. When Jesus qualifies "righteousness" by saying that he is going to the Father, this expresses the right relationship to God: acting as God's agent, fulfilling God's command to speak God's word, and the command to lay down his life. As one who has always done his duty to God, he is welcome in God's presence. But many see their duty to God as putting Jesus to death and exterminating his disciples (16:1–2). Thus, their relationship with God is tragically wrong; their true duties are left unfulfilled, and they dishonor God with wrongdoing.

(False) Judgment. On the principle that "as you judge, so you are judged," the enemies of the group share the judgment of the ruler of this world. And those who judge unjustly will be judged by the same judgment (7:24; 8:15; 9:16, 24). Instead of judging Jesus justly as God's agent, they judged him according to appearances (7:24) and as having a demon (8:48; 10:20). But Jesus has already judged this ruler: "Now shall the ruler of this world be cast out" (12:31). Thus

---

[431] A. E. Harvey, *Jesus on Trial* (1976), 108–9.

[432] D. A. Carson, "The Function of the Paraclete in John 16:7–11," *JBL* 98 (1979), 547–66.

[433] R. E. Brown, *Gospel According to John* (1970), ; 2.705; and T. G. Brown, *Spirit in John* (2003), 221–28.

the Advocate will attest to the goodness of Jesus and support and confirm his conviction of the world.

Another Advocate/Jesus' Replacement. The following synopsis of the Johannine remarks about the Spirit may help us identify the source of the Spirit; his role and function; and his relationship to Jesus.

	14:16–17	14:26	15:26	16:12–14
Source	And I will ask the Father, and he will give you another Advocate.	The Advocate . . . whom the Father will send in my name . . .	When the Advocate, the Spirit of truth who comes from the Father,	When the Spirit of truth comes . . .
Role and function	Another Advocate: perpetuate Jesus' words to group	Advocate: He will teach you everything, and remind you of all I have said.	Advocate/Spirit of truth: He will testify on my behalf.	Spirit of truth: He will guide you into all the truth . . . declare to you the things that are to come.
Relationship to Jesus	I will ask the Father.	. . . send in my name . . . remind you of all that I have said to you	. . . whom I will send from the Father . . . to testify on my behalf	He will glorify me . . . take what is mine and declare it to you.

With regard to the source, the Father "gives" and "sends" the Advocate, or the Advocate "comes from the Father." Jesus brokers the Advocate, "asking the Father" or "sending from the Father" or "sending in my name." Concerning his role, he is thrice named "Advocate" and "Spirit of truth." Advocate, we saw, refers to a witness who supports and encourages a person on trial, as well as a "witness on Jesus' behalf" (15:26). We know, moreover, that his primary role is to broker Jesus to the group. First, he "teaches" and "reminds" the disciples of Jesus' words;[434] and he "testifies" to Jesus and "glorifies" him. Concerning the Advocate as "Spirit of truth," at 14:16–17 we argued that "truth" has two meanings in this Gospel. First, as the mediator of Jesus' words, the Advocate acts honestly and accurately, hence truthfully. And because "truth" has to do with loyalty and faithfulness, the Spirit is therefore reliable and steadfast in bringing Jesus' words to the group. Finally, his relationship to Jesus is that of broker to the broker, for "He will not speak on his own" (16:13). However, there are suggestions that this Advocate and Spirit of truth may exceed his role of

---

[434] See M. E. Boring, "The Influence of Christian Prophecy on the Johannine Portrayal of the Paraclete and Jesus," *NTS* 25 (1978), 113–23; and Eskil Franck, *Revelation Taught: The Paraclete in the Fourth Gospel* (Uppsala: Gleerup, 1985).

broker, for he will "teach you everything" (14:26) and "declare to you things that are to come" (16:13), perhaps even things not spoken by Jesus.

No rivalry exists here between Jesus and Spirit. The premier activity of the Spirit is to communicate knowledge: to teach and remind, to testify, and to guide. For the most part, the Spirit brings nothing new nor speaks independently of Jesus. Thus the Spirit, who is "another" Advocate, and Jesus are in complete harmony. Yet the Spirit is not simply Jesus' replacement but functions as the broker or mediator who assures access of the group is access to the absent Jesus.[435]

Parallel Advocates. Many scholars have noted parallels between what is said of the Advocate in John 14–16 and what is claimed by Jesus in the rest of the Gospel.[436] For example:

1. As Jesus is "in" the disciples (13:33; 14:20, 23), so is the Advocate (14:16–17).
2. Jesus was not received by the world (1:11; 5:42; 12:48); nor is the Advocate (14:17).
3. Jesus was not known by the world but only by believers (8:19; 10:14; 16:3), and so is the Advocate (14:17).
4. Henceforth the world will not see Jesus but only believers will (14:19; 16:16–17), the same as for the Advocate (14:17).
5. Over forty times in John 1–12, Jesus states that he is sent by the Father, as is said of the Advocate (14:26; 15:26).
6. As Jesus comes from the Father into the world (5:43; 16:28; 18:37), so does the Advocate (15:26; 16:7, 13).
7. Jesus gives testimony (5:31 ff.; 7:7; 8:13–20), as does the Advocate (15:26).
8. Jesus does not speak of or by himself, but as he was told (7:17; 8:26–27; 14:10), and similarly for the Advocate (16:13).
9. As Jesus reveals and discloses secrets (4:25; 16:25), so does the Advocate (16:13–14).
10. Just as Jesus glorified the one who sent him (12:28; 17:1, 4), the Advocate does likewise (16:14).

Thus, the Spirit of truth is "another Advocate," yet a copy of the original and in service to the first Advocate. Because he is sent by God, he loyally serves God's interests; inasmuch as he dwells in the clients, he is likewise loyal to them. Like the other Advocate, he makes an excellent broker because of his fit in the worlds of both patron and clients.

---

[435] T. G. Brown, *Spirit in John* (2003), 209–11.
[436] R. E. Brown, "The Paraclete in the Fourth Gospel," *NTS* 13 (1967), 126–27; J. L. Martyn, *History and Theology* (1979), 148–50; and T. G. Brown, *Spirit in John* (2003), 189–92.

JOHN 16:16–24 – NOT KNOWING AND KNOWING

16 "A little while, and you will no longer see me, and again a little while, and you will see me."

17 Then some of his disciples said to one another, "What does he mean by saying to us, 'A little while, and you will no longer see me, and again a little while, and you will see me'; and 'because I am going to the Father'?"

18 They said, "What does he mean by this 'a little while'? We do not know what he is talking about."

19 Jesus knew that they wanted to ask him, so he said to them, "Are you discussing among yourselves what I meant when I said, 'A little while, and you will no longer see me, and again a little while, and you will see me'?

20 Very truly, I tell you, you will weep and mourn, but the world will rejoice; you will have pain, but your pain will turn into joy.

21 When a woman is in labor, she has pain, because her hour has come. But when her child is born, she no longer remembers the anguish because of the joy of having brought a human being into the world.

22 So you have pain now; but I will see you again, and your hearts will rejoice, and no one will take your joy from you.

23 On that day you will ask nothing of me. Very truly, I tell you, if you ask anything of the Father in my name, he will give it to you.

24 Until now you have not asked for anything in my name. Ask and you will receive, so that your joy may be complete.

Scrutinizing Jesus' Words. Jesus makes a confusing statement: "A little while, and you will no longer see me, and again a little while, and you will see me" (16:16). The first part closely resembles an earlier remark: "In a little while the world will no longer see me, but you will see me" (14:19), which provoked no questions or anxiety, but that is not the case in 16:16. The dynamic here resembles the familiar pattern of statement–misunderstanding–clarification. But we find here no false hearing of Jesus' words (see 8:51–52), nor false understanding. Here the disciples simply do not grasp his words at all, as they repeat the words accurately and separate them into four distinct units: (1) "You will not see me," (2) "You will see me," (3) "I go to the Father," and (4) "a little while"? Finally, they honestly confess: "We do not know what he is talking about" (16:18). They react differently from Nicodemus, the synagogue members at Capernaum, and the sons of Ishmael (8:31–58). They neither attempt to catch Jesus in his words nor lead him to futility in explaining them.

The author treats their questions as a topic statement of two items, which Jesus will explain. Because he "knew that they wanted to ask," he comments on two puzzling points: "You will not see me" (16:20–21) and "You will see me" (16:22–24). He does not give a word-for-word explanation but rather an equivalent. "*You will not see me*" means that the disciples will "weep and lament" while others rejoice. He explains this by way of a simile about a woman first in the pains of childbirth but filled with joy when she holds her child: "So you have pain now" (16:22). "*You will see me*" means that, after weeping, they will have joy that no one can take from them. But Jesus' explanation of this changes the original word; instead of their seeing him, he remarks, "but I will see you again." And when he sees them, then they will have access to the Father in Jesus' name, an access so favorable that "if you ask *anything* of the Father in my name, he will give it to you" (16:23). Thus, when he sees them, they will "see me" in their petitioning the Father through his name and experiencing "joy." The tone and rhetorical function of this catechism is that of comfort and exhortation rather than a matter of revelation of secrets or knowledge.

Telling Time, Once More. We observed earlier that "time" in this Gospel is not calibrated by clock or calendar. Now, in the Farewell Address, we find considerable interest in time, but we must sort out if the author considers this "time" past, present, or future. The problem is compounded because not all cultures have the same interest in and celebration of past, present, and future.[437]

Past. The patriarchs Abraham, Jacob, and Moses are mentioned, but not so much to consider them examples of past covenants or special deeds but as present points of comparison for Jesus, who is "greater than" all of these; "Abraham saw my day" speaks to the eternal existence of Jesus, for Abraham came into being and died but Jesus says "I AM."

Present. As is typical of ancient cultures, the Gospel focuses on present time. We are all familiar with "today"-oriented remarks such as "Sufficient for today . . ." (Matt 6:34), "Give us today our daily bread" (Matt 6:11), "Today this Scripture is fulfilled in your hearing" (Luke 4:21), and "Today you will be with me in paradise" (Luke 23:43).[438] "Present" describes what it means to "have" eternal life in the here and now (3:15–16; 5:24; 6:40, 47, 54) or to "abide" in the vine. We are told of an hour so imminent that it is "now here" (4:23; 5:25; 12:23; 16:32). "Now the Son of Man has been glorified" (13:31), but the present quality of this declaration will extend to the "lifting up" of Jesus and his full return to the Father. The "present," then, may consist of several days or even months once a process has begun.

Future. This poses a serious interpretive problem, for it has been recently argued that the New Testament was primarily present oriented, with secondary

---

[437] B. J. Malina, "Christ and Time" in *Social World* (1996), 179–214.
[438] See B. J. Malina, "Christ and Time," in *Social World* (1996), 183.

concern for the past; the future was a lesser part of the New Testament world.[439] Not only this, but Jesus often confesses that he does not know the future date of the coming disaster (Mark 13:32) because the "future" belongs only to God: "It is not for you to know the times or periods that the Father has set by his own authority" (Acts 1:7). What, then, does "future" mean to the ancients? And what do we make of prophecies in this Gospel, especially in the Farewell Address? Is there a "future"?

Present Is "Future." The future normally refers to things occurring far ahead of the present and unrelated to it.[440] The future is *not* the harvest that follows the sowing of grain (12:24), *nor* the birth of a child carried nine months in the womb (16:20–21). Sowing and pregnancy are present time events, which are inaugurated now and perdure until completion. What is known and expected, then, does not belong to the future. Similarly, many prophecies in the Farewell Address declare a process now under way in which a bad effect will occur, followed by a good effect (14:3; 16:18). Four times, moreover, Jesus makes his predictions intensely "present"-oriented because he tells the disciples now in order to remove the fear or terror that is predicted to happen later (13:18; 14:29; 15:11; 16:4). Thus the rhetorical aim of telling the predictions is to give a present and full "joy" to the disciples (15:11), a "joy" that cannot be taken from them (16:20–22). Moreover, the time lapse between "now" and the fulfillment of the predictions is "a short while" (13:33; 14:19; 16:16–19), an attempt to keep the terminus of the prediction calculable and therefore immediate.

Time and the Advocate. What, then, of the Advocate? Is he oriented toward the past, present, or future? We argue that the Advocate-Spirit is predominately present focused. Admittedly he has access to the past, for his main role is that of making it present to the disciples: "But the Advocate, the Holy Spirit . . . will remind you of all that I have said to you" (14:26). He is, moreover, the "other" Advocate, whose career exactly parallels that of Jesus and who functions as the present replacement for Jesus. As Tricia Brown argued, he is the broker who secures for the disciples access to Jesus, past and present. This Spirit, then, is normed by the past because what he "reminds" the group of and what he speaks to them conform to Jesus' words: The Spirit "will not speak on his own" but will "take what is mine and declare it to you" (16:14). But does this Spirit have

---

439 The Greco-Roman world, with its sybils and oracles, sought to know the future. But Israel's diviners, augers, soothsayers, and so forth were condemned (Deut 18:10–14). Moreover, the ancients accepted that in the course of a farewell address, a patriarch may give predictions of the future because he was thought to belong both to the present world and to the future one he was about to enter. See B. J. Malina and R. L. Rohrbaugh, *Commentary on the Synoptics* (2003), 361–62.

440 Gail O'Day, in "'I Have Overcome the World' [John 16:33]: Narrative Time in John 13–17," *Semeia* 53 (1991), 153–66, applies literary notions of time, according to which there are two times: "retrospection" (which looks back in time) and "temporal analepsis" (which anticipates).

a future orientation? Yes, it would seem, for Jesus says, "He *will* declare to you the things that are to come" (16:13).

JOHN 16:25–33 – FIGURES AND PLAIN SPEECH

25 "I have said these things to you in figures of speech. The hour is coming when I will no longer speak to you in figures, but will tell you plainly of the Father.
26 On that day you will ask in my name. I do not say to you that I will ask the Father on your behalf;
27 for the Father himself loves you, because you have loved me and have believed that I came from God.
28 I came from the Father and have come into the world; again, I am leaving the world and am going to the Father."
29 His disciples said, "Yes, now you are speaking plainly, not in any figure of speech!
30 Now by this we believe that you came from God."
31 Jesus answered them, "Do you now believe?
32 The hour is coming, indeed it has come, when you will be scattered, each one to his home, and you will leave me alone. Yet I am not alone because the Father is with me.
33 I have said this to you, so that in me you may have peace. In the world you face persecution. But take courage; I have conquered the world!"

Speaking in Figures/Speaking Plainly. It seems best to examine three patterns in 16:16–33 whereby the disciples are transformed in various ways. They change from asking questions to not asking questions, from hearing Jesus speak in figures to hearing him speak plainly, and from not knowing to knowing.

Questions/No Questions. The disciples ask three questions in 16:17–18 to discover the meaning of Jesus' statement in 16:16. Oddly enough, the disciples seem not to speak them to Jesus, who must guess what is on their minds, which Howard Bream has argued is a typical motif in the prophetic scenario here.[441] True prophets do not need questions asked of them, but false ones do. Thus, after an appropriate transition, the disciples will find themselves in the ideal position where they will know that Jesus knows all things and that questions are a thing of another age: "You do not need to have anyone question you."

Figures/Plain Speech. Jesus responds to the disciples' questions in 16:17–18 with "figures of speech." The first is a simile comparing their current crisis with childbirth labor (16:20–21). In this comparison, someone experiences a liminal

---

[441]   Howard N. Bream, "No Need to Be Asked Questions: A Study of Jn. 16:30," in J. M. Myers, O. Reimherr, and H. N. Bream, eds., *Search the Scriptures* (Leiden: Brill, 1969), 59–74.

stage of pain and suffering, with an appropriate new role assumed at the end of the process. The woman becomes a mother, and the disciples become the harvest from the grain of wheat. Jesus tells the disciples that they are transitioning from hearing things in figures to hearing them plainly: "I have said these things to you in figures of speech. The hour is coming when I will no longer speak to you in figures, but will tell you plainly of the Father" (16:25). The plain sense of this states that "the hour is coming" when this transition will occur. Jesus makes a complete statement about his own transition, which thus far the disciples have not understood: "I came from the Father and have come into the world; again, I am leaving the world and am going to the Father" (16:28). As "plain" as this seems to the Gospel audience, many narrative characters have thus far found this to be "figurative" speech (6:41–42; 7:27, 33–35). The disciples, however, declare: "Now you are speaking plainly, not in any figure of speech!" (16:29). They boast of exceptional knowledge, "Now we know that you know all things," and then claim, "Now by this we believe that you came from God" (16:30b). We should be suspicious of these claims to a status they do not yet enjoy, like Peter's boasts in 13:36–37. As Jesus did with Peter, he now challenges their claims to know and believe: "Do you now believe? The hour is coming, indeed it has come, when you will be scattered" (16:32). The time notation indicates that they are not finished with their liminal period of learning and discipleship; moreover, the testing of their belief will prove that they do not measure up to the grade. Despite their claims, they are still in a time of figures, not plain speech.

Not Knowing/Knowing. The critical question is always, "*Who* knows *what* and *when*"? Jesus knows all: He knows that his disciples wish to ask him questions (16:19) and, in fact, they boast that they know that Jesus knows all (16:30). The disciples, however, do not know much. They do not know what Jesus meant in 16:16–18. Whatever they know from him is now in figures. Although they are promised that when "the hour comes" they will know plainly, this has not yet happened. Therefore, although the disciples are in the process of transitioning out of the liminal state of asking questions, not knowing, and knowing only in figures, the completion of the process is not yet here.

Asking. Eight times in 16:16–33 the verb "ask" appears. Lest we assume that to mean petitionary prayer, consider what is asked for and how. First, the disciples were "asking" among themselves about the statement of Jesus (16:19); this is not a petition, nor is it a prayer. Furthermore, Jesus knows what they wish to ask and explains without any questioning of him by them. At the end of the figure, Jesus says, "Until now you have not asked for anything in my name," but when the hour of labor is over, "you will ask nothing of me" (16:23), for their petition will be directed to God as a prayer: "If you ask anything of the Father in my name, he will give it to you" (16:23b). Again, Jesus tells his disciples that "in that day you will ask in my name" (16:26). But, as before, he steps aside and disclaims any mediation: "I do not say to you that I will ask the Father on your behalf"

(16:26). The Patron "himself loves you," for God knows that the disciples believe fully in Jesus. All asking is directed to God, who is sometimes approached "in the name of Jesus" and sometimes immediately (16:26–27). What is asked for? Because the content of this discourse is "knowledge" of some sort, we suggest that the group petitions for various forms of knowledge, revelation, and the like. Even knowledge that is not requested is made available, such as the prediction of scattering. Formerly, we noted that the primary functions of the Advocate/Spirit were those of exhorting, encouraging, and confirming.

JOHN 17:1–5 – JESUS AT PRAYER

1 After Jesus had spoken these words, he looked up to heaven and said, "Father, the hour has come; glorify your Son so that the Son may glorify you,
2 since you have given him authority over all people, to give eternal life to all whom you have given him.
3 And this is eternal life, that they may know you, the only true God, and Jesus Christ whom you have sent.
4 I glorified you on earth by finishing the work that you gave me to do.
5 So now, Father, glorify me in your own presence with the glory that I had in your presence before the world existed.

A Priestly Prayer? A long tradition labels this a "high priestly" prayer,[442] which is rooted in two items. First, the seamlessness of Jesus' garment (19:23–24) has been compared to the high priest's robe similarly described in Josephus (*Ant.* 3.161) and Philo (*Flight* 110–12). Second, the Letter to the Hebrews shaped Christian understanding of the crucified Jesus as high priest,[443] which has surely affected the interpretation of John 17. "Priests" functioned as mediators and brokers, the social roles by which we understand Jesus' dealings between God and the disciples in this Gospel. Although all priests are brokers, not all brokers are priests. The seamless garment Jesus took off before his crucifixion is thin evidence for his identity as a priest.

Types of Prayer. As we observed regarding Jesus' prayer at Lazarus' grave (11:41–42), there are many types of prayer besides petitionary prayer. In his study "What Is Prayer?" Bruce Malina uses social-science materials to define the meaning of prayer and sort out its types.[444] Although not all of the types he identifies

---

[442] See R. Schnackenburg, *Gospel According to St. John* (1982), 3.433 no. 2.
[443] See Ceslas Spicq, *L'Épître aux Hébreux* (Paris: Gabalda, 1952), 1.109–38; see also R. E. Brown, *Gospel According to John* (1970), 2.920–22.
[444] B. J. Malina, "What Is Prayer?" *TBT* 18 (1980), 214–20; and B. J. Malina and R. L. Rohrbaugh, *Commentary on John* (1998), 246–47. See also J. H. Neyrey, "Prayer," in *Interpreting the Bible* (2001), 349–80.

are present in John 17, his typology greatly expands our ability to understand more precisely the prayers in John. Malina's seven types of prayer can be further summarized into two basic classes: prayers to have an effect on God (petitionary, regulatory, and interactive) and prayers of interaction with God (self-focused, heuristic, imaginative, and informative).

Prayers to Have an Effect

Petitionary prayers seek to obtain goods and services: "Now, Lord, look upon their threats, and grant to your servants to speak your word with all boldness" (Acts 4:29); "Give us this day our daily bread" (Matt 6:11).

    Regulatory prayers seek to control and command God to order people and things about on behalf of the one praying. We distinguish the verb "to pray (for)" (*euchomai*) from "to pray against" (*araomai*), the latter translated as "to curse."[445] The former expresses one's wishes for oneself but the latter one's wishes regarding others.[446]

    Interactional prayer seeks to maintain emotional ties with God. Laments in the psalter ask God a question, not requesting information but protesting God's apparent inactivity: "Why do you hide your face? Why do you forget our affliction"? (Ps 44:24). The one praying complains to God: "Why are you doing this or allowing it to happen?"[447]

Prayers of Interaction

Self-focused prayers identify the self to God, such as, "From now on all generations will call me blessed; for the Mighty One has done great things for me" (Luke 1:48–49) and "O Lord, my heart is not lifted up, my eyes are not raised too high" (Ps 131:1–2).[448]

    Imaginative prayer creates an environment of one's own with God: prayers in tongues and those recited in languages unknown to the one praying.

---

[445] Simon Pulleyn, *Prayer in Greek Religion* (Oxford: Clarendon, 1997), 70–77.

[446] S. Pulleyn, in his *Prayer in Greek Religion* (1997), 83, cites this curse by a rider against his rival: "Bind, tie down, fetter, strike with a javelin, overturn, finish off, destroy, kill, crush Eucherius the charioteer and all the horses."

[447] Patrick Miller, *They Cried to the Lord* (Minneapolis, MN: Fortress Press, 1994), 71–72.

[448] See F. Gerald Downing, "The Ambiguity of 'The Pharisee and the Toll-Collector' (Luke 18:9–14) in the Greco-Roman World of Late Antiquity," *CBQ* 54 (1992), 80–99. Joachim Jeremias's (*The Parables of Jesus* (New York: Charles Scribner's Sons, 1963), 142, cites this prayer: "I thank you, O Lord my God, that you have given me my lot with those who sit in the seat of learning, and not with those who sit at the street corners; for I am early to work, and they are early to work; I am early to work on the words of the Torah, and they are early to work on things of no moment. I weary myself and they weary themselves; I weary myself and profit by it, while they weary themselves to no profit. I run, and they run; I run toward the life of the Age to Come, and they run towards the pit of destruction" (*b. Ber* 28b).

Informative prayers convey acknowledgment, praise, and respect. They honor God by confessing God's sovereignty and majesty: "Know that the Lord is God; he made us and we are his" (Ps 110:3); "I will confess you among the gentiles and sing to your name" (Rom 15:9; Ps 18:49). They also honor God by a unique name, such as Savior, Almighty, or Father: "O Lord, our Lord, how majestic is your name in all the earth (Ps 8:1)." Finally, they honor God by praising, revering, glorifying, and magnifying him for his benefits and by telling and exalting his wondrous deeds: "The heavens declare the glory of God" (Ps 19:1); "Great is the Lord and greatly to be praised in the city of our God" (Ps 48:1). It is time to use this typology to interpret the prayers in John 17.

John 17 and Types of Prayer. It is a commonplace among commentators to divide John 17 into three sections (vv. 1–8, Jesus' prayer for himself; vv. 9–19, Jesus' prayer for his disciples; and vv. 20–26, Jesus' prayer for those whom his disciples will recruit), thus reducing the entire prayer to a series of petitionary prayers.[449] But while John 17 contains many prayers of petition, it also expresses prayers of other types and purposes. The following diagram attempts to sort out and classify these other prayers.

John 17	Prayer Text	Classification
v. 2	Glorify the Son that the Son may glorify You.	petitionary
v. 3	This is eternal life, that they (ac)know(ledge) You the only true God, and Jesus Christ whom You have sent.	informative
v. 5	Glorify me in your own presence with the glory which I had with You before the world was made.	petitionary
v. 6	I have manifested Your name to the men whom You gave me out of the world.	self-focused
vv. 6–8	Yours they were, and You gave them to me, and they have kept Your word. Now they know that everything you have given me is from You; for I have given them the words which You gave me, and they have received them and know in truth that I came from You; and they have believed that You sent me.	self-focused
v. 9	I am praying for them; I am not praying for those in the world, but for those whom You have given me, for they are Yours.	self-focused + petitionary
v. 10	All mine are thine; and thine are mine; and I am glorified in them.	self-focused
v. 11	Keep them in Your name, which You have given to me, that they may be one, even as we are one.	petitionary

---

[449] For example, R. E. Brown, *Gospel According to John* (1970), 2.748–51, and with minor variations, C. H. Talbert, *Reading John* (1992), 224–31.

v. 12	While I was with them, I kept them in Your name, which you have given me; I have guarded them and none of them is lost but the son of perdition.	self-focused
vv. 13–14	But now I am coming to You; and these things I speak in the world, that they may have my joy fulfilled in themselves. I have given them Your word, and the world has hated them because they are not of the world, even as I am not of the world.	self-focused
v. 15	I do not pray that you should take them out of the world, but keep them from the Evil One.	petitionary
v. 16	They are not of the world, even as I am not of the world.	self-focused
v. 17	Sanctify them in Your truth.	petitionary
vv. 18–19	As You sent me into the world, so I have sent them into the world. For their sake I consecrate myself, that they also may be consecrated in truth.	self-focused
vv. 20–22	I do not pray for these only, but also for those who believe in me through their word that they may all be one; even as You, Father, are in me and I in You, that they may be in us, so that the world may believe that You have sent me.	self-focused + petitionary
vv. 22–23	The glory which You have given me, I have given them, that they may be one, even as we are one, I in them and You in me, that they may be perfectly one, that the world may know that You have sent me and have loved them even as You have loved me.	self-focused
v. 24	Father, I desire that they also, whom You have given to me, may be with me where I am, to behold my glory which You have given me in Your love for me before the foundation of the world.	petitionary
vv. 25–26	O just Father, the world has not known You; but I have known You; and these know that You have sent me. I made known to them Your name, and I will make it known that the love with which You have loved me may be in them, and I in them.	self-focused

Petitionary Prayer. In this long prayer, Jesus, the sender, communicates *petitions* to God, requesting various benefactions for God's clients. Petitionary prayer is best considered as a request for transformation of status.[450] For example, petitioners seek to change their situation from disaster, famine, guilt, and death to salvation. Moreover, although enjoying a good status, they may petition for new benefaction and greater favors, such as glory, constancy, and sanctification. In John 17, we can identify two forms of petition: *petitions for himself* ("glorify your Son," 17:1; "glorify me in your own presence," 17:5) and *petitions*

---

[450] See the commentary on John 13:4–20; and also J. H. Neyrey, "Prayer, in Other Words," in *Interpreting the Bible* (2001), 373–77.

for the disciples ("I am asking on their behalf," 17:9; "protect them in your name," 17:11; "I ask you to protect them from the evil one," 17:15; "Sanctify them in the truth," 17:17; "I ask . . . also on behalf of those who will believe in me through their word," 17:20; "I desire that those also, whom you have given me, may be with me where I am," 17:24). All will be changed and transformed.

Mission Accomplished.[451] A second type of prayer, "self-focused" prayer, occurs frequently in John 17. It contains two elements: speaking in *first-person speech* ("I made manifest . . . "; "I kept them in your name"; "I have given them your word") and *celebrating the record* of God's past good deeds. Unlike the transformation sought by petitionary prayer, self-focused prayer celebrates the current role and status of the one praying in relation to God. Such a prayer does not tell God anything God does not already know but rather expresses fidelity and constancy in the service of God. Jesus declares that he has perfectly fulfilled what God sent him to do:

- I have glorified you on earth (v. 4).
- I have manifested your name (vv. 6, 26).
- I have given them the words which you have given me (vv. 8, 14).
- I have kept them in your name (v. 12a).
- I have guarded them (v. 12b).
- I have sent them into the world (v. 18).
- I have consecrated myself (v. 19).
- I have given them the glory which you have given me (v. 22).

Unlike his petitions, Jesus now confesses to God and before his disciples his fulfillment of his own apostleship. He has glorified God on earth, manifested to the disciples the divine Name and kept them in it, gave divine words to them, and extended his work by sending them into the world.[452] This is not only a communication to God but also revelation to Jesus' disciples of paramount secrets, his "whence and whither" and his role as God's broker.

Informational Prayer. A third type of prayer occurs in 17:3, where Jesus models the ideal confession: "And this is eternal life, that they may know you, the only true God, and Jesus Christ whom you have sent." The traditional monotheistic confession, "the only true God," is evident, but surprisingly Jesus is now

---

451 F. Gerald Downing, in his "The Ambiguity of 'The Pharisee and the Toll-Collector,'" *CBQ* 54 (1992), 80–99, concluded that both prayers in Luke 18 were "self-absorbed," a very negative classification that would not do justice to Jesus' "self-focused" prayer in John 17.

452 Although he seems to consider "prayer" only as "petitionary" speech, Ernst Käsemann, in his *The Testament of Jesus: A Study of John in the Light of Chapter 17* (London: SCM Press, 1968), 5, commented on the variety of Jesus' speech in John 17: "This is not a supplication, but a proclamation directed to the Father in such manner that his disciples can hear it also. The speaker is not a needy petitioner but the divine revealer and therefore the prayer moves over into being an address, admonition, consolation and prophecy."

part of this confession: "know . . . and Jesus Christ whom you have sent." Mere "knowing" of God is not enough, for even if the demons know that God is one (James 2:19), they do not acknowledge God. Jesus speaks of confession, loyalty, and acknowledgment here; honor is at stake rather than knowledge. And acknowledging the Patron necessarily includes the Patron's agent and broker. One cannot truly honor the Patron without honoring the one whom the Patron sent with words and power (see 5:23).

JOHN 17:6–12 – NEW FOCUS OF PRAYER: THE DISCIPLES

6 "I have made your name known to those whom you gave me from the world. They were yours, and you gave them to me, and they have kept your word.

7 Now they know that everything you have given me is from you;

8 for the words that you gave to me I have given to them, and they have received them and know in truth that I came from you; and they have believed that you sent me.

9 I am asking on their behalf; I am not asking on behalf of the world, but on behalf of those whom you gave me, because they are yours.

10 All mine are yours, and yours are mine; and I have been glorified in them.

11 And now I am no longer in the world, but they are in the world, and I am coming to you. Holy Father, protect them in your name that you have given me, so that they may be one, as we are one.

12 While I was with them, I protected them in your name that you have given me. I guarded them, and not one of them was lost except the one destined to be lost, so that the scripture might be fulfilled.

Name of Names. Four times in this prayer Jesus declares that he has "made your name known to them" (17:6, 26) or petitions that they should be "protected in your name" (17:11, 12). The "name," then, seems to be a revelation as well as a guarantee of safety. But which "name" is this? Not "God" or "Lord," names that Jesus has never used to describe himself, but rather the "name" that he reveals is "I AM" (8:24–25, 28, 58; 18:5–6), which we saw is shorthand for the name of God revealed to Moses (Exod 3:14) and taken up by Israel's prophets.[453] If "I AM" expresses divine existence, which is eternal in the past and imperishable in the future, then we ask if Jesus' revelation of it also contains this content. "Before Abraham came into being, I AM" (8:58) contrasts mortal existence, which begins (8:58) and ends in death (8:52), with divine existence, which has

---

[453] See R. E. Brown, *Gospel According to John* (1970), 2.755–56; C. H. Talbert, *Reading John* (1992), 226–27; and J. H. Neyrey, *Ideology of Revolt* (1988), 213–20.

no beginning or ending. Similarly, when Jesus says, "When you have lifted up the Son of Man then you will know that I AM" (8:28), this "lifting" means his death, the apparent end of his existence. But this death will be the occasion in which Jesus' imperishable existence will be manifest (see 10:17–18). Thus "I AM" in these comparative texts contrasts mortal and immortal existence, even as it declares that Jesus "IS" forever, just as God eternally exists.[454] Jesus does not merely reveal a secret name; this name embodies his eternity in the past and imperishability in the future. How will this name guard or keep the disciples? If eternal existence is meant, then God's eternal faithfulness and power hold the group in safety. Therefore, only one is lost, Judas, but not the others.

A CLOSER LOOK – THE MEANING OF NAMES

Many ancients argued that the Deity was ineffable, unknowable, and unnameable. Although no name can identify God's essence, names may describe God's actions. But these thinkers were generally elite philosophers, not typical authors of Greco-Roman or New Testament literature. In fact, it was a mark of honor for a Greco-Roman deity to be "many-named." Cleanthes' "Hymn to Zeus" begins with "Most glorious of immortals, honored under many names." And in a Hellenistic poem, Artemis as a little girl sat on her father's lap and asked for a special gift that would put her on a par with her brother: "Give me many-namedness."[455] Nevertheless, the ancients clearly understood that a person's name might indicate personal names; nicknames; names derived from occupation, origin, and affiliation; and patrifiliative names. What follows is clear evidence that the ancients understood the multiple meanings of names:

Caius was the proper name; second name, in this case Marcius, was the common name of *family or clan*; and the third name was adopted subsequently, and bestowed because of some *exploit*, or *fortune*, or *bodily feature*, or special *excellence* in a man. So the Greeks used to give surnames from an *exploit*, as for instance, Soter (Savior), and Callinicus ("Winner"); or from a *bodily feature*, as Physcon (Fat-paunch) and Grypus (Hook-nose); or from a *special excellence*, as Euergetes (Benefactor) and Philadelphus (Generous); or from some *good fortune*, as Eudaemon (Prosperous), the surname of the second Battus. And some of their kings have actually had surnames given them in *mockery*, as Antigonus Doson ("Always Promising") and Ptolemy Lathyrus ("Lentils"). (Plutarch, *Coriolanus* 11.2–3; emphasis added)

---

454 Eternal existence is a hallmark for true deities; see J. H. Neyrey, "Without Beginning of Days or End of Life," *CBQ* 53 (1991), 439–55.

455 Cited in J. M. Bremer, "Greek Hymns," in H. S. Versnel, ed., *Faith, Hope and Worship: Aspects of Religious Mentality in the Ancient World* (Leiden: Brill, 1981), 194–95. See also Dale Eickelman, *The Middle East: An Anthropological Approach* (Englewood Cliffs, NJ: Prentice-Hall, 1989), 55–59.

Whence and Whither. Throughout this Gospel, people endlessly debate whence Jesus comes and whither he goes. Jesus himself made this a key thematic issue at times (3:13) and provoked discussion of it (6:41–42; 7:25–31, 41, 52). Knowing the answer means knowing Jesus' true character as a heavenly being, which is correct life-giving knowledge. The author now makes this motif quite thematic in John 13–20:

Text	Whence	Whither
13:1–3	He had come from God.	. . . and was going to God
16:17		I go to the Father.
16:28	I came from the Father and have come into the world.	I am leaving the world and am going to the Father.
16:30	We believe you came from God.	
17:5	. . . that I had in your presence before the world existed.	Glorify me in your own presence with the glory . . .
17:8	They know that I came from you; they have believed that you sent me.	
17:11		I am coming to you.
17:13		I am coming to you.
17:18	As you have sent me into the world.	
17:25	these know that you have sent me.	

Jesus attests to God that his disciples now know whence he came and whither he goes. Thus the mentor certifies that his disciples have learned the right knowledge in their liminal state. Finally, the materials here overlap with the meaning of "I AM," inasmuch as they speak to an uncreated eternity in the past (17:5a) and an imperishable future (17:5b). If "I AM" speaks to duration, then "whence/whither" speak of relationships, not space (1:18). Finally, this differs from the "return" pattern we saw earlier, in which Jesus declares that he "goes away" and "comes back" (14:2–3, 18, 28; 16:16–18); the disciples never seem to have figured that out.

Group Glue. Jesus petitions that God "keep" the disciples, meaning that God should guard and defend them and hold them together as one flock: "so that they may be one, as we are one" (17:11). Balancing this is Jesus' own prayer that "I have 'kept' them in your name" (17:12). In addition, Jesus "guarded them" so that no one is lost, except the son of perdition" (17:12). Thus "keep" means that God should be attached to the disciples, just as Jesus is. Moreover, Jesus is also said to "keep" attached to God: "I know Him [God] and I keep his words" (8:55). Likewise the disciples are also exhorted to "keep" their attachment to God and Jesus in a variety of ways. Because the hallmark of true disciples or Jesus' sheep is that they hear his voice and "keep" his words and commandments, they, too, must be attached to Jesus.

> If anyone *keeps my word*, he will never see death (8:51–52).
> If you love me, you will *keep my commandments* (14:15).
> Who has my commandments and *keeps them*, I will love him (14:21, 23).
> If you *keep my commandments*, you will abide in my love (15:10).

Yet the disciples must also be attached in loyalty to other disciples, which Jesus expresses in the exhortations to "remain" (15:1–8) and to "love" (15:9–17). Thus, in regard to the disciples, both God and Jesus "keep" them in the sense of shepherding them, defending them, and bonding with them (i.e., being "one" with them). Because the group is under attack (16:1–2), its greatest danger is apostasy and cowardice. Jesus' prayer, then, petitions God to provide social glue to keep them attached to God and to himself.

JOHN 17:13–26 – PRAYERS FOR FUTURE DISCIPLES

13 But now I am coming to you, and I speak these things in the world so that they may have my joy made complete in themselves.

14 I have given them your word, and the world has hated them because they do not belong to the world, just as I do not belong to the world.

15 I am not asking you to take them out of the world, but I ask you to protect them from the evil one.

16 They do not belong to the world, just as I do not belong to the world.

17 Sanctify them in the truth; your word is truth.

18 As you have sent me into the world, so I have sent them into the world.

19 And for their sakes I sanctify myself, so that they also may be sanctified in truth.

20 "I ask not only on behalf of these, but also on behalf of those who will believe in me through their word,

21 that they may all be one. As you, Father, are in me and I am in you, may they also be in us, so that the world may believe that you have sent me.

22 The glory that you have given me I have given them, so that they may be one, as we are one,

23 I in them and you in me, that they may become completely one, so that the world may know that you have sent me and have loved them even as you have loved me.

24 Father, I desire that those also, whom you have given me, may be with me where I am, to see my glory, which you have given me because you loved me before the foundation of the world.

25 "Righteous Father, the world does not know you, but I know you; and these know that you have sent me.

26 I made your name known to them, and I will make it known, so that the love with which you have loved me may be in them, and I in them."

In, But Not of, the World. During the Word's sojourn in the world, relations with it became increasingly hostile: "He came unto his own and his own received him not (1:11)." From the first trial in 5:16–18, Jesus' enemies have repeatedly sought to kill him. This world, then, metamorphosed from the object of God's love (3:16) to the focus of his judgment (12:47–49; 16:8–11). But with Jesus' imminent departure from the world, he remarks on it for the purpose of confirming the disciples beset and besieged by the same world. The following chart summarizes how Jesus speaks of the world in radically dualistic terms.

World	Johannine Disciples
1. Cannot see the Advocate	but the disciples see him (14:17)
2. Does not know the Advocate	but the disciples know him (14:19; 17:25)
3. Jesus does not manifest himself to the world	but manifests himself to them (14:22)
4. Gives no peace	but Jesus gives them peace (14:27)
5. Hostile power	but Jesus overcomes the ruler of this age (14:30; 16:33), and protects them from the Evil One (17:15)
6. Hatred of disciples	but love by Jesus and love for one another (15:18; 17:14)
7. Rejoices	but disciples weep and lament (16:20)
8. No prayer of Jesus for world	but prayer for disciples (17:9)

From this we learn the following. First, "world" is not a geographical location any more than Galilee and Judea are. It is rather wherever one finds enemies. Second, almost all references to "world" in the Farewell Address are dualistic contrasts between it and Jesus' disciples; they are on opposite sides of every issue: knowledge, revelation, and manifestation; social attitudes, such as love versus hatred, and rejoicing by the disciples versus their weeping and lamenting; and social experience, such as war versus victory/peace. Finally, this type of discourse leads to a powerful sense of elitism in those *not* of this world. Jesus prays for them alone, and God is petitioned to guard and protect them alone. Another Advocate, moreover, labors on their behalf. Hence, their struggles are ennobled and their identity confirmed as the select few.

Stuck in This World. Jesus is from above, but his enemies are from below; he is not of this world, but they are (8:23). He told his disciples that they, too, are not of this world and are hated by it (15:18–25; see also 7:7). He repeats this critical "geographical" identification marker: "The world has hated them because they do not belong to the world, just as I do not belong to the world" (17:14). Like Jesus, they are "aliens" in an alien land: "They do not belong to the world, just as I do not belong to the world" (17:16). But whereas he leaves this hostile place, they do not, so Jesus prays for them: "I am not asking you to take them out of the world, but I ask you to protect them from the evil one" (17:16).

Sanctify in Truth. At risk is group solidarity, for if the shepherd is struck, will the sheep be scattered? God's "protection" must take the form of "sanctifying them in the truth." On the one hand, "sanctify" relates to concepts of "clean" and "cleansing" seen earlier. The word of Jesus makes the disciples "clean" (15:3); the attention of the vine dresser to the branches "cleanses" them (15:6). The result is "remaining"; that is, loyalty and faithfulness to the group's ideology and confession. On the other hand, Jesus declares that "For their sakes I sanctify myself, so that they also may be sanctified in truth" (17:19). Whether we translate the verb here as "sanctify" or "consecrate," we suggest that someone or something is set aside from ordinary use and dedicated uniquely to God. One is reminded of the verb "to seal" in 3:33 and 6:27, which can be translated as "to accredit as an envoy" (*LSJ* 1742). "To sanctify" is to remove an object from the profane world and dedicate it exclusively to God. As regards Jesus, God set him apart and "sent him into the world" (17:18) in total service of God's word; Jesus, too, sets the disciples apart and sends them into this hostile world: "I have sent them into the world" (17:18b). One purpose of this language is to hallow the task of faithfulness to the group's ideology; the task is noble and worth the effort. Indeed, "truth" here expresses the notion of faithfulness, as well as the notion that the word that Jesus revealed to the disciples is authentic. Thus they are set aside for the service of the truth, even as they are supported in faithfulness to the group.

"One" and "In." Although the author said in 10:31 that God and Jesus are "one," the meaning there had to do with equality between God and Jesus in eschatological power over death.[456] But, in 17:21, Jesus petitions God about the current and future disciples "that they may all be one," which cannot refer to equality but rather to unity or relationship, a constant theme in John 17. This unity, first expressed as "one," is amplified by reference to "in": the Father "in" Jesus, Jesus "in" God, and the disciples "in" Father and Son. John gives us other images of "one" and "in": make our home in them (14:23); abide in them (15:3–8); words abiding in the disciples (15:7); and keeping them "in" your name (17:17). "Home" is not a physical building but a metaphor for a household and its relationships. Oddly, the disciples never go to the "many rooms" in the Father's house; rather, God and Jesus "make their home" in the disciples. "Abide" or

---

[456] Paul used the same expression about himself and Apollos in 1 Corinthians 3:8 – he who plants and he who waters are "one"; that is, "equal."

"remain" metaphorically refers to physical attachment of branches to the vine, and also to adherence to Jesus, his words, and the group's ideology about him. "Words" can abide not necessarily written on parchment but in mind and heart; if disciples remain in the word, the word is surely "in" them. Therefore, "one" and "in" speak to the unique relationship that disciples have with Jesus and through him with God. And the uniqueness of this triple relationship becomes the object of Jesus' prayer, that it survive and grow.

Johannine "Our Father"? William O. Walker argues that John 17 strongly resembles the synoptic "Our Father." He claims that "the basic contents, to a somewhat lesser degree the overall structure, and occasionally at significant points the actual language of the High Priestly Prayer can best be understood as a reworking and expansion of the basic themes of the Lord's Prayer in terms of the specifically Johannine theology."[457] Let us examine this suggestion.

Father. The address to God as "Father" (17:1, 11, 21, 24, 25) constitutes the clearest link between the two prayers. But addressing God as "Father" is such a common feature of Jesus' Johannine prayers (11:41; 12:27–28) that dependency on the Our Father here is difficult to show.

Name. When Jesus mentions God's "name" four times (17:6, 11, 12, 26), his self-focused prayer declares that he has faithfully manifested it; he is not praying that God's name be exalted, as in the Our Father. Moreover, this name is not "Lord," "God," or "Father," but "I AM," the name shared by Jesus himself. Thus the reference to God's name in John 17 is less a celebration of God's honor and more an exaltation of Jesus.

Hallowed Name. Jesus declares that in the past he revealed the name only to disciples and now petitions that God keep the disciples in it. This differs from the Our Father, which prays that God's name be acknowledged by all, both now and forever. Does the picture change if we consider as synonyms of "hallowed" terms such as "glory" and "glorify"? Only once in the prayer does Jesus say that he has "glorified" God (17:4), an action in the past, not the present or future. Rather, Jesus himself petitions for glory from God (17:1, 10, 22, 24).

Kingdom. "Kingdom" appears only twice in this Gospel: with respect to a status transformation needed to enter the kingdom (3:3, 5); and as a statement that the "kingdom" of Jesus is not of this world (18:36). While we hear of God's "house" or "household" (14:2), these are not places but relationships. Instead of disciples going to God's house, Jesus and God will come and dwell in them (14:23). We do not know "where" the disciples will be when they "behold my glory" (17:24),

---

[457] William O. Walker, "The Lord's Prayer in Matthew and John (Matt 6:9–13 and Jn 17)," *NTS* 28 (1982), 238. See the commentary on 12:27–28, where some resemblance to the synoptic "Our Father" is indicated.

but it will be in this world, not out of it. "Kingdom" in the Our Father, then, does not match anything in the prayer in John 14–17.

Will Be Done. Jesus himself knows that God has a special "will" for him. His bread is to "do the will of him who sent me" (4:34); and God's will for him is that he "not lose one of them" (6:39). And God's will for the crowds and disciples is "that you believe in him whom God has sent" (6:29). Jesus' self-focused prayer in John 17 acclaims that he has done God's will: "I have accomplished the work which you gave me to do" (17:14). Hence, the prayer involving God's will is not about any future completion of the cosmic plan of God or an exhortation for disciples to obey the will of God but mainly a celebration of Jesus' current attention to the affairs of God.

Daily Bread. We have noted that the disciples are instructed to practice petitionary prayer, asking in the name of Jesus for whatever they need. We have no evidence that their asking would be for material benefactions such as foods or healings. More likely, these petitions are for knowledge, revelation, and the like. Yet the petition in the Our Father unabashedly requests food for subsistence peasants. Finally, we note that all petitions in John are made through Jesus and in his name, something very foreign to the synoptic prayer.

Forgive Trespasses. Although the Gospel tells us of terrible violence and hostility toward the disciples, they are never instructed to offer forgiveness for personal affronts. Yes, Jesus gives power to the disciples to forgive and retain sins (20:23), but never are they told to forgive insults and injury to themselves.

Lead Not into Temptation. Jesus declares that he himself has "guarded them, and none is lost but . . . " (17:12); he petitions God "to keep them from the Evil One" (17:15). Like Jesus, the disciples are aliens in an alien land, which seeks their ruin. Unlike Jesus, however, they do not leave this world but remain in it in all its hostility (17:9, 11, 14–16). Pray as they might, they will face great enemies (16:1–2).

What do we know if we know all this? First, we do not know if the Fourth Gospel is consciously redacting the Our Father. But we do know that despite some verbal parallels, the logic and dynamic of both prayers differ radically. In John 17, Jesus does *not* teach the disciples to pray as he does in the synoptics. Rather they hear *his* own unique prayer, which no disciple could ever imagine praying. Moreover, in keeping with the self-focused nature of this prayer, Jesus is as much the center of the prayer as God is; Jesus declares that *he* manifested "the name"; *he* seeks glory from God; *he* declares that he has accomplished God's will. John 17, we think, is an extraordinary compendium of Johannine Christology. The argument just presented persuades us that the prayer in John 17 is very different from the Our Father. A more interesting question might be: Could the synoptic churches pray the prayer in John 17? Could the Johannine group pray their Our Father?

JOHN 18:1–11 – I LAY DOWN MY LIFE . . . NO ONE TAKES IT FROM ME

1 After Jesus had spoken these words, he went out with his disciples across the Kidron valley to a place where there was a garden, which he and his disciples entered.

2 Now Judas, who betrayed him, also knew the place, because Jesus often met there with his disciples.

3 So Judas brought a detachment of soldiers together with police from the chief priests and the Pharisees, and they came there with lanterns and torches and weapons.

4 Then Jesus, knowing all that was to happen to him, came forward and asked them, "Whom are you looking for?"

5 They answered, "Jesus of Nazareth." Jesus replied, "I am he." Judas, who betrayed him, was standing with them.

6 When Jesus said to them, "I am he," they stepped back and fell to the ground.

7 Again he asked them, "Whom are you looking for?" And they said, "Jesus of Nazareth."

8 Jesus answered, "I told you that I am he. So if you are looking for me, let these men go."

9 This was to fulfill the word that he had spoken, "I did not lose a single one of those whom you gave me."

10 Then Simon Peter, who had a sword, drew it, struck the high priest's slave, and cut off his right ear. The slave's name was Malchus.

11 Jesus said to Peter, "Put your sword back into its sheath. Am I not to drink the cup that the Father has given me?"

Arrest. Like all good narratives, this one tells us all we need to know at the beginning of this part of the story. *Who?* Jesus and the inner circle of disciples. *Where?* A garden beyond the Kidron Valley. *When?* In the late evening. *How?* The place is already known to Judas because "Jesus and his disciples often gathered there." This is not the Gethsemane of the synoptics, where Jesus prayed in anguish as the disciples slept. Rather, the narrative focus highlights Jesus' control and power: Jesus "knows all that is to happen" (18:4), and he controls all of the action in the narrative, both in the question–answer exchange and in suppressing Peter's violent defense.

Questions and Answers. With few exceptions, those who ask questions of others do so to challenge them.[458] This happens regularly in the synoptic Gospels when Jesus' enemies put him or his disciples on the spot with questions. Here,

---

[458] J. H. Neyrey, "Questions," *CBQ* 60 (1998), 657–66, 670–78.

Jesus asks the questions; and by taking the lead in this confrontation, he exercises control over the situation: "Whom do you seek?" The soldiers might answer a question with a question, "Who are you?" but they follow the script, which emphasizes Jesus' authority: "Jesus of Nazareth!" His answer, "I AM," both identifies himself and communicates power, another aspect of control. "Drawing back and falling to the ground" is not the typical gesture of armed soldiers before an unarmed man. But if shoved back, then they have met a superior force; if overwhelmed, they are not in control. The pattern repeats, as Jesus again asks and they answer. Still in control, Jesus commands the soldiers to let his disciples go. He not only asks questions but commands the soldiers who have come to seize him. Thus he manifests complete control over the situation: He speaks the first and last words. He lays down his life; no one takes it from him (10:18).

Swords and Stuff. Peter, who protested that he would lay down his life for Jesus (13:37), seemingly acts that part now by drawing a sword and striking the slave of the high priest. Swords? Wherever would a peasant get a sword? Curiously, the only mention we have of Gospel characters having swords, much less using them, is in the arrest scene. Yet Jesus forswears swords for both an ethical reason ("Those who live by the sword perish by the sword," Matt 26:52) and a theological reason (Jesus' arrest is God's "cup" or "will"). Peter appears to manifest loyalty and even courage. But should he succeed, the will of God would be frustrated (see Mark 8:32–33). So, Jesus, in total control of his own fate (10:17–18), stops Peter from derailing the story: "Put your sword into its sheath."

The Noble Shepherd. From the investigation of this motif in 10:10–18, we retrieve certain elements that apply here as well. (1) Jesus *voluntarily accepts* his death: He knows what will befall him (18:4), comes forward and does not flee, and allows himself to be captured. (2) His arrest and death *benefit* his disciples in that he commands that they be let go. Thus, "This was to fulfill the word that he had spoken, 'I did not lose a single one of those whom you gave me'" (18:9). (3) He is *unvanquished* in this: The soldiers fall to the ground (18:7); even as he is captured, he speaks commands. (4) *Virtue*, courage, and faithfulness in "drinking the cup which the Father has given" (18:11) motivate his actions – a noble beginning to a noble death.

Judas, the Parody of Discipleship. We saw in 1:36–50 a pattern of discipleship that occurs frequently in the narrative. A disciple speaks of Jesus to another, inviting him to "come and see"; when this person is in Jesus' presence, Jesus comments on him in a way that confirms the new relationship. This pattern is found in five stories: disciples to others (1:35–50); the Samaritan woman to her fellow villagers (4:27–30); Martha to Mary (11:28–33); Mary Magdalene to Simon and the Beloved Disciple (20:1–10); and finally the disciples to Thomas (20:24–25). But in 18:3–11 Judas is hardly catechizing the soldiers whom he leads to Jesus. They certainly do not acclaim Jesus by any title, nor does he have a confirming word for them. The process in 18:3–11 seems to be a parody of the discipleship pattern, which accentuates how perverse Judas[459] and the soldiers are. Far from becoming disciples, they seek Jesus' destruction.

JOHN 18:12–27 – BOLD PUBLIC SPEECH INSIDE THE HIGH PRIEST'S HOUSE

12 So the soldiers, their officers, and the Jewish police arrested Jesus and bound him.

13 First they took him to Annas, who was the father-in-law of Caiaphas, the high priest that year.

14 Caiaphas was the one who had advised the Jews that it was better to have one person die for the people.

15 Simon Peter and another disciple followed Jesus. Since that disciple was known to the high priest, he went with Jesus into the courtyard of the high priest,

16 but Peter was standing outside at the gate. So the other disciple, who was known to the high priest, went out, spoke to the woman who guarded the gate, and brought Peter in.

17 The woman said to Peter, "You are not also one of this man's disciples, are you?" He said, "I am not."

18 Now the slaves and the police had made a charcoal fire because it was cold, and they were standing around it and warming themselves. Peter also was standing with them and warming himself.

19 Then the high priest questioned Jesus about his disciples and about his teaching.

20 Jesus answered, "I have spoken openly to the world; I have always taught in synagogues and in the temple, where all the Jews come together. I have said nothing in secret.

21 Why do you ask me? Ask those who heard what I said to them; they know what I said."

22 When he had said this, one of the police standing nearby struck Jesus on the face, saying, "Is that how you answer the high priest?"

23 Jesus answered, "If I have spoken wrongly, testify to the wrong. But if I have spoken rightly, why do you strike me?"

24 Then Annas sent him bound to Caiaphas the high priest.

25 Now Simon Peter was standing and warming himself. They asked him, "You are not also one of his disciples, are you?" He denied it and said, "I am not."

26 One of the slaves of the high priest, a relative of the man whose ear Peter had cut off, asked, "Did I not see you in the garden with him?"

27 Again Peter denied it, and at that moment the cock crowed.

---

[459] Charles C. Torrey, in his "The Name 'Iscariot,'" *HTR* 36 (1943), 51–62, argued that "Iscariot" derives from a word meaning "deceit," "fraud," or "falsehood." Judas is "the false one." See William C. Van Unnik, "The Death of Judas in Saint Matthew's Gospel," *ATR Supplementary Series* 3 (1974), 44–57.

Annas. The patriarch of the reigning high priestly clan, Annas,[460] must have lived in a palace in Jerusalem. Like all elites, he is served by many retainers: porters who guard his gate (18:16), soldiers who enforce his will (18:3), police to attend and guard him (18:22), and slaves to maintain his household.[461] His palace would have a courtyard large enough for many soldiers to gather, as well as formal chambers for public matters, such as the one where Jesus was questioned. Annas, then, is a rich, powerful elite of very high role and status. One does not sass such a person.

Jesus' Judean Trial. Although the synoptics narrate that Jesus was put on trial before "the elders, both the chief priests and the scribes, who led him away to their council" (Luke 22:66), John only says that Jesus was brought before the high priests Annas and then Caiaphas (18:24, 28). What happened to the Judean trial? Readers are reminded of the commentary on John 10:22–39, which appears to be a Judean trial of Jesus moved to an early part of the story. But in one sense the Judean trial of Jesus has been occurring since the healing of the crippled man in John 5. Jesus was accused first of breaking the Sabbath law and then of blasphemy (5:16–18); subsequent trials took place at the feast of Booths (7:10–52; 8:12–59). Jesus is again on trial in absentia in the controversy over the healing of the man born blind (9:13–34). He was interrogated and charged with blasphemy on the feast of Dedication (10:30–39), and finally the Judeans tried, convicted, and sentenced him to death in absentia (11:45–52). In 18:19–24, although no charge is made, Jesus is subjected to the judge's scrutiny and investigation. Thus the scene before Annas is both a forensic inquiry and more significantly the last occasion for Jesus to model for his disciples bold, public testimony on behalf of the Christ.

More Question and Answer. Annas knows something about Jesus' teaching and his disciples; evidently his secret service has kept him well informed.[462] But his "questioning" seeks to find some fault in order to accuse Jesus (e.g., Mark 12:13; Luke 11:54); it is hostile probing. There will be no conversion here, even if Jesus indeed tells him all. Deflecting the challenge, Jesus states how honorable a person he is: "I have spoken openly to the world; I have always taught in synagogues and in the temple, where all the Jews come together. I have said nothing in secret" (18:20).[463] Public, transparent, and bold – Jesus has acted with great honor. Far

---

[460] On Annas (or "Ananas"), see James C. VanderKam, *From Joshua to Caiaphas: High Priests after the Exile* (Minneapolis, MN: Fortress Press, 2004), 420–24.

[461] On the retainer class in antiquity, see Gerhard E. Lenski, *Power and Privilege: A Theory of Social Stratification* (Chapel Hill: University of North Carolina Press, 1984), 243–48; and Richard L. Rohrbaugh, "The Social Location of the Markan Audience," *BTB* 23 (1983), 114–27.

[462] See J. H. Neyrey, "Secrecy," in *What Is John?* (1998), 79–109.

[463] Jesus spoke either "openly" or "boldly". Either rendering of the word *parrēsia* brings out the social value of public, bold speech; see W. C. Van Unnik, "The Christian Freedom of Speech in the New Testament," in his *Sparsa Collecta: Part Two* (Leiden: Brill, 1980), 269–306.

from trying to keep himself from the fray, Jesus challenges Annas with his own volley of questions and insults: "Why do you ask me? Ask those who heard what I said to them; they know what I said" (18:21). In speaking thus, Jesus crosses a social line and causes Annas to lose face, an intolerable situation. Hence a nearby officer strikes Jesus on the face, saying, "Is that how you answer the high priest?" (18:22). Annas' loss of face is redressed by that of Jesus, for a slap in the face was a paramount shame. Yet this is hardly a demonstration of "turn the other cheek" (Matt 5:39), for Jesus' next question puts the shame back on Annas and the officer: "If I have spoken wrongly, testify to the wrong. But if I have spoken rightly, why do you strike me?" (18:23). Again, Jesus has the last word. From the community's point of view, Jesus has not been shamed, nor has he lost face, because he speaks with boldness in public to people of power and status. He acts as an honorable hero here.

Did He or Didn't He? Despite the claim in 18:20 that Jesus keeps no secrets, we find ample data in the narrative suggesting an elaborate process of secrecy. All religions have secrets; and not everyone knows all things at the same time. Experts define secrecy as, "The mandatory or voluntary, but calculated concealment of information, activities, or relationships."[464] Jesus, the great revealer, is also the great concealer. The secrecy process in the Fourth Gospel has four elements.

Information Control. Anthropologists distinguish outright and indirect secrecy. Outright secrecy includes *lying* (others to Jesus, 8:44, 55; and Jesus to others, 7:1–10, *deception* (Jesus accused of "leading others astray," 7:12, 47), *evasion* (parents of man born blind to Pharisees, 9:21–22), *hiding oneself* (Jesus in 8:59; 12:36; 14:22; God and others in 12:38–40; coming to Jesus at night in 3:2; 19:39) or *hiding information* (anti-language in 3:3–10), *secret transmission of information* (11:28), *riddles* (10:1–6; 16:25, 29), *double-meaning words*,[465] the pattern of public versus private discourse (11:28 vs. 7:4, 13, 26; 10:24; 18:20–21), Johannine asides, footnotes,[466] and irony.[467]

---

[464] S. K. Tefft, "Secrecy as a Social and Political Process," in *Secrecy* (1980), 320.

[465] D. A. Carson, "Understanding Misunderstanding in the Fourth Gospel," *TynB* 33 (1982), 61–91; E. Richard, "Expressions of Double Meaning and Their Function in the Gospel of John," *NTS* 31 (1985), 96–112.

[466] The special information provided to insiders includes translation of Semitic terms into Greek (1:38, 41, 42; 4:25; 5:2; 9:7; 19:13, 17; 20:16); notice of special times and places (6:4; 7:2; 9:14; 10:22–23; 11:17); customs revealed (4:9; 19:40); recollections of the disciples (2:22; 12:16); in-group explanations of actions or situations (2:9; 4:2; 7:5, 39; 11:51; 12:6; 19:36–37; 21:19). See J. J. O'Rourke, "Asides in the Gospel of John," *NovT* 21 (1979), 210–29; and M. C. Tenney, "The Footnotes of John's Gospel," *BSac* 117 (1960), 350–64.

[467] Irony, the disparity of knowledge between the narrator/audience and actors in a story, may include claims to knowledge (6:42; 7:27, 41–42; 9:29) mocked by insiders; assumptions (4:12; 7:15; 8:53, 57) that the audience knows to be false; and unconscious prophecy and testimony (2:10; 7:3–4, 35–36; 8:22; 11:48, 49–50; 12:19). See P. Duke, *Irony in the Fourth Gospel* (1985).

Entrusted Disclosure. Jesus declares in 14:21–22 and 17:6, 11, 12, 26 that he does *not* manifest himself or God's secret name to the world but discloses secrets only to loyal disciples. Because "no one has ever seen God," knowledge of this God is brokered only by Jesus, and even then, not to all (1:18; 5:37; 6:46). Insiders and outsiders are distinguished by being "in the know," including people who began "not in the know" but who are subsequently enlightened (John the Baptizer, 1:31–33; the man born blind, 9:24–25). Some statement–misunderstanding–clarification patterns lead people into knowledge of Jesus' secrets, whereas other instances of it confirm the audience's inability to know anything spiritual. Some receive special revelations, such as the Samaritan woman (4:25–26), Martha (11:25), and Mary Magdalene (20:17–18). Not everybody knows all things. Finally, the gossip network discloses knowledge to select insiders (1:35–51; 4:28–30; 11:3, 28; 11:45–51; 12:21–22; 20:17, 24).

Espionage: Discovering Secrets. Throughout the narrative, outsiders constantly ask questions such as, "How can this be?" (3:4, 9; 6:42, 53; 8:33; 12:34), "Who are you?" (8:25, 53; 12:34), "Who can it be?" (13:24–25), "Why do you do this?" (1:22, 25; 13:37; 14:22), or "What business is this of yours?" (21:22–23; see also 2:4). People endlessly scrutinize Jesus' words to discover his secrets. Jesus' enemies are constantly seeking information about him (5:13–15; 11:46–47). Jesus' discourse has been subject to intense scrutiny throughout the forensic proceedings against him in Chapters 5, 7, 8, 9, 10, and 18:33–19:11. Eventually, espionage will lead to putting Jesus on trial, where formal attempts will be made to learn his secrets (18:19–21).

Ambiguity. Things are seldom what they seem: Jesus' *healings*, which appear to violate the Sabbath (5:9–10; 7:21–23; 9:14); *judging by appearances* (7:24; 8:15); and *thinking one knows something* (insiders, 11:11–13; 13:29; 20:15; outsiders, 5:39, 45; 16:2).

Secrecy and Character Differentiation. The fact that Jesus knows all things confirms him as the unique Word of God who alone speaks the words of God (1:18). All other characters in the narrative, moreover, may be classified as insiders or outsiders in terms of what they truly know. And even among the insiders, some know more, thus confirming their high status within the group.

Disciple	Knowledge	Status
	what does this character know?	
John the Baptizer	*knowledge*: Lamb of God . . . I saw the Spirit descend and remain . . . the Son of God	*witness*: even in the prologue, he is the premier witness; speaks in defense of and in confession of Jesus; sends his disciples to Jesus; no envy of Jesus

Andrew, Philip, Nathanael, and other traditional disciples	*knowledge*: Jesus is Messiah . . . the one of whom Moses and the prophets wrote . . . Son of God and King of Israel.	*genuine insiders*: moderate status because the Christological information is "low Christology"; conduits of information to others
Nicodemus	*knowledge*: Jesus is a teacher come from God.	*low status*: comes at night; knows with earthly knowledge; never leads others to Jesus
Peter	*knowledge*: Jesus is the Holy One of God.	*insider*: but until 21:15 of ambiguous status; limited knowledge about Jesus; depends on others for knowledge; never brings information to others
Samaritan woman	*knowledge*: Jesus is greater than our father Jacob . . . a prophet . . . the Messiah; she receives a Christophany.	*significant insider*: transformed from "not in the know" to very much "in the know"; possesses very important knowledge, especially a Christophany; serves as conduit of information to others
Man born blind	*knowledge*: Jesus is a prophet . . . cannot be a sinner . . . must be authorized by God . . . Son of man	*very high status as insider*: transformed from "blind" to "in the know"; receives a Christophany; bold confession of Jesus in public; conduit of information about Jesus to others, even if others refuse it
Martha	*knowledge*: Jesus is the Resurrection and the Life . . . the Christ, the Son of God, he who is coming into the world.	*still higher status*: a beloved disciple; led from solid knowledge to still higher knowledge; special Christophany; conduit of information to others
Mary Magdalene	*knowledge*: Rabbi; great mystery revealed to her	*very high status*: called by name; transformed from "not in the know" to "in the know"; special Christophany with very esoteric knowledge; conduit of information to others
Beloved Disciple	*knowledge*: knows identity of the traitor; sees and believes at the tomb; recognizes Jesus on the shore	*highest status* in the group: most beloved by Jesus and physically closest to him; always maximally "in the know"; conduit of information to others

Is Jesus dissembling when he tells Annas that he has always spoken openly in public for all to hear? Or is this another ironic statement, which clues the reader in to the fact that Annas, like so many others in the Temple, could never understand Jesus, even if he heard him speak? Because they are not his sheep, they cannot hear his voice. Nothing Jesus could possibly say to him would find a home in Annas, for he is the enemy of God's Word.

What Does Peter's "Denial" Mean? If to "know" or "acknowledge" Jesus means to show loyalty to him, then "to deny" breaks all ties of commitment, friendship, and loyalty. Thus we find elsewhere in the New Testament Jesus or God saying to someone, "I have never known you" (Matt 7:23; 25:12; Luke 13:25–27), which severs the relationship. An apt parallel to this is found in the Talmud: "And the rabbi said 'Ben Kappara, I have never known you.' He (Ben Kappara) realized that he (the rabbi) had taken the offense to heart, and so submitted himself to (the disability of a) reproof for 30 days"(*b. Moed Katan* 16a). Moreover, when we hear Paul talking about Christians being "known by God," this signals election and favor (1 Cor 8:3; Gal 4:9). Conversely, if disciples fail to follow group policy, they are "not known": "Whoever does not know [this] is not known" (1 Cor 14:38). Thus Peter's "I do not know the man" breaks all ties of loyalty with Jesus; all relationship ceases. Peter now stands intimidated in the midst of Jesus' enemies (see 9:22; 12:42).

Shepherd and Sheep. We should compare the events here with Jesus' description of the noble shepherd in 10:1–18, for in this we can discern the plot of the current narrative:

Shepherd in 10:1–18	*Shepherd in 18:1–27*
1. Going in and going out: "He will go in and out and find pasture" (10:9).	1. Going out and going in: "he went forth with his disciples . . . a garden, which he and his disciples entered" (18:1)
2. The place of the sheep in the Shepherd's life: "I lay down my life for my sheep" (10:10–11, 14).	2. Shepherd in place of the sheep: "If I am the one you want, let these others go" (18:8).
3. Shepherd's voluntary death: "No one takes my life from me; I lay it down of my own accord" (10:18).	3. Not a victim, but one who offers his life (18:8)

The symmetry between John 10 and John 18 reinforces our acknowledgment of Jesus as the Noble Shepherd. How noble of this shepherd to go voluntarily to a death that will benefit others! During this narrative there is another shepherd who is "noble," namely the Beloved Disciple. It is certainly courageous to enter the palace of Jesus' enemies and later to stand beside Jesus on the cross. Fear never keeps him from a public expression of loyalty. But his current relationship with Peter deserves attention, for the choreography of 18:16 indicates that the Beloved Disciple is the shepherd, Peter the sheep, and the maid at the door the doorkeeper who opens for the shepherd.

Noble Shepherd in John 10	Beloved Disciple as Shepherd in John 18
1. *Shepherd enters by the door*: "He who enters by the door is the shepherd of the sheep" (10:2).	1. *BD enters by the door*: "As this disciple was known to the high priest, he entered . . . while Peter stood outside at the door" (18:15).
2. *Gatekeeper recognizes him*: "He who enters by the door is the shepherd of the sheep. To him the gatekeeper opens" (10:2–3).	2. *Gatekeeper recognizes him*: "So the other disciple, who was known to the high priest, went out and spoke to the maid who kept the door" (18:16).
3. *He leads the sheep in/out*: "He calls his own sheep by name and leads them out. When he has brought out all his own, he goes before them, and the sheep follow him" (10:3–4).	3. *He leads the sheep in*: "Peter stood outside the door. . . . The other disciple spoke to the maid who kept the door and brought Peter in" (18:16).[468]

As we saw in 13:37, Peter claimed the role and status of the shepherd, boasting that he had the stuff of "noble" shepherds: "I will lay down my life for you." All talk! Jesus will eventually transform Peter into a chief shepherd (21:15–18), when his loyalty is strong enough and when he truly is ready to "glorify God by his death." But not now.

JOHN 18:28–40 – JESUS FACES THE "FRIEND OF CAESAR"

28 Then they took Jesus from Caiaphas to Pilate's headquarters. It was early in the morning. They themselves did not enter the headquarters, so as to avoid ritual defilement and to be able to eat the Passover.

29 So Pilate went out to them and said, "What accusation do you bring against this man?"

30 They answered, "If this man were not a criminal, we would not have handed him over to you."

31 Pilate said to them, "Take him yourselves and judge him according to your law." The Jews replied, "We are not permitted to put anyone to death."

32 (This was to fulfill what Jesus had said when he indicated the kind of death he was to die.)

33 Then Pilate entered the headquarters again, summoned Jesus, and asked him, "Are you the King of the Jews?"

34 Jesus answered, "Do you ask this on your own, or did others tell you about me?"

35 Pilate replied, "I am not a Jew, am I? Your own nation and the chief priests have handed you over to me. What have you done?"

---

[468] J. H. Neyrey, "Footwashing," in *Social World of the First Christians* (1995), 209–10.

36 Jesus answered, "My kingdom is not from this world. If my kingdom were from this world, my followers would be fighting to keep me from being handed over to the Jews. But as it is, my kingdom is not from here."

37 Pilate asked him, "So you are a king?" Jesus answered, "You say that I am a king. For this I was born, and for this I came into the world, to testify to the truth. Everyone who belongs to the truth listens to my voice."

38 Pilate asked him, "What is truth?" After he had said this, he went out to the Jews again and told them, "I find no case against him.

39 But you have a custom that I release someone for you at the Passover. Do you want me to release for you the King of the Jews?"

40 They shouted in reply, "Not this man, but Barabbas!" Now Barabbas was a bandit.

Setting the Stage: The Roman Trial. The choreography of this scene describes how Jesus and Pilate four times "go in" (18:28, 33; 19:1, 9) and "go out" (18:29, 38; 19:4–5, 12). It would be a mistake, however, to label these movements as transitions from "public" to "private."[469] When officials such as Annas, Caiaphas, and Pilate hold audiences like this, they are always "public." This is not a private tête-à-tête but a public meeting because it occurs in the forum in which political figures conduct civic affairs.[470]

Those of the Truth Hear My Voice. Although Pilate is not the last person to hear Jesus' voice, he marks a convenient place to reflect on the significance of this motif in the narrative. Of course, "hearing" is much more than attending to mere physical sound, also expressing attachment to Jesus as shepherd and the process of becoming a disciple. Outsiders hear noise; insiders hear their names, revelation, and summons.

We know that many simply do not hear at all (5:37); they cannot understand "because they cannot bear to hear my words" (8:43). Nor do authentic sheep of Jesus' flock listen to the voice of other shepherds, but instead flee from them "because they do not know the voice of strangers" (10:5). Thus there appears to be a spectrum of kinds of listeners. Nicodemus, for example, listens to Jesus' words but hears nothing; no change occurs in him (3:3–5). Although the people of Sychar hear the voice of the woman at the well, they finally dismiss her voice: "It is no longer because of what you said that we believe, for we have heard for ourselves, and we know that this is truly the Savior of the world" (4:42). Who, then, hears Jesus in such a way as to become an insider, even an elite in the group?

---

[469] J. H. Neyrey, "Despising the Shame," *Semeia* 69 (1996), 121–22; but see R. E. Brown, *Gospel According to John* (1970), 2.857–59.

[470] For a fuller understanding of "public" and "private," see J. H. Neyrey, "Teaching You in Public and from House to House," *JSNT* 26 (2003), 75–79, 87–88, 93–95.

1. John the Baptizer hears the voice of the bridegroom (3:29).
2. The dead will hear the voice of the Son of God and those who hear will live (5:25).
3. All in the tombs will hear his voice and come forth (5:29).
4. The sheep hear his voice and he calls his own sheep (10:3).
5. The sheep follow him because they know his voice (10:4).
6. I have other sheep . . . and they will heed my voice (10:16).
7. My sheep hear my voice, and I know them, and they follow me (10:27).
8. Everyone who belongs to the truth listens to my voice (18–37).

To round out this motif, we note that Jesus actually calls some people by name who are true insiders and elites: "Lazarus, come forth" (11:42), "Mary" (20:16), and "Simon, son of John" (21:15). Although we know the names of many people, both disciples and outsiders, Jesus speaks only these names. We are informed, moreover, that some disciples have "heard and learned from the Father" and so have come to Jesus (6:45), but others who are not of God cannot hear the words of God (8:47). Finally, we know that Jesus, too, hears the words of God (3:32; 5:30; 8:40) and that God in turn hears Jesus' words (9:31; 11:41–42; 14:24; 15:15). Thus Jesus, the consummate insider with God, hears the Father's words and is attached to God, just as his disciples hear his words, either because God teaches them or because they are insiders who grasp the secret and so are strongly attached to Jesus. Like "know," then, "hearing" and being "called by name" are indices of true discipleship and insider status.

Shape of the Story: Choreography of a Roman Trial. The typical Roman trial contains the following elements.[471]

Arrest. Jesus was *"arrested"* by the retainers of the Temple elites (18:3, 12–14).

Charges. Back in 11:45–52, we learned that envy drove the process against Jesus,[472] although earlier the elites *accused* Jesus of being a deceiver (7:13, 47) and a lawbreaker (9:24). But later we are told that they have "hated me without cause" (15:25). Ironically, his accusers will claim that it is "not lawful" for them to put Jesus to death themselves, although they have tried repeatedly to do so and even condemned him to death in absentia (11:45–52), which was contrary to their law (7:51). But in 18:29–31 we hear no charge, which emphasizes the illegality of the proceedings. The chief priests seek a death penalty but do not specify which evil or crime of Jesus' deserves this. All they can say is that Jesus is an "evildoer" (18:30).

---

[471] See A. N. Sherwin-White, *Roman Society and Roman Law* (1963); and Henry J. Cadbury, "Roman Law and the Trial of Paul," in F. J. Foakes Jackson and Kirsopp Lake, eds., *The Beginnings of Christianity* (Grand Rapids, MI: Baker Book House, 1979), 5.297–312.

[472] John 11:47–48. See J. H. Neyrey and R. L. Rohrbaugh, "He Must Increase, I Must Decrease," *CBQ* 63 (2001), 476–81; and A. C. Hagedorn and J. H. Neyrey, "Envy," *JSNT* 69 (1998), 38–50.

Judicial Inquiry (Cognitio). Although we observed a brief judicial inquiry of Jesus before Annas, the formal inquiry by the judge occurs when Jesus stands before Pilate. The questioning is about kings and kingdoms, political reasons why Jesus should be executed, if true. Yes, he is a king, but no, his kingdom is not of this world. So where is the danger to Rome? In the question–answer exchange, Pilate asks questions, apparently for information to judge rightly, and Jesus answers. As with most questions, Pilate's are challenges, yet in this context Jesus testifies to the truth about himself. Hence, he models the way disciples should act in comparable crises (see Matt 10:17–20; Luke 21:12–19); he speaks plainly and boldly about the Christ, whatever the consequences. There is no possibility of Pilate hearing his voice and becoming one of his sheep (10:3–4, 27) because when Jesus extends this possibility, "Everyone who belongs to the truth listens to my voice" (18:37), Pilate mocks his voice: "What is truth?" (18:38).

Verdict. Nevertheless, Pilate declares Jesus innocent of all crimes (18:38).

Judicial Warning. Luke labels the next event correctly by considering it a judicial warning, a punishment administered to those found to be disturbing the public peace; it was followed by expulsion (Luke 23:16). Hence the soldiers scourge Jesus and mock him, after which Pilate displays this chastened prisoner to the crowds. We are reminded of how the Romans "taught Paul a lesson" when on three occasions they beat him with rods (2 Cor 11:23–25).

Verdict and Sentence. Trials always end with a judgment, either innocence and release or guilt and sentence, usually immediately imposed. But Jesus' trial goes through a completely new cycle; hence the verdict and sentence are postponed. The new cycle begins with a fresh accusation: "He makes himself the Son of God."

Elements of a Roman Trial	First Part of Trial (18:1–19:4)	Second Part of Trial (19:5–16)
1. Arrest	"The band of soldiers seized Jesus and bound him" (18:1–11).	(Already arrested)
2. Charges	"If this man were not an evildoer . . ." (18:29–30)	"We have a law and according to that law he ought to die" (19:7).
3. Judge's Cognitio	"Are you the king of the Jews?" (18:33–38).	"Where are you from? . . . Do you not know that I have power . . ." (19:8–11).
4. Verdict	"I find no crime in him" (18:39).	"I find no crime in him" (19:6).
5. Acquittal or sentence	—	"'Shall I crucify your king'? 'We have no king but Caesar!' He handed him over to be crucified" (19:12–16).
6. Judicial warning	Chastisement and release (19:1–4)	—

Barabbas. Although we are historically certain of the structure of Roman trials as just listed, no historical data exist for the release of Barabbas in 18:38–40.[473] Although the evangelists agree that it was a "custom" for the procurator to release a prisoner, they disagree concerning the legal status of Barabbas. Some identify Barabbas as a "rebel who committed murder in an insurrection" (Mark 15:7; Luke 23:19),[474] others as "a robber" (John 18:40; see also 12:6), which might indicate that he was a rebel.[475] There is a certain staged quality in juxtaposing Jesus with Barabbas, for several things happen:

1. *Injustice.* A murderer is set free while an innocent man is condemned.
2. *False judgment.* The crowds once more judge unjustly and so bring judgment upon themselves.
3. *The real rebel goes free.* If Barabbas is a "rebel" who was engaged in an insurrection to cast off Rome's power, according to Pilate's *cognitio* (18:33–38), then Jesus, the genuine king, appears as no threat to Caesar. His kingdom is not of this world and so his followers do not fight to prevent his being handed over to the Jerusalem elites (18:36).
4. *Irony.* The "chief priests" declare loyalty to Caesar (19:15) despite choosing the rebel Barabbas, the revolutionary.

JOHN 19:1–5 – IRONY: SHAME LEADS TO GLORY

1 Then Pilate took Jesus and had him flogged.
2 And the soldiers wove a crown of thorns and put it on his head, and they dressed him in a purple robe.
3 They kept coming up to him, saying, "Hail, King of the Jews!" and striking him on the face.
4 Pilate went out again and said to them, "Look, I am bringing him out to you to let you know that I find no case against him."
5 So Jesus came out, wearing the crown of thorns and the purple robe. Pilate said to them, "Here is the man!"

---

[473] See Robert L. Merritt, "Jesus, Barabbas, and the Paschal Pardon," *JBL* 104 (1985), 57–68. Although he concurs that "there was no custom of *privilegium paschale* in the Roman Empire or in Judea" (p. 67) in other times and places in the ancient world, prisoners were released at festivals.

[474] On Barabbas as a revolutionary, see Paul Winter, *The Trial of Jesus* (Berlin: De Gruyter, 1961); and S. G. F. Brandon, *The Trial of Jesus* (London: Granada Publishing, 1968), 25–29, 140–150. A critique of these is found in M. Hengel, *Was Jesus a Revolutionist?* (Philadelphia: Fortress Press, 1971).

[475] On social banditry, see R. A. Horsley and J. S. Hanson, *Bandits, Prophets and Messiahs* (1985), 48–69.

What Hurts Worse, Pain or Shame? Israelite floggings were restricted by law (Deut 25:3) and custom (*m. Makkoth* 3.10–14) to thirty-nine lashes (see Acts 5:40; 2 Cor 11:24). In contrast, Roman floggings consisted of three types: beating (*fustigatio*), flogging (*flagellatio*), and scourging (*verberatio*). They administered the first as a judicial warning (Luke 23:15; 2 Cor 11:25), the second for serious crimes, and the third as part of the death sentence. Roman citizens were exempt from this last, which was restricted to slaves, rebels, and criminals. Although such beatings were extremely painful, they were the lesser of the pains endured here. Beatings were generally publicly administered to shame the offender and to warn others who would see it inflicted. Such gruesome spectacles were also for the entertainment of the crowds. So, all eyes watched as the sentenced person was stripped naked. Even in the Mishnah we read that one-third of the blows were given to the front of the body and the rest to the back, suggesting that the person being flogged was beaten on the tenderest parts of the body – the thighs, groin, and belly – as well as the back and buttocks. In the case of Jesus, the scourging is downplayed in the narrative, whereas his mocking as king is emphasized.[476] In an honor–shame world, the insults, humiliations, and mockery would crush the soul as no whip could. Warriors, at least, were trained to endure pain with nobility and courage.[477] Suffering was likened to a school where one becomes "perfect" (Heb 5:9). But shame is never deflected: This challenge (scourging of the body, a mockery of the spirit) has no riposte. There will never be revenge for being slapped in the face (19:3). But being stripped before all and fixed naked[478] to a cross bring shock to the soul long before the body fails. Shame kills.

Crown of Acanthus. All evangelists who mention Jesus' "crowning" indicate that the crown was made of "acanthus," a thistle type plant with broad saw-toothed leaves.[479] A "crown" would easily be made by positioning the leaves vertically around the head and securing them with a cord. The effect, then, mimics the rays of light springing from the head, an image used to portray

---

[476] The flagstone floor of the residence of the Roman soldiers in Jerusalem contains markings scratched in it for games, such as a "king" game (basileus = king), but most scholars date this well after the time of Pilate and Jesus; see Marie Aline de Sion, *La Forteresse Antonia a Jerusalem et la Question du Pretoire* (Jerusalem: Franciscalium, 1955), 139–42.

[477] John J. Pilch, "'Beat His Ribs While He is Young' (Sir 30:12): A Window on the Mediterranean World," *BTB* 23 (1993), 103–10. The victim's silence during torture was a mark of honor (see Isa 53:7; Cicero, *In Verrem* 2.5.162; Josephus, *War* 6.304).

[478] On the shame of being stripped naked, see Jerome H. Neyrey, "Naked," in John J. Pilch and Bruce Malina, eds., *Handbook of Biblical Social Values* (Peabody, MA: Hendrickson, 1998), 136–42.

[479] Frederick Danker (*BDAG*, 34) notes that "acanthus" refers to useless, thorny weeds growing in fields, "esp. the common weed Ononis spinosa, cammock." The point we make here is that "thorn" or "thorny" refers to something more like a thistle than the long spikes of a hawthorn.

gods and monarchs on coins.[480] The point of this type of crown is mockery and dishonor, not torture. Again, shame, not pain.

JOHN 19:6–16 – WHEN WILL THIS TRIAL END?

6 When the chief priests and the police saw him, they shouted, "Crucify him! Crucify him!" Pilate said to them, "Take him yourselves and crucify him; I find no case against him."
7 The Jews answered him, "We have a law, and according to that law he ought to die because he has claimed to be the Son of God."
8 Now when Pilate heard this, he was more afraid than ever.
9 He entered his headquarters again and asked Jesus, "Where are you from?" But Jesus gave him no answer.
10 Pilate therefore said to him, "Do you refuse to speak to me? Do you not know that I have power to release you, and power to crucify you?"
11 Jesus answered him, "You would have no power over me unless it had been given you from above; therefore the one who handed me over to you is guilty of a greater sin."
12 From then on Pilate tried to release him, but the Jews cried out, "If you release this man, you are no friend of the emperor. Everyone who claims to be a king sets himself against the emperor."
13 When Pilate heard these words, he brought Jesus outside and sat on the judge's bench at a place called The Stone Pavement, or in Hebrew Gabbatha.
14 Now it was the day of Preparation for the Passover; and it was about noon. He said to the Jews, "Here is your King!"
15 They cried out, "Away with him! Away with him! Crucify him!" Pilate asked them, "Shall I crucify your King?" The chief priests answered, "We have no king but the emperor."
16 Then he handed him over to them to be crucified. So they took Jesus,

Trial Resumed. The trial will not end because "the chief priests and the officers" raise a *new charge* that warrants the death penalty: "He has made himself the son of God" (19:7). Readers have heard regularly how Jesus is charged with "making himself" something, – equal to God (5:18; 10:33; see also 8:53), "Son of God" (9:7), or "king" (19:12).[481] The charge is false because we know that whoever Jesus is and whatever he does, God has made him such. Although

---

[480] H. St. J. Hart, "The Crown of Thorns in Jn 19:2–5 (with two plates)," *JTS* 3 (1952), 66–75.
[481] In antiquity, people were constantly "making themselves" something; that is, claiming a new and higher status or role (Acts 5:36) (*kenodoxos* and *alazōn*; see Acts 8:9; 12:22–23; Josephus, *War* 2.55, 60; Josephus, *Ant.* 17.272, 278).

Jesus responded to such charges in the narrative, he offers none here. Yet this new charge prompts a new *cognitio*, in which Pilate aggressively questions Jesus, based on the judge's power to extract speech from the accused. Pilate joins the many who ask *whence* Jesus comes (19:9). Although Jesus' silence could mean that he is rendered "speechless" and so loses the contest,[482] we best interpret it as a posture of authority. By refusing to speak to Pilate, he defends his honor by this gesture. Pilate ironically claims power to release or crucify Jesus, power that all the other players in this drama hold in contempt. Although we know that Pilate cannot hear Jesus' voice (18:37), Jesus nevertheless speaks in order to refute Pilate's claims to power. He claims that all power resides in God, whence Jesus has come. Finally, the judge judges justly that Jesus is innocent (19:12).

Irony: Who Has the Power? Pilate claims power to release or crucify Jesus but is himself subject to the power of the crowd. Furthermore, his power is contingent on the emperor's patronage, which can be removed by the stroke of a pen.[483] Ostensibly to maintain Caesar's "friendship," Pilate seats himself on his official judicial throne (*bema*) with a full panoply of soldiers and all the trappings of military power. But his claim to power is empty, for when he says "Behold your king," the crowds smartly challenge this title and Pilate's attempt to release Jesus. So much for power! And by consulting the crowd to ask "Shall I crucify your king?" Pilate proves that he has lost control of the events. No, he does not have power to release or to crucify Jesus (19:10); this belongs to others.

"Friends" of Caesar. Patronage is the appropriate scenario in which to view the Judean questioning of whether Pilate is a "'friend' of Caesar" (see the commentary on 15:14–15). "Friend" here refers to a client who depends on a patron for wealth, power, and status.[484] If Pilate was the loyal "friend" of Caesar, he would not tolerate another king, a rival to Caesar. In another ironic gesture, the chief priests themselves protest loyalty to Pilate's patron, "We have no king but Caesar," a truly bizarre claim. For, in becoming "friends" of Caesar, they have forsworn friendship with Israel's God. Meeks cites the conclusion of the Great Hallel, which indicates how shameful this crowd is for rejecting its one and only King.

---

[482] J. H. Neyrey, "Questions," *CBQ* 60 (1998), 678.

[483] Philo writes that after a conflict between Pilate and the Jerusalem leaders, they "sent letters of supplication to Tiberias" (*Gaius* 301–3); such reports eventually occasioned the emperor Vitellius to suspend Pilate in 37 CE. See E. M. Smallwood, "The Date of the Dismissal of Pontius Pilate from Judea," *JJS* 5 (1954), 12–21.

[484] Josephus described a circle of aristocrats as "persons of power among the Friends of the King" (*Ant.* 12.298); Antiochus wrote to his "Governors and Friends" (*Ant.* 12.134). See P. A. Brunt, "'Amicitia' in the Late Roman Republic," *Proceedings of the Cambridge Philological Society* 191 (1965), 1–20.

From everlasting to everlasting thou art God;
Beside thee we have no king, redeemer, or savior;
No liberator, deliverer, provider;
None who takes pity in every time of distress or trouble.
We have no king but thee.[485]

A CLOSER LOOK – WHAT KIND OF CHARACTER IS PILATE?

Appointed in 27 CE, Pilate was removed from office in 37 CE. The Gospels all imply that Pilate lacked courage (Mark 15:15; Matt 27:24–25); having declared Jesus innocent, he nevertheless "handed him over to them to be crucified." Yet his contemporaries called him "inflexible, harsh and obdurate."[486] For example, Philo's *Embassy to Gaius* recounts how Pilate brought golden shields into Jerusalem, a bold show of power and contempt (298–305). Josephus relates several crises provoked by Pilate. On one occasion, he brought standards of the Roman legion secretly into Jerusalem, which caused a riot among the people; only when troops faced the people, who did not back down, did Pilate remove them (*Wars* 2.169–74). On another occasion, he confiscated the treasury called "Karbona" to build an aqueduct. In the face of the ensuing turmoil, Pilate had soldiers dressed like the locals mingle with the crowd and then attack them (*Wars* 2.175–77). Why, then, do the evangelists present a radically different Pilate? Some argue that they present Jesus and his disciples as unthreatening to Rome's hegemony, hence the apologetic interpretation of the scene. Pilate finds Jesus innocent, Matthew says that his wife had a dream suggesting the same, and the executioner eventually acknowledges Jesus to be a blessed and God-favored man.

King of the Judeans. During the synoptic Passion Narrative, Jesus is titled "prophet," "Christ," "Son of God," "Son of Man," and "King of the Judeans," the last of which becomes the premier status marker in John. From beginning to end, this title has been the most consistently used label for Jesus, from Nathanael's acknowledgment ("Son of God, King of Israel," 1:49) to the crowd's attempt to make him king (6:16), to the controversy over Jesus' descent from David (7:43), and then the discourse on the true shepherd (10:1–18), the background of which echoes David's prior status as both shepherd of his father's sheep and then shepherd of Israel. This metaphor was then extended to Israel's other kings.[487] Next, the crowds acclaim him "king" as he enters the royal city (12:13, 15), which

---

[485] W. A. Meeks, *The Prophet King* (1967), 77.
[486] See Carl Kraeling, "The Episode of the Roman Standards at Jerusalem," *HTR* 35 (1942), 263–89; and Daniel R. Schwartz, "Pontius Pilate," *ABD* 5.395–401.
[487] Johannes Beutler, S. J., "Der alttestamentlich-jüdische Hintergrund der Hirtenrede in Johannes 10," in Johannes Beutler, S. J., and Robert T. Fortna, eds., *The Shepherd Discourse in John 10 and Its Context* (Cambridge: Cambridge University Press, 1990), 23–30.

is the narrative background for Pilate's interrogation of Jesus as king (18:33, 37) and mockery (19:3, 12–15, 19–21). What content might an audience invest in the title "king"?

Scholars now know that many men who either styled themselves as "kings" or were acclaimed by others as such rose up in revolt against Rome's crushing taxation policies. Jesus' feeding of 5,000 with enough bread that all "ate their fill" is a political statement on behalf of overtaxed peasants; hence they seek to make him "king" (6:15). But in 18:33–37, we learn that despite how others interpret him, he has no ambitions to rule Israel as Caesar does because "my kingdom is not of this world" (18:36). If his kingdom was like any other political rule, then his soldiers would surely defend him (18:10–11). But he is not of this world, nor is he from below (8:23). Moreover, unlike most figures surveyed by Horsley and Hanson,[488] Jesus does *not* "make himself King" (19:12), just as he does not make himself "equal to God" or make any other ambitious honor claim. In Johannine irony, others make Jesus "king," first the Roman soldiers (19:1–3) and then Pilate (19:19–22). But the person who truly ascribes honor to Jesus is his heavenly Father.

Kingly Benefaction. What benefaction does Jesus the King mediate? What power does he wield? He tells Pilate that he "bears witness to the truth" (18:37), indicating that his paramount benefaction is unique knowledge of God and God's words (1:18). Yet he has also brokered: *inducement* (foods to eat and abundant wine to drink), *power* (healings and raising of the dead), *commitment* (beloved disciples, friends, vine for the branches), and *influence* (the Word who reveals God and God's words). Inasmuch as all ancients equated kingship with power, we are given a special view of Jesus' eschatological power in the Passion Narrative: He lays down his life voluntarily, and is no victim; he has power to lay down his life and power to take it back; and a curious scholarly reading of 19:13 suggests that Pilate seats Jesus on the procurator's own throne, thus making Jesus the judge.[489]

Crowned and Enthroned. Kings must be publicly enthroned, for which they experience a status-transformation ritual as they assume their new role and status. So, too, of Jesus. Pilate's *cognitio* of Jesus in 18:33–38 establishes *that* Jesus is a king. The judicial warning administered in 19:1–4 ironically serves as his crowning and public acclamation as king. It has long been observed that the scourging of Jesus is followed by a tableau that resembles the acclamation of

---

[488] R. A. Horsley and J. S. Hanson, *Bandits, Prophets, and Messiahs* (1985), 5–87.

[489] Ignace de la Potterie, in his "Jesus King and Judge according to John 19:13," *Scripture* 13 (1961), 97–98, cites this text from Justin: "And they clothed him with purple and set him on the seat of judgment saying, 'Judge righteously, King of Israel'" (Gospel of Peter 7) and "They tormented him and set him on the judgment seat, and said, 'Judge us'" (*1 Apology* 35).

Caesar by the Roman army, now ironically acted out on Jesus.[490] He is *crowned* with a crown of acanthus, *robed* in a purple robe, *acclaimed* king ("Hail, King of the Jews"), *honored* and *acknowledged* by the soldiers bending their knee before him, and the synoptics add a fifth item, a *reed scepter* placed in his hand. As the story is told, the Romans mock his vain claims to royal status, dishonor him, and thus prove his claims to be empty. By their actions, Jesus should be utterly humiliated and reduced to zero social worth.[491] But in the eyes of the evangelist, this ironically serves as a status-elevation ritual, whereby Jesus is invested with royal status.[492] Readers have already been conditioned to know that Jesus' "lifting up" is both his crucifixion, his being lifted back to heaven (3:14; 8:23; 12:32), and his glorification (12:23; 13:31–32; 17:1, 5). Finally, the crucifixion of Jesus may be read as the enthronement of the king, the cross being his throne, with the title fixed to it ironically acknowledging his role and even the Romans agreeing to it. Thus the Romans mock Jesus as king even as the Israelites reject every other king, God included, but Caesar (19:15). But insiders see an entirely different scene, namely, Jesus' enthronement as Lord and King.

JOHN 19:17–30 – IT IS ACCOMPLISHED

17 and carrying the cross by himself, he went out to what is called The Place of the Skull, which in Hebrew is called Golgotha.

18 There they crucified him, and with him two others, one on either side, with Jesus between them.

19 Pilate also had an inscription written and put on the cross. It read, "Jesus of Nazareth, the King of the Jews."

20 Many of the Jews read this inscription, because the place where Jesus was crucified was near the city; and it was written in Hebrew, in Latin, and in Greek.

21 Then the chief priests of the Jews said to Pilate, "Do not write, 'The King of the Jews,' but, 'This man said, I am King of the Jews.'"

22 Pilate answered, "What I have written I have written."

23 When the soldiers had crucified Jesus, they took his clothes and divided them into four parts, one for each soldier. They also took his tunic; now the tunic was seamless, woven in one piece from the top.

---

[490] Josef Blank, "Die Verhandlung vor Pilatus: Jo 18:28–19:16 in Lichte johanneischer Theologie," *BZ* 3 (1959), 62; and W. A. Meeks, *The Prophet King* (1967), 69–72.

[491] David Rensburger, in his *Johannine Faith and Liberating Community* (Philadelphia: Westminster, 1988), 93–94, interprets this scene as Pilate's humiliation of the Judeans by the sarcastic presentation of a Roman's interpretation of Israelite messianic hopes.

[492] P. Duke, *Irony in the Fourth Gospel* (1985), 131–32.

24 So they said to one another, "Let us not tear it, but cast lots for it to see who will get it." This was to fulfill what the scripture says, "They divided my clothes among themselves, and for my clothing they cast lots."

25 And that is what the soldiers did. Meanwhile, standing near the cross of Jesus were his mother, and his mother's sister, Mary the wife of Cleopas, and Mary Magdalene.

26 When Jesus saw his mother and the disciple whom he loved standing beside her, he said to his mother, "Woman, here is your son."

27 Then he said to the disciple, "Here is your mother." And from that hour the disciple took her into his own home.

28 After this, when Jesus knew that all was now finished, he said (in order to fulfill the scripture), "I am thirsty."

29 A jar full of sour wine was standing there. So they put a sponge full of the wine on a branch of hyssop and held it to his mouth.

30 When Jesus had received the wine, he said, "It is finished." Then he bowed his head and gave up his spirit.

The "Shame" of the Cross. Paul echoes popular sentiment about crucifixion when he states that Greeks consider it "folly" or "shame" and Judeans a "stumbling block" (1 Cor 1:23). The author of Hebrews rightly calls it "shame" (12:2). Various classical authors communicate a sense of the process of crucifixion, which at every step entailed progressive humiliation of the victim and total loss of honor.[493]

A CLOSER LOOK — SHAME AND THE CROSS

What was crucifixion like? Who was crucified? Crucifixion was the appropriate punishment for slaves (Cicero, *In Verrem* 2.5.168), bandits (Josephus, *War* 2.253), prisoners of war (Josephus, *War* 5.451), and revolutionaries (Josephus, *Ant.* 17.295). *Status Degradation Rituals*: Public trials created a new identity for the accused, namely a shameful person. *Flogging and torture*, especially the blinding of eyes and the shedding of blood, generally accompanied the sentence (Josephus, *War* 5.449–51 and 3.321; Livy 22.13.19; 28.37.3; Seneca, *On Anger* 3.6; Philo, *Flac.* 72; Diodorus Siculus 33.15.1). According to *m. Makkoth* 3.12, victims were scourged naked, both to the front and back of the body. Often they befouled themselves with urine or excrement *m. Mak.* (3.14). Those condemned were forced to *carry the cross beam* (Plutarch, *Delay* 554B). Property, normally only clothing, was *confiscated;* hence the accused were further shamed by being stripped naked (see Diodorus Siculus 33.15.1).[494]

---

[493] Martin Hengel, *Crucifixion* (London: SCM, 1977), 22–32; and Jerome H. Neyrey, "Honor and Shame in the Johannine Passion Narrative," *Semeia* 68 (1994), 113–15.

[494] On the shame of being stripped of one's clothing, see J. H. Neyrey, "Nudity," *Biblical Social Values* (1998), 136–38.

Victims *lost power* and thus honor through the pinioning of their hands and arms but especially by the mutilation of being nailed to the cross (Philo, *Post.* 61; *Somn.* 2.213). Executions served as crude forms of *public entertainment* as crowds ridiculed and mocked the victims (Philo, *Special Laws* 3.160), who were affixed to crosses in an odd and whimsical manner, including impalement (Seneca, *Consolatio ad Marciam* 20.3; Josephus, *War* 5.451). *Death by crucifixion was often slow and protracted.* Victims suffered bodily distortions, loss of bodily control, and gross enlargement of the penis.[495] Ultimately deprived of life, they lost the possibility of gaining satisfaction or vengeance. In many cases, victims were denied honorable burial; corpses were left on display and *devoured by carrion birds and scavenger animals* (Pliny, *H. N.* 36.107–108).

This list indicates how shameful certain events were in the Johannine Passion Narrative. Because Jesus was considered a revolutionary ("King of the Judeans"), crucifixion was the appropriate death. Kinds of death were status-specific; criminals, revolutionaries, and slaves were crucified, whereas Roman elites either committed suicide or were beheaded. Although Jesus was scourged as a "judicial warning," the process was no less ugly than a scourging in preparation for death. Inasmuch as his clothes were confiscated, we presume that he was crucified naked.

Because he later shows his hands to Thomas, we conclude that he was nailed to the cross (see 20:25, 27); Luke's mention of his "hands and feet" (24:39) implies that his feet were likewise nailed.[496] The process of dying, which might last days, is accelerated here because of the approaching Feast. The Temple elite press to have the legs of those crucified broken. Regarding mutilation, Jesus' side is speared, although his legs are not broken. Had the bodies been left on the cross, they would have either rotted or become food for scavenging birds and animals.[497]

Family Honor Defended. This Gospel implies that Jesus is the eldest son of an elderly widowed mother. As part of a son's duty to "honor"[498] his mother, he was to provide male protection and support for her when he died. Females without such guardians would be vulnerable because others would perceive their families

---

[495] Leo Steinberg, *The Sexuality of Jesus in Renaissance Rome and Its Modern Oblivion* (New York: Pantheon, 1983), 82–108. The phenomenon was known also in antiquity; see M. Hengel,*Crucifixion* (1977), 68, note 2.

[496] In a recently discovered tomb was found an ossuary with the bones of a crucified man; see V. Tzaferis, "Jewish Tombs at and near Giv'at ha-Mivtar, Jerusalem," *IEJ* 20 (1970), 18–32; and N. Haas, "Anthropological Observations on the Skeletal Remains from Giv'at ha-Mivtar," *IEJ* 20 (1970), 38–59. A sketch of crucifixion based on this may be found in J. H. Charlesworth,"Jesus and Jehohanan: An Archeological Note on Crucifixion," *ExpT* 84 (1973), 147–50.

[497] It is estimated that the crucified hung about six feet off the ground, making it easy for dogs to chew into the groin and gnaw into the soft belly tissue.

[498] On Jesus' honoring of his mother, see S. van Tilborg, *Imaginative Love* (1993), 9.

as unconcerned for their reputations, that is, they would be "shame-less." As Jesus dies, certain intimates appear at his cross, at such proximity as to conduct conversation. He addresses his mother not by her familial role, "mother," but as "woman," as he did earlier (2:4). Very much in control, he commands her to accept the Beloved Disciple as her "son," protector, and support: "Woman, behold your son!" Correspondingly, he changes the role and status of the Beloved Disciple to that of son, fictive kin but guardian nonetheless, of the woman: "Behold your mother."[499] The hero's mother, then, comes under the protection of a Beloved Disciple: "And from that hour the disciple took her into his own home" (19:27).

Jesus' Dying Words. Although all evangelists record some dying word by Jesus, we have three sets of different words:

Mark 15:35	"My God, my God, why have you abandoned me"?	(Ps 22:1)
Matthew 27:46	"My God, my God, why have you abandoned me"?	(Ps 22:1)
Luke 23:46	"Father, into your hands I commit my spirit."	(Ps 31:5)
John 19:28	"And to fulfill the Scriptures perfectly, he said, 'I thirst.'"	(Ps 69:1)
John 19:30	"It is finished."	

Except for John 19:30, these words all come from Israel's collection of psalms; that is, they are sanctioned prayers. Thus all evangelists dramatize Jesus praying to God as he dies.[500] We know from previous study of prayers in the Fourth Gospel that petitionary prayer is only one kind of prayer that Jesus prays (see "self-focused" prayer in John 17). Thus Jesus' "I thirst" should be considered a self-focused address to God that has little to do with wine and parched lips but rather is to ensure a lively relationship with God. Just as the bystanders utterly misunderstood Jesus' "My God, my God . . ." and thought that he called Elijah to rescue him, so, too, the soldiers here take Jesus' words literally and offer him a drink. The meaning, however, lies elsewhere.[501] The "cup" he drinks, we are told, is that presented by the Father (18:11).[502] If so, it expresses Jesus' full obedience to drink that cup, obey the divine will, and achieve the work for which he was sent.

The End. Yet Jesus says another word, "It is finished" (19:30), which like so many expressions of Jesus contains many meanings. On the one hand, it might express to outsiders that Jesus was worn down by his crucifixion and begs for death; on the other hand, the verb "finish" suggests a victory cry of faithfulness to his task

---

[499] S. van Tilborg's *Imaginative Love* (1993), 7–13, 94–96, notes that Jesus also honors his Father by fulfilling the paternal will, which is his death.

[500] J. H. Neyrey, *Honor and Shame* (1998), 151–61.

[501] One should link Jesus' "thirst" with his claim that others who drink of his water will never thirst again (4:13–14; 6:35; 7:37); just as "drink" has a literal and a spiritual meaning, so, too, does "thirst."

[502] R. E. Brown, *Gospel According to John* (1970), 2.929–30.

and perfection in its performance (see 13:1).[503] We presume that the evangelist understands "It is finished" as being addressed to God. Thus, it functions, like "I thirst," as a self-focused communication to God.

Pentecost and Cross? Many find ambiguous the remark that Jesus "handed over his spirit" (19:30), which may mean simply that he expired (i.e., ran out of breath) or that he bestowed the Spirit (i.e., "pentecost"). Again, this Gospel asks us not to be literal minded, especially in this scene. Hence the pentecost interpretation is not far-fetched because John's Gospel indeed compresses resurrection, ascension, and pentecost to one day (20:17–23). This, then, would be a superior benefaction achieved by Jesus' death. Moreover, only elite insiders standing around the cross would thus receive this spirit (Jesus' mother and mother's sister, the Beloved Disciple, and Mary Magdalene), confirming their elite status. Finally, inasmuch as he declared power to lay down his life and power to take it back, Jesus himself would seem to control the precise timing of that death. No one takes his life from him; he lays it down when and how he wishes.

Explanations of the Death of Jesus. We find in the Fourth Gospel six different ways of talking about and giving meaning to the death of Jesus.[504]

(1) Israel's Scriptures provide an apologetic argument that God has a will or plan observable in the Scriptures, which argues that there is a providential guiding of Jesus:[505]

2:12	(Ps 69:9) "Zeal for your house has consumed me."
3:14	(Num 21:9) "As Moses lifted up the serpent in the desert"
19:36	(Exod 12:46) "Not one bone of it shall be broken."

(2) Jesus predicts his death, indicating prophetic knowledge of it and thereby control (2:19; 10:11–18; 12:32–33; 13:21–30; 18:9, 32).

(3) Emphasis on the unjust, illegal proceedings against Jesus serves to dispel the gossip that he died as a criminal or a sinner.[506]

(4) Distinctive Johannine modes of talking about Jesus' death often use ambiguous or double-meaning words, such as "lift up" (8:28; 12:32–33); "glorify" (7:39; 13:31; 16:14; 17:1); "going away" (7:33–36; 8:21–22; 13:33, 36; 17:24); "going

---

[503] R. E. Brown, *Gospel According to John* (1970), 2.930.

[504] For a survey of motifs, see Godfrey C. Nicholson, *Death as Departure: The Johannine Descent–Ascent Schema* (Chico, CA: Scholars Press, 1983), 4–9.

[505] See also 13:18 = Psalm 41:9; 15:25 = Psalm 35:19; 19:24 = Psalm 22:18; 19:28 = Psalm 22:15; 19:37 = Zechariah 12:10.

[506] His trial is illegally conducted in his absence (11:45–53); he is unjustly manhandled by his interrogator (18:18–24); a traitor betrays him (18:1–9); and although his judge three times declares him innocent (18:38; 19:4–6, 12), he is sentenced to crucifixion.

back to where he was before" (6:62; 13:1–3; 17:5); "going to better pasture" (10:1–6, 14:2–4); and "laying down his life" (10:17–18; 11:50–53).

(5) The positive effects of Jesus' death are found in expressions such as John's labeling of him as "Lamb of God who takes away the sin of the world" (1:29). But the shepherd–sheep motif offers the most suggestive parallels. The Noble Shepherd draws all to himself (8:28; 10:16; 11:51–52; 12:32); by drawing them, they hear his voice (10:3, 26–27; 18:37) and they "go in and go out and find pasture" (10:3), which may include "eternal life" (10:27–29). The Noble Shepherd, as we saw, lays down his life for his sheep (10:11; 18:14).

(6) The high Christology described in 5:21–29 provides the most pregnant interpretation of the death of Jesus. Jesus claimed to have God's two powers, in particular God's eschatological power: He has "life in himself" (5:26) and power to raise the dead (5:25, 28–29). Later Jesus claims power to lay down his life and power to take it again (10:17–18). His death, then, does not mean what death means for mortals, for he "has life in himself" and "power to lay it down and take it back." In short, death is the occasion when Jesus manifests the greatest of all powers.[507]

JOHN 19:31–42 – THE BODY OF JESUS: MUTILATION? OR RESPECT?

31 Since it was the day of Preparation, the Jews did not want the bodies left on the cross during the sabbath, especially because that sabbath was a day of great solemnity. So they asked Pilate to have the legs of the crucified men broken and the bodies removed.

32 Then the soldiers came and broke the legs of the first and of the other who had been crucified with him.

33 But when they came to Jesus and saw that he was already dead, they did not break his legs.

34 Instead, one of the soldiers pierced his side with a spear, and at once blood and water came out.

35 (He who saw this has testified so that you also may believe. His testimony is true, and he knows that he tells the truth.)

36 These things occurred so that the scripture might be fulfilled, "None of his bones shall be broken."

37 And again another passage of scripture says, "They will look on the one whom they have pierced."

---

[507] J. Massingberd Ford, in "'Mingled Blood' from the Side of Christ (John XIX.34)," *NTS* 15 (1969), 337–38, argues from rabbinic texts that an animal was still kosher if from it came "mingled" blood and water.

38 After these things, Joseph of Arimathea, who was a disciple of Jesus, though a secret one because of his fear of the Jews, asked Pilate to let him take away the body of Jesus. Pilate gave him permission; so he came and removed his body.

39 Nicodemus, who had at first come to Jesus by night, also came, bringing a mixture of myrrh and aloes, weighing about a hundred pounds.

40 They took the body of Jesus and wrapped it with the spices in linen cloths, according to the burial custom of the Jews.

41 Now there was a garden in the place where he was crucified, and in the garden there was a new tomb in which no one had ever been laid.

42 And so, because it was the Jewish day of Preparation, and the tomb was nearby, they laid Jesus there.

Mutilation? Sacrifice? Mutilation of corpses was common in antiquity.[508] But the explanation for events described in John 19:31–34 provides an ironic take on this motif. Because of the sacredness of the approaching feast, which was so sacred that the high priests would not enter Pilate's quarters (18:28), Jesus and his co-crucified cannot remain dead and exposed. Hence, at the priests' request, Pilate had the legs of two criminals broken to hasten their deaths. Jesus, who was already dead, was speared, but why? To prove death? To mutilate? Very literal readings, but not in accord with our author's penchant for hiding spiritual meanings in literal matters, as in the case of "I thirst." To outsiders, the scene is mutilation; to insiders, Jesus is likened to the Passover lambs that at that hour were being slaughtered for the feast. The author secures this reading by citing two Scriptures, the first one from the Passover haggadah about the preparation of the lamb (Exod 12:46), and a corroborating passage (Zech 12:10). Seeing is not believing. Seeing is not even knowing.

Johannine Characters. We continue to examine how the Johannine group would evaluate the characters in the Passion Narrative and by what criteria. Two criteria emerge as most important. The first is knowledge: What do they know? do they possess any insider knowledge? And second, do they speak boldly in public about Jesus or are they secret, cowardly figures? Let us assess the dramatis personae in John 19, comparing, contrasting, and ranking them.

Chief Priests. Since John 5, they have sought to kill Jesus; they envied him so intensely that they plotted against him (11:47–52). Unsatisfied with Pilate's disciplining of Jesus, they demanded his death. And, finally, they protested to the title over the cross. Not just outsiders, they are wolves attacking shepherd and flock.

---

[508] Mutilation of corpses was particularly shameful when done to a fallen warrior; see Achilles' treatment of Hector's body in the *Iliad*; 1 Samuel 31:9–10; 2 Samuel 4:12; Josephus, *Ant.* 20.99.

Pilate. He, too, is an outsider, for he cannot hear Jesus' voice (10:5, 27; 18:37) and knows nothing, despite a lengthy *cognitio* of Jesus. When Jesus speaks to Pilate about his kingship and kingdom, he cannot understand spiritual things, like other deaf interlocutors from below. What Pilate says publicly about Jesus ("Behold your king," 19:14) is by no means a public confession of him.

Beloved Disciple. The consummate insider, he follows Jesus into Annas' palace and stands at the cross, thus proving his courage and public loyalty. As the disciple physically closest to Jesus at supper, he learns the identity of the traitor. And at the cross he becomes the fictive brother of Jesus and son of Jesus' mother, indications of exceptionally high status.

Woman and Mother. The evangelist imagines a radical character change in Mary since her appearance at Cana. Whereas at Cana she challenged Jesus to solve a family problem, her posture at the cross is that of great public loyalty. If formerly she did not know "the hour" of Jesus, she is sharing it now. And if Jesus' remarks to her at Cana seemed to lack respect, at the cross she is honored by having a noble disciple appointed as the guardian of her honor. Although we cannot say that Jesus' mother is distinguished by knowledge or revelations, her status is most honorable by virtue of her public stance at the cross and by association with the premier disciple. Although addressed as "woman," she acts the role of "mother," at least of the Beloved Disciple.

Mary of Cleopas and Mary of Magdala. The first Mary is Jesus' aunt, "his mother's sister," whose presence at the cross suggests a relationship of loyalty to Jesus; unlike the "brothers" (7:1–7), she appears to be a loyal, blood relative of Jesus. Mary Magdalene is only mentioned here; nevertheless, she demonstrates intense public loyalty to Jesus.

Joseph of Arimathea. All Gospels mention that Joseph comes forward to bury Jesus, although they disagree about his social status. Some state that he was a "member of the Sanhedrin" (Mark 15:43; Luke 23:50) or a rich man (Matt 27:57), all of which indicate high social status. John, however, omits all of this, commenting only that he was a "disciple of Jesus, though a secret one for fear of the Jews" (19:38). Joseph is thus linked to the "many authorities [who] believed in him, but for fear of the Pharisees did not confess it" (12:42). It is unclear if his public act of burying Jesus finally cancels the stigma of his secret discipleship.

Nicodemus. The ambiguity clouding Joseph also clings to Nicodemus. He, too, keeps the label of a "night-time" visitor, which negatively labels him as a "fearful, secret disciple," a fitting companion to Joseph. What are we to make of the immense volume of spices that he brings? So extraordinary an amount is often taken as a parody of his piety or as a sign of his conviction that Jesus is dead and starting to decompose.[509] Thus we conclude that Nicodemus knows nothing and so far has lacked courage.

Noble Death and Honorable Burial. Although all the Gospels relate that Joseph of Arimathea arranged for Jesus' burial, only John tells of a burial marked throughout by respect and honor.[510] Joseph and Nicodemus are high-status persons. The tomb has never been used, and so is not contaminated with dead men's bones. The volume of spices, even if an exaggeration, is a powerful mark of respect, such as might be used for royalty. The linen cloths in which Jesus was wrapped are difficult to identify, much less interpret. Some scholars, following Mark, claim that Jesus was wrapped in a shroud, but very little evidence exists to support a type of mummy wrapping.[511] Moreover, the narrator tells us that when Peter and the Beloved Disciple entered the empty tomb, they found "the linen wrappings lying there, and the cloth that had been on Jesus' head, not lying with the linen wrappings but rolled up in a place by itself" (20:6–7).

Judean Burial Customs. The narrator simply states that all happened according to "Judean burial customs,"[512] which were indeed quite simple. Typically, a corpse would be washed, presumably by female relatives, which is not mentioned in the Gospels. Depending on family wealth, oils and/or spices would be rubbed over the body, after which it would be wrapped in some cloth (nudity, even in death, is shameful). Finally, the body would be carried to a grave or tomb cut into rock, across the entrance to which a round stone was rolled. Burial garments, spices, and a new tomb are mentioned here. All in all, it was an honorable burial.

JOHN 20:1–10 – MANY WITNESSES TO AN EMPTY TOMB

1 Early on the first day of the week, while it was still dark, Mary Magdalene came to the tomb and saw that the stone had been removed from the tomb.
2 So she ran and went to Simon Peter and the other disciple, the one whom Jesus loved, and said to them, "They have taken the Lord out of the tomb, and we do not know where they have laid him."

---

[509] For the negative interpretation of Nicodemus, see D. D. Sylva, "Nicodemus and His Spices (John 19:39)," *NTS* 34 (1988), 148–51; M. de Jonge, *Jesus: Stranger* (1977), 32–33; and W. A. Meeks, "The Man from Heaven in Johannine Sectarianism," *JBL* 91 (1972), 54–55.

[510] Raymond E. Brown, *The Death of the Messiah: From Gethsemane to the Grave* (New York: Doubleday, 1994), 2.1258–65.

[511] R. E. Brown, *Death of the Messiah* (1994), 2.1264–65.

[512] S. Safrai, "Death, Burial and Mourning," in S. Safrai and M. Stern, eds., *The Jewish People in the First Century* (Philadelphia: Fortress Press, 1976), 2.773–87.

3 Then Peter and the other disciple set out and went toward the tomb.

4 The two were running together, but the other disciple outran Peter and reached the tomb first.

5 He bent down to look in and saw the linen wrappings lying there, but he did not go in.

6 Then Simon Peter came, following him, and went into the tomb. He saw the linen wrappings lying there,

7 and the cloth that had been on Jesus' head, not lying with the linen wrappings but rolled up in a place by itself.

8 Then the other disciple, who reached the tomb first, also went in, and he saw and believed;

9 for as yet they did not understand the scripture, that he must rise from the dead.

10 Then the disciples returned to their homes.

What Does "Resurrection" Mean? If we were reading the synoptic Gospels and Acts, "resurrection" would mean God's vindication of Jesus; that is, God's raising him up: "You killed him, but God raised him" (Acts 2:23; 3:14–15). By a splendid posthumous honoring, God delivered the perfect riposte to those who shamed his Son. Or, taking a clue from Daniel 7:14, one could argue that the person rejected on earth by mortals is vindicated in heaven by God. "Resurrection," then, means the undoing of shame, the final victory over enemies, and the glorification of the Noble Hero. But it means more, for God's "raising" also means raising Jesus to God's very throne and establishing him in a new role and status. Hence, when the New Testament cites Psalm 110:1, "The Lord said to my lord, 'Sit at my right hand,'" they understand that in addition to God's raising Jesus from death, "God made him Lord and Christ" (Acts 2:34–36).

But John's narrative uniquely speaks of the "resurrection" in other terms that emphasize Jesus' two powers and his equality with God. We recall how in 5:21–29 Jesus explains that he had God's eschatological power. God gave him all judgment, to have life in himself, to be honored equally with God, and to call in dead from their tombs to resurrection of life or judgment. This states that Jesus has power to call others to life, at which point he will exercise his future role as judge of all. His later remarks to Martha ("I am the resurrection and the life," 11:25) and the raising of Lazarus (11:44) function to confirm this power. But Jesus claimed that, just as God has life in himself, so, too, does Jesus "have life in himself." Because God is immortal, the same must be true of Jesus. Moreover, when the Noble Shepherd describes his fate to his sheep, he dramatically claims: "I lay down my life in order to take it up again. No one takes it from me, but I lay it down of my own accord. I have power to lay it down, and I have power to take it up again" (10:17–18). Thus, Jesus is no victim, nor does he receive an unanswerable challenge; hence he does not need vindication or restoration to honor by God. "Resurrection" means here that the figure who has "life in himself" will raise himself or will "take it [my life] again." In this Gospel alone, then, Jesus' own power effects his resurrection; God does not raise him.

Comings and Goings. The synoptics report simply that some women who had observed where Jesus was entombed visited the tomb and reported back to the disciples. John refines this and fills it with extraordinary narrative detail. Mary Magdalene, who stood with Jesus' mother and aunt at the cross and who presumably attended Jesus' burial, comes alone to the tomb. But she immediately goes back to give the "bad" good news to Simon and the Beloved Disciple. When she tells them "I do not know where they have taken him," she begins the refrain that she will repeat again and again. They come, confirm her "bad" good news, and go away. She comes back to the tomb, only to be told in 20:17–18 to go back to the disciples, this time with good news. What does all this busy coming and going mean?

Comparison and Contrast Again. Earlier, the evangelist contrasted Peter and the Beloved Disciple in many ways.[513] When Jesus announced the traitor, no one knew who it was. But because the Beloved Disciple was physically closest to Jesus, Peter asked him for the information. One knows, the other doesn't (13:21–26). Closeness to Jesus and access to esoteric information regularly distinguish Peter from the Beloved Disciple. Second, after Jesus' arrest, the Beloved Disciple plays the role of shepherd to Peter's sheep. He provides entrance through the gatekeeper into Annas' palace (18:15–18). The Beloved Disciple stands publicly beside the cross, but Peter has long ago denied any relationship to Jesus. Finally, the author contrasts them once more when Mary tells both of them the same message at the same time, after which both start out together running to the tomb. But differences immediately occur: The faster one arrives first but waits for the slower one. Thus Peter, who runs more slowly and arrives later, is shown deference by being allowed to enter the tomb first. Although both enter the tomb and make the same inventory of the burial clothes, Peter, the first to enter, understands nothing, but the other disciple, who enters last, is first in insight: "He saw and he believed."[514] The author's penchant for classifying the status of disciples by what they know is operative here. There is no question where the author's favor lies, nor is this the last act in his comparison of the disciples.

---

[513] Consult the commentary on 13:21–27. See also J. H. Neyrey, "Footwashing," in *Social World of the First Christians* (1995), 209–13.

[514] B. J. Byrne, in his "The Faith of the Beloved Disciple and the Community in John 20," *JSNT* 23 (1985), 83–97, argues that the "faith" of the Beloved Disciple is related to the blessing in 20:29 on those who believe but have never seen. He is, then, the model of their faith.

JOHN 20:11–18 – NOW SHE KNOWS "WHERE"

11 But Mary stood weeping outside the tomb. As she wept, she bent over to look into the tomb;

12 and she saw two angels in white, sitting where the body of Jesus had been lying, one at the head and the other at the feet.

13 They said to her, "Woman, why are you weeping?" She said to them, "They have taken away my Lord, and I do not know where they have laid him."

14 When she had said this, she turned around and saw Jesus standing there, but she did not know that it was Jesus.

15 Jesus said to her, "Woman, why are you weeping? Whom are you looking for?" Supposing him to be the gardener, she said to him, "Sir, if you have carried him away, tell me where you have laid him, and I will take him away."

16 Jesus said to her, "Mary!" She turned and said to him in Hebrew, "Rabbouni!" (which means Teacher).

17 Jesus said to her, "Do not hold on to me, because I have not yet ascended to the Father. But go to my brothers and say to them, 'I am ascending to my Father and your Father, to my God and your God.'"

18 Mary Magdalene went and announced to the disciples, "I have seen the Lord"; and she told them that he had said these things to her.

Mary, Finally "In the Know."   By now, we are alert to Johannine characterization markers, double-meaning terms, and gender considerations. First, we note how frequently Mary tells others that "I do not know" where Jesus is: "We *do not know where*" (20:2); "*I do not know where*" (20:13); "*Tell me where*" (20:15).[515] Although elsewhere "not knowing" may constitute a character defect, as this narrative progresses, Mary will be given a knowledge that summarizes all information about "where" Jesus goes. Her illumination begins when Jesus, like a shepherd calling his sheep by name, addresses her as "Mary."[516] This sheep knows her shepherd and responds "Rabbouni . . . my teacher." Moreover, her quest to know "where" Jesus has gone occasions the last stage of the revelation of "whence" Jesus comes and "whither" he goes. Yet finding "where" Jesus' body lies proves to be insignificant, for she comes to know the ultimate "where" of Jesus. Thus, she is transformed from "not in the know" to wonderfully "in the know," from not knowing "where" Jesus' body lies to attempting to touch it or cling to it. As the first insider to whom the Risen Jesus manifests himself, she enjoys high status as an intimate and informed disciple. At this point, she knows Jesus better than any other disciple in the narrative.

[515] See Paul Minear, "'We Don't Know Where . . .' John 20:2," *Interpretation* 30 (1976), 125–30.

[516] See R. E. Brown, *Gospel According to John* (1970), 2.694.

"Where" Is Jesus Going? Most do not know "whither" Jesus goes (7:33, 36; 8:14), mainly because they are flesh and think earthly thoughts.[517] But Mary Magdalene and the disciples to whom she brings Jesus' message know that "whence" means heaven, the realm of God and the heart of God (1:18). The disciples, moreover, were told in Jesus' Farewell Address that he was going to the Father (14:12, 28; 16:5, 7, 10, 17; 17:11, 13). But "where" might also be considered as some earthly location where Jesus and the disciples meet, for he promised that he is "coming" to them (14:3, 18, 20, 23, 28).

How Information Traveled in Antiquity. The social sciences aid us here by distinguishing four ways in which news and information travel. "News" refers to the reporting of facts or events, including the "fame" of Jesus to surrounding villages (Matt 9:26; Luke 4:14). "Recruitment" not only tells something about Jesus but invites the hearers to act on the knowledge. Speech is "commissioned" when God or Jesus formally dispatches a speaker who speaks a specific message, such as the *kerygma* (Matt 28:16–20; Acts 10:42). "Gossip," however, means critical speech about an absent third party.[518]

A CLOSER LOOK — HOW INFORMATION/NEWS TRAVELS IN A
NONLITERATE CULTURE

1. *News* ("telling" and "hearing")

   Mary to Jesus: "When the wine gave out, the mother said to Jesus . . ." (2:3)

   Official: "When he heard that Jesus had come from Judea to Galilee . . ." (4:47)

   Samaritan Woman: "Come, see a man who told me all I ever did. Can this be the Christ"? (4:29)

   Martha and Mary: "The sisters sent a message to Jesus: 'Lord, he whom you love is ill.'" (11:3)

   Martha to Mary: "The teacher is here and is calling for you." (11:28)

   Crowd: "A great crowd heard that Jesus was coming to the feast . . ." (12:12)

   Mary Magdalene to Peter and the Beloved Disciple: "They have taken the Lord out of the tomb . . ." (20:2)

   Disciples to Thomas: "We have seen the Lord." (20:25)

---

[517] P. Minear, "'We don't know where . . .,'" *Interpretation* 30 (1976), 134–35.

[518] See Richard L. Rohrbaugh, "Gossip in the New Testament," in John J. Pilch, ed., *Social Scientific Models for Interpreting the Bible: Essays by The Context Group in Honor of Bruce J. Malina* (Leiden: Brill, 2001), 239–59; and P. J. J. Botha, "Paul and Gossip," *Neotestamentica* 32 (1998), 267–88.

2. *Recruitment*: "X finds Y and says 'Come and see'" (1:35–51)
3. *Commissioned speech*

John to followers: "I myself did not know him; but he who sent me
   to baptize with water said to me, 'He on whom you see the Spirit
   descend and remain, this is he who baptizes with the Holy Spirit.'
   And I have seen and have borne witness that this is the Son of God."
   (1:33–34)
Jesus to Mary Magdalene: "Go, tell my brethren that I am ascending…"
   (20:17–18)
God to Jesus/"the Word"
"The word which you hear is not mine." (14:24)
"I have given them your word." (17:14)

4. *Gossip*

Every "division" in the crowd contains something critical about the
   absent Jesus.
Disciples to John: "He is baptizing and all are going to him."
   (3:26)
Healed paralytic to Judeans: "The man told the Judeans that it was
   Jesus who healed him." (5:15)
Witnesses inform the Pharisees about Lazarus: "Some went … and
   told them what Jesus had done." (11:46)

At the start, Mary functions as a conduit of information, first "bad" news to
the disciples about the empty tomb and then "good news" to all the "brethren."
In 20:1–2, no one deputized her to bring this news, nor can she be said to
play any role at this point. She simply functions in the informal network of
communicating "news." But after Jesus calls her by name and manifests himself
to her, he *authorizes* her to bring *a specific message* of great importance to *specific
people*: "Go to my brothers and say to them, 'I am ascending to my Father
and your Father, to my God and your God" (20:17). Jesus' words contain two
elements: an authorization ("Go to my brothers and say . . .") and a specific
message ("I am ascending to my Father and your Father").[519] Thus authorized
to speak a unique message, her status rises significantly because of the content
of the message, and she enjoys some formal role as broker or messenger.[520] But
is the role that of an "apostle"?

---

[519] Her message is vastly superior to the "travel plans" told the women in Mark 16:7 and
   Matthew 28:7, 10.
[520] For a comparison of Mary Magdalene and the Samaritan woman on this point, see J. H.
   Neyrey, "What's Wrong with This Picture?" *BTB* 24 (1994), 86–88.

Mary's Status and Role? Interpreters must carefully distinguish between status and role, for a person may enjoy high status but play no significant role.[521] A *status* is "a recognized position that a person occupies within society. . . . [It] determines where he or she fits in society in relationship to everyone else."[522] A "role," however, is defined as "the socially recognized position of a person which entails rights and duties." Roles have to do with behavior: "It provides a comprehensive *pattern* for behavior and attitudes; it constitutes a *strategy* for coping with a recurrent type of situation; it is *socially identified*; it is subject to being played recognizably by *different individuals*; and it supplies a major basis for *identifying* and *placing* persons in society.[523] Put simply, status defines who one *is* socially (slave, female, gentile, leper, etc.), whereas role defines what one is expected to *do* socially on the basis of status. One *has* a status, but one *plays* a role (king, priest, teacher, mother, prophet, etc.). Paul, for example, has low status in the eyes of many ("Last of all, as to one untimely born, he appeared to me") but nevertheless claims the role of an apostle: "I am the least of the apostles, unfit to be called an apostle" (1 Cor 15:8–9). Yet he claims and defends the formal role of "apostle" (1 Cor 9:1; 15:10), which entailed certain "rights" (1 Cor 9:4–12) and "duties" (9:16–17). Unlike Paul, Mary Magdalene enjoys very high status, but does she play a role?

Role and status are quite controversial in the Fourth Gospel, even to the point of being a theme of their own in the narrative.[524] In the section called "Characters" in the introduction to this commentary, we listed the roles that many of the dramatis personae play in the Fourth Gospel. Now we consider status in relationship to those roles. This becomes quite subjective until we resolve the issue of the author's criteria for evaluating characters, which are specific to this Gospel and representative of its value system. We identify six criteria used to indicate high or low status: (1) physical closeness to Jesus (anointing his feet, reclining on his breast, clasping his feet, touching his hand and side); (2) bold public acknowledgment of Jesus; (3) receipt of selected disclosure, secrets, and special knowledge; (4) imitation of Jesus (grain of wheat; greater love . . . to lay down one's life); (5) labeled as "beloved"; and (6) being called by name. With these in mind, we report on the characters as they appear in the narrative in terms of both role and status, beginning with Jesus and ending with Simon Peter.[525]

---

[521] A. Paul Hare, "Groups: Role Structure," *IESS* 6.283–88; Morris Zelditch, "Status," *IESS* 15.250.

[522] Raymond Scupin and Christopher DeCorse, *Anthropology and Global Perspective* (Englewood, NJ: Prentice-Hall, 1995), 280.

[523] Ralph Turner, "Role," *IESS* 13.551–52.

[524] R. E. Brown, in his *Community of the Beloved Disciple* (1979), 80–88, describes how the Johannine group "counterposes itself over against the kinds of churches that venerate Peter and the Twelve" (p. 83). It is an axiom of Johannine scholarship to compare and contrast the Beloved Disciple with Peter.

[525] A complete list would include kinship roles, such as those of Jesus' mother and brothers, as well as the roles of Abraham, Jacob, Moses, and Isaiah. In addition to the roles of priest, high priest, and scribe, one might ask whether the Pharisees have a role.

Person	Authorization	Status	Role and Duties	Duration
Jesus	"Sent" by God (3:17, 34; 6:57; 11:42; 17:3, 8; 20:21)	*Highest possible status:* "No one has ever seen God but the Son" (1:18); "No one has ever gone up to heaven but the Son of Man who came down from heaven" (3:13).	*Agent/Broker:* Speaks God's words to disciples; performs the works of God; exercises God's two powers *Duties:* To do the will of the Father (5:30; 12:27–28), which includes speaking to, praying for, and defending the group, mediating the Advocate, and being the Noble Shepherd and Vine	Because he is eternal in the past and imperishable in the future, his role endures forever.
John the Baptizer	"There was a man sent from God" (1:6).	*Very high status:* "He was a burning and shining lamp" (5:35).	*Premier witness:* "He came to testify to the light, so that all might believe through him" (1:6–7). *Duties:* "Witness" before foe and friend; "decrease, not increase" (3:30).	Role lasted all his adult life
Samaritan Woman	"Go, call your husband and come here" (4:16).	*High status:* Jesus reveals insider information to her.	*Ambiguous role:* Told to call her "husband," she calls the whole village; she speaks a question, not a confession (4:29). *Duties:* To call her husband	If a role, it is quickly terminated (4:42).
Disciples	"I sent you to reap that for which you did not labor" (4:38); "As you have sent me into the world, so I have sent them into the world" (17:18);	*High status:* But someone has already sown the word; they are in second place.	*Apostles/agents:* A recruiting and speaking role *Duties:* "To reap," i.e., to speak on Jesus' behalf	Continues over time
	"For I have set you an example, that you also should do as I have done to you" (13:15).	*Very high status:* Imitation of Jesus; only leaders perform this action.	*Servants of hospitality:* Role restricted to leaders of group, presumably at group meal/worship *Duties:* To extend hospitality; to perform servant tasks	Continues over time

		High status: extension of Jesus' role	*Apostles/agents:* Sent by Jesus; empowered with Spirit to purify and to control entrance and exit of group *Duties:* To serve as agents of purification; to guard group's boundaries	Continues over time
	"As the Father has sent me, so I send you." When he had said this, he breathed on them and said to them, "Receive the Holy Spirit. If you forgive the sins of any, they are forgiven them; if you retain the sins of any, they are retained" (20:21–23).			
Judas	Authorization unclear	*Dual status:* In Jesus' eyes, low; in eyes of disciples, moderate	*Kept the common purse* (12:6; 13:29) *Duties:* Utterly failed, for "he was a thief" (12:6); instead of giving to the poor, he led soldiers to Jesus (13:29)	Short duration
Mary Magdalene	"But go to my brothers and say to them, 'I am ascending to my Father'" (20:17).	*Very high status:* Physical proximity to Jesus; special knowledge, bearer of unique message	*"Messenger"/"Broker":* Formally "sent" to speak a specific message[526] *Duties:* To bring Jesus' revelation to the "brothers"	Duration limited; unless she continues to "tell my brothers" the message
Simon Peter	"Simon son of John, do you love me more than these"? "Feed my lambs" "Tend my sheep"; "Feed my sheep" (21:15–17).	*Very high status:* Eventually, Simon draws physically close to Jesus and becomes Jesus' successor as shepherd	*Leader:* Not just fisherman, but shepherd of Jesus' flock *Duties:* To be Noble Shepherd (pasture; defense); to lay down his life for the sheep (21:18–19)	Continues over time

According to our criteria for status, Mary has four of them: bold, public loyalty (present at his crucifixion and death); physical proximity to Jesus; information

---

[526] Many note that the Fourth Gospel is reluctant to use the term "apostle" for disciples, except those known as "traditional" (4:38; 17:20; 20:21), because Jesus alone is the "apostle," the one who was sent. If there is conflict between traditional apostles and members of the Johannine group, one would not expect the latter to be called by their role. See R.E. Brown, *Community of the Beloved Disciple* (1979), 81, 186, 188.

of the highest order; and being called by name. Because of two criteria (desire to touch Jesus; bearer of the unique message about "whither" Jesus goes), we evaluate her status as very high indeed. Except for the Beloved Disciple, she can be said to have the highest status in the Gospel.

As regards roles, we should keep track of three things: authorization (expressed by "send/sent" and "go"); the task authorized; and the duration of the actions mandated. God authorizes and sends some persons to speak (John the Baptizer, Jesus, and the Advocate); Jesus himself sends others to do various tasks, which include speech (4:16; 20:17), forgiveness of sins by virtue of the Holy Spirit (20:21), and feeding lambs and sheep (21:15–17). The duration of these roles seems to be a lifetime, or at least a very long time. Except for 17:20, one finds in the Fourth Gospel neither a commission to announce a Gospel (Matt 28:18–20) nor a mandate to witness to Jesus (Luke 24:48; Acts 10:40–43).[527] Mary, then, is sent by Jesus to a specific audience to deliver a distinct revelation, two formal elements of a "role." But how long will she play this role? Nothing in the text indicates that she will ever play her role again. But what role does she have?

We have argued that "apostle" is a charged role because it belongs uniquely to Jesus, the agent or apostle of God.[528] Moreover, because of the symmetry between God sending Jesus and Jesus sending the disciples (20:21), it would seem that the (traditional) disciples function in many of the ways that Jesus did. It is only to them that the Spirit is sent to give them access to Jesus' words, presumably to teach and preach (14:25; 15:26; 16:13–14). The disciples to whom the Risen Jesus appears are commissioned to the role of purificators, a task practiced strictly within the group (see 1:29; 8:21, 24; 16:8). These ongoing roles and tasks are apparently confirmed by their acknowledgment in other Gospels and the letters of Paul. The data indicate that Mary Magdalene indeed has a role, but what role? It is not that of an "apostle," although she has a speaking role.

Gender and Role. In general, it was customary for females to speak only with the males of their households or kinship groups (1 Tim 2:12; 1 Cor 14:33–36). Second, whereas the commissioning of male disciples in the synoptic Gospels implies that they will travel from city to city and town to town, speaking to strangers in "public" space, Mary is not thus commissioned any more than was

---

[527] In Matthew 10:17–20, Jesus commissions disciples to bear testimony on his behalf in court. In the Fourth Gospel, John the Baptizer is authorized to testify to Jesus (1:32–34), but Jesus is the premier witness (8:18). Only in 15:26–27 are the disciples described as witnesses. Many other witnesses attest to Jesus, such as his works (5:36; 10:25), Moses (5:45–47), and Isaiah (12:41). "Witness," then, emerges as a genuine role with authorization, specific duties, and duration.

[528] P. Borgen, "God's Agent," in *Religions in Antiquity* (1968), 138–44; G. W. Buchanan, "Apostolic Christology," *SBLSP* (1986), 172–82; and A. E. Harvey, "Christ as Agent," in *Glory of Christ in the New Testament* (1987), 239–50.

the Samaritan woman.[529] Mary will not speak to strangers, especially strange males. Nor does she travel to Galilee or Samaria or beyond. She is sent to "my brothers," who are fictive kin whom she already knows and who know her, but to no one else. Third, the apostles and others so commissioned will preach the Gospel about Jesus. But Mary speaks only one word, albeit an extraordinary revelation, and once spoken, she will have fulfilled her duty to Jesus and "my brothers." It stretches the text to claim that she kept saying the same words to the same people. Fourth, whereas the apostles' roles endured throughout their lives, it is difficult to say the same thing of Mary. The Gospel does not envision her continually catechizing the disciples nor forming part of a missionary team. She recruits no one. Her high status remains, but not her role.

A Touching Scene. On only two occasions does Jesus touch someone in this Gospel. First, he smears a paste of dirt and spit on the eyes of a blind man (9:6), and later he washes the feet of the disciples (13:5). Rare, too, are the notices that others touch Jesus. Curiously, all of these occur in the part of the narrative dealing with Jesus' death, burial, and resurrection. Mary anoints Jesus' feet "for the day of his burial" (12:7); and the Beloved Disciple was "reclining next to Jesus" (13:23), so close that he could ask for secret information. Annas' attendant slaps Jesus in the face (18:22), and Jesus' body is scourged, nailed to the cross, and mutilated by a spear. In burying Jesus, Joseph and Nicodemus must have handled the corpse when carrying it to the grave. But on the day of the resurrection, Mary is restrained from touching Jesus' feet, whereas Thomas demands to touch his hands and side.[530] There seem to be gender issues involved in that Mary of Bethany as well as Mary Magdalene are allowed to touch Jesus' feet, a gesture of intimacy and high status (see Matt 28:9). In contrast, head, hands, and side are touched by males, where the issues are honor/shame and challenge but not intimacy. Moreover, Jesus *shows* the disciples (20:20) and then Thomas his hands and side (20:27), which suggests a special revelation that establishes them as reliable witnesses to his beyond-death state. But touching and being touched emerge as criteria of status and honor.

---

[529] Scholars commonly label Mary Magdalene an "apostle," a "witness," a "quasi-apostle," a person with a "mission," or a "disciple" – all implying some formal role. Using imprecise notions of "role" and "status," they uncritically affirm more than the Gospel does. See Raymond E. Brown, "The Roles of Women in the Fourth Gospel," *TS* 36 (1975), 688–99; Turid Karlsen Seim, "Roles of Women in the Gospel of John," in Lars Hartman and Birger Olsson, eds., *Aspects on the Johannine Literature* (Uppsala: Almqvist and Wiksells, 1986), 63, 67–70; and Dorothy Lee, "A Partnership of Easter Faith, The Role of Mary Magdalene and Thomas in John 20," *JSNT* 58 (1995), 39–46.

[530] The woman who proposed to carry the body ("I will take him away," 20:15) now grabs Jesus. It is unclear whether Jesus forestalls her touching him or stops a prolonged touching of him (20:17). See Harold W. Attridge, "'Don't Be Touching Me': Recent Feminist Scholarship on Mary Magdalene," in Amy-Jill Levine, ed., *A Feminist Companion to John*, Vol. II (New York, Sheffield Academic Press, 2003), 140–66; and S. van Tilborg, *Imaginative Love* (1993), 199–207.

JOHN 20:19–23 – APPEARANCES AS COMMISSIONINGS

19 When it was evening on that day, the first day of the week, and the doors of the house where the disciples had met were locked for fear of the Jews, Jesus came and stood among them and said, "Peace be with you."

20 After he said this, he showed them his hands and his side. Then the disciples rejoiced when they saw the Lord.

21 Jesus said to them again, "Peace be with you. As the Father has sent me, so I send you."

22 When he had said this, he breathed on them and said to them, "Receive the Holy Spirit.

23 If you forgive the sins of any, they are forgiven them; if you retain the sins of any, they are retained."

Appearances as "Call Narratives." Why does Jesus appear at all? When we make a synopsis of the various appearances to the male disciples, we discern two functions in them. First, the Shepherd continues his search for lost sheep, as in the case of Cleopas and his companion, who "had hoped that he [Jesus] was the one" (Luke 24:13–33). Jesus' appearance to Thomas belongs in this category, for although once part of the group, he later refused to believe the Gospel of the apostles that Jesus had risen (John 20:25). The majority of resurrection appearances, however, function as formal commissionings of the disciples as "apostles." These are they of whom Acts says: "God allowed him to appear, not to all the people but to us who were chosen by God as witnesses.... He commanded us to preach to the people and to testify that he is the one ordained by God as judge of the living and the dead" (Acts 10:40–42). But to appreciate the formal shape of "commissioning stories," let us examine the biblical form known as the "call narrative,"[531] which consists of five parts:

1. Introduction: who, where, when
2. Confrontation/reaction: Because heavenly beings may destroy as well as build up, they are received with fear; reassurance in the form of "Be not afraid!" may be necessary.

---

[531] Norman Habel, in his "The Form and Significance of the Call Narratives," *ZAW* 77 (1965), 297–323, pioneered the study of God's appearances to Moses, Gideon, Jeremiah, and Isaiah. Benjamin Hubbard, in his *The Matthean Redaction of a Primitive Apostolic Commissioning: An Exegesis of Matthew 28:16–20* (Missoula, MT: Scholars Press, 1974), applied Habel's idea to Matthew. Jerome H. Neyrey, in his *The Resurrection Stories* (Wilmington, DE: Michael Glazier, 1988), further applied the model to the appearances in 1 Corinthians, Luke, and John.

3. Commission
4. Objections: Not uncommonly, those commissioned object. Reassurances such as "Do not fear!" may occur again. Signs may be given as proof of both God's favor and power.
5. Conclusion: departure of God or angel

The Johannine resurrection appearances follow this schema closely:

Elements of Call Narrative	John 20:19–25	John 20:26–29
1. Introduction	"When it was evening on that day, the first day of the week, and the doors of the house where the disciples had met were locked for fear of the Jews"	"A week later his disciples were again in the house, and Thomas was with them."
2. Confrontation/ reaction and reassurance	"Jesus came and stood among them and said, 'Peace be with you.' After he said this, he showed them his hands and his side. Then the disciples rejoiced when they saw the Lord. Jesus said to them again, 'Peace be with you.	"Although the doors were shut, Jesus came and stood among them and said, 'Peace be with you.'"
3. Commission	As the Father has sent me, so I send you.' When he had said this, he breathed on them and said to them, 'Receive the Holy Spirit. If you forgive the sins of any, they are forgiven them; if you retain the sins of any, they are retained.'"	
4. Objection; reassurance and sign		"Then he said to Thomas, 'Put your finger here and see my hands. Reach out your hand and put it in my side. Do not doubt but believe.' Thomas answered him, 'My Lord and my God!'
5. Conclusion		Jesus said to him, 'Have you believed because you have seen me? Blessed are those who have not seen and yet have come to believe.'"

By way of introduction, we learn in 20:19 that it is evening of the first day, in Jerusalem, presumably in the supper room, with only ten disciples in attendance. Jesus terrifies these disciples not known for their loyalty (16:32), who are hiding behind locked doors for fear of their enemies. But he reassures them with "Peace be with you" and with a demonstration of his hands and side. No, he is not a ghost, nor does he reproach them for his wounds nor threaten them with vengeance for disloyalty. Most importantly, he commissions them, first breathing the Spirit on them and then verbally authorizing them, "As the Father has sent me, so I send you." But to do what? One expects them to be set aside for the role of apostle, preacher, and evangelist; yet, they are authorized to deal with sins, even within the group. They informally play another role, as they tell their Gospel to the first person they encounter, namely Thomas: "We have seen the Lord" (20:25). We do not know why Thomas was absent from the group, but in this Gospel, being apart from or scattered from the flock or in any way separated from the vine indicates a serious fault or failure, a sin that needs to be forgiven. Hence, the disciples' telling Thomas their Gospel is also a call for his repentance to rejoin the group and to believe its good news. This fails, for Thomas makes an arrogant demand of Jesus. His sins are retained.

Sins Forgiven, Sins Retained. On the one hand, many "Judeans" consider Jesus a sinner, either because he does not observe the Sabbath (5:10–13; 7:22–23; 9:16, 24, 25) or he "makes himself" equal to God (5:18; 10:33–34; 19:7). Alternatively, they evaluate him as a corruption in their midst, one who "leads astray" the people and the police (7:12, 47–49). But the author has much to say about other sinners.

1. *Unbelievers.* All who reject Jesus and harass his disciples are sinners according to the Johannine code. Those who do not believe in Jesus are condemned by this very act (3:18), as are those who love darkness rather than light (3:19). And those who do not believe that Jesus is "I AM" will die in their sins (8:24).
2. *Liars and murderers.* Jesus exposes as liars and murderers (8:44) those who falsely claim to be his disciples (8:32).
3. *Hypocrites.* Some claim to see but are truly blind. How can these sinners be forgiven? (9:41).
4. *Dropouts.* In addition to enemies and unbelievers, some drop out of the group (6:60–65).
5. *Judging unjustly.* All who judge unjustly according to appearances or who condemn the innocent and release the guilty are sinners.
6. *Refuse his commands.* Some will not "love one another" or "abide in the vine" or "keep my word." These sins mark them as people who lack loyalty.
7. *Cowards.* People who come to Jesus in secret (Nicodemus, Joseph of Arimathea) and others who are afraid to speak publicly in favor of Jesus (9:22; 12:42) keep the stigma of cowardice.

Which sins, then, are forgiven and which retained? Although Thomas, who rejects the good news of the apostles, is a sinner, he is eventually forgiven by virtue of Jesus' appearance to him and his continued association with the disciples (21:2). Judas, on the other hand, is not forgiven. Peter, who denied loyalty to Jesus (18:25–27), is processed in 21:1–19 into an intimate relationship with Jesus, indicating forgiveness of his cowardice. It is doubtful, however, that hard-core unbelievers, liars and murderers, hypocrites, and unjust judges are ever forgiven. Hence, Jesus' commission in 20:22–23 would seem to extend only to in-group ritual behavior.

Holy Spirit and Forgiveness. We are familiar with community judgment scenes from Matthew 18:15–20 and 1 Corinthians 5:1–13. But John 20:22 is unique in that the Spirit is given for the express purpose of forgiving or retaining sins. What does the evangelist gain by this linkage? One is reminded of the earlier scene in 16:8–11, where the new Advocate will conduct a judgment of the world's sins; he will convict the world of sin, (false) righteousness, and (false) judgment. The Spirit, presumably inspiring one or another member of the group, orchestrates a judgment scene. And because one of the Spirit's chief characteristics is knowledge, the Spirit also knows what is in the human heart and can read secrets and detect ambiguity and deception. Jesus gives to the disciples in 20:21–22 both the Spirit and the power to judge and retain. And, as we observed in regard to "judgment" as an element of worship in John 16:8–11, so we expect that the forgiveness and retention of sins will be an element of the worship of the group.

Resurrection, Ascension, and Pentecost. All evangelists tell of the transit of Jesus from death to life and from this world to the right hand of God. But whereas Luke distinguishes resurrection (24:13–48), ascension (Acts 1:6–9), and Pentecost (Acts 2:1–4) as three temporally distinct events, John seems to have compressed them into one day: resurrection, "ascending to my Father," and "Receive the Holy Spirit." As in the case of Jesus raising himself from the dead (10:17–18), so, too, he ascends by his own power, which the synoptic Gospels could not possibly say. This ascension, moreover, is unique because it represents Jesus' return to where he was before. A pattern appears over and over in the Gospel that Jesus is a heavenly figure who descends to this realm and ascends back to heaven (1:1–18; 3:13–14; 6:62; 13:1–3). His death is his "lifting up" (8:28; 12:32). He returns to the glory that he had with God before the world began (17:5, 24). And his ascension provides the full and final answer to the question of "whither" he goes. Yet having said that, Jesus remains very much present to his disciples, as his many appearances in Jerusalem and Galilee illustrate.

JOHN 20:24–31 – DEMANDS, DEMANDS, DEMANDS

24 But Thomas (who was called the Twin), one of the twelve, was not with them when Jesus came.

25 So the other disciples told him, "We have seen the Lord." But he said to them, "Unless I see the mark of the nails in his hands, and put my finger in the mark of the nails and my hand in his side, I will not believe."

26 A week later his disciples were again in the house, and Thomas was with them. Although the doors were shut, Jesus came and stood among them and said, "Peace be with you."

27 Then he said to Thomas, "Put your finger here and see my hands. Reach out your hand and put it in my side. Do not doubt but believe."

28 Thomas answered him, "My Lord and my God!"

29 Jesus said to him, "Have you believed because you have seen me? Blessed are those who have not seen and yet have come to believe."

30 Now Jesus did many other signs in the presence of his disciples, which are not written in this book.

31 But these are written so that you may come to believe that Jesus is the Messiah, the Son of God, and that through believing you may have life in his name.

Call Narrative Continued. When Jesus returns, the "call narrative" form continues to be operative, but only its second half. The introduction and confrontation are as before, but the commission is skipped as Jesus takes up the objection of Thomas, the fourth item in the form. Thomas issued a shameful challenge to Jesus by demanding proof (20:25). Jesus' riposte is to give Thomas just what he asked for (20:27). Rarely do people get the signs they ask for. But here Jesus acts to transform Thomas from sinner to saint. He speaks to him in imperatives: "*Put* your hand . . . *Be* not faithless, but believing." Although we do not hear Jesus giving him the same commission as the others (20:21–22), later we see him with the disciples who go fishing (21:2), suggesting that forgiveness of his sin has occurred.

If at First You Don't Succeed. Why split the narrative this way? The answer lies in recognizing some of the distinctive Johannine themes and ways of telling the story. Thomas resembles Nathanael in that the latter mocked the story initially told him about Jesus. How can anything good come from Nazareth (1:46)? But despite his objections, Nathanael did "come and see" Jesus and so received special information and praise. Thomas objected when disciples "evangelized" him, but he remained with the group and eventually received special access to Jesus. But Thomas differs from all other characters in that he does not simply receive from others knowledge about Jesus. He is moved to make the most exalted acknowledgment of Jesus' status and role in the Fourth Gospel, "My Lord and my God!" (20:28). Thomas earlier saw Jesus raise Lazarus from the dead, which at the time was a "sign," not a demonstration of Jesus' eschatological power (11:7–16). But with his access to the body of the Risen Jesus, he is schooled to acknowledge that Jesus indeed has God's eschatological power to "have life in himself" and to "lay down his life and take it again." Now there is ample proof that Jesus is "equal to God" and that he has God's two powers: creative ("God") and eschatological ("Lord").

Signs, Seeing, and Believing. These final verses are generally described as the conclusion of the "sign source," the earliest stratum of the Johannine Gospel.[532] They argue that signs and miracles, when understood, occasion people like the man born blind to acknowledge Jesus as "the Christ, the Son of God" and so have life "in his name." First, the titles just named are worthy conclusions to an early Christology that argued that Jesus' miracles should warrant acceptance of him as an agent sent from God. Although Nicodemus hints at this (3:2), others make the connection (6:14–16), especially the man born blind (9:30–33). The "signs" mentioned in 20:30–31 might simply be the previous seven signs of the "sign source" or the epiphanic events narrated in John 20–21.[533]

Written in a Book. How curious to find the author saying that these signs are "written in a book," while admitting that there are many other signs "*not* written." In Luke's preface, he claims to have consulted previous accounts of the words and deeds of Jesus, indicating sources such as the Q-Source and at least Mark (1:1–3).[534] We learn in 20:30–31 of a written source used by the fourth evangelist. Although all admit that 20:30–31 was the original ending to some collection of signs, there is another ending to the whole Gospel in 21:24–25, in which we find the final redactor of the Gospel claiming that he has "written these things."

How Does One End a Book? Some hear in 20:30–31 echoes of the refrain that frequently concludes the account of Israel's kings. For example, of Solomon the historian writes: "Now the rest of the acts of Solomon, all that he did as well as his wisdom, are they not written in the Book of the Acts of Solomon?" (1 Kings 11:41; see also 14:19; 15:31; 16:27). Closer to the time of the Fourth Gospel, the author of 1 Maccabees writes of Judah: "Now the rest of the acts of Judah, and his wars and the brave deeds he did, and his greatness, have not been recorded, for they are very many" (9:22).[535] Others point to the Hellenistic world,

---

[532] See R. T. Fortna, *Gospel of Signs* (1970). For an exhaustive report on the proponents and critics of the sign source, see G. van Belle, *Sign Source* (1994).

[533] See G. van Belle, *Sign Source* (1994), 398–404.

[534] R. T. Fortna, *Gospel of Signs* (1970), 223.

[535] See C. H. Talbert, *Reading John* (1992), 257–58; in addition to 1 Maccabees, he cites Lucian, *Demonax* 67, for a similar type of ending.

where authors honor their subject by commenting on how long it would take to recount Diogenes' words or stories about Hipparchia.[536] Hence audiences are likely to understand that 20:30–31 is the narrative's ending. And they would also understand that the primary feature of the narrative is the honor of Jesus, for the "signs" were written to acclaim Jesus as the Christ, the Son of God.

JOHN 21:1–8 – GONE FISHING

1 After these things Jesus showed himself again to the disciples by the Sea of Tiberias; and he showed himself in this way.

2 Gathered there together were Simon Peter, Thomas called the Twin, Nathanael of Cana in Galilee, the sons of Zebedee, and two others of his disciples.

3 Simon Peter said to them, "I am going fishing." They said to him, "We will go with you." They went out and got into the boat, but that night they caught nothing.

4 Just after daybreak, Jesus stood on the beach; but the disciples did not know that it was Jesus.

5 Jesus said to them, "Children, you have no fish, have you?" They answered him, "No."

6 He said to them, "Cast the net to the right side of the boat, and you will find some." So they cast it, and now they were not able to haul it in because there were so many fish.

7 That disciple whom Jesus loved said to Peter, "It is the Lord!" When Simon Peter heard that it was the Lord, he put on some clothes, for he was naked, and jumped into the sea.

8 But the other disciples came in the boat, dragging the net full of fish, for they were not far from the land, only about a hundred yards off.

Appendix? Epilogue? Scholars still debate whether John 21 was added to the original Gospel or was part of it.[537] As noted, John 20 contains a complete presentation of the resurrection of Jesus from empty tomb, to appearances, to formal commissioning of the disciples. So when readers compare John 20 and John 21 they notice that in many ways John 21 returns to material that occurred earlier in the Gospel; for example Peter's denial (18:17, 25–27), resolved in

---

[536] C. S. Keener, *Gospel of John Commentary* (2003), 1214–15.

[537] In support of John 21 as an addition, see R. E. Brown, *Gospel According to John* (1970), 2.1066–85. For John 21 as the original conclusion, see John Breck, "John 21: Appendix, Epilogue or Conclusion," *SVTQ* 36 (1992), 27–49. Narrative scholars tend to argue for authenticity, such as Beverly Gaventa, "The Archive of Excess: John 21 and the Problem of Narrative Closure," in R. Alan Culpepper and C. Clifton Black, eds., *Exploring the Gospel of John* (Louisville, KY: Westminster John Knox, 1996), 240–54.

21:15–18; shepherd and sheep (10:11–16), resolved in 21:15–18; the special knowledge of the Beloved Disciple (13:25–27), repeated in 21:7; and the special status of the Beloved Disciple (19:25–27), at least touched upon in 21:20–23.[538] Conversely, we find materials that are strikingly different or new; for example, John 21 is entirely focused on the mission of the Johannine group.

Gone Fishing. It is striking that so many disciples are named here at one time: "Simon Peter, Thomas called the Twin, Nathanael of Cana in Galilee, the sons of Zebedee, and two others of his disciples" (21:2) – the Beloved Disciple would apparently be one of the "two others." We know that three are fishermen by trade, but of the piscatory skills of the rest we have no record. Most importantly, Simon Peter takes a leadership role in this enterprise. The story sounds familiar because at the start of Luke's narrative Jesus directs Peter to fish and catch a large school of fish. Once we have compared Luke and John, we will be in a better position to comment on how the story is functioning in John.

Luke 5:1–10	*John 21:4–8*
1. Disciples present: "James and John, sons of Zebedee, who were partners with Simon" (5:10)	1. Disciples present: "Simon Peter, Thomas called the Twin, Nathanael of Cana in Galilee, the sons of Zebedee, and two others of his disciples" (21:2)
2. Jesus commands them to fish: "When he had finished speaking, he said to Simon, 'Put out into the deep water and let down your nets for a catch.'" (5:4)	2. Jesus commands them to fish: "He said to them, 'Cast the net to the right side of the boat, and you will find some.'" (21:6)
3. Fished all night, caught nothing: "We have worked all night long but have caught nothing." (5:5)	3. Fished all night, caught nothing: "They went out and got into the boat, but that night they caught nothing." (21:3)
4. Obedience and great catch: "'Master . . . if you say so, I will let down the nets.' When they had done this . . ." (5:5–6)	4. Obedience and great catch: "So they cast it, and now they were not able to haul it in because there were so many fish." (21:6)
5. Nets did not break: "They caught so many fish that their nets were beginning to break." (5:6)	5. Nets did not break: "Simon Peter hauled the net ashore, full of large fish, a hundred fifty-three of them; and though there were so many, the net was not torn." (21:11)
6. Peter's reaction: "But when Simon Peter saw it, he fell down at Jesus' knees, saying, 'Go away from me, Lord, for I am a sinful man'"! (5:8)	6. Peter's reaction: "When Simon Peter heard that it was the Lord, he put on some clothes, for he was naked, and jumped into the sea." (21:7)

[538] On features that do and do not represent Johannine style, see R. E. Brown, *Gospel According to John* (1970), 2.1080. See also Francis J. Moloney, *Glory Not Dishonor: Reading John 13–21* (Minneapolis, MN: Fortress Press, 1998), 182–83.

7. Jesus called "Lord": "Go away from me, Lord." (5:8)

7. Jesus identified as "Lord": "That disciple whom Jesus loved said to Peter, 'It is the Lord!'" (21:7)

8. Catch of fish symbolizes mission of all and specific commission of Peter as "Chief Fisherman": "From now on you will be catching people." (5:10)

8. Catch of fish symbolizes mission of all and confirms the specific commission of Peter as "Chief Fisherman": "Simon Peter hauled the net ashore, full of large fish, a hundred fifty-three of them." (21:11)

This comparison suggests the following. (1) In both, the inner circle of disciples is present. In Luke, the two sets of brothers join Jesus in the boat and later are with him at the Transfiguration and in Gethsemane, whereas in John, most of the original disciples are here, as well as those who know and confess remarkable things. (2) In Luke, Peter is the central figure who is commissioned as "fisher of many." But except for John 6:68, Peter has never been a "leading" or "first" disciple in the Fourth Gospel. (3) In both, nothing successful happens until Jesus occasions a catch of fish. (4) In both, a ritual occurs with the catch of fish. In Luke, Peter is transformed from mere fisherman to "Fisher of People" (Luke 5:10). In John, however, although his status as a fisherman is confirmed, better roles await him in 21:10–19.

But the comparison also reveals important differences. The Lukan version functions both as a miracle of plenty and a commission, whereas the Johannine one is first an appearance of the absent Jesus and then a miracle symbolic of plenty – all leading to a commissioning. The Johannine narrative keeps its focus on Peter as fisherman and provider of food for the group, and finally as shepherd. Hence, John 21 focuses on Simon Peter in terms of two roles: fisher and provider of food and noble shepherd. Thus "fisherman," a traditional label for Peter, while confirmed here, is by no means all that Jesus would assign him. "shepherd," a hotly contested role thus far, will be finally ascribed to Peter (see the commentary on 18:15–16).[539]

Like Night and Day. The distinction that this Gospel regularly makes between day and night is echoed here, but not in the dualistic sense seen earlier. Whereas "night" was the time of fear for Nicodemus (3:2), when people are unable to work (9:4) and when Judas practices his treachery (13:30), here it is simply a period when success is absent. But with day, work can be done, people can come into the light, and success occurs.

"In the Know." We know that the author distinguishes people "not in the know" from those "in the know." Some remain "not in the know" because, like Nicodemus (3:3–10), they are earthly persons and from below. Others are transformed "into the know" after Jesus gives them epiphanies and revelations.

[539] J. H. Neyrey, "Footwashing," in *Social World of the First Christians* (1995), 207–13.

Mary Magdalene best exemplifies a person who thrice declares "I do not know where. . . ." But when Jesus calls her name, he transforms her into one of the elite people "in the know." Because she recognizes the shepherd's voice, Jesus can make a selective disclosure of his greatest secret (20:17–18). So, at first no one in Peter's boat "knows" the person on the shore telling them where to cast their net; all are "not in the know" (21:4). But the Beloved Disciple comes to know and in turn enlightens the others: "It is the Lord" (21:7).

Peter, Nudity, and Clothing. First of all, *gymnos* can mean totally naked or "without an outer garment"; that is, with merely a loin cloth.[540] Peter puts on an *ependytes*, a garment put on over another garment. Minimally, we learn that Peter is transformed from scantily to normally clad. But why? Why should a laborer be ashamed of his working clothes? Inasmuch as clothing and nudity are highly susceptible to cultural meanings related to honor and shame or purity and pollution, we had best look here for an answer.[541] Whereas slaves and captives might labor totally naked before their masters, which would confirm their shameful status, when they come into the public presence of their superiors, they must be suitably clothed. Whereas it was shameful if one's clothes were taken away (19:23–24), it was correspondingly aggressive and shameful for a man to expose himself to another. But Peter's "nudity" among his co-workers is neutral, neither shameful nor honorable. But to come into the presence of the Risen "Lord," he must be honorably clad. "Nudity" would shame the Lord. All, then, is a matter of honor.

Rivalry That Won't End. Although this epilogue to the Gospel tells Peter's glorious story, the Beloved Disciple is also on the scene and always in some contrast with Peter. Now, for the fourth time, these two figures are contrasted: Peter asks the Beloved Disciple for knowledge of the traitor he does not have (13:25–26); the Beloved Disciple arranges for Peter's access to Annas' palace (18:15–16); both run to the tomb, enter, and see the same thing, but only the Beloved Disciple believes; and now the Beloved Disciple "knows" Jesus, whereas Peter and the others do not. Shortly, a fifth contrast will be narrated, Peter challenging the status of the Beloved Disciple. These data suggest that a dominant theme in John 21 is leadership, either official roles credited to Peter (fisherman, table host, or noble shepherd) or exalted status credited to the Beloved Disciple (most knowledgeable or deathless). Once the Beloved Disciple was physically closest to Jesus (13:22–25), but now Peter seeks the same by jumping from the boat and rushing to Jesus. Physical closeness to Jesus, we saw earlier, constitutes a high-status marker.

---

[540] Frederick Danker (BDAG, 3rd edition, 208) cites instances where sailors are described as *gymnos* at their labors.

[541] J. H. Neyrey, "Clothing" and "Nudity," in *Biblical Social Values* (1998), 21–27 and 136–42, respectively.

JOHN 21:9–14 – BREAKFAST ON THE BEACH

9 When they had gone ashore, they saw a charcoal fire there, with fish on it, and bread.

10 Jesus said to them, "Bring some of the fish that you have just caught."

11 So Simon Peter went aboard and hauled the net ashore, full of large fish, a hundred fifty-three of them; and though there were so many, the net was not torn.

12 Jesus said to them, "Come and have breakfast." Now none of the disciples dared to ask him, "Who are you?" because they knew it was the Lord.

13 Jesus came and took the bread and gave it to them, and did the same with the fish.

14 This was now the third time that Jesus appeared to the disciples after he was raised from the dead.

Peter as Apprentice Host. This meal echoes other traditions of Jesus both feeding his disciples and eating with them. In John 6:1–13, Jesus miraculously produced abundant bread and fish from a mere five loaves and two fish to fill thousands. The disciples' inability to solve the food problem then (6:5–10) contrasts with Jesus' ability to work this great sign, a pattern repeated here. Moreover, in several resurrection appearances, Jesus himself eats some of the disciples' food for the express purpose of demonstrating that he is alive and not a ghost (because ghosts do not eat: Luke 24:37–43; see also Acts 1:3; 10:41). But this does not seem to be the issue here. Finally, Luke narrates that Jesus broke bread with Cleopas and a companion in an inn near Emmaus (24:30–31). But the eating here, although similar in some respects to these other feedings, has an entirely different purpose.

Jesus has all matters in hand: a charcoal fire, fish roasting on it, and bread. Nevertheless, Jesus commands all of them to bring their fish hither: "Bring some of the fish you have just caught." Simon Peter takes the lead, boards the boat, and hauls the net ashore. Peter is now more than chief fisherman, for he is in a liminal process to learn how to be a chief host whose role it is to feed the sheep. He will formally assume this role in the next episode when Jesus designates him "shepherd" who will "Feed my lambs, feed my sheep."

Meals and Ceremonies. In the commentary on John 13:4–20, we made the distinction between status transformations and ceremonies. Some ritual actions celebrate how people are changed from one role or status to another: an unmarried female to a mother; a man and woman to husband and wife; a living person to a dead one; an outsider to an insider; and the like. These transformations begin in the present and look to the future, so that current changes abide and determine future roles and statuses. Other actions ceremonially confirm role and status in a group or institution: All birthdays, anniversaries, and feast days confirm the honor and worth of the persons or events in the past. They look to the past and bring meaning and worth from it to the present. The premier example of ceremony in the New Testament is the meal, especially the *agape* meal and the Eucharist.[542] Thus we examine the meal here as a ceremony, not a status transformation.

Three key questions arise in examining a meal.

(1) *Who* eats *what* with *whom*? Jesus eats with the elite inner circle of his disciples. Moreover, he hosts the meal and serves the food: "Jesus came and took the bread and gave it to them, and did the same with the fish" (21:13). The roles of all are apparent: Jesus, who is Shepherd of his flock, pastures his sheep. As Risen Lord, he continues the great benefaction he brokered in an earlier meal (6:1–13). The disciples confirm their status as elite insiders by eating Jesus' food in the very presence of their Risen Lord: "Now none of the disciples dared to ask him, 'Who are you?' because they knew it was the Lord" (21:12).

(2) *Patronage and reciprocity.* As a superior broker, Jesus provides God's clients with abundant food, giving it as an altruistic gift for which there is no possible reciprocity.

(3) In terms of *body symbolism*, all eat, so to speak, with their eyes opened (they know the Lord). Although no one washes hands before eating, this has never been an issue in this Gospel. Their mouths eat "holy" food that Jesus provides. Peter is now properly clothed.

A Great Fish Story. They catch "153" large fish. Is "153" just a very large number (see Matt 18:21–22) suggesting abundance of fish caught, or might it have some symbolic or cryptic meaning? Other commentators who have surveyed the options provide us with this summary.[543] Most attractive is Jerome's comment on Ezekiel 47:9–12: "Writers on the nature and properties of animals, who have learned the *Halieutica* in Latin as well as in Greek, among whom is the learned poet Oppianus Cilix, say that there are one hundred and fifty three kinds of fish."[544] Other interpretations include a mathematical reading of "153" as the sum of certain numbers, such as 1 to 17 or a combination of perfect numbers such as 7 and 10, and gematria, which finds numerical equivalents in the letters of special words, such as Simon = 76, fish = 77. Jerome's interpretation has the advantage that it supports the plain meaning of the incident; namely, that the catch relates to future successful recruitment (see 4:35; 10:16; 12:32). His "153" means a comprehensive number that includes all species of fish. It suffers

---

[542] See J. H. Neyrey, "Ceremonies in Luke-Acts," in *Social World of Luke-Acts* (1991), 361–87; and his "Meals, Food and Table Fellowship," in Richard L. Rohrbaugh, ed., *The Social Sciences and New Testament Interpretation* (Peabody, MA: Hendrickson, 1996), 159–82.

[543] R. E. Brown, *Gospel According to John* (1970), 2.1074–76; and George Beasley-Murray, *John*, 2nd ed. (Nashville, TN: Thomas Nelson, 1999), 401–4.

[544] The translation is that of E. C. Hoskyns, *The Fourth Gospel* ed. (1950), 554.

a serious drawback in that modern editions of Oppianus do not include this passage, which urges caution about its probative value here.[545]

JOHN 21:15–19 – FINALLY, ANOTHER "NOBLE" SHEPHERD

15 When they had finished breakfast, Jesus said to Simon Peter, "Simon son of John, do you love me more than these?" He said to him, "Yes, Lord; you know that I love you." Jesus said to him, "Feed my lambs."
16 A second time he said to him, "Simon son of John, do you love me?" He said to him, "Yes, Lord; you know that I love you." Jesus said to him, "Tend my sheep."
17 He said to him the third time, "Simon son of John, do you love me?" Peter felt hurt because he said to him the third time, "Do you love me?" And he said to him, "Lord, you know everything; you know that I love you." Jesus said to him, "Feed my sheep.
18 Very truly, I tell you, when you were younger, you used to fasten your own belt and to go wherever you wished. But when you grow old, you will stretch out your hands, and someone else will fasten a belt around you and take you where you do not wish to go."
19 (He said this to indicate the kind of death by which he would glorify God.) After this he said to him, "Follow me."

From Fisherman to Shepherd. Peter's role as fisherman looks to the boundaries of the group; that is, recruitment of outsiders. But the role of shepherd looks to what is within that boundary; that is, to the care and feeding of insiders. Peter already enjoys the role of lead "fisherman" (21:1–3), who recruits others to join him in fishing. In contrast, Jesus' triple command to Peter, "Feed...feed...feed," constitutes a status-transformation ritual for him. He now assumes a new role that he did not have before. Jesus mandates that Peter act toward the flock as Jesus himself did.

Since John 13, Peter has been in the liminal phase of a status-transformation ritual, which typically consists of four stages: separation, liminality, transformation, and acknowledgment. Peter *separated* himself long ago with his recruitment by Andrew (1:41–42). In addition to traveling with Jesus and being tested by him (6:67–71), Peter begins a distinctive *liminal period* with Jesus' washing of his feet (13:6–9). Typically, his liminal experience includes a search for knowledge (13:7, 24–25), receiving rebukes (13:36–38), taking risks (18:15–17), and even

---

[545] Robert M. Grant, "One Hundred Fifty-Three Large Fishes," *HTR* 42 (1949), 273–75. See also P. R. Ackroyd, "The 153 Fishes in John XXI.11 – A Further Note," *JTS* 10 (1959), 10; J. A. Emerton, "The 153 Fishes in John xxi. 11," *JTS* 9 (1958), 86–89; and J. A. Emerton, "Some NT Notes," *JTS* 11 (1960), 329–36.

failure (18:25–27). We argued earlier that Peter failed the test to become an elite disciple, courageous in confession and bold in loyalty (see the commentary on 13:36–38). Jesus himself declared Peter unfit for the role of noble shepherd because of his cowardice. Finally, Peter is *transformed* by Jesus into the role of shepherd (21:15–18). *Acknowledgment* is provided, but only by the readers, not the characters of the narrative.

The Magic Moment. Peter's transformation ritual occurs after the meal in which he assists Jesus in feeding the disciples. Because Peter has previously failed to show the virtues of a "noble" shepherd (i.e., loyalty and faithfulness), Jesus tests him with a triple question – "Do you love me?" – to which he responds affirmatively: "Yes, Lord, you know that I love you." The audience, of course, knows that each question–answer exchange corresponds to each of Peter's failures of loyalty in 18:17, 25–27. Jesus now declares him ready for the new role, three times mandating that Peter, the new shepherd, *feed* Jesus' sheep. Shortly, matters of courage will again be discussed in regard to Peter's future death. But suffice it to say that Jesus, who reads hearts, knows what is in Peter's, just as he did earlier when exposing Peter's bluster and boasting (13:38). The fact that Jesus asks if Peter loves[546] him "more than these" other disciples suggests some sort of ranking among them.

Peter, a Noble Shepherd. Peter is not just constituted shepherd, but indeed a "noble" one.[547] From the discussion of the motif of "noble shepherd" in 10:11–18, we know that six criteria are generally in play. A death is "noble" when it is beneficial, voluntary, virtuous, and unique; and noble deaths are those of people who die unvanquished and are followed by posthumous honors. Jesus declared that he voluntarily "lays down his life for his sheep" (10:11, 15). His courage leads him to stand between the wolf and his sheep. He was no victim and "no one takes my life from me." Jesus, then, is the original "noble" shepherd. But at the beginning of the period of Jesus' arrest and death, Peter boasted that "I will lay down my life for you" (13:37), a "noble" claim that proved to be all words and no substance. Nevertheless, the character of Peter knows of this criterion of a noble death. Peter repents of that failure in the current declarations of "love" of Jesus. Shepherd, but "noble" shepherd? How will Peter die? When Jesus tells Peter, "You will stretch out your hands, and someone else will fasten a belt around you and take you where you do not wish to go" (21:18), the audience knows that all previous failures at being "noble" are erased because Jesus knows both Peter's heart and his future. As the author explains Jesus' cryptic words, we learn that Peter will die a death that will glorify God (21:19), just as Jesus' own death was

---

[546] Readers are referred back to the discussion of "love" in the commentary on 15:11–17. Two different verbs are used here for "love" (ἀγαπαω, φιλεω), the latter verb used to designate "beloved" ones, such as Martha, Mary, and Lazarus, as well as the Beloved Disciple. It is unclear if Simon Peter is now given that high status.

[547] See J. H. Neyrey, "Noble Shepherd," *JBL* 120 (2001), 267–91.

both his own glorification and the glorification of the Father. Hence, Peter is transformed into a shepherd, even a "noble" shepherd.

Resurrection Appearances and Commissionings. Most appearances[548] of the Risen Jesus function as commissionings of apostles to be Jesus' witnesses in Jerusalem, Judea, and the ends of the earth. In the exposition of John 20:19–25, we described the form of a biblical commissioning (i.e., "call narrative") and argued its importance for understanding that particular resurrection appearance. Although the Risen Jesus appears throughout John 21, only the conversation with Peter in verses 15–19 functions as a commissioning scene. Formerly, no individual disciple was transformed by the Risen Jesus: *all* disciples were "sent" (20:19–25) and *all* were declared "witnesses" (Luke 24:48; Acts 10:41–42). But here Jesus commissions a specific individual, Peter, to feed the lambs and sheep of the flock. Then he commands Peter: "Follow me." Peter is transformed, then, to a new role and a new status. "Follow" strongly suggests complete imitation of Jesus, especially by a death that will give God glory, just as Jesus' did.

JOHN 21:20–23 – CONTROVERSY ENDS EVEN THE EPILOGUE

20 Peter turned and saw the disciple whom Jesus loved following them, the one who had reclined next to Jesus and asked at the supper and had said, "Lord, who is it that is going to betray you?"
21 When Peter saw him, he said to Jesus, "Lord, what about him?"
22 Jesus said to him, "If it is my will that he remain until I come, what is that to you? Follow me!"
23 So the rumor spread in the community that this disciple would not die. Yet Jesus did not say to him that he would not die, but, "If it is my will that he remain until I come, what is that to you?"

Doesn't Everybody Die? Apparently, some early Christians did not think so. For example, in 2 Timothy 2:17–18, the author condemns Hymenaeus and Philetus for the gangrenous doctrine they preach: ". . . claiming that the resurrection has already taken place." One might understand this as an elitist remark that the true believer has already passed from death to life. Similarly, one finds Paul taking to task Corinthian disciples who apparently say similar things by virtue of their elite or charismatic status (1 Cor 4:8). Yet even in the Fourth Gospel, Jesus himself declares that believers experience a dramatic transformation: "Anyone

---

[548] See the commentary on John 20:19–28; see also J. H. Neyrey, *Resurrection Stories* (1988), 84–97.

who hears my word and believes him who sent me has eternal life, and does not come under judgment, but has passed from death to life" (5:24). Moreover, the narrative stresses how shocking it is for a beloved disciple like Lazarus to die. So, we know from within the Fourth Gospel and from other Christian writings that there was discussion over whether elite disciples die.[549]

Final "Statement–Misunderstanding–Clarification." Peter, who is walking with Jesus, observed the elite Beloved Disciple "following them." We have argued elsewhere that questions in antiquity generally have an aggressive or challenging aspect to them. Thus, Peter's question, "What about him?" is hardly a request for information but a reopening of the rivalry between him and the Beloved Disciple. Peter wants to know the status of this disciple, who has upstaged him thus far. His question, moreover, functions as an honor challenge to Jesus in that Jesus is pressured to give information that he may not care to divulge. Hence Jesus effectively tells Peter that the other disciple is none of his business: "If it is my will that he remain until I come, what is that to you? Follow me!" (21:22). But this is not the end of the crisis.

Jesus' statement (21:22) is misunderstood: "So the rumor spread in the community that this disciple would not die" (21:23). This misunderstanding, if correct, would boost the elite status of the Beloved Disciple. So, a confirmation is needed, which, in this case, although it denies the misunderstanding, repeats the original words of Jesus: "If it is my will that he remain until I come, what is that to you?" (21:23b). This kind of clarification makes the correct pattern distinctive: There is no revelation, no hidden meaning.

JOHN 21:24–25 – THE LAST ENDING

24 This is the disciple who is testifying to these things and has written them, and we know that his testimony is true.
25 But there are also many other things that Jesus did; if every one of them were written down, I suppose that the world itself could not contain the books that would be written.

Two Endings Compared. The second ending, although it parallels the first ending in some ways, differs significantly. The data of John 21 are both "deeds"

---

[549] In addition to 5:24, there are many statements of "realized eschatology" in the Fourth Gospel suggesting a belief that elites or true believers are already in possession of life: "God sent his son so that whoever believes in him shall not perish but have eternal life" (3:16); "This is the bread come down from heaven, that a man eat of it and not die" (6:50); "Who eats my flesh and drinks my blood has eternal life" (6:53); "Whoever lives and believes in me shall never die" (11:26). See also the misunderstanding over "never dying" in 8:51–52.

(catch of 153 fishes) and "words" ("Feed my sheep"). Moreover, the remark in 21:24 focuses on testimony of certain select witnesses that has been written down, so one might expect more emphasis on sayings of Jesus and about Jesus than on actions or signs.

John 20:30–31	*John 21:24–25*
1. Signs Jesus did: "Now Jesus did many other signs in the presence of his disciples which are not written in this book."	1. Things Jesus did: "There are also many other things that Jesus did."
2. Written: "But these are written . . ."	2. Written: " . . . if every one of them were written down . . . "
3. Purpose of writing: Propaganda – " . . . so that you may come to believe that Jesus is the Messiah, the Son of God, and that through believing you may have life in his name."	3. Purpose of writing: Praise – "I suppose that the world itself could not contain the books that would be written."

Who Stands Behind the Testimony and the Writing? The remark of the author that "This is the disciple who is testifying to these things and has written them" has caused considerable difficulty among commentators, for it could be taken in many ways.[550] First, is the same person "testifying" and "writing"? It seems most unlikely that a disciple of Jesus – that is, a peasant laborer – was educated sufficiently to *write* a complex story such as this Gospel. Moreover, as has been pointed out, "write" may mean simply that the one testifying *caused his testimony to be written* by a trained scribe. Just as Pilate himself did not scourge Jesus (19:1) but caused it to be done, neither did Pilate himself write the title over Jesus' cross but caused it to be written (19:19).[551] Second, who might this figure be? Four options emerge in the discussion: the elders at Ephesus; the author, using the editorial "we" (3:2, 11; 20:2); the writer and others on behalf of others;[552] and the author and the Johannine group to which he belonged. Put simply, the one who testifies is most likely the Beloved Disciple, and the one who writes favors his version of Jesus' words and deeds. Thus, the Beloved Disciple has the last word at the end of John 21. Although he may not enjoy the role of "chief

---

550 G. Beasley-Murray, *John* (1999), 413–15; R. E. Brown, *Gospel According to John* (1970), 2.1123–25; and Richard Bauckham, "The Beloved Disciple as Ideal Author," *JSNT* 49 (1993), 21–44.

551 J. H. Charlesworth, *The Beloved Disciple* (1995), 25.

552 The Muratoran Canon says the author was urged by others to write the Gospel: "The fourth of the Gospels, that of John, (one) of the disciples. When his fellow-disciples and bishops urged him, he said: Fast with me from today for three days, and what will be revealed to each one let us relate to one another. In the same night it was revealed to Andrew, one of the apostles, that, while all were to go over (it), John in his own name should write everything down" (W. Schneemelcher, *New Testament Apocrypha* [Philadelphia, PA: Westminster, 1963], 1.43).

shepherd" now that Simon Peter has been so named, the Beloved Disciple still enjoys exceptionally high status because he is the first Easter believer and the first to recognize the Risen Lord. He was, moreover, the person most intimate with Jesus, most courageous, and perhaps most favored if he escapes death. All of this qualifies him as an elite figure superior to all of the disciples of Jesus. Given his proximity to Jesus, who is "the Truth," certainly "his testimony is true."

Final Praise to Jesus. The conclusion of the second ending is couched in a hyperbole, which honors Jesus by claiming that his deeds and words would require a library as large as the world to house them. Just as 20:31 honors Jesus by arguing that these and other "signs" acclaim him "Messiah, the Son of God," so 21:25 honors Jesus not by a title but by attesting to the volume and value of all he said and did. It is commonplace to cite parallels to this type of hyperbole, one of which is sufficient here:

If all the heavens were sheets of paper, and all the trees were pens for writing, and all the seas were ink, that would not suffice to write down the wisdom I have received from my teachers; and yet I have taken no more from the wisdom of the sages than a fly does when it dips into the sea and bears away a tiny drop.[553]

The parallel provides the right touch, for the emphasis shifts back from the one who testifies and causes to write to the object of this activity, namely Jesus, who is a hero whose words and actions are so many and so worthy that they cannot be transcribed adequately by mortals.

---

[553] *T. Sopherim* 16:8; in addition to this, R. E. Brown's *Gospel According to John* (1970), 2.1130, cites Qoh 12:9–12 and Philo, *Posterity* 144, *Drunkenness* 32. See *Str-B* 2.587.

Scriptural Index

Subject Index